ITEM 021 353 997

G000268979

WD PS

The Life
and Campaigns of
General Hughie
Stockwell

The Life and Campaigns of General Hughie Stockwell

*From Norway,
through Burma, to Suez*

by

J. P. Riley

Pen & Sword
MILITARY

First published in Great Britain in 2006 by
Pen & Sword Military
an imprint of
Pen & Sword Books Ltd
47 Church Street
Barnsley
South Yorkshire
S70 2AS

Copyright © J.P. Riley, 2006
ISBN 1 84415 504 8

The right of J. P. Riley to be identified as Author of this Work has
been asserted by him in accordance with the Copyright,
Designs and Patents Act 1988.

A CIP catalogue record for this book is
available from the British Library.

All rights reserved. No part of this book may be reproduced or transmitted
in any form or by any means, electronic or mechanical including photo-
copying, recording or by any information storage and retrieval system,
without permission from the Publisher in writing.

Typeset in Sabon by
Phoenix Typesetting, Auldgirth, Dumfriesshire

Printed and bound in England by
Biddles Ltd, King's Lynn

Pen & Sword Books Ltd incorporates the Imprints of Pen & Sword
Aviation, Pen & Sword Maritime, Pen & Sword Military, Wharncliffe Local
History, Pen & Sword Select, Pen & Sword Military Classics and Leo
Cooper.

For a complete list of Pen & Sword titles please contact
PEN & SWORD BOOKS LIMITED
47 Church Street, Barnsley, South Yorkshire, S70 2AS, England
E-mail: enquiries@pen-and-sword.co.uk
Website: www.pen-and-sword.co.uk

Contents

Acknowledgements

I would like to acknowledge the help of a great number of people and organizations in the writing of this book. I am indebted to them all and thank them for their kindness and their patience. Many are listed in the bibliography and sources, but those not listed by name include the following individuals: Polly Hope, Anabel Wright, The Lady Reilly (Anette, née Stockwell, Hugh's first cousin), Madge Crocker, Brigadier A.C. Vivian CBE, the late Lord Parry of Neyland, Mr Jamie Owen, Major E.C. Lanning, late RWAFF, the late Colonel B.G.B. Pugh OBE TD, Nigel Anderson MC, Myles Stockwell, Mrs Susan Sonnak, Tessa Trappes-Lomax, Major H.J.E. Jones MC, the late Lieutenant Colonel Neville Bosanquet, the late Major Peter Kirby MC TD DL, Rear Admiral E.F. Gueritz CB OBE DSC, Ian Moody Esq, Lieutenant Colonel Guy Goldsmith, the late General Sir Anthony Farrar-Hockley GBE KCB DSO MC BLitt, Major Barney Griffiths, Major Johnny Westbrooke, Dr Kate Morris, Major Sir Anthony Tritton Bt, Major General P.B. Cavendish CB OBE DL, Sir Philip Goodhart Kt, General Sir Richard Worsley GCB OBE, Hugo Meynell Esq, David Russell Esq, Major General F.G. Caldwell OBE MC▪, Mrs Susan Balance, Major General Sir Roy Redgrave KCVO, Air Chief Marshal Sir Thomas Prickett KCB, Mr Diccon Wright, Rt Hon Lord Morris of Aberavon KG QC, Mr Illtyd Harrington, Mr Peter Lindley Jones. I would also acknowledge and thank the following institutions:

Lieutenant Colonel Peter Crocker, Curator, The Royal Welch Fusiliers Museum and Archives; Chris Hobson, Annie Maddison, Sarah Landa-Font, Sue Barrett, and the Staff of the Library, Joint Services Command and Staff College; Mr Andrew Orgill, Senior Librarian, The Royal Military Academy, Sandhurst; Dr P.J. Thwaites MA MSc DMS AMA MIMgt, Curator of the Sandhurst Collection; Dr T.E. Rogers, Honorary Archivist, Marlborough College; Mr A.D. Richardson, Headmaster of Cothill House; Mr Vernon Scott and the *Western Telegraph*; Mr Ron Watts, Hon Curator, and Mr John Davies MA Dip Lib MIInfSci, Hon Secretary, the Pembroke Dock Museum Trust; John Harding and the staff of MOD Historical Branch (Army); Staff of the Public Record Office, Kew; Mrs Kate O'Brien and the Staff of the Liddell Hart Centre for Military Studies, King's College London; Marie Lewis,

Pembrokeshire County Record Office, Haverfordwest; Martyn Lockwood and the Staff of the Essex Police Museum, Chelmsford; Lieutenant Colonel Peter Hall, British Liaison Officer at the *Führungsakademie der Bundeswehr*, Hamburg; Library Staff at the *Führungsakademie der Bundeswehr*, Hamburg; Major W. Sharpe MBE, Regimental Secretary, and the staff at Regimental Headquarters, the Royal Highland Fusiliers, in Glasgow; Major W. Shaw MBE and the staff at Regimental Headquarters the Royal Highland Fusiliers (Princess Margaret's Own Glasgow and Ayrshire Regiment); The Imperial War Museum Sound Archive and IWM Department of Photographs; Dan Kurzman and the Sussex Academic Press, for permission to quote from *Genesis 1948*; HE the Ambassador and the Staff of the Embassy of Israel; Staff of the Hagana Archive; Regimental Headquarters of the King's Own Royal Border Regiment; Debbie Usher, librarian at the Middle East Studies Centre, St Anthony's College Oxford; Anita Brady and the library staff, Royal College of Defence Studies; Brigadier Ahmed Aideed Al Masareh, Director of Moral Guidance, JHQ Jordanian Army; Mr Amjad Adaileh, Director Arabic Press Department, Communications and Information Division at the Royal Hashemite Court, Amman, Jordan; Ms Alia Al-Kadi, Press Officer Communications and Information Division at the Royal Hashemite Court, Amman, Jordan; Peter Lindley Jones and the Staff of the Kennet and Avon Canal Trust; Lieutenant Colonel Derek Armitage and the staff of the Museum of Army Flying; Gillian Owen and British Waterways; Caroline Jones and the staff at the Waterways Archive; Gregory W. Pedlow and the SHAPE Archive.

Maps

Glossary of Terms and Abbreviations

AA	Anti-Aircraft
AA & QMG	Assistant Adjutant and Quartermaster General. The senior administrative staff officer in a divisional HQ.
AB	Army Book
ADC	*Aide-de-camp*, personal assistant to a General officer.
ALC	Assault Landing Craft
ALFSEA	Allied Land Forces South-East Asia
BEF	British Expeditionary Force
BEM	British Empire Medal
BGS	Brigadier General Staff
BLA	Burma Liberation Army
BM	Brigade Major
BPAFL	Burmese People's Anti-Fascist League
CB	Companion of the Order of the Bath
CBE	Commander of the Order of the British Empire
CEPS	Central Emergency Planning Staff (Malaya)
CIGS	Chief of the Imperial General Staff
Cpl	Corporal
CMG	Commander of the Order of St Michael and St George
CO	Commanding Officer; Cabinet Office Papers (in the PRO)
COHQ	Combined Operations Headquarters
CP	Command Post
CSI	Companion of the Order of the Star of India
CTC	Combined Training Centre, Inverary

CVO	Commander of the Royal Victorian Order
DAA & QMG	Deputy Assistant Adjutant and Quartermaster General. The senior administrative staff officer in a brigade HQ
DCIGS	Deputy Chief of the Imperial General Staff
DCM	Distinguished Conduct Medal
DFC	Distinguished Flying Cross
DL	Deputy Lieutenant (of a county)
DLAW	Director Land-Air Warfare
DRA	Director Royal Artillery
DSC	Distinguished Service Cross
DSO	Distinguished Service Order
DUKW	'Duck' – an American amphibious vehicle
FARELF	Far East Land Forces
FRGS	Fellow of the Royal Geographical Society
GCB	Grand Commander of the Order of the Bath
GCIE	Grand Commander of the Order of the Indian Empire
GHQ	General Headquarters
GOC	General Officer Commanding — the Major General commanding a division or district
GOC-in-C	General Officer Commanding-in-Chief — Lieutenant General or General commanding a command or an army
GSO 2	General Staff Officer Second Grade - a Major
GSO 1	As above - First Grade - a Lieutenant Colonel
HLI	Highland Light Infantry
HMIAS	His Majesty's Indian Auxiliary Ship
IASC	Indian Army Service Corps
INA	Indian National Army
ISA	Israel State Archives
IWT	Inland Waterways Transport (Burma)
IZL	*Irgun Zwai Le'umi.* Jewish terror group
KAR	King's African Rifles
KBE	Knight of the Order of the British Empire
KCB	Knight Commander of the Order of the Bath
KCL	King's College London

KCMG	Knight Commander of the Order of St Michael and St George
KCVO	Knight Commander of the Royal Victorian Order
KRRC	King's Royal Rifle Corps
LCS	Landing Craft (Support)
LCpl	Lance Corporal
LH	Liddell Hart Centre for Military Studies, King's College London
LMG	Light Machine Gun
MA	Military Assistant
MBE	Member of the Order of the British Empire
MC	Military Cross
MCP	Malayan Communist Party
MEC	Middle East Studies Centre, St Anthony's College Oxford
MELF	Middle East Land Forces
MG	Machine Gun
MI(R)	Military Intelligence (Research) – the forerunner of SOE
MLC	Mechanized Landing Craft
MM	Military Medal
MMG	Medium Machine Gun
MPAJA	Malayan People's Anti-Japanese Army
MRLA	Malayan Races Liberation Army
MSM	Meritorious Service Medal
MVO	Member of the Royal Victorian Order
NCAC	Northern Combat Area Command
NCO	Non-Commissioned Officer
NDC	National Defence Company
OBE	Officer of the Order of the British Empire
OTC	Officers Training Corps
PRO	Public Record Office, Kew
PUS	Permanent Under-Secretary, a very senior civil servant
QM	Quartermaster
RA	Royal Artillery
RAC	Royal Armoured Corps
RAMC	Royal Army Medical Corps
RAOC	Royal Army Ordnance Corps

RASC	Royal Army Service Corps
R Craft	Raiding Craft
RE	Royal Engineers
REME	Royal Electrical and Mechanical Engineers
RHQ	Regimental Headquarters
RMC	Royal Military College, Sandhurst
RMLI	Royal Marine Light Infantry
RNVR	Royal Naval Volunteer Reserve
RUC	Royal Ulster Constabulary
RWAFF	Royal West African Frontier Force
Sgt	Sergeant
SOE	Special Operations Executive
STC	Special Training Centre, Inverailort
SWB	South Wales Borderers
TA	Territorial Army
Tac HQ	Tactical HQ. The command post of a battalion, brigade or divisional commander
TD	Territorial Decoration
Teggart Fortress	A reinforced concrete bunker complex used to dominate areas and as a base for operations in internal security operations (i.e. Palestine)
TEWT	Tactical Exercise Without Troops
V Force	Burmese irregular force with British officers, employed chiefly in intelligence gathering and scouting
WO	War Office papers (in PRO)
WOII	Warrant Officer Class II – Company Sergeant Major

The Life
and Campaigns of
General Hughie
Stockwell

Introduction

The year 2006 marks the fiftieth anniversary of the Suez operation, an operation that marked the nadir of British amphibious operations, only twelve years after the launching of the greatest amphibious landings the world has ever seen in Normandy. It marked, too, a low point in relations between the wartime Western allies and laid the foundations of the Franco-American split which caused the French withdrawal from the NATO integrated Military Structure in 1964, a split which is still in evidence today. It was the precursor to the Sandys Defence Review which ended conscription, focused British military power on the continent of Europe for the next thirty years, but at the same time created the expeditionary capabilities which allowed the Falklands campaign to be successfully executed twenty-six years later.

The Anglo-French land force commander at Suez was Lieutenant General Sir Hugh – Hughie – Stockwell, who was at that time Commander I British Corps in Germany. At first sight this was not perhaps a logical choice. But on closer inspection, Stockwell was almost self-selecting because of his familiarity with the type of operation involved, and with the components of the force. He spoke French fluently. He had a background in amphibious operations beginning with his service in Norway in 1940, through his time as Commandant of the Special Training Centre at Lochailort in 1941, and beyond, to his command of an amphibious battalion in 29 Independent Brigade during the highly successful invasion of Madagascar in 1942. He had commanded 6th Airborne Division in Palestine during the evacuation in 1948, where he had secured the vital port of evacuation at Haifa. Most recently he had been the Commander of land forces in Malaya under the CIGS of 1956, the famous Field Marshal Sir Gerald Templer.

As well as all this, Stockwell had a tremendous record as a commander during the Second World War. After Madagascar he had commanded 29 Brigade in Burma, first in the Arakan, and then detached from Fourteenth Army to Stilwell during the long campaign down the railway corridor. In 1944 he had taken command of the 82nd (West African) Division back in Arakan, until its disbandment in 1946. He was well known by the West Africans, having served with the Nigeria Regiment from 1930 to 1935, and by the

1

Supreme Commander, Lord Louis Mountbatten, who said of him: 'You could not find a better divisional commander.' By 1956, significantly, Mountbatten was First Sea Lord.

During the Second World War, Stockwell had risen from Major to Major General in four years, and had been awarded the DSO, CB, CBE and three mentions in despatches. He was knighted for his part in operations in Palestine. His personal courage was legendary, while his magnetism, leadership, humour and intuitive grasp of command in battle made him quite simply adored by those he commanded. He achieved all this without ever having been near the Staff College.

This book is, therefore, a study of command in battle, using one of the most consistently successful British generals of the Second World War. According to received wisdom, a man like Stockwell, who was not a Staff College graduate, should never have achieved as much as he did. But here was a man who could spot an opportunity, exploit it, and win – even against a truly formidable enemy like the Japanese. Secondly, the work explores several areas of operations, using previously unpublished personal memoirs and other original papers, which have hitherto received little attention, or have untold stories: given all that has been written about the Second World War, it is surprising that this is still possible. These areas include a view of Gubbins's operations around Bodø in 1940 and the dismissal of Trappes-Lomax; the invasion of the Vichy French island of Madagascar, the first successful British amphibious operation since Quebec in 1759; the operations of 36th Infantry Division under Stilwell in Burma; and the operations of the 82nd (West African) Division – if anyone deserves the title of 'Forgotten Army', it must be the 90,000 Africans who fought in the Burma-India theatre. Thirdly it gives a personal view from a senior commander of post-war operations in Palestine and Egypt, areas that are still to this day running sores. It describes anti-terrorist operations in Malaya, arguably still the text-book example of how to defeat insurgency. Finally, it describes how these experiences informed Stockwell's peacetime command, including the training of officers and men, the higher direction of defence, and NATO.

Chapter One

Going for a Soldier, 1903–1923

Hugh Charles – Hughie – Stockwell was born on 16 June 1903 in Jersey where his father, H.C. (also Hugh Charles) Stockwell was serving as a captain in the 2nd Battalion Highland Light Infantry. The family connection with the British Army was a strong one, and it was obvious from an early age that Hughie was destined for the Army. Hughie's grandfather, Charles Stockwell, was a Seaforth Highlander who had retired as a major general; of his six children, four went into the Army. Grandfather Stockwell had a twin brother, Clifton, a colonel in the Lincolnshire Regiment, who had two sons; the younger of these cousins was Inglis, who joined the Royal Welch Fusiliers, and who was to play an important part in Hughie's early military service.

In September 1902 Hughie's father married Gertrude Emily Forrest, an Australian lady with all the toughness and strength of character of people from that country. Gertrude was the daughter of the late Mowbray Stenhouse Forrest, a millionaire from New South Wales, and Elizabeth Kite. Elizabeth's father was Thomas Kite, who been shipped out to Australia having been convicted of theft, but on his death in 1876 he had left the equivalent of four million pounds sterling to his ten children, so that Gertrude brought with her a welcome injection of funds to the family. Hughie was their first child and their only son.

In 1905, the Stockwell family went out to Lucknow in India, where Hughie's father joined the 1st Battalion Highland Light Infantry, commanded by his eldest brother, Geordie. Here it remained until late 1910. India in those days was but a vague memory to Hughie in later life, but from his earliest years he began to absorb much of Army life – his earliest memories were of riding down on his pony to watch the battalion parade early in the morning due to the climate. His world would have been that described by Veronica Bamfield, who later married a fellow Royal Welch Fusilier:

Nice bungalows, servants, ponies, pets and picnics; oil lamps and frilly drawing-rooms. Day after day went by in enjoyable monotony, often beginning very early in the morning with a ride round the perimeter of the station, but never venturing farther afield because that would mean

3

going into villages where Indians lived. Back at home, the *syce* (groom) would be waiting at the stables to take the horses.

Hughie himself recalled that:

> I do remember the shaking of the bungalow during a minor earthquake while father was stationed at Dinapur in the foothills of the Himalayas, in the middle of the night, so frightening. I do remember being beaten with mother's silver handled brush and father's shame at the imprint of the angels embossed on the back of the brush on my bottom! I just remember my birthdays and the tennis parties. I don't remember attending the Regimental school of the HLI at Lucknow, a fact of which I was reminded just recently by a Mr Mann who wrote to say he was one of the 'scholars'.

It is not surprising that he did not remember the local school since these were often hit-and-miss affairs, dependent on the availability of either regimental teachers, or else a lady schoolmistress. In theory, all army schools were regularly inspected and the pupils medically examined; the teachers' and doctors' reports were supposed to follow a child from school to school. In practice, the curriculum would have been restricted to learning the ABC, and singing nursery rhymes and 'God Save the King'. No attempt was made, however, to teach the children, or indeed the wives, the local languages, customs or history. It also meant that the children of officers did not have to mix with box-wallahs – the merchant and business class. Mixing with tradespeople? Unthinkable! As Veronica Bamfield remarked: 'Nowhere in the world have so many opportunities been missed as were missed by the army wives in India.'

For the newcomer to India, the extremes of climate were very marked and as seasonal temperatures rose, the families were moved to a hill station, accompanied by up to two-thirds of the battalion. In young Hughie's case this meant moving up to Chakrata, or Dinapur, or Nowshera in the foothills of the Himalayas: first by road, and then by march route, when he was conveyed in a 'dandy' – a form of litter carried on the shoulders of two stalwart porters. Later, he remembered:

> the early morning starts with hurricane lamps waving and the shouting and assembly for the day's march. I was to have so many dawns to face in my life ahead, all of them full of the mystery of the breaking day and the sorrows and joys of each new day. I still find it an exciting experience to be up and away as light breaks across the sky.

The HLI Regimental journal described one such march, from Meerut to Chakrata, from 28 March to 9 April 1905:

The band marched in front, and the pipers and buglers in the centre of the Battalion, so we had music the whole way – a great thing – and kept everyone in good spirits. A very nice grass camping ground. The band played for an hour in the evening; there was also a parade for instruction in fixing the new bayonet, with which we had only been supplied the previous evening . . .

Second day, Khatauli, 105/8 miles – 'Reveille at three a.m., march off at 4 a.m.' thus ran the orders. The first morning everything was rather late, the men not being yet in practice at striking tents, loading transport, and getting their breakfasts in a short time . . . We had 'coffee shop' after marching about six miles . . .

Thirteenth day, Chakrata, 15½ miles . . . At the end of the climb we were rewarded by a magnificent view of the 'snows', 60 or 70 miles away, and varying from 22,000 to 25,000 feet high . . . as we got to our new comfortable quarters, I fancy that the majority considered that there were worse places than Chakrata.

Up in the hills, the quarters were heated by log fires kept going by supplies from local hillmen. Water would be brought round by *bhistis*, milk in large cans by the *dudh wallah*, and rations by a corporal from the battalion for the families who were on the strength. There would have been few shops, but native traders would visit from the nearest bazaar, and there were peaches, apricots and lychees growing wild on the hillsides. The family photograph album shows the bungalow at Nowshera – a large and comfortable wooden building, faintly suburban in style, and with a number of staff: the head servant or *khitmatghar* and a boy to assist him; a bearer; a cook; the *mascalchi*, who looked after the lamps, fires and nursery; a nursery boy; a *dhobi*, or washerman; the syce; the *mali*, or gardener and his assistants; and a sweeper who attended to the ablutions and the thunderbox. There is certainly, in the photograph, an *aya*, or nanny, and it is odd that Hughie seemed to have no memory of her.

For Hughie's parents, life in a hill station would have meant a round of diversions in addition to military duty – safaris, shooting trips on elephants, riding to hounds to hunt jackal, tea dances, club dances, dinners, picnics, gymkhanas, polo, garden parties, balls. Although it was quite possible in those days to live well on one's pay in India, cutting a dash in society meant spending a good deal, and it was here that most of Gertrude's money was spent.

Hughie did recall the leisurely voyages to and from India in P&O troopships through the Mediterranean and the Suez Canal, where the occupation of a first-class cabin brought such benefits as fruit and biscuits with the early morning tea! He also recalled visits to Australia, where his mother took him twice to stay with her mother, Granny Forrest, a kindly and remarkable woman. Elizabeth, or more usually Betty, Hughie's eldest sister, was born during one of these visits in 1909. But perhaps for most children, it was the smells of India which were the most evocative of sensations:

Do many British children know what a dead tiger smells like? . . . The smell of the earth soaking up the first rain of the monsoon, of watered Lucerne, of roasting *gram* (chickpea) from the servants' godowns, of tobacco smoked on the roadside in a communal pipe and the tremendous, heady, bitter smell of something in the Simla bazaar – you never forgot and you longed to smell it again. Sometimes it nearly came back in the smell of autumn leaves burning, or varnish, or packing cases, but never the same.

In 1910, Hughie's father was posted as Adjutant to the 3rd (Special Reserve) Battalion of the Regiment, whose headquarters were at the Regimental Depot in Hamilton. By now it was already clear to the young Hughie that his father had a very short temper, was uncommunicative to small boys and generally had little time for him – in short, an altogether 'Victorian papa'. As is often the way, he was kindly and indulgent to his grandchildren in later life, as Susan Sonnak, his granddaughter, remembered.

At Hamilton, Hughie started the second phase of his education, the first having been the unremembered spell in Lucknow, at Cothill House, a prep school near Abingdon. Here he came under the headmastership of M.J. Daughlish, whom Hughie described as 'a superb man of real character, a bachelor, kind, severe, gentle and amusing – a fine games player'. He also later remarked that 'he would beat you if he thought you deserved it – idle, scruffy or lazy. I was devoted to him and he had a great influence on my early life.' This is a revealing comment, and goes a long way to explain how Hughie's character developed during his years at school and later in the Army. Given what we know of his father, and Hughie's lack of any real relationship with him, it is also unsurprising.

In 1912 his father decided to leave the Army to become a Police Chief Constable – a not unusual thing for a retiring army officer to do in those days. He succeeded in becoming Chief Constable of Colchester but the First World War began in August 1914 while the school holidays were on, and although life at Cothill ran along fairly smoothly, activity within the family became far more exciting and varied. Hughie's father had rejoined the Army as Assistant Provost Marshal of the 10th Division, which was forming up at Colchester to go to France. By November 1914 the battle lines began to stabilize after the early fluid battles, and Hughie senior found himself based at Poperinghe not far from Amiens, which was in turn within comparatively easy reach of Paris. So, a flat having been found, Gertrude, never daunted, set off with her four daughters and two servants in November 1914 to settle there, to be joined in the Christmas holidays by Hughie, who travelled by himself, aged 11. He could not later recall the preliminary arrangements of all his moves, but he did remember embarking on the MV *Sussex* at Newhaven for Dieppe. The ship 'was packed solid and I was befriended by a group of nurses heading for their field hospitals, who saw me off the boat and onto the train to Paris, to be met by Mother'.

Hughie, even at this age, had a way of getting on with all sorts and conditions of people, and of making friends easily. He therefore quickly found chums among the local French boys and American expatriates. He also learned to speak good French, which would stand him in very good stead at various times in his life. From time to time his father appeared on short leaves from the front. Gertrude obviously had plenty of the spirit of adventure in her to take on the move to France, and all that went with it, including doing a regular shift at the British soldiers' canteen, known as 'the Corner of Blighty', in the Place Vendôme. As well as this, she worked as a volunteer in the French soldiers' canteen at the Gare de Lyon on the night shift, and on occasions Hughie used to go with her.

By the end of 1916 two things had occurred. First, Gertrude found life increasingly difficult in Paris with the ever-pressing problem of food, and the demoralizing effect the terrible battles being fought out at Verdun and on the Somme was having on the French population. She therefore decided to move further south and found a villa on the west side of Nice. Secondly, in May 1917, Hughie's sojourn at Cothill came to an end, and he was sent to Marlborough College.

In the years before, during and just after the First World War, Marlborough was one of the most popular schools to which Cothill boys would move. In order to keep fees low, expenditure was stinted on everything but the teaching, with the result that despite being housed in some fine buildings, Marlburians took a perverse pride in being able to survive poor food, little heating, and no privacy. Right up until the end of the Second World War, Marlburians going into the Army often declared it to be an easy life after the rigours of the College! Overshadowing everything in Hughie's time at Marlborough, to a far greater extent than at Cothill, was the War. On 21 June 1917, *The Marlburian* identified the astonishing total of 3,039 old boys serving in the armed forces, at least six of whom, including the poet Siegfried Sassoon, were serving in the Royal Welch Fusiliers, the regiment that Hughie was later to join. In all, 742 Marlburians were killed during the course of the War. When the War finally ended in November 1918, the paralysis of grief and shock which was felt, allied to the fact that many older pupils and young masters had left to join the forces, must have severely limited the ability of the College to resume a normal life. 'It was uncanny,' wrote one old Marlburian during the First World War, 'to look across chapel to the back row and realise that within six months half the boys there would be dead.' Every week someone was notified of a brother or a friend, and in some cases a father or uncle, killed, wounded, captured or missing. The pages of *The Marlburian* throughout – and after – the War are filled with lists of casualties, appointments and promotions in the Services. The celebrations which accompanied the announcement of the Armistice on 11 November 1918 were not surprisingly noisy, bearing in mind that the prospect of death or wounds had suddenly been lifted from the older boys.

Hughie's father was a major by 1918, and retired again in March 1919 with the rank of lieutenant colonel, returning at once to Colchester as Chief Constable. Hughie's schooldays were almost over now, and given his family background, there could be no possible doubt about his future career. After achieving the School Certificate, in the Lent term of 1920, he was therefore placed in the Army Class, which prepared boys for the competitive entrance examinations for the Royal Military College, Sandhurst. Hughie passed the exam at the first attempt and left Marlborough in December 1920 to begin his chosen career in the Army. It was a career for which the prevailing culture of his early life and school had prepared him well: physical fitness and obedience to discipline was the most obvious evidence of this, but the culture went much deeper then. Despite the anti-military and anti-war mood of the post-First World War years, the ethos of military service was much closer to that of the society from which the Army was drawn than it is now, after more than fifty years since the end of the Second World War, and more than a generation of multiculturalism. Society, even after the War, was relatively stable and homogenous; the culture and tradition of service was particularly marked in the class from which officers like Hughie Stockwell were drawn. There was then no need to explain what military service stood for – the evidence was plain to see in the aftermath of War, and the maintenance of an empire which reached its zenith in 1921. Few questioned the right – and duty – of Britain to rule that empire; no one questioned Crown immunity; there was no Health and Safety legislation; there was no European Court of Human Rights – there was no Europe; and, above all, the tendency to litigation at the drop of a hat was unheard of. People of all classes accepted that they might enjoy the rights and privileges which came from citizenship of the British Empire, but that these rights had to be bought by acceptance of duties and responsibilities. Military or civil service was inextricably bound up with this understanding. Hughie's final report from Marlborough, written by Patteson, his housemaster, must therefore be read in the light of this prevailing culture:

> A gentleman he is first, with a fine sense of right and wrong and the courage of his convictions. I can't imagine Hugh Stockwell doing a mean or ungentlemanly act; it's a contradiction in terms. He is also a fine little sportsman, [he was 6 feet 1½ inches tall!] he has already experienced both success and disappointment and shown that he knows how to treat both these impostors, and to estimate them at true worth. Leadership he has in plenty – not forced or assumed but natural and therefore compelling.

When one had been a senior boy at an English public school in the early years of the last century, with all the rights, responsibilities and privileges which went with that position, it was easy to feel important: the acclaim of the juniors, the easy terms with masters, the small boy coming running to the shout of 'fag', the study and the common room – all conspired to place the eighteen year old (especially if he was an accomplished sportsman), on a

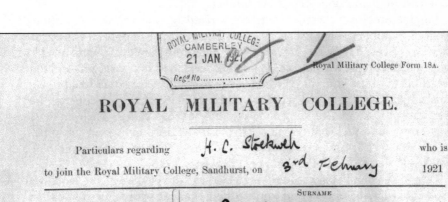

Royal Military College Form 18A.

ROYAL MILITARY COLLEGE.

Particulars regarding H. C. Stockwell who is
to join the Royal Military College, Sandhurst, on 3rd February 1921

ROYAL MILITARY COLLEGE
CAMBERLEY
21 JAN. 1921
Regd No.....................

Name in full ... ... (IN BLOCK CAPITALS)	**SURNAME** STOCKWELL **CHRISTIAN NAMES** HUGH CHARLES
Date of Birth	16ᵗ JUNE 1903
Religion	Church of England
Schools where educated { 1. Private ... 2. Public ... 3. Crammer ...	M.J. Dauglish Esq, Cothill House Abingdon Marlborough College Wilts.
Whether desirous of entering Cavalry, Infantry or Indian Army	Infantry

The Cannons Colchester Permanent address of Parent or Guardian.
Any change to be notified as it occurs.

H.C.Stockwell (late Captain Higld. L.I. etc) Signature of Parent or Guardian.
Father Stating relationship of latter, if any.*

Hugh C. Stockwell. Signature of Gent. Cadet.

Note—This return should be carefully filled in and forwarded without delay, addressed
to the Assistant Commandant, Royal Military College, Camberley, Surrey,
Postage to be prepaid.

* State rank (if any) or whether Revd., Mr., Mrs., Miss, etc.

Hugh Stockwell's joining certificate as a gentleman cadet at the RMC Sandhurst in 1921
(RMA Sandhurst Collection).

pinnacle of achievement which he might never surpass. Sandhurst very rapidly took care of any notions of self-importance.

Hughie Stockwell, aged seventeen, arrived to join the Royal Military College, Sandhurst, on 3 February 1921. The College had only emerged from its wartime role during the previous year. Each company was commanded by a lieutenant colonel who had seven other officers, two staff sergeants and four sergeants to assist him, all of whom were carefully selected and had distinguished war service. These were tough, brave men, of proven courage, but who had a deep understanding and sympathy for their cadets. Their influence was profound. Stockwell remained at the RMC until he passed out on 21 December 1922, and was gazetted as 23894 Second Lieutenant H.C. Stockwell, Royal Welch Fusiliers, on 1 February 1923.

Despite his family background in the Service, the young Hughie Stockwell probably, nonetheless, viewed joining the Regiment with some trepidation. Officers like Hughie Stockwell were not so much joining the British Army, as joining their regiment – it was the regimental ethos which dominated the prevailing military culture, reinforced by the value that society in general at that time placed on tradition. Regiments played on this for all it was worth, despite the effect of mass casualties in 1916 on particular areas caused by regional recruiting in the New Armies. It was generally felt – and probably rightly so – that men would fight better with a sense of loyalty to their comrades, and of belonging to a family, than they would for more abstract ideas: regimental associations, distinctive uniforms, the teaching of regimental history, the appointment of royal personages as colonels, all reinforced the sense that the individual belonged to, and owed his first loyalty to, his regiment. Arthur Bryant summed up the general feeling then and in the years which followed when he said:

> The safety and honour of Britain depend not on her wealth and administration, but on the character of her people. This in turn depends on the institutions which form character. In war, it depends, in particular, on the military institutions which create the martial habits of discipline, courage, loyalty, pride and endurance.

Hughie had probably never heard of Sir Garnet Wolseley's *Pocket Book*, but before he grew much older he would recognize what Wolseley had said on the same subject that 'the soldier is a peculiar being that can alone be brought to the highest efficiency by inducing him to believe that he belongs to a regiment that is infinitely superior to the others round him.' This was, and to a great extent remains, one of the Army's great sources of strength – faith in the Regiment, no matter how large or small, was unquestionably with its members.

10

Chapter Two

Pembroke Dock, 1923–1926

Stockwell was ordered to report to the 2nd Battalion Royal Welch Fusiliers on Wednesday 28 February 1923, sixteen days after his commission was gazetted. The battalion was stationed at Llanion Barracks, Pembroke Dock in West Wales, whence it had moved in December 1922 on completion of a tour of operations in Ireland. The prospect was one of enjoying his first real freedom after the constraints of Marlborough and Sandhurst, and of embarking properly on a military career. The 11.15 am train from Paddington was due at Neyland, the port for the Irish steam packets, at 7.00 pm. The horsebox with the Monk and Judy – his horse and dog – was hooked to the back of the train and when Dick Martin, the Assistant Adjutant, met him at the station, he said, 'Quick, I hope your mess kit is easily get-at-able, as you have to change and be in the Mess by 8.00 pm.' 'But,' Stockwell replied, 'I have a hungry horse and a dog in the back of the train!' This caused Dick no little embarrassment and the rest of that dark February evening was a shambles, getting across to Pembroke Dock by the ferry, and then the horse to a stable and his kit to the Mess, where he retired, in his own words, 'shaken and hungry'.

As the next day was St David's Day, 1 March, and the Regimental Day, no one was much concerned with the welfare of a brand-new subaltern. Stockwell was awoken at dawn by a drummer boy, who burst into his room demanding half-a-crown to pin a leek on his Service Dress cap, while the Regimental Band and Corps of Drums were belting forth 'Reveille' outside the Officers' Mess. In accordance with immemorial custom, St David's Day was a day of celebration. There would be games of rugby or soccer, and the officers competed at steeple-chasing. The officers and sergeants would serve the soldiers' lunch at midday and in the evening the fabulous St David's Day dinner took place in the Officers' Mess – Stockwell remembered being just sober enough to take his turn standing with one foot on his chair and the other on the table, to eat the leek. The rest of the night he later admitted was more or less oblivion, after beer all day, sherry before dinner and champagne flowing throughout dinner.

He found himself posted to D Company, commanded by Captain 'Casso' Lloyd, who had fought through the War, had been wounded twice and had,

11

therefore, not kept step with others in the Regiment. Lieutenant Colonel C.C. ('Crump') Norman, who had been wounded three times during his service in West Africa and on the Western Front, and who would later become Inspector General of the Royal West African Frontier Force, commanded the battalion. Among the field officers there were several men who had held high rank during the War, and now held brevet rank. They represented a fearsome array of battle experience for a young officer: take, for example, Brevet Lieutenant Colonel John Minshull-Ford, who had been wounded four times during the War, had been awarded the DSO and MC and had been mentioned in despatches six times; he had commanded a brigade, would eventually command a division and be Colonel of the Royal Welch Fusiliers from 1938 to 1942. Then there was Brevet Lieutenant Colonel William Garnett, or 'Buckshee', also a wartime brigade commander with pre-war service in South Africa, China and India; he too had won the DSO and had been mentioned in despatches four times. D.M. ('Tim') Barchard, the Adjutant – an important figure in the life of any subaltern – had been taken prisoner at the Battle of Langemarck in 1915, and had a deep and lasting loathing for the Germans. These were men whose background was in war, and whose business was fighting. They had little time for the niceties of the staff, and their influence on the post-war generation was profound. Stockwell described their influence thus:

Looking back on my first three years in the Army and my early days as a Regimental Officer, there is little doubt that with the experienced influence of the many senior officers who had all survived the war in various theatres of conflict, we absorbed a great deal of knowledge: we learnt the responsibilities of an officer, we learnt the basic tenets of leadership, we were knocked into shape and, although it seems much of our time was carefree and gay, those years – certainly for me – shaped my future life in my profession.

On 12 May 1924, Hugh Stockwell's uncle, Lieutenant Colonel C.I. (Inglis) Stockwell, took over command of the battalion. CI had commanded 164 Infantry Brigade in the 55th Division during the First World War and later in Ireland, was eight times mentioned in despatches, and had been awarded the DSO and the Croix de Guerre. Frank Richards described him as 'cool as a cucumber', having 'plenty of guts', but being a 'first class bully'. Siegfried Sassoon agreed with this assessment, and in *Memoirs of an Infantry Officer*, CI appears as the overbearing character Kinjack.

His command was memorable. CI Stockwell was determined that some at least of his young officers should pass the promotion examinations, both practical and written. He personally taught tactics and set test papers, which he corrected with much care. He was a superb teacher and all his candidates passed with flying colours at their first attempt. One result was that Hugh Stockwell, having passed the examination, was promoted to Lieutenant on

1 February 1925. CI insisted on the study of military history, and set the subalterns to examine in detail the exploits of the Regiment in France, Italy, Gallipoli and Mesopotamia. Hugh Stockwell himself was given an insight into CI's personal diary he had kept through the War – it was, he recalled, 'a brilliant record of those ghastly battles in France during the First World War'.

2 RWF was probably only some 450 to 500 strong at this time, barely half its established strength. During the latter stages of the First World War, infantry battalion and company organizations had become very flexible, with platoons formed into sections of riflemen, Lewis gunners, bombers, and rifle-grenadiers; Vickers medium machine guns and light mortars were operated at company level. Since 1919, however, infantry battalions had reverted to a more traditional organization suited to imperial policing. The battalion consisted of four rifle companies and a Headquarters Wing. Clothing and equipment was very much that in use during the late war, and was already looking obsolescent. Like most line regiments, the Royal Welch Fusiliers maintained two regular battalions in peacetime, which were of markedly different character. As the home battalion under the Cardwell system, 2 RWF was responsible for training and finding drafts for the 1st Battalion of the Regiment, which was stationed at Lucknow in India, and the battalion Digest of Service is full of notifications of such drafts being sent off.

For the company officers in the home battalion, duties were simple and work finished by lunchtime so that they spent much of their time shooting, hunting, playing games and amusing themselves as best they could on limited pay. In winter soccer, rugby, tug-o'war, boxing, shooting and hunting were the main pastimes, and in summer, athletics, cricket, golf, tennis and swimming. Boxing was especially popular, with coaching and exhibitions every evening by the Regiment's great boxing star and European Champion, Johnny Basham.[1] In May 1923, the battalion entered a team for the Army Boxing Tournament at Aldershot, and came fourth – Dick Martin became officers' heavyweight champion, Hughie's contemporary, Meyrick Ap Rhys Pryce ('Ap') lost the middleweight final on points, Llewellyn Gwydyr-Jones (always known as 'Gwydyr') likewise the lightweights, and Geoffrey Taunton-Collins was knocked out in the second round of his event.

Borrowing a Bleriot motor car from a friend, Stockwell went off on leave to Colchester, a considerable journey then, taking three dogs with him: Judy the Labrador, Flash (a nondescript liver and white half-spaniel) and Winkie, his Sealyham. There was not all that much room in the Bleriot and by the time Stockwell had stowed his kit on board and had the dogs sitting loose beside him, they were pretty well hull down. In this fashion they set off on a bright morning from Pembroke Dock and were going well, when, near the small town of St Clears and going down a hill at a good 40 mph, the dogs saw a rabbit run down the road and into the hedge. They took off straight away and in his anxiety to grab hold of some of them, Stockwell and the car sailed full tilt into the ditch and turned over – not a good way to start his leave. There

13

was nothing for it but to walk into St Clears, where he managed to find a garage that would recover the car, which did not look as if it could ever be made to run again. However, in due course it was and Dick paid the bill. In the meantime, Stockwell decided to go on by train. First he had to get a few pounds from a bank – there were no cheque cards then and precious little in his bank account in London, the *Westminster* at 36 St James Street. By the time the local manager had put him through a gruelling cross-examination before he parted with a fiver, Stockwell and the dogs got to London too late to catch the last train out of Liverpool Street for Colchester. As he was not exactly mobile with three dogs, a suitcase, a double-handled bag and a twelve-bore shotgun, he and the dogs curled up together and slept in the waiting room at Liverpool Street station, to the surprise of a number of local drunks, who used the accommodation regularly. A somewhat bedraggled outfit finally fetched up to the surprise of his father and mother, who must indeed have been long suffering to accommodate such a lot of lodgers.

Under CI's instructions, the officers ran a concert party – the Red Dragons, based on Burnaby's popular and long-running West End revue *The Co-optimists*, and supported by a string band formed from the Regimental Band. Mrs Garnett was their soprano, and other members included Mrs Moody and her husband Bill, Gwydyr, Frederick Shove at the piano, Stockwell and Winnie Pringle, the soubrette, who was married to Jack Pringle, a quiet and dour Australian serving with the Regiment. She was a professional from the London stage and set the whole group alight with her gaiety and vivacity as the young men flirted and danced with her. Stockwell was an enthusiastic member, as one friend remembered:

> Some who knew him well in his early days say that he would have done very well on the stage; he was certainly a born entertainer when he wished to be. On one or two very special private occasions, I saw him tap-dancing to a piano accompaniment as well as anyone on Broadway.

The Red Dragons performed in Tenby and elsewhere; they certainly had fun doing it, though whether it amused the audiences Stockwell often wondered.

As the summer returned once more, the companies marched off for five days' training in camp at Freshwater. Then, in August 1925, the battalion was ordered to London to take over the guard duties on the royal palaces and the Bank of England for six weeks. These public duties were only rarely allocated to line or colonial regiments, and to take responsibility for the security of the Sovereign was a rare privilege. That it was granted to the Royal Welch Fusiliers was recognition of the Regiment's outstanding war record, and of the fact that no less a person than His Majesty the King was Colonel-in-Chief of the Regiment. The battalion, dressed in drab khaki rather than the scarlet of the Guards, began to undertake guards on Sunday, 23 August 1925. Apart from guard duties there were some distractions:

Most of us didn't have enough money to hit London too much of a crack, but we did manage to get out on the town sometimes. One particular late night or early morning, I was returning to the Mess with Tim Barchard from the *Little Club* which we had made our night head-quarters. We were both in tails and white ties if you please, and it was not long before reveille. A soldier stuck his head out of a barrack room window and shouted out 'Look you there's Mr Stockwell in his hunting kit!'

The battalion returned to Pembroke Dock on 25 September 1925 and in May 1926 undertook security duties during the General Strike, which passed without incident. Stockwell himself then went off on a long course at the School of Musketry at Hythe:

eleven weeks on the rifle and light machine gun. I suppose it took so much time as the methods of instructions were so long winded . . . Hubert Pritchard was known as 'Snip' in the Regiment, as on joining he had said in the Mess 'If any of you chaps are going to London, let me know and I can put you in touch with a "Snip"!' He was at Hythe with me, and somehow became involved with a fake cross-channel swim. It was highly organised by the course: posters, and even aircraft from Hawkinge aerodrome dropping leaflets over Folkestone announcing the early arrival of the swimmer. 'Snip' dressed as the Mayoress on the beach and everybody rallied around as extras to make a suitable welcome, to the body which had in fact dropped into the ocean only a hundred yards or so out, well covered in grease! It was enormous fun and gave the holiday-makers a free show and a diversion from the task of building sandcastles.

The alleged swimmer was none other than 'Joe' Vandeleur, later to command the Irish Guards during Operation Market Garden in 1944 – six feet seven inches of the British Army's finest. Moreover, the oarsman in the dinghy was, of course, Hugh Stockwell. Joe Vandeleur, well smeared with grease and swathed in a voluminous bathing suit, cap and goggles, was rowed out to just beyond the horizon by Lieutenant Stockwell and dropped in the sea. Together they approached the crowded beach, Stockwell rowing and Joe swimming. But oh, calamity! On getting out of the sea it could be seen that all the grease had been washed away, and Vandeleur was immediately recognized by one of the Hythe instructors who happened, by great bad luck, to be on the beach. 'Second Lieutenant Vandeleur!' he shouted, and chased both Joe and Stockwell across the beach, and into the School.

In the aftermath of the General Strike, but primarily influenced by reductions in the size of the Royal Navy following the end of the First World War, came the closure of the Royal Dockyard. Arguably, the town has never properly recovered from the blow, even with the arrival first of the Royal Air Force in 1939, and then the establishment of the oil-refining industry in the 1970s. Many tradesmen moved to find work at the dockyards in Portsmouth, Plymouth and Chatham, establishing small colonies of Pembrokeshire folk in those towns. It was with some relief, therefore, that on 8 November 1926, 2 RWF departed the atmosphere of deep depression in the town to join the British Army of the Rhine in the Occupied Zone of Germany.

Notes
1 John Michael (Johnny) Basham (1889–1947). He enlisted into the Regiment in 1911 and served throughout the First World War. He was British Welterweight Champion 1914–1920, and British and European Middleweight Champion in 1921. See his biography by Alan Roderick, *Johnny! The Story of the Happy Warrior* (Newport, 1990).

Chapter Three

The Rhine Army, 1926–1929

The British Army of the Rhine had originally comprised some 273,000 men, twelve divisions of first-class troops which had marched into the Rhineland in 1918 in the immediate aftermath of the Armistice. It had taken responsibility for one of the bridgeheads astride the Rhine – the city of Cologne, where an excellent relationship had developed between the Army and the German people. To comply with the Locarno Pact of 1925, the Rhineland was gradually demilitarized in tranches, from north to south. The British Army of the Rhine, which had been steadily reducing from the time that the Peace of Versailles had been signed, evacuated Cologne at the end of 1925, and moved south to the area of Wiesbaden. The last troops and families left Cologne on 30 January 1926.

In Wiesbaden, the situation was markedly different from that in Cologne. The area was far more rural than Cologne, and this, added to the transfer of some powers from the occupation forces back to local *Kreis* (county) officials, reduced contact at all levels. As time went on, however, reasonably cordial relations were established. As for the town itself, go there today and you will find a large modern city with more than 300,000 inhabitants – and with a foreign military garrison: the Americans. In 1926 its population was about 102,000, and it was a popular centre for recreation and tourism as well as being the administrative capital of the state of Hesse-Nassau. It boasted a fine *Kurpark*, a *Kurhaus*, or Civic Centre, in the neo-classical style, mineral baths, and many fine baroque buildings such as the theatre and the *Neues Museum*. Its historic connections with Britain and the British Army were underlined by the Waterloo memorial in the town centre. For those – like most young officers in the British Army, Stockwell included – less inclined towards culture, the town boasted many restaurants, *Bier Kellern*, dance halls, hotels and nightclubs. It was, therefore, the natural centre for the social life of the men of the British Rhine Army and their families.

By 1926 the British Army of the Rhine consisted of GHQ located in Wiesbaden itself, along with its Army troops, and two infantry brigades, the 1st and 2nd Rhine Brigades. 2 RWF was to join the 1st Brigade, and took over a series of three small, dispersed barracks: two in Bingen, and one in

Sicherstein, where the reserve ammunition and explosives for the Army were stored.

During the move from Pembroke Dock, Stockwell was assigned the task of being Officer Commanding the families. In those days, most infantry battalions had relatively few married officers and men with wives 'on the strength'; in the case of 2 RWF this amounted to no more than 100 women and children all told:

> I had to assemble them with their children and kit, and keep a fatherly eye on them till they were finally settled in their new quarters. I think we crossed from Dover to Ostend, though the official line of communication was via Harwich and the Hook of Holland. I had them all on board and then off again to the train at Ostend, it seems easy enough to say but I remember being in a constant panic of counting heads at each stage of the journey.

The men of 2 RWF and their families found themselves on arrival in the charming small town of Bingen, which at that time boasted a population of about 14,000. The barracks at Bingen had recently been evacuated by the French and to 2 RWF's way of thinking were in a poor state of cleanliness. 'We had,' recalled Stockwell, 'a deuce of a time getting them up to the standard that we were accustomed to.' The Officers' Mess was in a lovely villa above the town and looked down across the Rhine, with vineyards all around. The officers had comfortable and well-furnished rooms with central heating – such a difference from the Mess at Llanion with coal fires for a lucky few in bedrooms, and a large fire in the ante-room. Stockwell shared a small flat with Hilary Pritchard (known as 'Lepro') in the Mess,[1] greatly to Stockwell's advantage, as Hilary was always extremely well equipped and provided for. This was indeed luxurious living! In addition, all ranks of the Occupation Army received additional pay: for a lieutenant this was a most welcome £1 8s 0d per week.

The British garrison, just as in Cologne and indeed just as in the Rhine Army which was established after the Second World War, was largely self-sufficient. It ran its own schools, shops, and youth organizations such as the Scouts and Guides. It had its own newspaper, the *Cologne Post and Wiesbaden Times*, which appeared twice weekly. It organized its own social and sporting affairs, including dances and shows at the Walhalla Theatre in Wiesbaden, which was run as a cinema as well as for drama and variety. The 2 RWF amateur dramatics troupe – the Red Dragons – all joined the Rhine Army Dramatic Society, taking part in productions of *War to the Death*, *Thanks*, and *A Man from Mars*. Sports were many and varied: horse shows, polo (at Erbenheim, south-east of Wiesbaden and next door to the suburb of Biebrich), cricket, soccer, rugby, boxing, tennis (at the Hohenzollern Hotel) and hockey were all actively pursued. A nine-hole golf course was taken over 3 miles north-west of Wiesbaden. The Army conducted its own military training and was subject

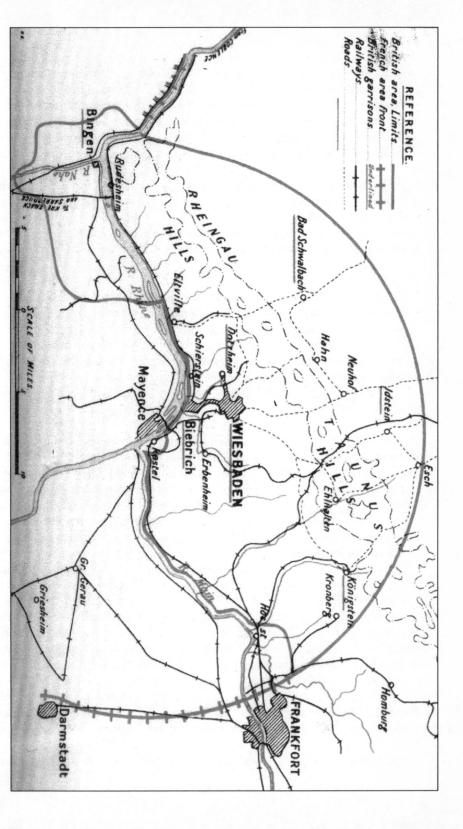

Map of the Wiesbaden Bridgehead, occupied by the British Army of the Rhine until late 1929, compiled by the Ordnance Survey Historical Section (Military Branch), 1943 (Crown Copyright).

to its own military laws. For the officers, life was therefore not much different from that in any other overseas station – social contact with the civilian population was discouraged, and German girls were much disapproved of.

Bingen was not the easiest of places to get back to after an evening out in Wiesbaden as it entailed catching the half past midnight train to change at 1.00 am at Frankfurt am Main, which was actually beyond Bingen, onto a *Schnellzug*, or express train, which went back northwards to Cologne and which stopped en route at Bingen at 1.45 am. The trains were invariably overheated and therefore very soporific, and it was not unusual for an officer with a good evening's draught on board to nod off, not surfacing until he reached Cologne. This would put him in barracks around breakfast time, still dressed in mess kit. Those with some wits about them would telephone the Guard Commander, who was usually decent enough to come down to the station to collect them:

> We had a totally wild, charming, inconsequential officer named René de Miremont, one of the company commanders. I fancy he enjoyed his evenings out. At any rate, returning to his house, which was just opposite the Mess, one morning at breakfast time in his Mess Kit, he was seen by a very newly joined supplementary reserve officer, one John Richardson, who on meeting him in the Mess before luncheon remarked 'You must have had a good night Sir,' which caused René to take off like a cork out of a bottle!

On 21 August 1927, C.I. Stockwell handed over command of the battalion to Lieutenant Colonel Patrick Butler, and departed for India. He left behind his wife, Hilda, who had died after a long illness and had been buried with full military honours in the British cemetery. For her husband, for her daughter Anette, and for Hugh Stockwell she was an incalculable loss – one who had always interceded on behalf of the younger generation when her husband and his contemporaries, having lived through the War, tended towards intolerance of youth and its foibles.

With C.I. Stockwell's departure, Captain Maurice Dowse became Adjutant, while Stockwell became the Cadre Officer, which he felt was a worthwhile and useful job, training young NCOs for promotion either to corporal, or from corporal to sergeant. When young officers joined the battalion, they too were required to complete a Cadre Course. Given a fairly free hand under the watchful eye of Maurice Dowse, Stockwell felt able to pass on much of what he had been learning and absorbing in his earlier years. These cadres were clearly very rewarding to run, especially as he was allowed the best NCO instructors, and his students were keen and competent. Stockwell was also the Battalion Musketry Officer, and developed a firm friendship with Sammy Metcalfe, the Musketry Sergeant and the chief musketry instructor to the Cadre.

The battalion rugby XV was still strong, and was now run by Garnett

Braithwaite,[2] a strong and powerful forward, together with Morgan Lloyd, Maurice Dowse and Jimmy Rice-Evans,[3] a dashing and experienced centre, who was later capped for the Army. With Stockwell himself, the team often included as many as seven officers and to everyone's delight, 2 RWF won the Rhine Army Championship. Along with playing in the Rhine Army rugby side, representing the battalion and the Rhine Army at hockey, and cricket in the summer, as well as learning to play polo, Stockwell was kept fully occupied and very fit.

Under the auspices of Woolly Alston, the officers had become fully engaged with polo, and Stockwell was despatched to Cheltenham to choose and pick up a dozen ponies from Mr Holman, who was a big dealer in this field. Stockwell's favourite was a pony called Hennemara. One of the leading lights was Luke Lillingston who would later ride round Aintree in the Foxhunters' Race over the Grand National. Another fervent player was Alan Heber-Percy who left to join the Welsh Guards and later killed himself at the first fence riding at Cheltenham.[4] Maurice Dowse was also a keen polo player. Stockwell himself was taught and helped greatly by friends of all ranks in the 8th Hussars in Wiesbaden, who were responsible for running the Rhine Army polo. They kindly asked him to be one of their players when taking two teams to play in a tournament at Vittel, about 50 miles (80km) south of Nancy in France:

Maybe we won one of the handicap tournaments as I have by me a decanter inscribed 'Polo de Vittel'. My chief memory is running out of cash and having to return to Wiesbaden travelling with the grooms and the ponies in the horse boxes.

Heber-Percy, Lillingston and others, including Stockwell, were clearly pretty wild young men, as an extract in the autobiography of Alan Heber-Percy's brother Cyril makes clear:

Alan . . . became inseparable friends with Luke [Lillingston] and 'Flossie' [Fox]. All three of them had larger allowances than perhaps was good for them. They bought racehorses and dogs, and had fast cars. They were in trouble with the German police and, of course, with their adjutant. They were put under open arrest; in fact they did everything one would expect of young men at that age, if their energies are not turned in the right direction (and theirs were not). They were out of one scrape into the next, first one of them, then another, or all together.

Despite what Heber-Percy says, the battalion was kept busy training, with training camps being held for annual field training at company and battalion level. These led on to more extensive brigade manoeuvres, which were regarded as considerable fun since they involved much movement around the German countryside. Stockwell's duties now included the billeting of officers, a task which entailed riding ahead during the afternoon and fixing the billets for the battalion with the local village *Burgomeister*. The Germans had the system well buttoned up: the soldiers went into the well-kept and roomy village barns, and the officers, according to rank, were housed in village houses with a Mess set up in the local school. It was rare for men to sleep out in the open. As Stockwell recalled, 'I learnt to be comfortable and warm when the opportunity appeared. I remember sleeping beneath well-filled feather quilts as if I had been pole-axed.' Once the battalion moved on next day, Stockwell would stay behind to sort out any problems and fix the compensation for any damage done. In the late summer of 1928 2 RWF took part in the Rhine Army manoeuvres at Fürfeld, about 30 miles (40km) south-west of Wiesbaden, where both the Rhine Brigades took the field. Stockwell was appointed galloper to Brigadier Maxwell-Scott, commanding the 1st Brigade, and so was able to ride out with him as he went about his affairs on the manoeuvres. He also had charge of a Scott motorcycle and sidecar to run errands, and occasionally – to his peril – to take the Brigadier in the sidecar.

Thus, with the many and various duties that came his way as a junior regimental officer – messing officer, transport officer, musketry officer, cadre officer, billeting officer and company officer – Stockwell was continuing to progress, and to acquire the basic responsibilities and techniques of soldiering which produce a professional officer. What seems markedly to have been missing, however, was any intellectual development. At some stage, Stockwell would have to sit further promotion examinations, as well as the dreaded Staff College entrance examination – a one-time opportunity which, if missed, could deny a man the chance to progress to high rank, at least in peacetime.

In the Mess at Biebrich one night at dinner a discussion arose concerning the merits of the city of Koblenz, north of Wiesbaden on the Rhine. Argument then turned to the distance, either by the road that ran along the side of the Rhine, or by a road that ran over the *Hohewurzel* (an offshoot of the Taunus Hills, north-west of Wiesbaden) through Bad Ems, which was just south-east of Koblenz. The former, it was thought, was about 64 miles, the latter about 56. When Stockwell piped up and said that he could walk to Koblenz from Biebrich in under twenty-four hours, he was taken up with a bet of £5 each from three of his brother officers, on the proviso that he started the next day. Waking up next morning and feeling somewhat foolish he presented himself at the Orderly Room and asked for twenty-four hours leave starting from midday. Leave granted, he duly set off, choosing the road over the *Hohewurzel* and through Bad Ems:

> There is nothing very remarkable about walking fifty-six miles, but untrained and done on the spur of the moment, it had its chances . . . I set out on my way to walk through the night. I walked for two hours at a stretch and halted for twenty minutes. Luckily the German propensities for staying up drinking all night enabled me to find a 'hut' open in Bad Ems at about 4.00 am, where I quaffed a couple of pints of lager.

Then having time on my side and my feet burning, and as it was raining, I lay down under a bench just clear of the town and fell into a deep sleep – to be woken two hours later by a motor bike roaring past my head. Then I put on my soft shoes and after a mile or so . . . I warmed to my work and eventually sailed over the hard cobble stones, up to the Koblenzer Hof at 10.50 am with an hour and ten minutes to spare, to demand a pint of lager, a bath and a telephone call back to Biebrich, to the somewhat startled Mess Sergeant.

Although the evacuation of the occupied zones was not due to be completed until 1935, hostility to the continuation of the Army as a whole was growing in Britain. Troop levels continued to be reduced and the new Labour government, elected on 31 May 1929, decided unilaterally to recall the Rhine Army by Christmas 1929. The contrast between the victorious march to the Rhine in 1918 and the evacuation could not have been starker. On the 28th day of the evacuation, 12 October 1929, 2 RWF was ordered to move to Assaye Barracks at Tidworth on Salisbury Plain. Crowds of well-wishers lined the platform at Wiesbaden station to wish the battalion God speed. General Thwaites himself was among them. At Trier, the train was met by the band and trumpets of a French cavalry regiment, the French bandmaster and trumpet major were invited to take wine with the officers, and many toasts were exchanged. The battalion arrived safely at Tidworth during the evening of 13 October, complete with its families, numerous horses, ponies and dogs, and, of course, the goat:

By 14th October all women and children had been evacuated and every billet handed over. This considerably facilitated the completion of the evacuation; even the bulk of the three hundred cats and dogs had disappeared, also the goat of the R Welch Fusiliers, which was to be let off with 28 days' detention on arrival at Tidworth, the new station of the battalion, while the lesser animals had to undergo the usual 3-months' quarantine.

With the comforts of Germany lost, a growing awareness that his finances were limited and likely to remain so on British Army rates of pay, it seemed to Stockwell that he should try to improve both his finances and his military outlook. He therefore began to look around the various opportunities for secondment which were then available to British officers, but for which one had to apply to get a vacancy. His fancy lit first on the Iraq Army, where pay and conditions seemed good – after a tour of duty there a man might well be better financially equipped. Unfortunately there were no vacancies, so a visit to London in early December 1929 took Stockwell to see a cousin of his who worked in the War Office, one Rupert Brett of the Oxfordshire and Buckinghamshire Light Infantry. Rupert worked in the Adjutant General's department – the branch which controlled all aspects of personnel, pay and conditions of service. After Stockwell had somewhat hesitantly explained his problem, particularly the financial side, Rupert immediately got on the telephone to Alec Telfer-Smollett at the Colonial Office, where he was the staff officer responsible for the Royal West African Frontier Force, saying, 'I have a young cousin of mine who has got to leave the country in twenty-four hours. Can you help?' 'Oh no,' Stockwell interrupted, 'it isn't really quite as bad as that.' Rupert replied, 'They'll get a move on if I tell them that – you'd better go over and see him now.' Stockwell duly presented himself to Alec, who was none other than the man who had put the Glengarry bonnet on his head at his Christening. Telfer-Smollett said he was sorry, but he could not get Stockwell away for a fortnight, when there would be a vacancy in the Royal West African Frontier Force. The two eventually agreed on his departure in one month, and Stockwell returned to Tidworth to put his affairs in order, and to get off home on leave.

On 1 January 1930, Stockwell sailed for Nigeria, leaving the 2nd Battalion Royal Welch Fusiliers after seven years of regimental service, during which the foundations of his military career had been well and truly laid.

Notes
1 Later Brigadier Charles Hilary Vaughan DSO, born 29 October 1905, commissioned 29 October 1926 from university. During the Second World War served with the Airborne Forces, making a significant contribution to their development. Retired 13 January 1949, died 28 March 1976. Changed his name by deed poll to Vaughan on inheriting the Nannau Estates, Dolgellau, in 1956. His obituary is in *Y Ddraig Goch*, June 1976. See also *Who Was Who*, Vol VII.
2 Later Lieutenant Colonel Garnett Edward Braithwaite, born 13 Nov 1904, commissioned 27 August 1924, commanded 1 RWF August 1943 to May 1944, retired 6 September 1947, died 16 November 1981.
3 Later Colonel James Alverstone Mackworth Rice-Evans, born 8 December 1907, commissioned 2 February 1928, retired 14 April 1957 having commanded 2 RWF 1947–1948, died 4 June 1980.
4 Alan Charles Heber-Percy, born 4 May 1907, commissioned 1 September 1927, transferred to Welsh Guards 1 September 1930, killed 7 March 1934.

Chapter Four

The West African Frontier Force, 1930–1935

'West Africa was still a land where the improbable was normal and the impossible occurred often enough to make life interesting.' So wrote the authors of the excellent *History of the Royal West African Frontier Force*, of conditions between the wars. However many uncanny things happened – and they did – the region had ceased to be the White Man's Grave of the previous century, thanks mainly to advances in medicine, improvements in sanitation and the adoption of prophylactic medications like quinine which controlled the scourge of malaria. Even with the improvements in communications and health, eighteen months' service without a break was considered quite long enough for a white man. (The author was the Force Commander in Sierra Leone from 2000 to 2001, and even today would subscribe to that view.)

In an Indian Army battalion, only about 2.5 per cent of the strength – ten or fifteen officers – would be Europeans. In a West African battalion, by contrast, about 14 per cent of the strength was European, and consisted of officers and NCOs from many regiments and corps of the Army who filled every position of responsibility. For these men, service with the RWAFF afforded the chance for promotion to local or acting rank and additional pay, combined with a much lower cost of living than in Britain. With the system of promotion by regimental vacancy that then pertained in the British Army, such men might be stuck for years as subalterns or captains in humdrum posts. A secondment in West Africa would bring freedom from the deadly routine of barracks, and greater responsibility, as well as the material benefits.

On New Year's Eve 1929, Hugh Stockwell set off from Euston Station in company with Leslie d'Arch Smith of the Suffolks to join the 4th Battalion of the Nigeria Regiment, RWAFF. Feeling rather homesick, the two spent much of the train journey joining in the strains of 'Singing in the Rain', played on Stockwell's portable HMV gramophone. The night of New Year's Eve was spent in the Adelphi Hotel in Liverpool, where the two enjoyed an altogether uproarious night of celebrations. Stockwell perhaps regretted this the next morning when he boarded the MV *Adda*, a comfortable ship of 8,000 tons of the Elder-Dempster Line, which was to call at Madeira, Bathurst in the Gambia, Freetown in Sierra Leone, Takoradi in the Gold Coast, and Accra – a total journey fourteen days. As a very junior member of the passenger list, Stockwell's cabin was in the very bowels of the ship, far from light, air and other hangover relief.

Going out to Africa for the first time in the 1930s it was noticeable how the old hands – especially those with one tour behind them – began to thaw out as the ship got nearer to the tropics. As they approached Madeira, Stockwell's cabin became more and more oppressively hot. Early one morning, he ventured to the upper decks to catch the cool of the day and was surprised to be greeted by laughter and chatter coming from the smoking room. Creeping up and looking in, he beheld many of the old hands – Coasters as they were known, or Waffs (pronounced Woff) – downing brandy and ginger ale before breakfast. Not able yet to face this alternative to early morning tea, Stockwell himself withdrew to a bath – salt water first, then fresh to wash off the salt – and breakfast. Sad to say, this clean living did not last long, for two days later, Stockwell too had adopted the West African habit of an iced brandy and ginger before breakfast. As he later remembered:

> The climate in the Gold Coast and Sierra Leone had such a high humidity that any drink you took was quickly sweated out, so to the uninitiated outlook the gin seemed to flow, but it was not to the extent that everyone fell flat on their faces from excess – it was just the normal intake!

And so to Lagos, from where it was a journey of over two days to the Regimental Headquarters of the Nigeria Regiment at Kaduna. It was a pity to miss seeing the tropical forest from the train as by dawn it was travelling through open country near Ilorin. Then there was a long wait in the steamy heat of Jebba, followed by the first sight of the mighty Niger River and the infamous Juju Rock. On arrival at Kaduna he was whisked away to a bungalow complete with servants, known in West Africa as boys. Bungalows at Kaduna were large, airy, handsome, and on arrival, everything was ready. The RHQ, where next morning Stockwell encountered the familiar figure of Colonel Crump Norman, turned out to be a miniature war office dealing with every aspect of the Nigeria Regiment, including the preparation of the annual estimates. Kaduna itself resembled the Indian cantonments of Stockwell's vaguely remembered childhood, especially in its layout. Instead of a magistrate, the civil power was represented by a local authority, a chief who was also lord of the mango trees. The station doubled as the administrative centre of the Northern Province and as such boasted an imposing secretariat, where files passed from one official to another with the appropriate decorum. Bill Edwards, who served with the Gold Coast Regiment, remembered that:

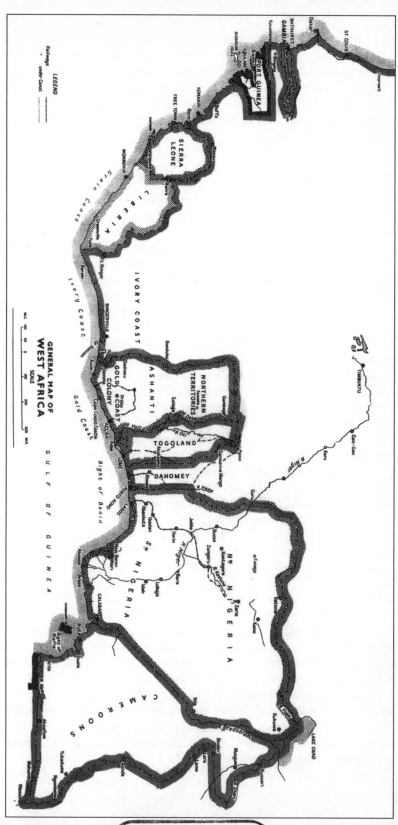

Source: Colonel A. Haywood and Brigadier F.A.S. Clarke, *The History of The Royal West African Frontier Force* (Aldershot, 1964).

Hillingdon Libraries

District Commissioners and District Officers in remote parts became very shy of other Europeans. A brother officer of mine on a recruiting drive . . . knew the form. He climbed onto the DO's veranda, signed his book and asked the boy if he could see the DO. Boy came back with a silver salver asking for a card. The DO would not see him because he had no cards!

The formalities over, Stockwell was ordered to report to the 4th Battalion, which was under the command of Lieutenant Colonel Ladas Hassell. The other battalions of the Nigeria Regiment were stationed on peacetime duties at Kaduna – along with the Regiment's Headquarters and Depot – Kano and Calabar. The 4th Battalion Headquarters were in the town of Ibadan, 100 miles north of Lagos on the main railway, along with three of the four rifle companies and the regimental mortar battery. From here, one detached platoon was maintained in the town of Agbor, while the fourth company was stationed in Lagos. The Nigeria Regiment had no service units – local contractors provided and delivered rations in barracks and on manoeuvres, while on operations, the civil service provided food. Medical care was in the hands of the West African Medical Service. Kaduna and Kano were popular stations on account of their cooler climate; Ibadan and Calabar were regarded as rather steamy. In the Northern Province the pungent tang of hot dust, flavoured according to locality, and especially noticeable when the harmattan blows, is a feature the south usually lacks. Once tasted, this dry, hot, earthy smell is never truly forgotten and one who has known it will, when meeting it unexpectedly after a period of years, be immediately transported back to the last encounter with it. Near Enugu there is a similarly evocative but sweet smell in the forest. Kaduna had its own smell, another during the mango season, and often the fragrance of exotic flowering trees and shrubs. Zaria had nothing except dust. As to Kano, it seemed to specialize in the odours of sweat, musk and leather, besides the indescribable stink of the dye pits. But the Kano smells were much nicer, as Stockwell would soon be able to testify, than Cairo or Suez. Ibadan, the headquarters of the 4th Battalion, was notable for being the largest African town in Africa – that is, the largest town created by and for Africans without the agency of Europeans. In 1930 it had a population of about 200,000 and was Yoruba in style, architecture and local government. By day its red clay houses with corrugated-iron roofs and hot, dusty red streets were full of trade and talk: West Africa from earliest times has been a clearing-house for trade from the interior, including slaves, and this kind of activity (without the slaving) still continued.

A description by Stockwell's fellow Royal Welch Fusilier, Philip Pritchard, gives a wonderfully vivid picture of the sort of life that Stockwell, as a young officer, would have found – indeed Stockwell's own account of his service contains many references that support Pritchard's account. Like Stockwell, he was posted to the 4th Battalion:

At Ibadan we lived in 'bush houses', that is houses built of mud, with grass roofs and matting 'doors' and 'window' coverings. Since we received five pounds a month Bush Allowance for this we were contented enough. The visit of the then Prince of Wales in 1925 had led to the construction of a very roomy and airy officers' mess and a squash court. The mess was not elaborate, but it was well laid out and comfortable. A long *punkah*, hand- or usually foot-operated, from behind a screen by a *punkah* boy, kept the dining-room coolish and the table reasonably clear of flies, flying ants and all the other winged insects which abounded. In those days no wives were permitted to join their husbands in the Nigeria Regiment and so consequently every officer lived in the mess. This led to a real regimental life and the building of houses for married officers and the arrival a few years later of their wives in the country detracted, in my humble opinion, from the pleasant mess life which had previously existed.

In fact this business of wives came to a head in July 1930 when Crump Norman gave approval for wives to go out to Nigeria, so long as the efficiency of the Regiment was not impaired, and suitable accommodation was available. He was also at pains to point out that such would be an 'exceptional privilege'. This approval did not find favour with the then Inspector General of the force, nor with the Colonial Office. After some correspondence it was agreed that so long as applicants were unmarried at the time of application to the force, subsequent permission to marry and bring a wife out to West Africa might be granted by the Commandant.

The soldiers of the RWAFF were first-class material. The author would agree that the general description of the West African soldier of 1930 still holds good today: keen as mustard, honest and loyal, spotlessly clean, hard as iron on campaign, and absolutely fearless when properly led. Superimposed on these qualities was a delightful, almost child-like, simplicity. 'His infectious smile and cheerful laugh were a great inspiration to those of us who had the privilege of training and leading him.' In Nigeria the great majority of the men were Muslim Hausas from the north, who were generally thought of as the fittest and hardiest men. Those from Ibadan were Yorubas, who had not enlisted in large numbers until the Second World War, but of whom their first field commander wrote: 'I never wish to see better soldiers.' The mainly Christian Ibos, a small minority, often made the best NCOs, as they had been educated by missionaries. There were also Fulanis, Kanuris and Shua Arabs as well as pagans from the Bauchi Plateau – not that religion ever seemed to be an issue in the Regiment as everyone joined cheerfully in each others' services. Men applying to join the Regiment were carefully vetted, and those chosen were enlisted for six years with the Colours.

There is no doubt that the experience of commanding these fine soldiers, so different from his fusiliers, was to make a lasting impression on Stockwell, adding a different perspective of leadership and giving him assurance in dealing with men of different backgrounds and nationalities which would be invaluable in the years ahead. Stockwell himself described them as 'wonderful to teach and to work with, they responded with such obvious enjoyment and loved being taught to handle their rifles and LMGs'. He also admitted, however, that he learned far more about them when he commanded a West African division in wartime, than he did during the whole of his peacetime service – but that is a not unusual experience.

Domestic arrangements for the men in barracks were simple, and have changed little during the intervening years. All men fed themselves, and to do so received either meat on the hoof, and the good-quality local vegetables which they supplemented by keeping goats and chickens; or else 'chop money' each week in addition to their pay – chop being the local term for food, or a meal of any kind, and Nigerians being especially partial to meat to supplement the staple ground-nut stew, unlike other West Africans who favour rice. 'Palm oil chop', a cut of meat cooked in the juice of the oil palm, was a standard dish for Europeans that was rumoured to have been invented through an accident in the kitchen! It was also possible to buy sausages, kippers and butter from the fortnightly mail train, which came up with a cold-store wagon. Meals were usually preceded by much gin, and followed by whisky and soda to replace the liquid sweated out during the day – at least, that was the theory. The juice of the oil palm was used by the men mostly in the form of 'palm wine', a rough, fermented drink made by bleeding the crown of the tree and leaving the juice for a few days. The results varied from dreadful to poisonous. Most of the men other than recruits had bush wives who would buy and cook food for them, and keep the huts and lines clean; in the case of Muslims, a warrant officer was allowed four wives, a sergeant three, a corporal two and a private one. Each company had a *magajia*, or head-woman, who was in overall charge of the cleanliness of the lines, which were thoroughly inspected at least once a week, and was responsible for the conduct of the women.

Stockwell was allocated the services of a houseboy called Victor, a Yoruba, who spoke some English, and as orderly, a tall, lanky Hausa called Alakeri Bagarami, recently joined, who spoke no English at all. It took Stockwell a while to get used to the living conditions after the sheltered life of a British Officers' Mess in Germany and Tidworth. His bush house contained only a table and chairs on loan, but thanks to the efficiency of Humphreys and Crook, his gear had arrived safely and was soon unpacked and comfortably installed.

There were some men who ticked off the days and weeks to the next leave. Not so Stockwell. Indeed he sometimes felt that the time flew all too quickly. With his grounding in polo in Germany, he took to the sport in Nigeria like a duck to water. Four chukkas three times each week kept him hard and fit, and he was able to afford a small string of polo ponies: Chance, Beverley, and Mendip – the latter described as 'a good type but too slow for tournament'. To keep three or four ponies was quite usual, and with African wages it was quite possible to afford a groom for each. The price of ponies was controlled by the club and there was a top limit of £30 on even the best animal – the aim was to keep the sport going, rather than encourage individuals to use it as a means of making money.

But it was not all sport, social events and parades. For one thing, the Hausa language had to be mastered, even though most soldiers knew Creole, or pidgin English – for often, British officers and NCOs would find themselves on detached duty in platoon strength in small towns or villages like Agbor, charged with protecting the District Officer or his assistant, or the doctor, all of whom would spend much time on tour. Stockwell himself later recalled that on one tour in 1930, he marched with his company 127 miles in six days through rough country. The troops would be kept busy with some training, but also with agricultural duties like grass-cutting or clearing bush by hand with machetes, except in the rainy season when the constant downpour made such work impossible. On those detachments, the British officers would live almost entirely on tinned food since fresh vegetables and fruit, bread, fish and meat which one could safely eat were very hard to obtain. In these out-of-the-way places, many of the uncanny things which people reported in the 1930s were ascribed to *juju* – that is, the supernatural powers attributed by native people to a magic charm or fetish.

In 1931 the Inspector General's report on the Nigeria Regiment concluded that the Regiment was 'in every respect ready for war', although venereal disease remained a significant problem among the men. The report also shows that Stockwell had qualified for promotion to Captain, and had achieved the colloquial standard in language qualification.

Stockwell was always popular with the ladies – no surprises there for he was good-looking, charming, well brought-up and, moreover, an accomplished dancer. While in Nigeria he had been introduced to Joan Garrard, whose sister Margery was married to Stockwell's Commanding Officer, Ladas Hassell. Joan was the youngest of the five beautiful daughters of Charles and Marion Garrard of Kingston Lisle, near Wantage in Berkshire; the others, apart from Margery, being Nancy, Kathleen and Hazel. Charles Garrard had been a senior partner in Garrard's, the goldsmiths and jewellers but on marrying a well-born wife had given up trade, retired to the country and devoted himself to hunting the fox with the Vale of White Horse foxhounds. He was soon almost bankrupt and was not unnaturally anxious to marry off his daughters. Nancy sadly had to be sent off to a mental hospital; Kathleen married Robin Laidlaw, a director of J & P Coats and chairman of the Clydesdale Bank; and Hazel married de Cronin Hastings, the owner of the *Architectural Press*. It was said that Hastings was in love with Joan, but he was well known for having a particularly cruel streak in his character. Joan disliked him, and one day while on a picnic threw his shoes over a cliff. In exasperation, he married her sister. Stockwell's daughter Polly remembered staying often with Hastings while a girl, at times when her parents were abroad, and recalled him as being a man of great culture and intellect, and a meticulous teacher, mentor and guide. But poor Joan, having disgraced herself, was sent off on the fishing fleet to join her sister and find a husband. Joan had grown up something of a tomboy, had almost no education, but could ride and shoot well. She and Stockwell became engaged and when he left Nigeria for his first leave back in Britain, on 28 August 1931, they were married on 9 December at Bramley in Hampshire. Their honeymoon was spent as one might guess – hunting in the Cotswolds and visiting the two families. But when Stockwell re-embarked for Nigeria on New Year's Eve 1931, Joan did not travel with him:

> As we sailed away, she was left standing on the jetty! Some leave! There was no home for us and I was to organise one when I got back. In the event the Ibadan hospital lent me one of their bungalows, and Joan was able to join me.

When Joan did arrive, Stockwell obtained leave to travel down to Lagos to meet her. Arriving the night before, he was up early next morning to join the pilot boat and so out to meet Joan's ship. She had had a happy and amusing voyage, and so the two departed back to the hospital bungalow in high spirits. Soon afterwards, Stockwell was able to buy a Ford pick-up truck and the two of them were able to go off in it for weekends with friends on shooting trips – with Victor and Alakeri perched on the top. The usual venue would be a rest house from which they would set out at daybreak, returning by 10.00 am for a good breakfast before the heat of the day. The quarry was plentiful: guinea hens, duck, pigeon and bush fowl, which resembled a large, yellow-billed partridge. A good bag of game was of course well received in the Mess at Ibadan, as a welcome change from stringy bullock, palm-oil chop and groundnut stew, but the meat went off so fast in the climate that it had to be eaten straight away.

At Ibadan, however, Joan found the daily routine irksome. Although polo continued to thrive, Joan was never able to join in as to her great disappointment and frustration, it remained very much a male preserve. So her time was taken up with going to market, giving orders to the houseboys and the cook, riding, reading books and periodicals – there was no wireless – and the club. 'I don't know what she did do a lot of the time,' said Stockwell later, 'she got browned off with sitting in a large circle in the club in the evening.' She learned Hausa and clearly would have liked more contact with the African women and African culture generally than the limited amount that was possible through the District Officer, without upsetting the social mores of the time. She also kept birds and grew flowers in her garden, part of which she and Stockwell replanted with grapefruit trees. Fortunately, neither Stockwell nor Joan was ever seriously ill – five grains of quinine and plenty of gin kept the malaria at bay.

Professionally, Stockwell was promoted to Captain on 25 June 1932, and found himself serving another new commandant, Colonel William Meredith, who had relieved Archie Ellis in March 1932. In October that year, Joan became pregnant. Just before Christmas, she and Stockwell made a trip north to Kaduna for the inter-battalion polo tournament and from there, Joan took the train to Port Harcourt where she picked up the boat to return to England to stay with her parents and have her child. When Joan and Stockwell's daughter, June Maryann, or Polly as she was always known, was born on 21 June 1933, he took his second spell of leave in Britain from 4 August to 28 December 1933. Being keen to get command of the battalion's machine-gun company, he was allocated a vacancy on the Company Commander's Course at the Machine Gun School at Netheravon in Wiltshire during his period of leave. He and Joan rented a small house in nearby Amesbury for the duration and after twelve weeks, he passed out top of the course, incidentally adding a welcome £1 per day to his pay. But soon it was back to Ibadan for Stockwell's third and final tour of duty in Nigeria.

This time, he and Joan travelled together, leaving baby Polly in the capable hands of Stockwell's mother Gertrude. They returned not to the bungalow but to a stone-built quarter in the barracks – one of only three in the station – that boasted the great attraction of a nearby swimming pool, a welcome alternative to the usual afternoon siesta. But leaving the baby at home was, Stockwell later admitted, a bad thing. Although the climate was not unhealthy, it was not a good thing to separate 'the child' – as Stockwell referred to her, rather than by her name – from her mother. A separation of twenty-one months at such a young age was one factor which, he felt, contributed to making her a difficult child. Of course, it is quite possible that this was partly due to the fact that she was her father's daughter – determined and strong willed.

Stockwell returned from leave to a new organization in the RWAFF, to which the Nigeria Regiment had been a victim during 1933. The four battalions had been transformed into six smaller ones, each commanded by a major with a headquarters, two rifle companies and a machine-gun section. Stockwell himself became Machine Gun Company Commander on 1 April 1933, but a short time later was made acting Area Quartermaster for No. 2 Area – the Southern Area. However, he was soon due to return to Britain for good – his success on the Machine Gun Course had caused him to be selected for an instructor's appointment and he left for home on 28 June 1935. Like all officers leaving Nigeria for the last time, Stockwell received the Hausa farewell, a long medley of bugle calls believed to be based on Hausa tunes played when the men went to war. It was played either at the home station or on the quayside, sometimes both. In most cases, those leaving experienced a feeling of deep regret at leaving Africa and the African soldiers. Philip Pritchard wrote of it thus:

Final drinks with the party who had come to see me off and futile attempts at conversation: more farewells to my orderly and a row of dejected servants as the whistle blew. Then, as the long, dusty train began to move very slowly, the bugles sounded. I stood at the window while all the figures on the platform became blurred in the dim light and, as the last sad notes of the Hausa Farewell rang out my compartment passed the buglers. Almost mesmerized, I remained staring out of the window long after the station lights had disappeared and the train, gathering speed, had plunged into the dark bush. There are some memories, grave or gay, which remain forever fresh.

Chapter Five

Home Service and the Phoney War, 1935–1940

Stockwell and Joan arrived home from Nigeria on 28 June 1935 and went straight on three months' leave. They immediately retrieved Polly from her grandmother's care and set about finding somewhere to live. In due course they were allocated a small, grey, suburban-looking house on the outskirts of the otherwise picturesque Wiltshire village of Netheravon, very close to the Small Arms School. Joan had now to embark on the nomadic life of an army wife, with its inherent difficulties like bringing up a family while constantly moving from posting to posting every two years or so. The wife of another Royal Welch Fusilier, Molly Bruxner-Randall, recorded forty homes in twenty years, the shortest spell of occupation being two weeks. At each move there were boxes to be packed and unpacked; the house to be scrubbed out to the satisfaction of the local housing commandant; curtains to be altered; furniture to be fitted in to houses of vastly varying sizes and shapes; and schools to be found for the children, and help in the house.

In October, Stockwell reported to the Netheravon Wing of the School where he was first to undertake a refresher course on the Vickers machine gun, and then, assuming he completed this successfully, he was to join the School staff as an instructor – which he duly did on 30 January 1936. Unfortunately, there are no surviving historical records of that period at the School, nor did Stockwell leave any souvenirs of his service there other than two or three group photographs; however, a flavour of life at the School can be gained from Stockwell's near contemporaries, John Masters and David Niven. Masters had this to say:

> The Small Arms School was the only one that every infantry officer had to attend . . . The [school], therefore, had more justification than most for its perfervid enthusiasm . . .
>
> But work was of secondary importance at this school. The students, twenty or thirty young officers from as many different battalions, were far from the overawing presence of their seniors, and the course only

lasted six weeks . . . Everyone wanted to emphasize the superiority of his regiment, so everyone refused to abate one jot of his regiment's peculiarities of dress, drill, or custom, and getting the group together on parade was in itself a circus.

Niven was rather more acerbic:

Gloom descended on me like a blanket.

My loathing of the Machine Gun School was only equalled by my pathological hatred of the Vickers Mark IV machine gun, a foul piece of machinery of such abysmal design that it was subject to countless stoppages, all of which we were supposed to be able to diagnose and rectify at a moment's notice.

Netheravon provided limited social life for a married captain with a young family but no private means, and most of what there was centred on hunting and polo at Tidworth. Still lurking on Stockwell's horizon was the spectre of the Staff College entrance examination. He had now completed the basic qualifications for entry to the examination: 'Good service in the field. Three years' service as Adjutant. Good service on the staff or as an instructor for two years.' He was by no means an intellectual, neither his temperament nor his upbringing had ever steered him in this direction, and certainly there was little encouragement in the Royal Welch Fusiliers for a Staff College education – service with troops and sporting prowess were far more important than a lot of damned quill-driving. But Stockwell was far from stupid. He had always dealt well with examinations in the past, and shown ample evidence of being intelligent, quick thinking and capable. According to him, he qualified twice in the examination, but was not selected for a Staff College place. This was a heavy blow and in a peacetime army it was likely to be a serious limitation to an officer's aspirations. In all likelihood, it would limit him to the rank of major. Fortunately Stockwell, like many others, would get the chance to overcome this handicap, and show what they could do in the coming war.

In the short term, however, some ground had to be made up, and further service on the staff seemed to be the best route. In doing this, Stockwell managed to get the best of both worlds – service on the staff, but also a return to his own Regiment after an absence of eight years. As part of the process of revitalizing the Army after years of neglect, Territorial Army infantry brigades were to be given a skeleton staff and on 23 January 1938, Stockwell was appointed Brigade Major of 158 (Royal Welch) Infantry Brigade. Soon after Christmas, therefore, Stockwell himself moved up to Wrexham while the family stayed for the time being in Netheravon until after the birth of their second daughter Anabel on 3 June 1938. By the time Joan and the girls joined him, Stockwell had found a small house near Morpeth in Cheshire.

36

In 1938, 158 Brigade was commanded by Brigadier Eric Skaife, with his head-quarters in Poyser Street, Wrexham. Skaife was something of an exception among officers of the Royal Welch Fusiliers at this time in that he had embraced the Welsh language and culture. During the First Battle of Ypres in November 1914 he was badly wounded, and captured, spending the rest of the war in prison camps in Germany, or interned in the Netherlands. Skaife was a natural linguist and already had a good command of Russian. During his captivity, he turned his attention to Welsh, and emerged with an excellent command of the language. In 1933 he had become a member of the *Gorsedd Beirdd Ynys Prydain*, and a Day President of the Wrexham *Eisteddfod*. After the Second World War, he was initiated as bard, and became Vice-President of the Honourable Society of Cymmrodorion. Among the officers and men of what was a strongly Welsh-speaking area, this gave Skaife a tremendous moral authority. Stockwell himself felt that Skaife did invaluable work with the Territorials, and for his own part, learned a very great deal about living and working with Welshmen.

Ordinarily, in a regular brigade, Stockwell would have had a number of other officers and NCOs to assist him in his duties. However, in a peacetime TA brigade the entire load fell on Stockwell, with only a chief clerk and a quartermaster sergeant to help with routine administration, which meant that much had to be delegated to the adjutants and quartermasters of the brigade's subordinate battalions. The benefit of this was that Stockwell himself had to get away from Brigade HQ and get to know the officers of the brigade both personally and professionally. Another benefit from being the only staff officer was undoubtedly the closeness of his relationship with Skaife. Even in a fully staffed brigade, as the author can well testify, this relationship between a brigade commander and his principal staff officer is a very special one, and it engenders many close and lasting friendships which endure throughout and beyond the military service of those involved.

158 Brigade consisted of four infantry battalions: the 4th, 5th, 6th and 7th Battalions of the Royal Welch Fusiliers, which were spread over a consider-able area of North Wales. The 4th and 5th Battalions each covered one county, Denbighshire and Flintshire respectively, in which there were some fair-sized towns, like Wrexham, Flint, Mold, and Queensferry. The 6th and 7th Battalions, by contrast, covered areas of dispersed, rural population: the 6th in Caernarvonshire and Anglesey, and the 7th in Merionethshire and Montgomeryshire.

The lean inter-war years had been felt as hard by the Territorials as by the Regular Army. Its establishment in 1938 was 170,000 but this was never reached – even as late as March 1939 it was 40,000 short of this figure. There were, too, chronic shortages of modern weapons, vehicles and equipment, and training was rudimentary. Transport was still mostly horse-drawn, or else required requisitioned civilian vehicles. Pay and allowances remained static, and annual camps had been cancelled in 1926 and 1932 to save money. One TA officer recalled that:

> On manoeuvres you saw private cars and tradesmen's vans with flags sticking up on them, pretending to be tanks. And batteries had to leave half of their guns at home because of the shortage of transport vehicles. That meant that the lessons of mobile warfare were never fully rubbed in.

Training was based on one night each week in the drill hall, about one weekend each month either in drill halls or on the rifle ranges, and two weeks' camp each year. This was when field training and manoeuvres took place and although most TA battalions preferred the independence of a battalion camp, it was usually the practice for a whole brigade to go into camp together – camp for 1938 took place at Ramsey on the Isle of Man, and in 1939, at Caernarfon. Camp was a strenuous time for the small numbers of regular permanent staff – the work of organizing it would start many weeks before and not finish until many weeks after it. Of course, there were social benefits too, such as sports and games, battalion and company dinners, and prize-giving ceremonies – most TA units had funds from which good prize money was given for a range of activities including shooting, bayonet fighting, physical training and various sports. Then there would be mess parties, and dances at Christmas and St David's Day. Not least among all these benefits was the fact that at this time Wales was dry on Sundays – no pubs were open – but a man belonging to the TA had a club, with its own licensed bar, close at hand!

During 1937 and 1938, TA units and formations began to be modernized. The annual bounty was restored to £5, travel allowances were paid and a marriage allowance introduced for men over twenty-one. Motor vehicles such as the 15cwt began to appear in place of horse transport at a scale of one per company. Some Bren gun carriers even appeared – at a scale initially of only one per battalion, but enough to start some driver training. In March 1939 the government decided to double the strength of the Territorial Army – more as an attempt to stave off conscription in peacetime, as well as allaying criticism in Parliament and in the press, than as a genuine act of preparation for war. It was intended that the existing Territorial Army divisions would all provide a nucleus of officers, NCOs and specialists, and up to two formed companies and their equipment, to form a mirror-image second-line division. For the 53rd (Welsh) Division, its second-line formation was based on one resurrected from the First World War – the 38th (Welsh) Division. The brigades carried on this mirror-imaging: in the case of 158 (Royal Welch) Infantry Brigade, its double was 115 (Royal Welch) Infantry Brigade. Going down a further level, three of the infantry battalions – 4th, 6th and 7th – each formed a second-line double, the 8th, 9th and 10th Battalions. Recruiting was brisk and the cadres of the new units and formations were generally formed without fuss, although at the cost of a loss of operational effectiveness in the parent units. Indeed, annual camps were chaotic as units struggled to cope with large numbers of new recruits and insufficient experienced instructors.

The whole brigade took part in the deeply impressive ceremony at Caernarfon Castle in the brilliant weather of July 1939 marking the 250th anniversary of the raising of the Royal Welch Fusiliers at Ludlow back in March 1689. The occasion was rich in pageantry, yet to many, heavy with foreboding. The Constable of the Castle, former Prime Minister David Lloyd George, summed this up in his address before handing over the keys of the Castle to Brigadier Eric Skaife:

> Should the menace to human liberties which now hangs in the firmament, like a dark thundercloud over our heads, burst into a raging storm, we shall all do our duty to save humanity from irretrievable disaster. It is a source of confidence to us that we know that this Regiment will once more face its responsibilities in a way which will be worthy of its glorious past and which will uphold that reputation for bravery which the Welsh people won in their age-long struggle for freedom.

'Dark thundercloud', 'irretrievable disaster', 'face its responsibilities' – quite a different mood from that of 1914. Most ordinary people were encouraged by the press to remain optimistic – there were, after all, the Maginot Line and the British fleet, even if things did go wrong. There was also a widespread feeling that the horrors of the First World War must never be repeated by further continental entanglements. Almost exactly a year before the outbreak of war, the *Daily Express* had this to say:

> In 1918 we were marching to victory, our courage high. In 1938 we are disturbed and distressed, asking each other whether there will be war and dreading the answer.

Even among more senior military officers, however much professional expertise they had gained between 1914 and 1918, there was a strong feeling that casualties on the scale of the First World War were not to be countenanced ever again – the ghost of 1 July 1916 could be felt hovering in the background of almost every operational planning group of the Second World War. Thus there was widespread support for Chamberlain's policy and enormous relief at the outcome of the Munich conference. The *Daily Express* reported the following:

> The policy of this journal is to be sympathetic to those in trouble and at the same time to look after our own affairs . . . For us, in Britain, in the midst of these troubled times, it is the duty of all, every man and woman,

to stand behind the Prime Minister, to support his deeds, to ratify his acts, to uphold his position.

But in the year following Munich, the mood changed, and a feeling of humiliated anger replaced that of relief. Rearmament gathered pace, conscription was introduced and the signs of war were everywhere; in the Stockwell household, the coming war was announced by the arrival of gas masks. Polly remembered being scared out of her wits at the sight of her father coming into the room one day, wearing his, looking like some appalling, bug-eyed monster. In the wider world, the TA was embodied – called out, in effect – on 1 September 1939. As the officer responsible, Stockwell received the order and issued instructions to the battalions at 9.00 pm that night. Key parties had already been called in and the BBC read out the Royal Proclamation over the wireless. In general, Stockwell reported that the system worked smoothly and well. The immediate task was to take over civil defence duties. The whole of Britain was divided into regions, each under a regional commissioner, who boasted almost unlimited powers in the event of a serious emergency. The Welsh Region had its HQ in Cardiff and consisted of the whole of Wales – incredibly, not the same area as was covered by the military district of Welsh Area and 53rd (Welsh) Division, which included Monmouthshire, Shropshire, Beachley and Herefordshire as well as Wales. To complicate matters further, the military command was divided into four zones, and the Welsh Area contained two of these, not contiguous with the divisional and brigade boundaries, placed under a Regional Commander tasked to assist the two Civil Defence regional commissioners. 158 (Royal Welch) Infantry Brigade's area covered the counties of Caernarvon, Anglesey, Flint, Denbigh, Merioneth, Montgomery and Shropshire. Thus from the start there was a misalignment of responsibility, accountability, and civil, military and financial authority – in short, a recipe for chaos before ever the enemy took a hand in the matter.

Although the system of calling the men in worked well, shortages of weapons and equipment had by no means been rectified when hostilities broke out, and the Territorials took the field armed mostly with weapons of the same type as those of 1918. Nor were other resources up to meeting the demands of modern war: for example, only one Royal Engineer bomb disposal NCO was allocated to 158 Brigade for the whole of North Wales. There were also serious shortages of accommodation and stores, spares, vehicles and equipment of all kinds. To remedy this, the units were dispersed around the zone in drill halls, church halls, schools, railway stations, community centres, sports pavilions and under canvas. 7 RWF, for example, reported that:

Life in Newtown during those early days was a busy one for all ranks. It had been expected that the Germans would carry out extensive air raids, so special attention was paid to A.R.P. measures, blackouts, slit trenches and alarm posts.

. . . finding accommodation for the troops was a problem. The old

40

woollen factory in New Road, Community House, Victoria Cinema and the Pavilion were all requisitioned and made use of. The cookhouse was erected outside the pavilion, whilst the dining room was inside.

However, although men had answered their call-up in large numbers, not all could be kept on. In 4 RWF, for example, 1,200 men were called up but over the next two weeks, 136 were discharged to work in the mines. Other men had continually to be found for specialist duties, and still more were found to be unfit for active service, so that units were shrinking rapidly. Stockwell and others described such a hurried process as 'a complete muddle – a badly thought out plan and badly executed'.

As was to be expected, the Civil Defence authorities leaned heavily on the military and, as time passed, their demands increased rather than lessened, which did not help the task of training the troops for war. Not the least of these demands was the harvest, clearly a matter of great importance to the survival of the country. This duty was given a priority second only to actual combat with the enemy, for all units except air defence – by 20 September, 158 Brigade was providing around 300 harvesters each day, a figure which was maintained until early October. So much for the views of one veteran of 1918 who thought that the programme would be 'a month's individual training, some company and battalion exercises, a fortnight each for brigade and divisional manoeuvres, and then the trenches, I suppose!'

One considerable advantage of mobilization for the Brigade Major was that a number of officers and NCOs were posted to the Brigade Headquarters staff, thus relieving Stockwell of many routine duties and allowing him to accompany the Brigade Commander on his rounds. The brigade in general, and Stockwell more personally, suffered a blow on 13 September when Brigadier Skaife was making his first round of visits to battalions, accompanied by Neville Bosanquet. They were rather late leaving the 7th Battalion in Newtown and had a long run to the 6th Battalion. The driver had been with Skaife for some years and had never had an accident, but trying to make up time, he drove the Humber staff car into a bus on the A55 Bangor–Conwy road, just outside a lunatic asylum near Bangor. The car was completely smashed and Bosanquet suffered back injuries. When he came to and reached Skaife he found that some nurses from the asylum had diagnosed a broken leg, had laid him on his back and bound his legs together. 'You look perfectly ghastly,' said Skaife. Both had to be admitted to hospital in Bangor, where they were conveyed in a passing Macfisheries van. Although Skaife returned briefly to duty on 6 October, he was too badly injured to remain in command and the next day he handed over to Brigadier J.P. Duke.

Had the brigade remained in North Wales, training and assisting with the harvest, Skaife would probably have been able to recover and continue in command. However, on 26 September orders were received for a move to Northern Ireland. All units were to be made up to War Establishment before departure, and on 4th October, drafts of reinforcements began to arrive,

41

making up the losses from discharges during the early period after mobilization. The move began by train and ferry on the 22nd, and was completed via Stranraer in a few days. The Headquarters arrived in Belfast on the 23rd and the GOC Northern Ireland District met Duke personally. The move was conducted under conditions of strict security, but even so, Lord Haw-Haw duly announced their arrival on the wireless.

It was not anticipated that the Germans would invade Ireland, although there was a possibility of seaborne raids, increased by the attitude of Eire, which maintained strict neutrality and retained control of the so-called 'Treaty Ports'. Air attacks on installations like the Harland and Wolff shipyard in Belfast, and Short's aircraft factories on Queen's Island and in Castlereagh were a possibility. There was also the threat of espionage and sabotage, since Germany maintained full diplomatic representation in Eire throughout the War, with consulates in some cases very close to the border. The chief cause of nervousness, however, was the possibility of increased IRA activity. This had already begun – from January 1939 onwards the IRA had conducted a bombing campaign in mainland Britain and in Northern Ireland. Although the Irish government passed the Offences against the State Act, this was more concerned with safeguarding its own state from subversion than with dealing with the IRA. Complaints by the Stormont government in Northern Ireland were loud and long, hence the despatch of troops.

Like Stockwell's mother during the First World War, Joan decided to follow the drum and, although strictly speaking families were not allowed to accompany officers and men on active service, Joan went to Northern Ireland under her own arrangements. The family moved into a house in Lisburn, an arrangement winked at by Brigadier Duke. Polly, being now five years old, went off to a local school close enough for her to use her bright yellow bicycle, which she proudly learned to ride in very short order.

Once established, the brigade was tasked to provide guards and security detachments, carry out route clearance operations and be prepared to assist the police in public order. However, Duke was determined that training for war was going to resume. A 'get fit campaign' was launched, with route marches working up to 25 miles, as well as courses for specialists like pioneers and carrier crews; weapon training and shooting; tactical schemes in the Mourne mountains; and a series of TEWTs – tactical exercises without troops, conducted on a map or cloth model – for the officers. By January, Stockwell noted a change in the character of the brigade:

The older TA NCO is gradually fading from the picture, and the younger men are taking their places, a large proportion of the younger NCOs coming from the first Militia called up.

By April 1940, the whole division had concentrated in Northern Ireland. Watching other units, and indeed other divisions, departing for the BEF in

France must have been deeply galling for the officers and men of 53rd (Welsh) Division, and not least for Stockwell himself. However, fate was about to hand him his chance, for on 20 April a sudden call was sent out for volunteers for irregular warfare units to go immediately on active service abroad – the Independent Companies had been born.

Chapter Six

Norway, 1940

In the early months of the Second World War, Allied military planning was much concerned with Scandinavia. After a false start over the abortive intervention in the Russo-Finnish War, the Allied Supreme War Council resurrected the idea of a campaign against Narvik and the iron-ore mines as part of an intensified strategy of economic warfare against Germany. Allied mining of Norwegian waters was to begin on 14 April and when Lulea opened in May it too would be mined. It was also known that Germany, which had already divined Allied intentions, and which was further convinced after the *Altmark* incident that Norway was at least passively in the Allied camp, was preparing plans to invade Norway. Hitler had in fact given orders to Grossadmiral Erich Raeder on 26 March to launch Operation *Weserübung*, in order to occupy both Denmark and Norway at the next new moon in early April.

In parallel with German preparations, conducted in conditions of great secrecy, an Allied force of divisional size was prepared to land in Norway to forestall the Germans. In addition, the Military Intelligence (Research) Branch of the War Office General Staff under Lieutenant Colonel Jo Holland, known as MI(R), was directed to make plans for amphibious raids on the Norwegian coast. He at once summoned Lieutenant Colonel Colin Gubbins to take charge of this project.

On 9 April 1940, German troops, assisted by total air superiority, invaded Norway by sea, and, with the help of Quislings, seized Oslo, Narvik, Egersund, Bergen, Kristiansand and Trondheim. The Germans had won the race and in doing so launched the first large-scale combined operation in which all three components of a recognisably modern military organization – land, maritime and air – were committed with equal weight under a unified command.

On 14 April, a British force – Avonforce – under Major General Pierse Mackesy, the GOC of 49th Infantry Division, was landed north of Narvik, and a second force was put ashore at Namsos on the 16th. Norway's long and rugged coastline could not be defended with the troops available and it was therefore decided to form a separate force to cover the coast between the defended areas at Namsos and Narvik, and prevent the Germans from setting up bases for air or U-boat operations. Meanwhile, Gubbins had been working up the raiding force plans and had produced a draft proposal for special units known as Independent Companies, smaller than a standard infantry battalion, but armed and equipped to operate in an independent role for up to a month. As time was pressing, the proposal was adopted. It was decided to raise these companies from volunteers drawn from the first- and second-line Territorial Army divisions still in Britain. The command of this scratch force fell on Gubbins.

Formal orders were issued on 20 April for the formation of the Independent Companies, each of which was to have an establishment of twenty-one officers and 268 men. Within each TA division, every brigade was to find a platoon, and every battalion a section. The high percentage of officers meant that a subaltern would lead each section. Companies would have their own support sections and would operate from a ship which would act as a floating base – because of this they were not allocated any transport, nor were there any proper logistic arrangements. That said, there is evidence that the equipment of the Independent Companies was superior to that of any other unit in Norway, with the soldiers carrying up to five days' rations of pemmican. Gubbins was very fortunate in the calibre of his officers, among whom were Charles Newman who later commanded 2 Commando and won the Victoria Cross at St Nazaire, and Ronnie Tod who subsequently commanded first 9 Commando and later 2 Commando Brigade. His intelligence staff consisted of Captain Andrew Croft of the Essex Regiment, and Lieutenant Commander Quintin Riley RNVR, both of whom were polar explorers and holders of the Polar Medal. Also going along with him was an American, Kermit Roosevelt, nephew of the late President Theodore Roosevelt. Roosevelt had spent his early life as a hunter and explorer, and during the First World War he had served as a volunteer in the British Army's Machine Gun Corps. In April 1940 he had just returned from a spell in the Finnish Army, and had rejoined the British Army as a volunteer in the Middlesex Regiment.

The first company, No. 1, was formed immediately on 20 April at Martock in Somerset, followed by the rest over the next forty-eight hours. Last but by no means least was No. 2 Company, which was first discussed on Sunday, 21 April 1940, when a conference of brigadiers was called at HQ 53rd (Welsh) Division in Belfast, in order to pass on the orders for the formation of the divisional company, and begin the procedures for selecting the Officer Commanding, officers and men of the company. Nominations from commanding officers to their brigade commanders came in at brigade conferences on 22 April. The chance of active service was not one that Hugh Stockwell was about to pass up. Moreover, being one of a very small number of regular officers in a TA division, he was well placed. Very fortunately, his Brigade Commander, Brigadier Duke, was understanding and well disposed, and was quite clear that such a company must have the best men available, whatever their rank – but he could well have dug his heels in and refused to part with his principal staff officer. Thus Stockwell found himself as one of three nominations for command of the company:

> spoke Brigadier about my chances and he said he would mention it to the Divisional Commander . . . Interviewed by the General – things began to look exciting. At 5.45 the telephone went and it was the General himself ringing up to say he had appointed me to command.

The company began to form at Ballykinler Camp the following day, although most of the men did not arrive until 25 April. Stockwell recalled the frantic course of events:

> Conferences with A and Q, everyone most helpful . . . Second-in-command appointed – I shall like him. Company starting to fill up with decent chaps. Went to Div HQ to fix up the officers with GOC.

The officers, NCOs and men of 2 Independent Company were drawn from all battalions in the division, and organized into three platoons numbered 158, 159 and 160 after the three brigades of the division, along with a support section. Stockwell's second-in-command was Captain Tom Trevor of the Welch Regiment, and there were thirteen other infantry officers, among them several Royal Welch Fusiliers well known to Stockwell. These included N.J.H. (Nigel) Anderson, Sir James Croft, cousin of Andrew Croft, and B.G.B. ('Puggie') Pugh, who commanded the support platoon. After medical and dental inspections and some training tests, no less than fifty-six of the soldiers had to be returned to their units as unfit, and only thirty-two replacements could be persuaded to volunteer in the time available – 'persuaded' because, as at least one account makes clear, a pretty liberal interpretation was put on the volunteer ethos. This from Sergeant (then Corporal) W.A. Jones of 6th Battalion Royal Welch Fusiliers, from Caernarfon in North Wales:

> Very soon after our arrival in Lisburn . . . our names appeared on battalion orders informing us that we were selected to join a force for a special mission for service in an area that was not disclosed at that time, and we were ordered to appear before the C.O. at the Orderly Room where we were informed by the C.O. a little about the task before us, without disclosing the final destination . . . he finally asked us if anyone felt that he did not wish to go, and out of those assembled only one declared that he did not wish to go, so therefore the rest of us became volunteers.

Even when volunteers were genuinely called for, there was no mention of destination, Arctic training or even winter sports of any kind, rather that they should have an interest in unusual and adventurous training.

On 1 May, Stockwell was summoned to the War Office, where map packs were issued – although 'map packs' rather overstates a bundle of papers which consisted of illustrated holiday brochures, touring maps and the like.[1] Stockwell made notes on the series of briefings he received:

> series of staff meetings, issue of pamphlets etc on irregular warfare. Not certain that all G1098 equipment could be provided in time especially: ice axes, alpine . . . sleeping bags, special boots, rucksacks, aluminium cooking utensils, primus stoves, kerosene containers, cap comforters, scarves, mittens, jerseys. Briefed on attacking railways, supply columns etc isolated en posts.

Sergeant Jones described what had been happening during his absence:

> We finally unloaded at Ballykinler, an Army barracks, the Headquarters of an Irish Regiment, and we were placed in wooden huts. While we were there, more men were arriving from the 53rd Welsh Division . . . I could not help noticing what a tough looking bunch of men they were, and I began to wonder what I had let myself in for. We had not been told [who] our company commander was to be, only that we expected him to arrive from the War Office at any time now. And when he duly arrived I was glad to see that he was another Royal Welch Fusilier by the name of Major Hugh Stockwell. Very soon after his arrival we were ordered to assemble in the canteen so that he could introduce himself to us. He spoke in a very confident and jovial manner, and he [said] also [that he] had noticed that we were a tough looking bunch, and that it was exactly what he wanted, and that he felt quite safe with [us] . . . he finally stated that he was more than confident that we would be able to cope, and give a good account of ourselves in these circumstances, and he wished us all the best of luck. Then he walked amongst the men talking to them individually as they moved about in the canteen. He spent a lot of time in the canteen with the men, which they greatly enjoyed.

From then on, 2 Independent Company was put through a rigorous programme of physical training, shooting and tactical schemes over the rugged terrain of the Mourne Mountains – more preparation than any other company had achieved, and which undoubtedly paid off later. Quantities of new weapons arrived, on which men had to be trained: a sniper rifle per section; two Thompson sub-machine guns per section; three Bren guns for the Support Section, one for each infantry section, and one for Company HQ; three Boyes anti-tank rifles for the Support Section, two per platoon and one for Company HQ.

On 3 May, the GOC 53rd Division visited the company, and on 8 May, they left Ballykinler and moved by ferry and train first to Glasgow, and then on to Leith. The soldiers' spirits were high. They were keen, eager and fighting fit, and after a boisterous night on the town the company embarked on 10

May on the MV *Royal Ulsterman*. Sergeant Jones recalled a few of the highlights:

> In the afternoon we were marched in full service marching order like pack mules to the waiting troopship . . . this boat had all the signs that it had been hastily converted from a passenger boat to a troopship, and there were double decker barrack room beds placed in every available space. It was to prove most uncomfortable for this voyage . . . at last we were informed that our destination was Norway, and we were issued with some Norwegian currency, and since we had been repeatedly lectured to expect some heavy enemy air attacks we had no reason to believe we were going on a shopping expedition.

At 9.00 pm on the 13th, the ship arrived at Bodø, the main port for reinforcement and supply of the expeditionary force. Here they met up with the rest of Scissorsforce, which had had seventy-two hours of severe fighting, marching and countermarching. The troops performed well, but rapidly found they were no match for the Austrian ski troops they encountered, and the exhausted men were withdrawn in a Norwegian coastal ship. Gubbins by this time presented a somewhat surprising appearance, described by Commander Bill 'Tiny' Fell as:

> the most unconventional General I'd ever seen, dressed in a khaki shirt, with sleeves cut off at the shoulders, a pair of slacks and enormous boots . . . he was very short and thickset with vast hairy arms that looked as if they could crush rocks and hung down almost to his knees.

In the wake of this withdrawal, Lieutenant General C.J.E. Auchinleck, who had assumed command of the Anglo-French military, and British air forces, in northern Norway, issued orders from his HQ for the Independent Companies to be formed into a light force and placed under 24 (Guards) Infantry Brigade, commanded by Brigadier the Hon William Fraser, despite the fact that the Independent Companies were known to have insufficient mobility, firepower and training for such a role. Already in 24 Brigade were the 1st Battalion Scots Guards, which was at Mo with No. 1 Independent Company, the 1st Battalion Irish Guards and the 2nd Battalion South Wales Borderers, both of which were located with Brigade HQ at Harstad. The specific task allocated to Gubbins was the denial of Bodø to the enemy while an airstrip there was completed.

No. 2 Company was initially to remain at Bodø, and Stockwell therefore disposed his platoons around the town. 158 Platoon moved off to the south to occupy a large fish-drying shed about 2 miles away, south-west of the harbour, at Langestranda, in which much salted fish was stored. From here, this platoon patrolled the town to control looting and look out for suspicious activity – Stockwell quickly came to the view that Quislings were active in the

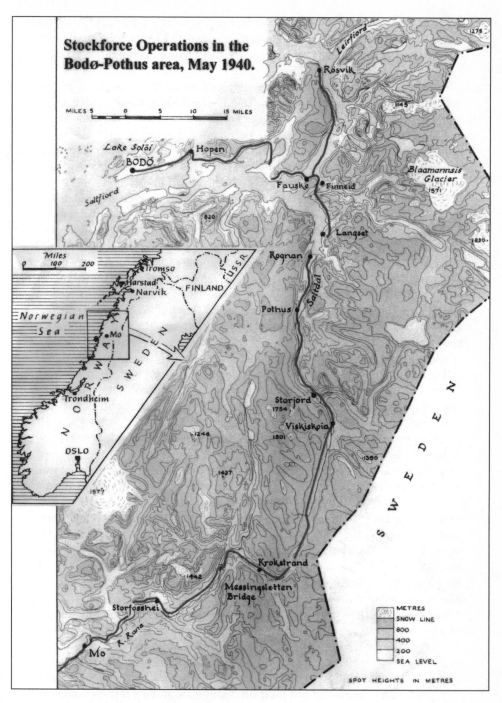

Source: T.K. Derry, *The Campaign in Norway, History of the Second World War,*
United Kingdom Military Series (HMSO London, 1952).

49

town and were somehow passing information to the Germans. With the assistance of an attached Norwegian officer, Second Lieutenant Sönothagen, he interviewed a number of suspects, several of whom, including the Chief of Police, were placed under military arrest.

Auchinleck's orders had also directed Brigadier Fraser to move with his HQ and the bulk of the Irish Guards to Mo. The Irish Guards and Brigade HQ were moved in small boats onto the Polish liner MV *Chobry*, while Fraser and some of his staff embarked on HMS *Somali*. But at this point the Germans took a hand – HMS *Somali* was attacked from the air and badly damaged, and had to make for Scapa Flow to effect repairs, carrying with her Brigadier Fraser who had been injured and had to be invalided home.

With the Brigade Commander gone, Gubbins, now an acting Colonel, was the senior officer and accordingly took command of 24 (Guards) Brigade on 15 May. But disaster struck again. News came through that German aircraft had attacked the *Chobry*, which was carrying 1st Irish Guards, about 30 miles short of Bodø in the Westfjord at midnight on the 14th. An incendiary bomb penetrated the ship and exploded near the senior officers' cabins, killing or wounding eight officers and 100 men, including the Commanding Officer and all the company commanders. The abandoned ship had to be sunk by British aircraft, all the battalion's stores and equipment were lost and the battalion had to return to Harstad to re-equip. Worse still, the losses included three light tanks, the only British armour in Scandinavia.

Two days later, on 17 May, 2 SWB and Brigade HQ were sent up from Harstad to Bodø on HMS *Effingham*, but taking an unusual route outside the Leads to avoid air attack the ship struck a rock close to Bodø. Stockwell and No. 2 Independent Company managed to salvage some 3-inch mortars, their ammunition and vehicles, including three Bren gun carriers, and, as related by Puggie Pugh, several cases of gin! However the SWB had lost most of their equipment and also had to return to Harstad while the *Effingham* was sunk by torpedoes. Gubbins, therefore, effectively had only one battalion – the 1st Scots Guards at Mo under the popular and respected Lieutenant Colonel T.B. Trappes-Lomax – and his Independent Companies. Worse, the Scots Guards were 135 miles away. The force at Mo was meant to protect the route north-wards towards Bodø and its airstrip. It was believed that the Germans had a mountain brigade in the area, possibly supported by light armour, and with air cover. As it turned out there was no armour, but the brigade was the advance guard of a division.

Gubbins decided that a personal visit was required and so he travelled south to Mo by road during 18-19 May. Meanwhile the Scots Guards and their Norwegian counterparts had withdrawn into the town from their positions south of Mo after the left flank had been turned by the advancing German mountain troops, and a parachute landing. When Gubbins arrived, he and Trappes-Lomax clearly did not hit it off. Gubbins wanted Trappes-Lomax to hold a perimeter in Mo long enough for evacuation by ship, but Trappes-Lomax objected as there was no cover of darkness and ships would be vulnerable to air attack down the length of Ranen fjord; nor could a sufficient perimeter be held for long enough as it would take twenty-two hours for the ships to arrive. All in all, Trappes-Lomax felt that a march to Bodø was preferable, especially since to evacuate by ship would risk leaving the road unprotected. Gubbins at length agreed. 'But,' Trappes-Lomax wrote, 'that he could have entertained the idea [of naval evacuation] throws some light on his military judgement.'

At this stage, Trappes-Lomax received instructions from Auchinleck to stand and fight on the south side of the plateau. He replied direct by signal, with a copy to Gubbins, that since the Scots Guards were the only troops in place, in order to keep his force intact and achieve the aim of covering Bodø, the best hope of stopping the Germans was north of the snow-bound plateau, where it would be harder for the enemy to outflank him. After a conversation with Lieutenant Colonel Arthur Dowler, the GSO1, Auchinleck's message was amended from defence to fighting withdrawal. Gubbins then wrote an order authorizing Trappes-Lomax to withdraw 'from any position you hold if in your opinion there is serious danger to the safety of your force'. Trappes-Lomax therefore selected three delaying positions and conducted a fighting withdrawal through them. Three salvaged Bren gun carriers from No. 2 Independent Company, which Stockwell had detached and sent forward under the command of Second Lieutenant Nigel Anderson, helped cover the withdrawal on 21 May with great skill. Two of the three carriers were destroyed in the action, but the task was successfully accomplished. As a result of this, Anderson was awarded the Military Cross, the first won by a Royal Welch Fusilier during the Second World War.

When Gubbins became aware of the Scots Guards' withdrawal he tried a damage limitation exercise by moving the forward elements of 1st Irish Guards, along with Stockwell's No. 2 Company, to a blocking position at Pothus, between Storjord and Rognan. As Stockwell's company HQ was preparing to move, a German aircraft bombed the area, hitting the wireless tent, killing two soldiers and wounding another eight.

Sergeant Jones recalled that the company travelled the 30 miles inland up the Saltdal fjord to Rognan in the fjord steamer *Bodin*, and from thence by a combination of route march and 3-ton lorries, which were repeatedly attacked by German aircraft on the narrow road which follows the Salt river as it flows into the fjord from the south, the only practicable route from Mo, since the country around was very mountainous, wooded and pitted with lakes. The road was therefore the natural focus for both the enemy and Stockwell's force. At the same time, No. 3 Independent Company was sent forward to occupy the high ground just west of Viskiskoia so that the Scots Guards could retire and take up a firm position astride the road. Having no transport, 3 Independent Company and a few Norwegian troops had to march from Rognan, and by the time they had got into position, the Scots Guards, not pressed by the enemy, had taken up their position to cover a demolished bridge over the Salt River.

51

The next day, the Germans appeared in front of the Scots Guards and attacked in strength, supported by aircraft and mortar fire. With the Bofors anti-aircraft guns out of action, only one 3-inch mortar available, and artillery support limited by poor radio communications, the Independent Company was driven back and the main position outflanked. Gubbins therefore ordered the acting Commanding Officer of the Scots Guards, Major H.L. Graham, to withdraw through Stockwell's position at Pothus – Graham was acting Commanding Officer because earlier that day Auchinleck had signalled Gubbins, relieving Trappes-Lomax of command. Gubbins felt that Trappes-Lomax had endangered the whole force by his actions, and he at once implemented the order.[2] The Scots Guards began to move back to Hopen.

While all this was in progress, Auchinleck decided to strengthen the position at Bodø by building an airstrip and bringing in more troops, including the remaining Independent Companies from Britain, and some French Chasseurs Alpins, so as to develop a base for counter-offensive operations.

It was clear therefore that the force at Pothus must now form a guard force, and to that end No. 4 Independent Company was sent up to reinforce the position. Stockwell, granted the local rank of Lieutenant Colonel, was directed to form and take command of this grouping, which was to be known as 'Stockforce', and hand over command of 2 Independent Company to Tom Trevor. Orders were issued at 7.00 pm on the 23rd, and Stockwell went forward with Captain H.C. McGildowny, the acting Commanding Officer of the Irish Guards, to have a look at the area. Opposite Pothus, a thickly wooded razor-backed ridge stuck out from the mountains and behind it a small tributary ran down into the Salt River. Stockwell decided to form his position at the hamlet around two bridges over the Salt River, which was wide and deep, and swollen with melt water. The main road bridge was a substantial girder construction carrying the road from west to east, and it was prepared for demolition; a second bridge, a few hundred yards downstream across the tributary, carrying a rough track over the ridge, was much smaller. This track continued along the eastern bank for about 3 miles until it too crossed the Salt by another small bridge. All in all, Stockwell decided that the position offered a good choke-point at which the advancing Germans could be held. The Germans could certainly outflank the position, but this could be checked, Stockwell felt, by positioning other troops on the flanks under the cover of the woods. 158 Platoon of No. 2 Independent Company, about fifty-five men, along with the Support Platoon under Captain Puggie Pugh, came up first at about 2.30 am on the 23rd, and Stockwell placed them in positions on the west and east sides of the river. Pugh remembered that he 'had with me three Bren guns and a 3-inch mortar. We got into position at 11.00 in the morning, having had to climb a very steep mountain side, covered with trees.' Sergeant Jones, who was a section commander in 158 Platoon on the other side of the valley, recalled that:

there were also many piles of wooden logs scattered about in this area . . . The German Air Force seemed to be quite active, as many aircraft

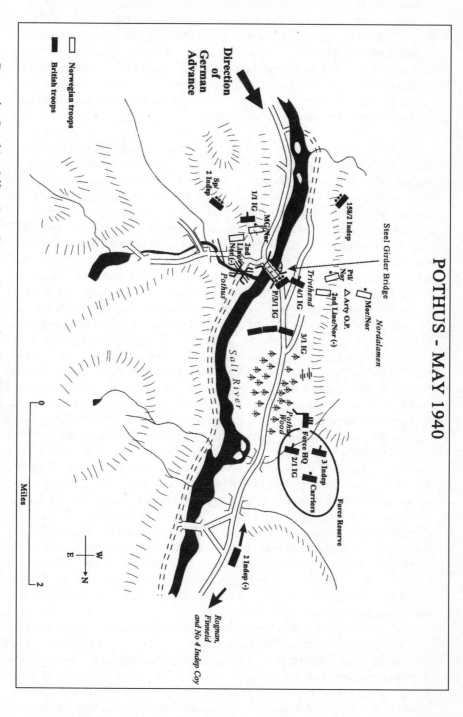

POTHUS - MAY 1940

Direction of German Advance

Norwegian troops

British troops

Steel Girder Bridge

Nordalamen

Ptl/Nor

MarNor

△ Arty O.P.

2nd Line/Nor (-)

158/2 Indep

Spr 2 Indep

1/1 IG

MG/Nor

2nd Line/Nor (-)

Pothus

Trivthend

P/3/1 IG

4/1 IG

3/1 IG

Salt River

Pothus Wood

Force HQ

2/1 IG

3 Indep

Carriers

Force Reserve

2 Indep (-)

Rognan, Finneid and No 4 Indep Coy

0   Miles   2

W   N   E   S

Drawn by Graphics Office, Joint Services Command and Staff College from original notes supplied by J.P. Riley.

could be seen flying overhead, but alas it was always 'theirs' and not 'ours' . . . we started off uphill in the woods to the high ground, and my section was positioned about 400 yards from platoon headquarters, we had ample supplies of Marmite and cocoa,[3] and very soon my position was being strafed by German aircraft, luckily with no casualties, and I moved my section slightly below the ridge, to where I found some crevices that the men could use during air attack, as it was fairly obvious that our position was already known.

They were followed by the Irish Guards who began to arrive at 10.00 am on the 24th. One of its companies, No. 1, covered the main bridge on the far side with a detached platoon from No. 3 Company on the bridge itself with an Engineer NCO who was responsible for preparing the bridge for demolition. Once the Scots Guards had passed through, this company and platoon were to be withdrawn and the bridge blown – but only on Stockwell's direct orders. The only method of communication to this forward company was by runner, since the signallers did not know how to operate the wireless set they had been given, and there was insufficient cable available to lay a tele- phone line. A second company, No. 3, covered the tributary and the river banks below the bridge, while No. 4 Company, on a plateau or terrace on the right of the position, was able to command a long stretch of road and river. In support of the British troops, a Norwegian patrol detachment under Captain Pedersen took up a position 400 yards west of the bridge; a machine- gun detachment under Captain Ellinger, and a half-company from the 2nd Line Battalion, joined No. 1 Company Irish Guards on the northern side of the bridge, with the other half company joining No. 4 Company Irish Guards. A Norwegian mortar section was deployed south-west of the bridge to cover the forward troops, while a troop of 25-pounder field guns, which had been brought up from Mo, also covered the main road. Once the bridge was blown, Stockwell thought, the Germans would have great difficulty in getting forward. As a backstop, Gubbins had ordered 4 Independent Company to adopt an intermediate position in front of Finneid to cover any subsequent withdrawal.[4] No. 3 Independent Company, which came up at 8.00 pm on the 24th, and the remaining company of the Irish Guards, No. 2, formed Stockwell's reserve which was co-located with his HQ about a mile to the north in Pothus Wood. Here they were to be joined by the balance of No. 2 Independent Company and the carrier section as it moved forward. Finally, two Indian Army officers, Major J.H. Prendergast and Captain R.A. Bailey, were attached to the force.[5]

Oral confirmatory orders were issued at noon. It was a hot, clear summer's day, and Stockwell spent much time going around the position, siting weapons and encouraging the men to give their best, in the knowledge that the hard- ships and dangers were being shared equally. The hot sun thawed the frozen Arctic soil and the men dug slit trenches with a will, 'smoking and chatting, beating off swarms of ants and midges, and quietly watching the German fighters overhead'. Some civilians appeared, and several members of the force reinforced Stockwell's view that not all Norwegians were strong in the Allied cause. Quintin Riley noted that 'The whole country is riddled with Quislings and the Hun knows everything. Their equipment, training and speed are infinitely better than ours and they have complete control of the air.' Sergeant Jones said:

My section spotted a civilian moving uphill towards our position. I ordered the men not to fire at him, but keep him under observation and allow him to come into our position. He was then held until my interpreter could find out more about him. The officer told me that he was just an ordinary Norwegian looking for his wife, and that the German position was about two miles away. He was allowed to go on his way, and I soon realised that he was returning by the same route that he had taken to come into my position . . . so shouted at him to stop. On hearing me, he started running away. His action convinced me that he was not an ordinary civilian.

As the men of Stockforce dug in, encouraged by Stockwell, other British and Norwegian troops began to appear down the road from the direction of the enemy, at first in twos and threes, many of them wounded. About 5.00 pm, the advance party of the Scots Guards appeared. Puggie Pugh thought that they were 'marching very well, as though they were on parade'. Eventually the short Arctic night fell and the temperature dropped. The men wrapped themselves up in blankets, greatcoats and leather jerkins, and some welcome rations appeared, brought up by lorry from Rognan. By midnight on 24 May, reasonably effective defensive positions had been completed. Soon afterwards, the troops heard the unmistakable sound of tired men tramping slowly along the road, and as they watched through the gloom the Scots Guards passed silently through the position. There was now nothing between the main position and the Germans except No. 1 Company Irish Guards and their Norwegian allies. Then, without warning, the girder bridge blew up at 1.35 am, leaving the troops on the far side unsupported. This, it later turned out, had been done by the Engineer NCO on the information received from an unidentified officer of the Scots Guards, in direct contravention of his orders.

The enemy was now reported to be closing up and to muster about 4,500 men from the 2nd Mountain Division and 181st Infantry Division. Puggie Pugh was the first to make contact. At about 8.00 am on 25 May the Support Platoon, now well positioned in the woods behind breastworks of rocks, stones and logs and with weapons sited to sweep the road, spotted a German motorcycle patrol. The platoon let the Germans get well along the road to a stretch which was fairly straight and level and without cover except for the ditches on either side. 'Then,' said Puggie, 'we opened up on them and I think got most of them.'

A fierce battle raged, often at close quarters, for the next thirty-six hours. It was Stockwell's first taste of combat – as it was for most of the men of Stockforce – and they were not found wanting. By 11.00 am the Support Platoon had been outflanked and Stockwell ordered them to join the Irish Guards around the girder bridge, a move which took about an hour by a round-about route. The last Bren gun carrier moved off the position 'a moment before a 4-inch mortar shell fell on the spot'.[6] Around the bridge, the guardsmen of No. 1 Company, who were well dug in and supported by artillery, machine-gun fire and the Norwegian mortars, held their ground resolutely. In the early afternoon of the 25th, five Heinkel aircraft began to attack the position, including Stockwell's HQ which was burnt out by incendiaries, while German infantry put in an attack. They were driven back, but gradually managed to outflank the position. Puggie Pugh remembered that:

I got my 3-inch mortar into action and we fought a desultory battle all that day until about 17.00 hours, when the Germans delivered a very determined attack and drove us off the hill on which we had established ourselves . . . it was very close country and my Bren guns had a very small field of fire. The Germans got within 50 yards of us before I saw any of them.

Eventually, Stockwell had to order a withdrawal. The guardsmen of No. 1 Company had worked their way down to the river and, as the bridge east of the main girder bridge had also been blown, had to cross the swollen stream under fire, hand-over-hand, using a rope made of rifle slings. This company eventually rejoined the force having crossed the Salt at the Brenne suspension bridge further downstream. The men of 2 Independent Company had to make their way along a track down the river to a small hanging footbridge about a mile below the reserve position. No. 2 Company Irish Guards crossed by the footbridge at 7.00 pm and by 4.30 am next morning had established themselves on Point 800, the highest peak in the area. No. 4 Company Irish Guards still held its position and by concentrated fire prevented any German move across the river. By about 8.00 pm Stockwell had as clear an idea of the confused situation as was possible. He could see that the German attack was being held, but was worried about being outflanked. As he was also clear that his task was to hold the Germans here, he had no option but to commit his reserve. The two companies were ordered across the river to a blocking position at the northern angle of the river confluence, where cliffs afforded some protection. By 4.30 am on the 26th, Stockwell felt that his left, southern, flank, was secure.

During the night, the Germans built a pontoon bridge upstream in order to switch the direction of attack onto the northern bank. This was observed and reported by Drummer Hughes of the Irish Guards who, with a Norwegian officer, was on OP duty:

We observed the enemy constructing a pontoon bridge. We immediately found a suitable OP and sniped but with little success as they seemed to sense where we were after the first few shots . . . we took it in turns to sleep and watch the pontoon bridge . . . They eventually found us out and gave us a burst of MG fire which was badly aimed and we came away unscathed.

By about 9.00 am on the 26th, the Germans, using this pontoon, had pushed the platoon of No. 2 Independent Company back onto the main position. Seeing this, and recognizing that the position was about to be penetrated, Stockwell personally led forward his only remaining reserve – the balance of 2 Independent Company, which had joined the force at 3.00 am on the 25th. The company moved uphill and managed for a time to prevent the Germans from pressing forward – surely one of those occasions when the qualities of judgement, personal courage and example which mark out the successful battlefield commander were most required.

While this action was in progress early in the morning on 26 May, Gubbins had been warned by signal that the British government had decided to begin an evacuation. Stockwell was therefore given modified orders to hold the Germans only for long enough to cover the withdrawal of Bodøforce, which was expected to evacuate between 1 and 3 June. The Germans kept pressing hard at Pothus, and at 11.30 am Gubbins therefore sent orders to Stockwell by wireless to carry out a withdrawal as far as Fauske, north of Rognan on the northern shore of the Saltfjord. This was to take place over severe, mountainous and thickly wooded terrain, which, being within the Arctic Circle, was covered in places by belts of perpetual snow and ice. The fighting was so close, and his flanks were so threatened by German and Austrian ski troops, that it was not until the middle of the afternoon that Stockwell was able to plan breaking contact, and early evening before this could be effected. The only means of passing orders was by runner or by face-to-face contact, and Stockwell only managed to meet up with McGildowney and the company commanders of Nos 3 and 4 Companies Irish Guards – Captains C.A. Montagu-Douglas-Scott and N.S.P. Whitefoorde – at about 4.00 pm at the corner of Pothus Wood. Shouting to make himself heard over the roar of German aircraft, he told them, 'Battalion HQ of the Irish Guards will withdraw at the discretion of the Commanding Officer. The forward company will withdraw at 1900 hours.' This did not leave Scott long to get back and organize the extraction of his company which was in close contact with the enemy.

From then onwards, Stockforce fought a vicious rearguard action – the most difficult operation of war – under continuous mortar fire and air attack. The move began just before 7.00 pm with 2 Independent Company concentrated in a covering position near the footbridge, from which it blocked the German advance in close fighting until 10.30 pm that night. Scott, with No. 4 Company of the Irish Guards, was at his wits' end trying to find a way of breaking contact at the bridge, when two Gloster Gladiator aircraft from the strip at Bodø appeared, seemingly from nowhere, and machine-gunned

57

the attacking Germans. This bought just enough time and space for the company to get away, but the respite was short-lived.

Stockwell meanwhile had sent orders by runner to those companies he had not been able to see personally. No. 2 Company Irish Guards was to move down and join the position at the footbridge, but the order never reached the company – instead, it went to 3 Independent Company. But Charles Newman could not get clear of the Germans and had to withdraw down the eastern side of the river to the head of the fjord. A Norwegian liaison officer eventually contacted No. 2 Company Irish Guards late that evening. 'Why haven't you gone?' he asked Lieutenant G.S. Brodrick. 'There has not been another man on these mountains these last three hours. You had better hurry if you want to get back, as the Germans have occupied Pothus Wood and are moving quickly on Rognan.' With the Germans on the road, No. 2 Company had no choice but to follow the same route as 3 Independent Company.

Whatever their route, the men of Stockforce now had to traverse 10 miles of extremely rugged terrain from Pothus to Rognan. As they fought their way yard by yard slowly northwards along the line of the road, the men destroyed ammunition dumps, blew up bridges and jetties, and created as many ad hoc obstacles to impede the Germans as they could. The Germans for their part worked their way around the flanks and down to the road at several points, ambushing parties whenever they could. 2 Independent Company was ambushed as it moved out of Pothus, by Germans who had infiltrated round their flanks, and the company took casualties. A battle went on for most of the day with the Welsh soldiers giving as good as they got: 'Platoons 159 and 160 had a running fight with the Germans in which they wiped out a machine gun post.' But the companies, often broken up in the darkness and confusion into small groups, somehow made their way to the village of Nestby, about 2 miles from Rognan, where Stockwell had organized a blocking position from two platoons of No. 4 Company Irish Guards under Captain Whitefoorde, and Captain Ellinger's Norwegian machine-gun detachment. Here, men sorted themselves out, found their comrades, and were moved off down the road in something approaching good order. To support the withdrawal, 1, 4 and 5 Independent Companies were all placed under command of Stockforce on the 27th, although 1 Independent Company reverted to Bodøforce command at 1.00 pm that same day, as did 3 Independent Company.

At Rognan, the road ended abruptly at the head of the fjord, providing a natural barrier to any further German advance, although it picked up again at Langset on the north shore, and there was a rough track around the edge of the fjord. The force was to move the 6 miles from Rognan down to Finneid by small boats, a precarious run of an hour each way. To carry this out, Tiny Fell, who was in charge of small boat operations, had assembled a flotilla consisting of a large ferry and ten armed fishing boats – known as 'Chuffers', or more often 'Puffers', each around 50 feet long and powered by a single-cylinder Bollinder engine. The engines were so temperamental that

Fell had had to co-opt Norwegian engineers and seamen to work them; many of these men were most unwilling and took any opportunity to jump ship. Added to this, the boats had just returned from a walrus-hunting expedition, and stank to high heaven. Fell, who later commanded 14th Submarine Flotilla, was described by Andrew Croft as 'a tall New Zealander who had spent twenty years as a submariner in the Royal Navy and had a way with men, who loved and followed him'. He recalled his arrival at Bodø and being briefed by Croft and Riley on the situation: 'They made [Stockwell's] plight sound like an adventure full of amusing incidents. Riley asked how many men each Puffer could carry. Fell thought about fifty, but Riley, an experienced polar traveller, suggested that this was too many: "Remember," he said, "they have full equipment and a lot of kit – the Army will never learn how to travel light."'

The Puffers, operated by Tiny Fell, Quintin Riley and Andrew Croft, made repeated runs to and from Rognan, often under air attack, and the task took longer than Gubbins and Stockwell had hoped. Inevitably, to get the men away, a lot of heavy equipment had to be left behind and destroyed, and demolition charges were laid under the wooden jetty at Rognan, timed to explode once the evacuation was complete. With things going slowly, there was only about a quarter of an hour left before the charges were due to blow, and the engine of the ferry, which Fell had flogged to get maximum speed, caught fire. Smoke and flames were pouring out of the funnel while the troops on board – about 350 men all told – tried unsuccessfully to put the fire out, bailing water with buckets, basins, their helmets and anything that would hold water. At almost the last moment, Fell, manoeuvring his Puffer with great skill and bravery, managed to pull the ferry clear. The ferry was only 50 or 60 yards away from the jetty when the charge blew, showering the troops with burning debris. As the ferry was towed slowly away, German cyclists entered the town and began firing on the boats. All the troops were, however, safely extracted except for No. 2 Company Irish Guards, which had had to make an arduous forced march of 20 miles over the bleakest mountain terrain to meet up with the force at Langset on the other side of the fjord. Luckily for them, each Norwegian town and village owned a municipal motor bus; Kermit Roosevelt commandeered the one in Fauske and set off along the fjord track to meet the guardsmen, bringing them back in two lifts with a man sitting on the roof as air sentry, while the charabanc rattled over the stony road.

As the force passed through 4 Independent Company, Stockwell ordered 2 Independent Company to reinforce it and come under Paterson's command. Major Paterson recounted that:

I had no sooner started talking about this than, BANG! Up went the bridge, the enemy were at our gates . . . I gave orders [by runner] . . . telling No 2 Coy to withdraw on their own but not to become involved, but before withdrawing to inform No 2 Platoon of my own Company

59

what they were doing. In order to be sure this message was carried out I sent my Intelligence Officer with it. Actually by the time he got there, they had started their withdrawal . . . We then sat and waited. After a short time the Boche got a mortar going and a machine-gun which covered the road between Fauske and Finneid with long range fire. Copland [Second-in-Command of the Company] came up in a car and got chased, also a lorry which turned up to get some explosives.

Stockforce consolidated that night at Fauske, with the Irish Guards and 2 Independent Company on a line north of Lakes Nedre and Övre, spread out to rest on the bleak terrain overlooking the village and covering the road which ran along the north side of the Saltfjord; the wounded were moved back by road to Bodø. The 27th dawned, dank and dreary, with plenty of attention from German aircraft. Stockwell and McGildowny set out to reconnoitre a holding position. At midnight, the troops marched out to occupy a new position on the Valnes peninsula, about 4 miles further west, where it could block the roads and approaches into Bodø. 5 Independent Company was placed on the right, 4 Independent Company in the centre, the Irish Guards held the left, and No. 2 Independent Company formed the force reserve; 1 and 3 Independent Companies meanwhile still held forward positions near Finneid. The men once again dug slit trenches, found what shelter they could in farms and barns and relieved the Norwegian cows of their milk!

During the 28th, the force consolidated the Fauske position. The Germans arrived early in the afternoon and engaged one of the platoons of 4 Independent Company. The company held on until dark and just before midnight, Stockwell ordered Paterson to adjust his position onto high ground overlooking Fauske.

As they did so, Gubbins was working on the evacuation plan, which Auchinleck had ordered to begin on the night of 29/30 May. Destroyers would take off Bodøforce over that night and the two successive nights. The stubborn defence of Stockforce, and the destruction of jetties, Puffers and all small boats not in immediate use, had temporarily halted the German advance at Rognan so that Gubbins had a breathing space in which to issue his orders. On receiving these late on the morning of the 29th, Stockwell quickly made a plan. The force HQ, No. 1 and No. 4 Independent Companies were ordered to move by truck and Puffer from Hopen to concentrate at Bodø, and there embark on 29 May. The Scots Guards, he knew, had been told to adopt a blocking position at Hopen, to allow Stockforce to move from Fauske on the 30th. No. 2 Independent Company and No. 3 Company Irish Guards would adopt an intermediate position at Mjones, with No. 5 Independent Company carrying out a delaying action to give them time to get into position. No. 3 Independent Company would also come under command again and would move as quickly as possible to Hopen with the remainder of the Irish Guards.

At this point, the Germans were not pressing hard, and 2 and 4 Independent Companies, which had begun to withdraw early, had been led back into position by Stockwell. He then issued orders to the CO of the Irish Guards and the commanders of 1 and 5 Independent Companies, and sent a warning order to Paterson at about midday, but with no details of time and place of rendezvous; whether this was poor staff work, or good security is not clear. The main body duly moved back on foot that night to Hopen, where Puffers picked the men up in relays and took them on to Bodø. As for 2, 3 and 4 Independent Companies, a typewritten order was sent by dispatch rider, telling them to be on a destroyer at Bodø at midnight. This reached Paterson at about 6.30 pm. Gathering up his platoons and loading them on to whatever transport he could find, Paterson made the rendezvous on time, blowing the Valnesfjord bridge on the way. There they joined Stockwell and his HQ, just in time to hear the whispered message along the quayside: 'Destroyers *Firedrake, Fame* and *Vindictive* coming alongside. Five minutes to board.' So Stockforce was successfully evacuated and moved to Harstad.

Stockforce was shipped from Norway back to Scapa Flow in the transport *Royal Scotsman*. The campaign in Norway was over. Stockwell would later recall ruefully how, despite being in command of the sea, employing some good troops and at times enjoying local superiority in numbers, the Allies were baffled by superior air power, intelligence and the momentum of the Germans' advance. It was a lesson he would not forget. But it had not been a wholly negative experience. Scissorsforce – and within it, Stockforce – had kept the field for a month in good order, and had enabled operations to continue elsewhere, especially at Narvik. It had fought skilfully in adversity and had been evacuated without loss. For Stockwell himself, the long years of training and service in Britain, Germany and West Africa had borne their first fruits. He had shown the ability to improvise, had faced up to enemy fire, held his nerve, and triumphed over challenges of command that would have confounded many who were his seniors in age and service.

Stockwell's achievement was made clear to all at the time in the citation from General Auchinleck, almost certainly drafted by Gubbins, which led to his being awarded the Distinguished Service Order:

> When placed in command of a mixed force of all arms at a difficult moment in the Rognan Valley operation, he showed great skill and energy in organising a defensive position within a short period, making the fullest use of ground, and by his energy and determination inspiring all ranks to stand and fight.
>
> He held his position successfully for 48 hours until ordered to withdraw. During the withdrawal towards a small and congested harbour [Rognan], close behind where the troops were embarking, he showed great courage and determination when part of his rearguard went astray. He immediately went back, collected two platoons, and went forward with them, and put them into action to stem the German advance.
>
> I cannot speak too highly of this officer's military capacity and

soldierly qualities, displayed at a time when the situation was most difficult, and troops who were under-trained and tired had to be inspired
with the idea of stubborn and successful resistance.

Notes
1 That said, Stockwell's papers from the campaign in King's College London
  contain a good quality Norwegian 1:100,000 map of Bodø and another of the
  Saltdal printed on linen. It is possible, of course, that he obtained these on
  arrival in Norway.
2 The Trappes-Lomax family papers contain an extensive correspondence
  between Trappes-Lomax himself and the authorities. Although his dismissal
  stood, there were clearly reservations about the matter – he finished the War as
  a Brigadier and was appointed CBE.
3 The Independent Companies often carried up to five days supply of pemmican.
  Quintin Riley said that the soldiers often refused to eat pemmican, but were
  quite content if it was called 'special Bovril', or 'Oxo' or 'Marmite' (From Pole
  to Pole, Annex B). It may be this to which Sgt Jones is referring.
4 Derry's official account does not mention No. 4 Independent Company;
  however it is clear from Charles Messenger's interview with the Company
  Commander, Major J.R. Paterson, that the company was indeed present.
5 The task of these officers was to pass reports to higher HQ in Urdu or
  Hindustani, in the hope that these would not be understood by the Germans.
6 The standard calibre of mortar in a German infantry division at this time was
  81mm.

Chapter Seven

Special Forces, 1940–1941

On his return from Norway, Stockwell received a complimentary letter from the GOC 53rd Welsh Division. Major General Wilson wrote that:

> I am both proud and delighted at the success which has obviously been achieved by No 2 Coy and its gallant commander – go on to further glories always remembering to temper valour with discretion . . . I hope you will send me an account of your adventures without any too modest covering up of gallantry so that I can issue it as an inspiration to the division to go and do likewise . . . I have naturally asked for my Co[mpan]y back again. It was the carefully selected cream of the division.

Wilson did not, however, get his men back. On 3 June, in the wake of the Dunkirk evacuation, Churchill had written to the Chiefs of Staff, directing that raiding forces were to be organized in order to keep the Germans tied down on the European coast, on the famous 'butcher and bolt' principle. The response from the War Office was Commandos, special units which would be billeted on seaside towns where they would live off the local economy and train, providing a pool of troops able to undertake raiding operations as required. The difference between the Commandos and the Independent Companies was that whereas the Independent Companies were formed to fight as small, self-contained units, Commandos, as originally envisaged, were to be trained to fight as individuals. There would be ten Commandos with No. 1 being formed from the Independent Companies. On 17 June 1940, Churchill appointed Admiral Sir Roger Keyes as Director of Combined Operations, with Sir Alan Bourne as his deputy, to take over responsibility for raiding operations, for the Combined Operations Development Centre, and for the Irregular Warfare Centre at Lochailort.

But in the short term it was a case of all hands to the pump for home defence; the Independent Companies were not, for the time being, formed into No. 1 Commando, but were divided into two groups and placed under the operational control of HQ Home Forces. On 20 July 1940, Stockwell was appointed to command one of these groups of Independent Companies. This comprised Nos 6, 7, 8 and 9 Companies and his command formed the basis of the anti-invasion defences of the Land's End Zone, based at Carbiss Bay in Cornwall.[1] Once again, Joan and the girls followed the drum and the family moved down from Scotland with Stockwell, and took a house on the seafront at Carbiss Bay.

The main tasks of the group were to protect the beaches, ports and harbours in the zone and in particular, the towns of Penzance, St Just, which also boasted a small aerodrome, and Porthcurno, the terminal for the trans-Atlantic telegraph cable. Manpower was badly stretched, for Nos 6 and 9 Companies were immediately detached to the Isles of Scilly, both to forestall an invasion, and to protect important, and highly secret, forward radar sites on the islands. Thus the defence of the rest of the peninsula was left to Nos 7 and 8 Companies, the local anti-aircraft artillery and searchlight units, and the Local Defence Volunteers. Much time was spent constructing coastal obstacles and defences, cratering roads, and building pill-boxes, trenches, bunkers and observation posts. On 14 July, HQ Southern Command ordered that the ports and harbours of Looe, Par, Mevagissey, Charlestown, Porthleven, Portreath, Appledore, Barnstaple and Bideford should be prepared for immobilization – a major task given the shortage of engineer assistance. The West Country was not a high priority for defence and there were shortages of everything from stores to radar units.

Stockwell also considered that it was important not to lose sight of the original purpose of the Independent Companies, and so he organized cadre courses to train the men in demolition and sabotage, in the use of weapons of all kinds, and in fieldcraft. There was also much emphasis on boat training. To run these courses he needed the help of the small boat training centres on St Mary's Island in the Scillies and at Newlyn. Here he was fortunate, for running them were his old friends from Norway, Quintin Riley and Tiny Fell. Resources were short: in the Scillies there were only three 12-oared cutters, three service whalers, four gigs and three 30-foot motor launches for boat towing. At Newlyn there were only three cutters and one 60-foot launch. These were indeed small beginnings, but until sufficient landing craft of all types could be developed, the tactics and techniques of amphibious operations depended on such as this. But it was heavy going. Riley wrote to his superior, Commander C.H. Pilcher RN, that:

> I have concentrated on watermanship . . . it sounds simple enough to shove the cutter off after the shore party has disembarked, anchor the boat, and return when ordered to the beach; but it takes much practice even to carry out a simple manoeuvre such as this, the importance of which is obvious if a raiding party is to be successfully withdrawn . . . In all the companies the men are beginning to understand the meaning

of silence and to realise the need for the strictest discipline, but they have a long way to go.

Meanwhile, as the Germans continued to build up their invasion fleet, tension mounted. On 7 September a serious invasion scare occurred when a large concentration of shipping was sighted south-west of the Isle of Wight – the codeword 'Cromwell' was received at 9.30 pm, indicating that the Germans were landing and the church bells were rung to sound the general alarm. Stockwell called an orders group where he passed on the information, received from above, that the Germans had landed at Plymouth with the intention of sealing off the peninsula as a bridgehead for further operations inland. Things rapidly returned to normal when the scare was exposed.

By September, the immediate threat of invasion had lifted, and the Independent Companies were returned to the operational control of the Director of Combined Operations. Although offensive operations had originally been envisaged in four phases – reconnaissance and experimentation including coastal raids; guerrilla warfare; deliberate tri-service attacks on carefully defined objectives; and then finally a full-scale re-entry to the European mainland – it was now felt that the first phase was better left to MI(R), and subsequently SOE. Combined Operations began, therefore, to focus very quickly on the third phase – deliberate attacks.

On 17 October, Stockwell, having presumably received orders from above, called a conference of his subordinate commanders and representatives of the small boat training centres. Quintin Riley was there and recorded that Stockwell's group was to be split up: Nos 8 and 9 Companies were to be combined with Nos 1, 2, 3, 4, and 5 Independent Companies in Dartmouth and Paignton to form No. 1 Special Service Battalion, later No. 1 Commando. Nos 6 and 7 Companies would combine with Nos 10 and 11 Commandos to form No. 2 Special Service Battalion.

To make good the deficiencies in training, the training organization was given a shake-up. On 30 October, with his command dispersed, Stockwell was posted to command the Special Training Centre (STC) at Inverailort Castle, Lochailort, in Scotland. This had begun life in May 1940 as the Irregular Warfare School under the aegis of MI(R), and was one of the schools that had been passed to the command of the Director of Combined Operations. Under MI(R), its task had been to train saboteurs; now it was to train the officers and NCOs of the Special Service Brigade. Clearly, the Commandant had to be a man possessed of special qualities. Given his background, character and experience in Norway, Stockwell was an obvious choice for this tough job. For the family, it was back once more to Scotland, with Joan and the girls moving into a house on the estate, and the girls attending a tiny country school nearby.

The results being produced at Inverailort varied from good to rank amateur. Bill Fell recalled how, at about this time, he had travelled up to Inverailort with Admiral Keyes to see a demonstration of a Commando landing. The landing was to be at 1.00 am and so, after a late dinner, they settled down to wait. Keyes went straight to sleep, and Fell got out his fishing rod to try for a sea-trout. The night wore on and there was no landing. Then:

> As dawn broke, I saw two figures standing by the Admiral: Andrew Croft and Quintin Riley. They had led the attack, landed noiselessly, and captured the Admiral and all the strong points. The Admiral woke up and said 'Splendid attack.' I thought this attack a good augury for the future of Combined Operations.

Lochailort lies at the eastern end of Arisaig Sound, an extremely wild, remote, bleak and mountainous region on the west coast of Scotland, about 22 miles west of Fort William in Inverness-shire. The headquarters of the Centre were in the castle at Inverailort belonging to the Laird, Francis Cameron-Head. The castle lay in the shadow of the north-facing side of a steep mountainous slope overlooking a cold, grim loch. The castle saw the sun only for an hour or two around noon each day and the funereal atmosphere was enhanced by the vulture-like wheeling of crows, rooks and buzzards. Around it, a camp of Nissen huts and tents sprang up to supplement the castle and various shooting lodges and crofts in order to house the first students, and a wild bunch of instructors who numbered among them, in addition to Lovat and the Stirling brothers, Freddie Spencer Chapman, 'Mad Mike' Calvert and Peter Kemp, a veteran of the Spanish Civil War.

Under Stockwell's direction, the school evolved from this ad-hoc beginning into a school capable of devising, organizing and running a variety of courses in irregular warfare. For example, there was one on offensive demolitions which, as well as dealing with the technicalities of explosives, bombs, detonators, improvised explosive devices and booby traps, also taught the tactics and techniques of raids. As the introduction to the course booklet put it, 'The object of this course is to teach you to destroy things quickly.' The school also taught street fighting, stalking, bayonet and sword fighting, and first aid. There were short courses on guerrilla warfare for formed units; three-week-long courses on fieldcraft and weapon training for junior NCOs; and weekend courses for the Home Guard.

Because the men of the Commandos were all volunteers, and therefore of higher calibre than might be expected in a normal infantry battalion, the instructors for such a school had to be as exceptional as the Commandant. To teach unarmed combat, there was Captain W.E. (Douglas) Fairbairn, a former policeman in the Shanghai European Concession, and a ju-jitsu black belt – reputedly the first awarded by the Kodokan Ju-jitsu University of Tokyo to a foreigner. Fairbairn was largely responsible for fostering a new and aggressive style of combat in the Commando forces, similar to that which had been prevalent at close quarters in the trenches during the First World War, but had subsequently been forgotten. He taught men never to hesitate, but to disable or kill an enemy using whatever weapons came to hand – if necessary with their hands. He later continued this training with members of Phantom, the SAS and with SOE operatives after the STC closed down.

To teach small arms, Stockwell found Captains P.N. (Wally) Walbridge and W.F. (Bill) Sykes. The latter was a cultured and affable man who had also been in the Shanghai police as a sniper. His chief addiction was big-game hunting and around Lochailort, the closest thing to big game was deer. 'Mad Mike' Calvert and Captain G.B. (Bobby) Holmes of the Royal Engineers taught all types of demolitions – 'everything from battleships to brigadiers'. Jim Gavin, a mountaineer who had been a member of an aborted Everest expedition with Freddie Chapman, planned for 1940, taught climbing. Jimmy Scott, a former polar explorer, holder of the Polar Medal, and expert in Arctic conditions, taught mountain and Arctic warfare. As he was also a close companion of Stockwell's friend from Norway, Quintin Riley, it is probable that Quintin recommended Scott for the job. Captain T.L.A. Clapton taught tactics, and Captain P.A.J. Garnons-Williams of the Royal Artillery taught observation and indirect fire support. Garnons-Williams was a relative of Major H.F. Garnons-Williams of the Royal Welch Fusiliers, and so was well known to Stockwell. To act as Medical Officer at the Centre, Stockwell summoned Captain Gerald Petty – 'Mad Gerry' – of the Royal Army Medical Corps. Petty was a pre-war Territorial Army officer, who was sufficiently fearless and eccentric to have caught Stockwell's eye. Reluctantly, Petty reported as ordered and went straight in to see Stockwell. 'Sir,' he said, 'the Commandos are a volunteer force; I do not wish to volunteer, I wish to return to my Field Ambulance.' 'You are quite right,' replied Stockwell. 'But this is not a Commando unit, it is a training unit with direct orders from the War Office. You will stay. On the other hand, this is a depressing place and friends quarrel, so you can go after three months.'

Much of the training at Inverailort was of the hard, physical sort, such as long-distance marches over the mountains by day and night under full load. David Niven did the course in 1940 and, remembered that: 'After two months running up and down the mountains of the Western Highlands, crawling up streams at night, and swimming in the loch with full equipment, I was un-bearably fit.' But this kind of thing was interspersed with more technical training. Stockwell himself joined in the practical aspects of the Centre, giving lectures and demonstrations on raiding operations, stressing the need for high-quality intelligence, rehearsal, clearly defined, limited objectives, and close co-operation between landing force and naval or air component. The remit of the Centre changed constantly: in June 1940, Stockwell was tasked to run courses to train an assault troop per infantry division – with the same basic techniques as the Special Service Brigade.

In July 1941, Stockwell's short term of command at the STC ended when he was appointed to command the 2nd Battalion Royal Welch Fusiliers. Short it may have been, but it was clearly highly effective as for his work at Lochailort he was mentioned in despatches. A letter from Brigadier Charles Haydon, Commander 1 Special Service Brigade, sets out Stockwell's achievements in unusually strong terms:

> We all of us owe you an extremely big debt of gratitude and no-one is more conscious of that than I am. You have had a devilish task to carry out and I do not believe that anyone else could have accomplished half as much in the face of the thousand and one difficulties with which you were confronted . . . The whole atmosphere of the place changed visibly while you were there and your staff are, I know, as sorry to lose you as we are.
>
> The only lucky ones are your Battalion. I can just imagine how much you are going to enjoy every moment of that command.

His battalion was part of 29 Independent Infantry Brigade, an amphibious formation. The appointments system seemed to be working – an officer with considerable experience in special, and specialist, operations was being posted to command a battalion in exactly that role.

Notes

1 G.F. Petty has stated in his autobiography *Mad Gerry – Welsh Wartime Medical Officer* (Newport, 1992) that Stockwell commanded No. 11 Commando in the raid on Guernsey on 14/15 July 1940, and was subsequently reprimanded for its lack of success. This is not true. The raid was conducted by No. 3 Commando under the command of John Durnford-Slater, and No. 11 Commando under Ronnie Tod. No personal reprimands were ever issued. See Charles Messenger, *The Commandos 1940–1946*, pp. 33-5.

Chapter Eight

The Invasion of Madagascar, 1942

Hugh Stockwell rejoined the 2nd Battalion Royal Welch Fusiliers as its Commanding Officer on 22 July 1941, twelve and a half years after he had left it in Tidworth as a mere captain. The men now wore battledress instead of the old service dress, and troops formed threes on parade rather than fours; but in terms of organization the battalion still looked superficially similar to that of 1930, with four rifle companies each of three platoons, and a Headquarter Company. This apparent similarity, however, masked some important improvements in capability. Each section had a Bren light machine gun, and each platoon a two-inch mortar and a Boyes anti-tank rifle. At battalion level, HQ Company included a signal platoon, a light machine gun platoon for air defence, a platoon of six 3-inch mortars, a defence platoon (the Corps of Drums), an assault pioneer platoon, a platoon equipped with the tracked Universal carrier, usually known as the Bren gun carrier, which provided mobile firepower, and the Regimental Band which in war doubled up as stretcher bearers. In 29 Independent Infantry Brigade, to which the battalion belonged, battalions also had a motorcycle platoon whose duties included some limited scouting, and dispatch riding.

The circumstances in which Stockwell moved to command his battalion were unusual even in wartime. In command at the time was Llewellyn Gwydyr-Jones, an old friend from Pembroke Dock days, who was senior to Stockwell. It was clear that Stockwell was marked for higher things, while Gwydyr would perhaps make one more step up – but Stockwell had to prove his ability in command of a regular infantry battalion. A friendly gentlemen's agreement was therefore reached whereby Gwydyr very gallantly stepped down and remained in the battalion as Second-in-Command. In modern times, this may seem a curious arrangement, but Gwydyr accepted it with his invariable good humour and courtesy. Not that there could there be any question about Gwydyr's ability to command – he had already proved it and would do so again many times over in the bitter fighting in Burma during 1943 and 1944. Gwydyr was a hard act for Stockwell to follow for he had a great affinity with people, and especially with his fusiliers. It may seem a cliché to say that they would follow him anywhere and do anything for him, but it was nonetheless true. He was a man of deep-set feelings which he kept closely guarded, under an extrovert, charismatic and urbane exterior; he also had the disarming habit of calling everyone 'my dear'.

As well as Gwydyr, there were some old friends from Pembroke Dock and Germany: John Vaughan commanded Headquarter Company, and the Regimental Serjeant Major was none other than Stockwell's old friend from his days as Cadre Officer in Germany, Sammy Metcalfe. But soldiering is a young man's business and twelve years is a long time in terms of the turnover of manpower in an infantry battalion. Many of the officers and men whom Stockwell had known in his earlier days had completed their terms of service and had been replaced by others. Stockwell's command group was made up of Captain George Demetriadi, the Adjutant; Captain James Willans, the Intelligence Officer; and Lieutenant Cliff Burton, the Quartermaster. His other subordinates, commanding the four rifle companies of the battalion, were Major James Vyvyan (A Company), Captain John Dickson (B Company),[1] Captain Brian Cotton (C Company) and Captain Michael Harrison (D Company). What was their impression of their new commanding officer? Most of them knew him by reputation only and this, from Norway and subsequent exploits as well as old soldiers' tales from the 1920s, was formidable. Also, the Royal Welch Fusiliers was a family regiment or it was nothing, and Stockwell came from a regimental family – it helped. There must have been some lingering unease about the manner of Gwydyr's replacement, but Gwydyr was the soul of loyalty and Stockwell's undoubted charm and charisma, his obvious qualities of leadership, his courage, and his intuitive grasp of military operations quickly put these to rest. It was not long before every man in the battalion recognized that here was a commanding officer who would not only take them into battle, but also lead them through it and out at the far side successfully. He had, as Henry Jones recalled, a fine, strong personality, always encouraging and positive, and possessed great charm and an excellent, twinkling sense of humour. Moreover, the men knew that here was a man who would not play games with their lives.

The 2nd Battalion Royal Welch Fusiliers had returned from India in 1940 after the fall of France, to join 29 Brigade, first under the command of Brigadier (later Lieutenant General Sir) Oliver Leese, and later under Brigadier John Grover. The other fighting units of the brigade were the 1st Royal Scots Fusiliers, under Lieutenant Colonel W.S. (William) Ritchie, 2nd East Lancashires under Lieutenant Colonel T.A. (Tom) Eccles, and 2nd South Lancashires under Lieutenant Colonel M.G.A.R. (Michael) West.[2] By March 1941, the brigade had reached a sufficient standard that it was sent for intensive training in combined operations around Loch Fyne, at the Combined Training Centre, Inverary and in the Orkneys. At the time of moving north, the commanding officers were told that there would only be time for ten days' training before an operation was to be launched, but three weeks later, after the fall of Crete, the brigade was stood down and normal training resumed. Demonstrations were given to King George VI and Prime Minister Winston Churchill at Scapa Flow at the end of June, and the results were mixed. Lieutenant, later Rear Admiral, Teddy Gueritz,[3] recalled that these 'registered about 8–9 on the Richter Scale of cock-ups even by the standards of Combined Ops at the time! Keyes was relieved as DCO soon after.' Churchill, still doubtless bearing the scars of Gallipoli, signalled after the demonstration:

> For the success of the operations for which they are being trained, perfect co-operation between units of all three Services is essential, and to achieve this, long, hard and patient training is inevitable. It was evident that this is cheerfully accepted and loyally carried out.

For several months, the battalions lived on troopships – in the case of the 2nd Royal Welch Fusiliers this was the *Ettrick*. Even though the *Ettrick* was a new ship and described as 'quite comfortable', it must have been with some relief that the battalion moved ashore on 14 July, first to Inverary, where further demonstrations were given to the CIGS and the American Ambassador on 19 July, and then, shortly after Stockwell arrived, to Dumfries on 25 July. Finally on 12 August the battalion moved to Selkirk. Here Joan and the girls moved once more, to a rented private house in the town.

Brigade training at Selkirk included rehearsing amphibious skills with beach assaults from landing craft, development of a bridgehead, and the breakout and advance inland. Some of this training was done under the auspices of the Royal Marine Division and as a result Stockwell got to know Major General Robert Sturges.[4] In October, Grover was promoted to Major General and assumed command of the 2nd Infantry Division. Brigadier Francis Festing,[5] known by the troops after the Madagascar operation as 'Front Line Frankie', took command of the brigade. Thereafter, training again stepped up to include co-operation with tanks, artillery and engineers, by day and night.

Training resumed relentlessly in early January. On 1 March 1942, the battalion war diary, written by George Demetriadi, recorded that: 'Today, in spite of the exigencies of war, all Royal Welchmen made a loyal attempt to recapture the spirit of St David's Day.'

It was nineteen years to the day since young Hughie Stockwell had joined 2nd Royal Welch Fusiliers at Pembroke Dock – most officers go through their early years with the unspoken ambition of commanding their battalion in years to come, but precious few achieve it. Stockwell had done so in a very respectable time frame, and, what was more, against the odds, given that he had not been to the Staff College. The War had given him his chance – and he had risen to it. What quiet satisfaction, mingled with pride, it must have given him to watch the youngest subaltern eat his leek, and to remember his own debut.

*   *   *

After St David's Day, training and exercises again resumed. Then, suddenly, on 20 March, with the brigade two days into an exercise, orders were received for a move from Selkirk that night:

> In the early months of '42 2 RWF was again moved to Loch Fyne, this time to do 'enemy' to a landing force of Royal Marines and this was known to be a rehearsal for an actual operation. Shortly after St David's Day 1942 the bn was for the third and last time doing tr[ainin]g in Loch Fyne. One morning without warning HMS *Karanja* steamed us back to Gaurock and that night the Bn was again in Selkirk, the exercise uncompleted. It had fallen to 29IB to do the operation for which they had provided the enemy during rehearsals. A move to Ceylon, with a view to operations to assist the Army in Burma, was used as the cover plan . . . and the troops whilst at Selkirk were told merely that we were re-embarking to do the exercise so suddenly postponed. The fitting of Topees hardly lent colour to the story.

It so happened that the DAA&QMG of the brigade, Major the Hon D.F. (David) Brand,[6] was away reconnoitring billets for the move of the brigade to an area in Fife which had been ordered before the exercise, and was to take place immediately afterwards. Festing was summoned to London for an operational briefing and Stockwell was placed in temporary command of the brigade. On 15 March, Stockwell received a telegram reducing the brigade's notice to move, and that evening he called a conference of the commanding officers and key staff to issue the movement orders. The brigade was to embark at Greenock on the 21st in HMS *Karanja*. No destination was given, indeed the men were told that they were re-embarking for the exercise, which was to be rescheduled. This, and the story of the move to Fife, allowed the brigade to move away from the Galashiels area without undue comment, and when Festing returned on 17th, preparations were well advanced. However, during the course of the next days, it became known that the whole of 29 Brigade Group had embarked in transports, with full mobilization stocks. Rumours began to circulate once more: was this really just another exercise? Or was it a change of station? Or could it be the real thing at last? These questions were partly answered two days later, as the war diary recounts:

> This morning [23rd March] the Commanding Officer in a short lecture pleaded guilty to the charge of having 'put one over' on us. We were, he said, bound for operations overseas, a fact which rendered patently obvious the necessity for the utmost secrecy until the last moment. The Battalion was getting its chance.
>
> The announcement was greeted by cheers on all sides which, if not indicative of a general feeling of exuberance, at least showed a valiant attempt to conceal any other which might be there.

What Stockwell knew, but the rest of the battalion did not, was their destination: the island of Madagascar, off the coast of East Africa.

The importance of the island of Madagascar lay in the fact that, with the Mediterranean still an area of contention with the Axis, the Allied main supply routes to North Africa, the Middle East, Australia and India, as well as one route to Russia, were by sea round the Cape of Good Hope and then northwards up the east coast of Africa. Twelve million tons of oil was passing this way each year from the Anglo-Iranian oilfields in Azerbaijan, roughly the equivalent of the civilian consumption of the British Isles, so that although most of this was going to Australia, this trade was putting back into the Allied pot the equivalent of what Britain was taking out. Most convoys passed through the Mozambique Channel between Madagascar and the continental coast. The entry of the Japanese into the War had cast a long shadow over the security of this route, and as early as the autumn of 1941 plans had been made to forestall a perceived threat to the island by Japanese forces. It was now thought possible that, given the scale of early Japanese victories thus far, their submarines, ships and aircraft might soon be able to threaten these routes. It was therefore vital to secure Madagascar, whose main harbour in the bay of Diego Suarez and its associated airstrip was large enough to hold a sizeable Japanese fleet with air support.

The Vichy French government controlled the island and the British view at this point was that either Vichy might reinforce it in the near future, thus making the task of capturing it more difficult, or, more likely, that Vichy troops would offer no resistance to a Japanese invasion. The Japanese already controlled Manila, Guam, Singapore, the Dutch East Indies, the Andaman Islands and Rangoon. With the benefit of hindsight, one might feel that the Japanese could not have held Madagascar for long, but at the time, things looked rather different.

The Vichy government was by this time entirely hostile to the Allied cause, for the preceding two years had seen bitter fighting between British and Empire troops and the French. The French colonial authorities were traditionally of an independent mind and were suspicious that the British would seize any French colony if it suited them. They were therefore disposed to fight, and the chances of the British receiving any warning of a Japanese threat to the island in time to react were felt to be slight – therefore the best means of anticipating such action would be to seize the initiative. Accordingly, in mid-March 1942, Operation Ironclad was launched, with the object of capturing the anchorage of Diego Suarez bay and the port of Antsirane. The rest of the island was of less importance, and the capture of the capital, Tananarive, and the only other sizeable cities, Tamatave and Majunga, could be carried out as subsequent operations.

The assault on Madagascar, which was to follow a long sea voyage, was therefore the second major combined operation of the War – if the fiasco of Dakar is counted as the first – and as it turned out was to be the only occasion other than the Falklands War of 1982, and later Iraq in 2005, in which a two-star Royal Marine general would command a force ashore. It was, moreover, the first operation on this scale since the Dardanelles twenty-seven years before, since when the techniques of amphibious landing operations had been completely revolutionized by the British. However, the commanders, staffs and troops of all three Services lacked any real experience.

Planning for the invasion had in fact begun by the Joint Planning Staff *before* the Japanese attack on Pearl Harbour under the codename Bonus, a fact which reveals considerable foresight and says much about the confidence of the government and the War Office in the ability of Allied forces in the Far East to withstand a Japanese attack. Matters reached a head in March 1942, with the Japanese capture of Singapore, Rangoon and Java, and the decision to attack Madagascar, using a modified plan developed by COHQ, was taken by the War Cabinet on 12 March. Rear Admiral Neville Syfret,[7] the Commander of Naval Force H, was nominated as the Combined Commander of the expedition. Force H normally protected Gibraltar, but had been replaced temporarily by a US force.

By this time, 102 RM Brigade was unavailable and so the assault force, which was designated Force 121 and which Sturges was nominated to command as Syfret's deputy, consisted of 29 Independent Infantry Brigade, No. 5 Commando, B (Special Service) Squadron of the Royal Armoured Corps (six Valentines and six Tetrarch light tanks), 455 Light Battery Royal Artillery and a troop of 19 Field Battery RA (four 3.7-inch howitzers and two 25-pounder guns, all with tractors) and 145 Light Anti-Aircraft Troop (four Bofors guns). Also in England was the 5th Infantry Division, with three brigades and divisional troops, preparing to embark for India. One of its brigades, 17 Infantry Brigade, was detached to Force 121. This brigade had received none of the training in amphibious operations given to 29 Brigade, and would not therefore be engaged in any assault landing, but used as a follow-up or second-echelon force. Because of the short time available for mounting the operation, the limited shipping and the rough nature of the terrain, vehicles and heavy artillery pieces in the force were reduced to a minimum. Enough stores for thirty days of combat operations were carried.

Force 121 sailed with seasickness widespread and as a result, morale was low – the general desire was to huddle in a corner and die. However by 25 March, the men were beginning to find their sea legs and PT parades, ship's rounds, and boat drills began to gain prominence; for Hugh Stockwell, it was the voyage to Norway all over again – albeit that there was the prospect of warmer weather – except that in order to try to maintain secrecy, many of the troops had been issued with Arctic clothing! Later, it was put about that the destination was Rangoon. This was reinforced on 31 March, when khaki drill uniforms were taken into service with great self-consciousness on the part of most, but with the old sweats affecting their usual nonchalance. One difference from the norm, however, was the issue of steel helmets in place of the topees that had been given out earlier.

The convoy which included 29 Brigade Group, and the whole of the 5th

Infantry Division, formed up at Liverpool. Once the convoy had formed, it represented one of the largest to have left Britain since the end of the First World War. The convoy sailed first to Freetown in Sierra Leone, arriving on 5 April, when the landing elements made rendezvous with the naval force assigned to the operation from Force H. The task group was to be further reinforced by elements of the Eastern Fleet. The force under Admiral Syfret's command therefore comprised the battleship *Ramillies* – the flagship; the fleet aircraft carriers *Illustrious* and *Indomitable*, each carrying a mix of Swordfish torpedo-bombers, Sea Hurricane fighters, Fulmar and Albacore light bombers; the seaplane carrier and HQ ship HMS *Albatross*; the cruisers *Devonshire* and *Hermione*; and escorts including eleven destroyers, six minesweepers, and six anti-submarine corvettes. During the voyage down, the staffs had been hard at work preparing an operational briefing for commanding officers; the only people who knew the final destination up to this point were Syfret, Sturges, the Senior Naval Officer Landing, Captain Aylmer Garnons-Williams, Festing and their key staff officers, a few commanding officers like Stockwell, and one NCO, Sergeant W. (Bill) Lonsdale, the Brigade Intelligence Sergeant. At Freetown, therefore, came the first opportunity for senior commanders to give outline orders and discuss plans with their opposite numbers and their subordinates, and put in hand the necessary deception and disinformation measures to help ensure secrecy. On 16 April, an additional floating reserve, 13 Infantry Brigade Group, also from 5th Infantry Division, was placed under command in the event of more serious opposition being encountered than was expected, or for use in subsequent mopping-up operations.

From Freetown, the force sailed on to Durban in South Africa in two convoys – a fast one carrying 17 and 29 Brigades, and a slower one carrying 13 Brigade and stores. Jim Stockman, a veteran of the campaign then serving with the 6th Seaforths in 17 Infantry Brigade, remembered some details of the voyage in an article in the *British Army Review*:

> What I remember most vividly about that time were the old Swordfish aircraft taking off jauntily from the carriers and joining in the hunt, and then making their precarious landings on return, destroyers hooting and shooting flares in signals we could not understand. At one point, I was approximately 300 yards from the *Indomitable* and was treated to a close-quarters display of landing Swordfish. We had never seen anything like it before and lined the deck to watch, fascinated by the pilots' skill and daring. The first one came down, was trapped by cables and pulled away . . . When the third Swordfish came in, however, there was a massive swell. The poor devil hit the deck and although the cables caught him, he slid on and went over the edge, slipping under the water with alarming speed . . . From conversations I had with the naval staff on our troopship, I discovered that he was lost, gathering that a pilot did not stand a chance going under in that type of aircraft.

On 15 April, Stockwell assembled the battalion for a talk in which he expressed great admiration for the wholehearted support he had received from all ranks since leaving Scotland. He was satisfied, he said, that every man was pulling his weight. However, the main reason for the talk was not mutual congratulation, but to stress the need for the utmost secrecy during the time that the convoy was to spend in South Africa – careless talk, as the contemporary poster put it, would certainly cost lives.

The convoy rounded the Cape on 18 April and made rendezvous at Durban on the 22nd, where it joined up with 13 Infantry Brigade. Together, the enlarged force severely taxed the limits of the port, which because of the situation in the Mediterranean was a main staging post for convoys to the Middle East and India. 2 RWF had passed through Durban on its way home from India in 1940 and had clearly had a whale of a time – the old hands expected to find the dockside lined with cars waiting to convey the troops to a paradise of beer and skittles. Alas, although the *Winchester Castle* was sung alongside by Pearl Griedle Gibson – the Lady in White – and the locals were hospitable, the enthusiasm of pre-war days had largely evaporated; two years of war, and weekly convoys, had bred too much familiarity with the military. The force sailed again in two convoys, under conditions of great secrecy, although there was much talk of Madagascar, despite the deception arrangements. The slow convoy sailed first on 25 April, the second, faster one on the 28th. Two days out from Durban, the destination was revealed to the troops, and D-Day for the invasion was fixed for 5 May.

Madagascar, the third largest island in the world, lies about 2,000 miles north of the Cape, and about the same distance from Colombo. The island is just over 1,000 miles from north to south, and 300 miles from east to west; its population in 1942 stood at about three million. The expedition was not intended to occupy the whole of this vast landmass, but to neutralize it and deny its use to the Japanese by occupying the key ports and facilities. The object of the attack, the sprawling port of Antsirane in the anchorage of Diego Suarez, had been completed as recently as 1935 and was well protected by coastal batteries. The anchorage lay on the eastern side of the island, very close to the northern tip. A glance at the map shows that the entrance to the harbour, known as Port Nievre, is only about 1,200 yards wide, making the anchorage almost landlocked. Although the seaward side was heavily defended, Antsirane and Diego Suarez itself could be reached from the west over land, as the island was only about 10 miles wide at this point. The French had, however, built some strong defensive positions on the western side of the island to deter such a course of action.

Intelligence estimates of the Vichy French forces on the island were good. A comprehensive briefing pack had been prepared in February 1942, and this was supplemented by reports from a team of SOE agents on the island, led by Percy Meyer and his French wife, Berthe. These reports estimated the Vichy forces at about 8,000, of whom three-quarters were native Malagasies, and

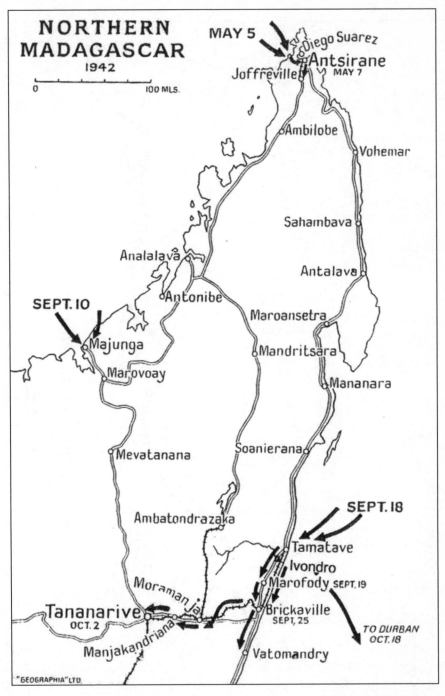

Source: Lieutenant Commander P.K. Kemp and John Graves, *The Red Dragons: the Story of the Royal Welch Fusiliers 1919–1945* (Aldershot, 1960).

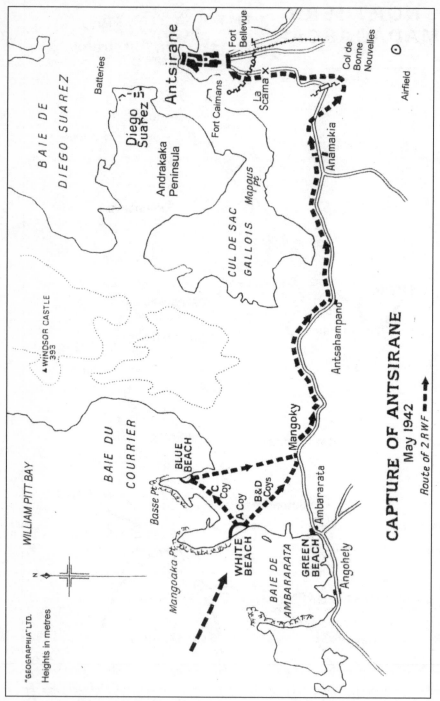

CAPTURE OF ANTSIRANE
May 1942

Route of 2 RWF ■ ■ ■ ►

Source: Lieutenant Commander P.K. Kemp and John Graves, *The Red Dragons: the Story of the Royal Welch Fusiliers 1919–1945* (Aldershot, 1960).

the rest mainly Senegalese regiments, although some Foreign Legion units were also believed to be present. At Diego Suarez itself there were thought to be between 1,500 and 3,000 troops whose chief task was to man the defensive forts with their heavy guns, of which there were eight, although intelligence had suggested nine. Supporting these land forces were some naval and air units: in the harbour were two small sloops, two armed merchantmen and five submarines; on the airstrip there were just four aircraft. The remaining seventeen Morane 406 fighters and ten Potez 63 bombers were 600 miles away at Ivato near Tananarive, unable to interfere with the operation without a refuelling stop, which did not exist. As things turned out, the Vichy troops 'fought professionally and furiously. No wonder our task force was so large.' The experience of Syria should have been enough to make this plain from the start.

On the morning of 4 May, Stockwell again called the battalion together for a final talk. 'He was,' George Demetriadi wrote, 'confident of success, at the same time stressing the importance of not underestimating the enemy. Short and straight was the order of the day. The sooner we finished the job, he said, the sooner we will be sailing back to Blighty.' That night, in fine weather and under a brilliant full moon, the ships were guided with immense skill through the unlit, mined and rocky channel, negotiating reefs, shoals, and unpredictable currents – a feat which the Vichy authorities considered to be impossible. The minesweepers even detonated two of the seventeen mines they swept, but despite the roar of these two explosions there was no response from the defenders ashore. Shortly before 1.00 am on 5 May the transports passed through William Pitt Bay and dropped anchor in the smaller Courrier Bay, out of range of the guns of a nearby French coastal battery. Stockwell recalled that:

> At 2040 hrs [on 4/5 May] the navigation lights on the island of Nosi Fati, placed there by the cutter Lindi, from which the previous S.O.E. landings in the island had been made, were seen; the convoy carried out the approach in perfect order in spite of considerable difficulties.

Admiral Syfret's task group lay offshore, ready to engage the defenders with gunfire or with aircraft. The assault plan called for landings on the west shore of the island's northern tip, where several suitable beaches would make for an easy landing. The initial assault would be made by 29 Brigade and No. 5 Commando in the *Winchester Castle*, which was taken close inshore by the intrepid Captain Newdigate. The Commando, reinforced by a company of the 2nd East Lancashires, was to land in Courrier Bay on three beaches codenamed Red North, Red Centre, and Red South, and capture two coastal batteries – there turned out to be only one, since the French had such confidence in the protection of the bay's natural defences – supported, if required, by the guns of HMS *Devonshire*. The main body of 29 Brigade would land further south at three beaches codenamed Blue, White and Green, the last being near the village of Ambararata. As a deception, the cruiser *Hermione* was to lie off the main harbour and bombard the fortifications, while dummy parachutists were dropped inland. The force would then advance eastwards, with 29 Brigade, supported by tanks, moving on Antsirane while the Commando advanced parallel to the main axis towards Diego Suarez. When both places had been secured, the final phase of the operation would be an assault on the Orangea peninsula, supported by naval gunfire. Sturges, who had served at Gallipoli with the Royal Naval Division and who therefore knew the penalty of not pushing inland rapidly from a beach landing, urged his subordinates that speed was of the essence, and that initial successes must be exploited rapidly and ruthlessly.

Before the assault commenced, Swordfish aircraft dropped copies of a leaflet signed by Admiral Syfret addressed to the Vichy Governor, inviting him to surrender. A reply was asked for by radio, or under a white flag. Thanks to the Royal Navy's near-perfect navigation, landing began to the minute at 4.30 am, about eighty minutes before sunrise; at the same time, the airfield and harbour were attacked with torpedoes, depth charges, bombs and machine guns – with devastation being wreaked on Vichy ships and aircraft. The submarine *Bévéziers* and the frigate *Bouganville* were sunk alongside; two other submarines which were out at sea were later sunk as they tried to attack the British force; and all French aircraft were destroyed. As a result, the French were unable to intervene in any effective way against the landing force. No. 5 Commando captured the battery – known as 'Windsor Castle' – without difficulty, and soon established that it was the only fortification in the area. The East Lancashires came ashore unopposed on Blue Beach, and the Royal Scots Fusiliers likewise on Green Beach, which was found to be unsuitable for any vehicles. Stockwell and the 2nd Royal Welch landed on White beach. Jim Stockman summed up the feelings of many that day:

> There is always a first time for everything, and we made many amphibious assaults later in the war which did not require so much psychological boosting. But the first assault always stands out so vividly, that huge block of ice slowly melting in the pit of the stomach. We really had no idea what to expect going into the attack this way, a situation that all the training and conditioning in the world will never produce the reality you anticipate.

Stockwell and his fusiliers found themselves in Ambararata Bay, among some deserted islands, under a full moon. Not a light was to be seen anywhere, but as on other beaches, SOE agents made themselves known, acting as guides and advisers. Stockwell and his command post team, along with A and C Companies, came ashore at 4.30 am, whilst B and D Companies were held in reserve. Henry Jones, second-in-command of D Company, recalled that 'We got into the landing craft in a heavy swell. One minute you were looking up at the side of the ship, and next minute you could see down her funnel! The result was that we all lost our breakfasts.'

The landing craft were unable to complete the approach to the beach because of a coral reef, so the men had to wade ashore, however this presented no difficulty at all, other than to discover that the beach was hard going for all vehicles except tracks, making Blue the only practicable beach for vehicles on the brigade front. The official accounts say that not a shot was fired, however Lieutenant Ray Simmons, commanding the leading platoon of A Company, recalled otherwise:

We had been told to expect little in the way of beach defences, but that there might be sharks in the water. As I was wading ashore I heard a big splash just near me, so I pulled out my pistol and shot at it. There was another splash and I fired again. Whatever it was – a crocodile I think – made off.

At 4.40 am the success flares went up, and B and D Companies immediately came ashore. As dawn was breaking, these two companies pushed forward to the village of Mangoky, which was found to be undefended. Within two hours, 2,000 men were ashore and at the front of the brigade main axis, Stockwell was pushing the Royal Welch forward, followed by the Scots Fusiliers from Green Beach, having left C Company to secure the perimeter at Blue Beach, and A Company to do the same at White Beach. C Company bumped into a group of Senegalese setting up a machine gun outside a village, but the position was rapidly stormed and the village burned. The Senegalese showed no inclination to press the issue and most of them dropped their weapons and fled into the bush. Festing and Stockwell, meanwhile, were well up with the leading companies in Bren gun carriers. It must have seemed all too easy.

As the sun came up, the heat and humidity increased until the temperature reached 100°F, and the troops slogged on along the single unmade road in a cloud of choking red dust which clung to their still-wet clothes. Water, it seemed, was likely to be a bigger logistic requirement than ammunition. Since little transport had been landed so far, the men were carrying as much as they could of their first-line scales: not just rifles, Bren guns, mortars and anti-tank rifles, but also boxes of ammunition, mortar bombs, radios and batteries. They were, Henry Jones remembered, going as fast as their legs would carry them, and so there was little leisure for the men to enjoy their first sights of this tropical paradise – the dense vegetation on each side of the road, trees and bushes sprouting bananas and other fruits not seen in wartime Britain, a glimpse of a brightly coloured bird. Stockwell further remarked in his report to the Colonel of the Regiment that:

The map provided was very inaccurate and of a small scale, 1/100,000. It seems regrettable that when planning this operation it had not been possible to obtain copies of the very excellent French maps which were subsequently discovered to exist and were to be bought at the modest price of 5 frs.

No French troops were seen until about 9.30 am, when an officer and three sailors were surprised and captured near the village of Anamakia by the motorcycle platoon of 2nd Royal Welch Fusiliers. Since Sturges had ordered that the first officer prisoner was to be sent off to the Vichy Governor with a copy of the surrender leaflet, the man was duly despatched in his own car. This, as it turned out, was a bad mistake, as the French were made well aware of the direction of the British main attack. In time, an answer was returned to Stockwell, who was with Festing at the time: the French would defend the town to the last man!

At about 10.45 am, the Carrier Platoon reported to Stockwell that the ground was clear as far as the village of Anamakia; C Company had now been released from its task at the beach and Brian Cotton was hurrying the men along the road trying to catch up with the rest of the battalion. But at about 11.15 am, the first opposition was encountered on a ridge called, rather inappropriately, Col de Bonne Nouvelle. The ridge was lightly defended with a trench system and a small garrison. Beyond it the main Vichy position, a sort of mini-Maginot Line, had rather alarmingly not been picked up by aerial reconnaissance. The position consisted of a trench system almost a mile and a quarter long with well-camouflaged strongpoints and concrete pillboxes on the forward slope. Behind this line was the main position, centred on two strong redoubts, Forts Caimans and Bellevue, each mounting 75mm field guns, mortars and heavy machine guns that covered the approaches and the obstacles. The position had obviously been well sited by professional soldiers who knew their business. The two forts were connected by an elaborate trench system, protected in front by a deep anti-tank ditch and on their flanks by mangrove swamps falling away to the sea.

The Vichy defenders in the forward positions opened fire on the leading carriers of the 2nd Royal Welch as soon as they came into view. Festing's carrier was up among them, and the first casualty was his driver who was hit in the hand. The big, ginger-haired figure of the Brigadier jumped out of the carrier, accompanied by a couple of staff officers, and took cover among the trees by the roadside. Shortly afterwards, when two Valentine and one Tetrarch light tank rumbled up the road, Festing hurried across, banged on the turret of the first Valentine with his stick to get the commander's attention and with the assistance of the tank was able to extricate himself from trouble. Having done so, he sent all available carriers to bring up the marching men more quickly, so that a flanking attack could be put in.

While this was going on, the tanks engaged the French line and at first it appeared that they had silenced the enemy machine guns. The gunners, however, had gone to ground and once the tanks had passed them, they opened up again on the infantry. Orders reached Stockwell to move up the

2nd Royal Welch and the men moved forward, the crash of artillery and mortars and the crackle of rifle and machine-gun fire clearly audible to the sweating fusiliers. Having talked to Festing and had a look at the position, Stockwell decided to seize the initiative and go in quickly with B and D Companies, rather than wait for A and C. Certainly, there was little advantage in waiting, for no more fire support would be available unless naval gunfire could be brought to bear, and delay merely allowed the defenders more time to prepare themselves.

By noon he had given orders to Dickson and Harrison, and all was ready for a right-flanking attack: B Company on the right and D on the left. With four Valentines in support, the battalion stormed the ridge in proper old-fashioned style at the point of the bayonet. Stockwell positioned himself on one flank in his carrier, with George Demetriadi in the centre of the two companies, controlling the rate of advance. Gwydyr, meanwhile, was watching matters from the driver's seat of a steamroller on the main road, a position which he was obliged to exchange for a ditch when the vehicle attracted a good deal of incoming fire. As the battalion advanced, bullets began whistling past Stockwell's ears, but from immediately behind him. He turned round quickly, exclaiming, 'My Goodness! They have got us from the rear!' only to find that his batman, Fusilier Jones, was firing from the hip straight ahead. 'Try the enemy, not me,' was Stockwell's advice to Jones – and the attack continued. It was not serious business, for the few Senegalese troops seemed more determined to get away than to hang on to their positions. The fusiliers, however, were taking no chances, for enemy snipers had been active. Michael Harrison was killed by a single shot, leading D Company up the forward slope, and Henry Jones took over command of the company. Jones saw the sniper running off and, more in hope than expectation, fired his revolver at the man. It was a lucky shot – the man's body was found soon afterwards. Lieutenant Ken Bonnell-Jones died, again from a single shot, leading his platoon against a machine-gun post. He and Harrison were buried near where they fell, on the Col de Bonne Nouvelle. By 2.00 pm it was all over, and the position was secure, apart from some desultory sniping which went on for some time, but most of the Senegalese in the end surrendered rather than face close combat with the bayonet. The fusiliers were quite exhausted, physically and emotionally, by what was for most their first taste of combat – but it was remarkable what a brew of hot tea could accomplish. By the time A and C Companies came up between 3.00 and 4.00 pm, and the battalion was together again, the men had quite recovered, even to the extent of a few derisory shouts about battle-dodging!

In the meantime, the two leading Valentines, followed by three Tetrarchs, had driven on and come up against the main position, where tank traps, pill boxes and ditches, all covered by the direct fire of weapons of every kind, brought them to a halt. Every tank was knocked out by accurate and sustained anti-tank fire from the forts. The remaining Valentines followed up, and two more were also knocked out, so that by 6.00 pm only one Valentine and three

Tetrarchs were battle-worthy. Festing by now had his entire brigade up close to the position, centred on a ramshackle group of buildings including an abattoir, a meat-packing factory and a hostelry known as Robinson's Hotel in the village of La Scama – it was in fact a store run by a Chinese who greatly endeared himself to the troops by giving out tea and food, refusing all offers of payment, until his stocks ran out.

While the troops took advantage of this unexpected bounty, Festing gave orders for a deliberate attack. The 2nd Royal Welch, having borne the brunt of the initial attack, was to reorganize and become the brigade reserve. The attack was to be led by the Scots Fusiliers, and the South Lancashires and East Lancashires were to follow. The attack got as far as the anti-tank ditch a few hundred yards in front of the position, and there halted. In the face of heavy fire, and with no cover, fire support or smoke to suppress the Vichy positions, further progress was impossible. The short tropical dusk was upon them and in the swiftly gathering darkness, Festing ordered all his units to form all-round defence; the Scots Fusiliers were to maintain contact with the enemy using patrols and snipers. Smoke from the British naval and air bombardment could be seen rising from the direction of Antsirane as Stockwell and the Royal Welch Fusiliers went into close perimeter. The men were surprised at how quickly the tropical night descended and soon the flicker of Tommy cookers announced the arrival of that essential tonic for the British soldier, a brew of tea. Most men were able to get some sleep, although Captain Charles Cunningham, the battalion's medical officer, was hard at work in his aid post at Robinson's Hotel, remaining at his post for thirty-six hours without a break.

Back at the beaches, 17 Brigade had begun to land at 11.15 am, once disembarkation of 29 Brigade had been completed. By midnight on 5 May, 17 Brigade and all 29 Brigade's vehicles had been successfully put ashore. Festing therefore issued new orders at 11.00 pm. The South Lancashires were ordered to work their way in darkness round the eastern flank of the two forts in the swampy, broken ground which fell away towards the sea shore. At 5.30 am on 6 May, all available carrier-based aircraft would bomb and strafe the enemy positions for thirty minutes, after which the South Lancashires would attack the position from the flank and rear. This attack would be the signal for the Scots Fusiliers and the East Lancashires to put in a frontal assault, supported by the guns of 455 Light Battery. The 2nd Royal Welch Fusiliers were to remain in reserve.

As dawn came, the aerial bombardment went in as planned, but nothing was heard of the South Lancashires. The frontal assault moved forward, but again fire was heavy – the defenders had plenty of ammunition and knew their ground. Their guns were ranged in and any movement attracted a fearsome amount of incoming fire. In the face of bursting artillery rounds and streams of tracer from machine guns, flesh and blood could make no progress. By 7.00 am, Festing broke off the attack.

The 2nd Royal Welch Fusiliers had woken early on 6 May to sniping.

Festing came up to join them, and he and Stockwell sat down under some trees, waiting for the attack to get under way. As they did so, the battalion photographer snapped them – about three minutes later, a salvo of French 75mm fire pitched all round and one exploded directly overhead, taking the smallest knick out of Stockwell's eye. Once the Scots Fusiliers' attack had been halted, signs of a Vichy counter-attack could be seen and felt. The British artillery near the meat factory came under counter-battery fire from French 75mm guns. Stockwell gave orders for the Carrier Platoon to move to a position on rising ground around Robinson's Hotel where they could fire into the counter-attacking troops; A Company was to occupy some high ground to the right of the road; and D and C Companies were to form a hasty defensive position to secure the brigade's flank on the left of the main road. This had the desired effect, although there were two further unsuccessful attempts at a counter-attack, and the battalion remained in position throughout much of the day, being fired on in desultory fashion by Vichy mortars and 75mm guns. Snipers were also active so that several times Stockwell hastily had to shift the position of his headquarters and take cover. At length, the fusiliers set fire to the undergrowth and, the wind being in the right quarter, this flushed the snipers out.

While this was going on, Sturges himself came up during the morning, bringing with him the Commander of 17 Brigade, Brigadier G.W.B. Tarleton. Moving carefully forward with Festing, they carried out a further reconnaissance. The situation now was that nothing had been heard from the South Lancashires, as all their radio sets had failed; the frontal assault had been halted in its tracks; and there were no means available to silence the French artillery. Without being sure of the support available from the fleet, Sturges was unwilling to come to any definite conclusion about further action, so he went back to Courrier Bay to confer with Admiral Syfret in the *Ramillies*. He was loath to ask much more of 29 Brigade for the time being – the men had already made a successful assault landing, marched 10 miles in tropical heat and thick dust, and made two assaults against strongly defended positions with little in the way of fire support. After comparing notes and ideas, Sturges and Syfret decided to continue to attack the Vichy main defensive position, shipping, troops and other installations with carrier-based aircraft and naval gunfire. While this went on, more artillery would be landed and got forward to concentrate on counter-battery fire, while at the same time, 17 Brigade would be moved up as fast as possible – perhaps by early evening – ready for a further major effort. It was known that No. 5 Commando had succeeded in reaching its objective in Diego Suarez, but without boats to cross the Port Nievre there was no way of bringing the Commando into action in the rear of the Antsirane position. Syfret suggested that as a diversion, HMS *Anthony* could put a landing party of fifty Royal Marines ashore on the quay at Antsirane, and this was built into the plan.

Orders for this reached Stockwell at about 4.30 pm. Explicitly, he was told to detach one company to reinforce the 6th Seaforths in 17 Brigade, and James Vyvyan duly went off with A Company. Once 17 Brigade had penetrated the main position, 2nd Royal Welch Fusiliers and 1st Royal Scots Fusiliers were to pass through and round them, and get into the town as quickly as possible. Actually, the situation was by no means as bad as the senior commanders feared. First, the landing operation was still going on very well: by 1.00 pm on 6 May, 14,000 troops, 635 tons of ammunition, 140 tons of fuel and 6,962 cans of water had been put ashore. Secondly, there was much to hope for on the main axis, for the South Lancashires had managed to penetrate into the enemy rear, capturing the pack-mules of the Vichy artillery, rushing isolated posts, and even overrunning the barracks in Ano Bozaka. Prisoners had been taken and the battalion was now established only 200 yards behind the enemy front line in some places, and hard against Fort Bellevue in others. As Sturges and Syfret agreed their plan, news of the South Lancashires reached Festing.

At about 7.30 pm, 29 Brigade began to shake out for the assault, and the Royal Welch Fusiliers took up position behind the 6th Seaforths and the 1st Northamptons. At about 8.00 pm the Royal Marines were landed. Around the same time, it was discovered that the threat posed by the South Lancashires had caused the Vichy troops in the defensive line to withdraw somewhat, so that the Scots Fusiliers, securing the start line for 17 Brigade, were able to push forward, supported by artillery fire from guns established on the Col de Bonne Nouvelle. The Seaforths, with A Company of the 2nd Royal Welch Fusiliers, pressed the attack hard, and penetrated the main position after some vicious fighting. Festing, who was as usual well forward, then ordered the Royal Scots and Royal Welch Fusiliers to move through and get into the town, leaving 17 Brigade to consolidate the position – which in the end took until around 3.00 am. As the two battalions moved forward they came under heavy fire from pillboxes on the road and from Fort Caimans, but in the dark they managed to slip through. Second Lieutenant Reginald Sparrow and his batman, Fusilier John Lloyd, were killed at a Vichy roadblock, while 'Sgt [R.O.] Jones did some splendid work at a machine-gun post.'

The 2nd Royal Welch Fusiliers entered Antsirane at about 1.00 am on 7 May – but found there was little to do. 17 Brigade's attack had been timed to coincide with the marines' landing, and the official accounts state that this diversion caused such complete panic among the Vichy garrison, that within two hours the fifty Marines had captured the whole town and its garrison of nearly 3,000 Vichy troops. Admiral Syfret called it 'a fine achievement brilliantly carried out, and in my opinion the principal and direct cause of the enemy's collapse', although this must be open to doubt. Under Gwdyr-Jones's direction, Henry Jones led D Company quickly down to the docks and there he met the marines as they landed – unopposed. The Vichy collapse was already an accomplished fact. Festing and Stockwell had the satisfaction of entering the Governor-General's residence, while Henry Jones went off to Defence Headquarters with one of his platoons, commanded by Lieutenant

Roddy Rainier, who was a fluent French speaker. There they found Colonel Claerebout, commanding the military garrison, and Captain de V. Maerten, the Vichy naval commander, who were unceremoniously dragged out of the building. Jones sent a message to Stockwell informing him of their capture; shortly afterwards Festing himself appeared, and gave Jones and Rainier a rocket for their rough handling of Claerebout and Maerten. Maerten had, however, recovered and told Rainier to take what he wanted from his wine cellar before being taken up to the Residence to make the surrender. Rainier needed no urging, for in civilian life he was a wine merchant! Before long, a good few choice bottles had found their way into the officers' and men's packs – which was just as well for soon afterwards a lorry sent by Festing appeared and carried off the rest.

Some mopping up was still needed around the forts, which had yet to capitulate. Some CQMS's parties moving into the town in the early dawn of D+3, for example, were engaged by 75mm over open sights from Fort Bellevue. But the most important task was to secure the surrender of the coastal batteries and garrison of Orangea – for until this was done, the British fleet could not enter the harbour. This task was given to Stockwell, being a good French speaker. When Sturges gave orders for him to lead the advance on land with a composite force of carriers drawn from across the brigade, Stockwell knew that he was negotiating from a position of strength. 17 Brigade was being prepared to assault the headland from the landward side, while the fleet and its aircraft had prepared a bombardment plan which was ready from 10.00 am on the 7th. Moreover it was clear that with the British capture of Antsirane and Diego Suarez, Vichy morale was close to collapse, and the Governor-General, M. Armand Annet telegraphed to the Vichy government that the situation was critical. A short bombardment by the fleet at 10.30 am on the 7th was enough to decide the issue – at 10.50 am, the garrison raised the white flag and at 2.00 pm that same afternoon the two forts of Bellevue and Caimans also surrendered. During the remainder of 7 May and into the next day, the troops were kept busy with large numbers of prisoners streaming in, although there seemed no sign of animosity either from the black soldiers or the French officers and NCOs. About 5.00 pm that evening, all prisoners were marched off to an internment camp and the men could relax for the first time.

It was at this point that the participants' views of the intelligence estimates of Vichy strength were revealed. Not only had they fought tenaciously but, as Jim Stockman recalled:

> our Brigade lined the surrender route, we were shocked to see what was still left of the allegedly small force. We lined up on either side of the road with fixed bayonets and stood to attention. The first senior French officer came marching along the road with a white flag. I shall never forget the sight. He had a sword drawn, bearing the flag, and his troops were marching on behind. The sight that passed us gave me a jolt in the

stomach. There were literally thousands of highly professional French, Foreign Legion and Senegalese troops, and with them, an impressive array of cannon, heavy mortars, machine guns, and boxes of ammunition . . . From what I saw that day, I imagine that the Vichy French garrison there had at least six times the equipment and professional troops estimated by Intelligence – which was why the battle for Diego Suarez was such a tough and bloody affair.

His view is supported by a large number of photographs of the surrender, however his impression that intelligence had failed is not borne out by the facts, as described earlier. The most likely explanation is that intelligence slightly underestimated numbers, and tired men, seeing all their enemies in one place, overestimated. What is clear is that the commanders at all levels recognized the importance of intelligence at every stage of planning, preparation and indeed to training, and in support of the assault itself. They analyzed the information available, used SOE agents, and by understanding the nature of the intelligence provided made sure it was disseminated to all appropriate levels in sufficient time for it to be effective. Festing accepted responsibility for his failure to task aerial reconnaissance in sufficient depth to identify the strength of the positions at Antsirane and reported this back to COHQ after the operation. Despite Jim Stockman's view, it can be said that the intelligence process came of age at Madagascar.

The successful achievement of all the expedition's objectives had taken a mere three days, at a cost of 389 all ranks killed, wounded and missing, nine aircraft and one minesweeper. French losses had been around 650 men, all their aircraft and ships were either destroyed or captured, and many prisoners were taken. Churchill took a keen interest – even meddling perhaps – but his influence was all-pervading; his military strategic direction was clear, he kept an eye on the art of the possible, and paid significant attention to the need to keep 29 Brigade, highly trained and valuable, in good shape for subsequent operations. In the aftermath of the operation, Churchill telegraphed to Sturges:

> Prime Minister congratulates you cordially upon swift and resolute way in which difficult and hazardous operation was carried through.
>
> He sends all ranks his best wishes and says that their exploit has been of real assistance to Britain and the United Nations. He was sure when he saw you at Inverary nine months ago that the 29th Brigade would make its mark.

The news of the successful assault came at a time when good news was at a premium, and its effect on morale at home was tremendous. 'It was in fact,' as Churchill remarked, 'for long months the only sign of good and efficient war direction of which the British public were conscious.' The press was equally enthusiastic. The *Evening Standard*, under the banner headline 'Madagascar: We Land to March on Navy Base', remarked that:

> All Britain will rejoice that the Allies have moved first. However this act, although long foreshadowed and fully justified, has further implications for the whole war. Both in Washington and London it is now accepted that Vichy's word is as bad as her bond. Neither can be trusted.

For Stockwell's fusiliers, it had been their first experience of combat, the vindication of all their hard training, and their first introduction to the tropical conditions they were to endure for the next three years. They had tasted victory – and their heads were up.

Sturges, who knew the Stockwells well from Selkirk, wrote to Joan in the aftermath of the first part of the operation:

> Hugh did very well, is doing very well, and is jumping out of his skin with fitness. I thought you might like to know this, because I was quite certain that he would never tell you himself. I would like to see him get command of a Brigade and hope that this may come along one day. He is far more fitted to be that, than I am to command a Division!! I think that Hugh enjoyed it – all of it, and just laughed his way through troubles.

Following the success of the initial attack, command of all troops in Madagascar passed to Lieutenant General Sir William Platt,[8] GOC-in-C East African Command. 13 and 17 Brigades were needed to move as soon as possible to rejoin the 5th Division in India, and 13 Brigade duly sailed on 20 May. 22 (East African) Infantry Brigade relieved 17 Brigade and it too left for India on 12 June. 29 Brigade took over garrison duties; 2nd Royal Welch Fusiliers were quartered in the Vichy barracks of Camp Méhouar and the Artillery lines in Antsirane, with platoons and companies detached for duty at various times in the docks, Fort Caiman, Windsor Castle and Joffreville. What must have been particularly galling, given the reason for Operation Ironclad, was an attack in Diego Suarez Bay by a Japanese midget submarine on 31 May, which succeeded in sinking a tanker and holing HMS *Ramillies*. The submarine was dealt with by gunfire from the *Ramillies* – the troops in Windsor Castle were able to watch the fireworks. Two Japanese naval officers were later picked up on the shore by patrols from the 2nd Royal Welch Fusiliers.

With the uncertain situation in Burma and on the frontier with India, and in the Middle East, no thought could be spared for further operations on Madagascar. Many in 29 Brigade were in favour of pushing on anyway – Brian Cotton, for example, stated a fairly widely held (if not strictly accurate) view that the advance on the south of the island 'was delayed by political and diplomatic back chat'. But like it or not, the force remained in occupation of the northern tip of the island for five long months, bottled up on a peninsula 100 miles long and 70 miles wide while carrying out training, coastal defence and internal security duties.

There was also time now for some relaxation. In addition to a drag hunt being started, the Royal Scots Fusiliers put on a July race meeting at Arrachart Racecourse, Diego Suarez, on 4 July, which was attended by large crowds of British servicemen, French civilians and locals. The race card records that Stockwell entered the 9 Indian Brigade Cup, a race over 3 furlongs, as a member of a team of three officers – it was an inter-battalion team event – for a cup presented by Festing. Stockwell rode a handsome grey pony called Activity II and his teammates were Brian Cotton on Little Fish, and John Dickson on George, which came in first thus winning the trophy. Stockwell and Gwydyr also entered the General's Cup, an individual event over 3½ furlongs. In the event, Stockwell himself did not ride, and Henry Jones took his place. As it had been all those years ago at Pembroke Dock, Gwydyr showed himself to be a fine horseman and won the race. The battalion's crop of trophies was completed by LCpl Jones of the Horse Transport Platoon, who rode to victory in the mule race! This Jones had been a kennel man at the Wynnstay Hunt before the War, and boasted a legendary tattoo of a hunt in full cry, which stretched across his torso, over his shoulder and down his back. The fox's brush was just visible as the quarry went to earth – in Jones's backside.

Back at home, once it was clear that the troops would be away for a considerable time, Joan and the girls moved to Ystumllyn, Pentrefelin, an old manor house and 300-acre farm in the depths of the countryside about 2 miles from Criccieth in North Wales. With them went no less a personage than the Regimental Goat of the 2nd Royal Welch Fusiliers, which remained with the family throughout their stay. The house was a perfect example of Tudor architecture, with large rooms and attics, its interior and furniture intact. It came complete with its own ghost, a black boy called Jack, who had lived as a servant in the eighteenth century. In the farmyard were a large duck pond with ducks and geese, chickens, ponies for the girls, cats and dogs. The rest of the farm was let to a neighbour and Italian prisoners of war worked the land and garden. It was a wonderful place for children, especially in wartime – the girls went to a school in Criccieth which had been evacuated from Walsall, but otherwise were free to roam the countryside, the cliffs and the beaches, swimming, riding and dodging an infestation of adders. Getting away was not easy, given wartime restrictions and petrol rationing, and the family had no car, just a pony trap. But one trip was made to Chester where Polly saw and fell in love with the ballet. Her constant demands for lessons eventually drove Joan to arrange for the Arts Educational Ballet School to be evacuated to Criccieth from London – and so Polly got her wish. After the War, Polly begged her father to buy the place, which was for sale for the princely sum of

£500, and which was the closest thing to a permanent home that the family had known – but he refused.

By early August matters had stabilized in the Middle East and in India, and the Chiefs of Staff issued orders for the occupation of the whole island of Madagascar. Admiral Sir James Somerville,[9] Commander-in-Chief Eastern Fleet, and Lieutenant General Platt were jointly empowered to direct operations, although the execution of the campaign was delegated to Major General Sturges and Rear Admiral William Tennant.[10] Tennant had no love for the Japanese, having been Captain of HMS *Repulse* when she was sunk off the east coast of Malaya. An old plan was resurrected for capturing the two secondary ports – Majunga on the west coast and Tamatave on the east – and moving from them on the capital, Tananarive. Sturges' plan called for three sequential operations. In the first of these, Operation Stream, 29 Brigade, reinforced by a KAR battalion from 22 East African Brigade and the South African armoured cars, was to make a surprise night assault landing at Majunga. The KAR and the armoured cars would then push inland to secure the route to Tananarive and, in particular, two key bridges. At the same time, No. 5 Commando would be landed further north to block the road from Maromandia and thus secure the flank of the landing force. Having secured these objectives, Operation Line would begin with the rest of 22 East African Brigade being landed, and then advancing as fast as possible to capture the capital. With 22 Brigade ashore, 29 Brigade would be re-embarked and moved round to the east coast for the third operation, Jane.[11] This was to be an assault landing at Tamatave, from which the brigade would advance to link up with 22 Brigade, establishing control across the island.

On 20 August the 29 Brigade group and No. 5 Commando embarked on HMT *Empire Pride* and the cargo ship *Ocean Viking*, and moved to Mombasa in Kenya, which was the HQ of both East African Command and the Eastern Fleet. There were few regrets at leaving Diego Suarez, and no one missed the conditions. However, the voyage to Mombasa was not the pleasant interlude that the trip from Britain had been. One victim remembered that:

> On a stuffy mess-deck eighty of us were herded. There was hammock space for twenty at most and men had to make their beds on the tables from which in daytime we ate. Cockroaches crawled in thousands over the walls and tables and the air at night, with all port-holes closed for black-out, was suffocating. In addition to our perspiring bodies all our kit had to be stacked in this meagre space and all our food eaten. The food was crude and greasy, slopped out from great bins like pigwash ...
> With relief I went ashore at Mombasa.

Once ashore, drafts of reinforcements from Britain were met and integrated into battalions. It was put about that they were destined for India, and the brigade carried out Exercise Touchstone on 30 August, a highly realistic rehearsal for the coming assault landing and a test of the defences of Mombasa. On 5 September, the whole force re-embarked – Stockwell and the Royal Welch Fusiliers in the *Empire Pride* – and moved off to rendezvous with 22 Brigade in the Mozambique Channel. At 5.00 pm that day, the troops were told of the plan.

Majunga, the objective of Operation Stream, was a pleasant seaport about 320 miles south of Diego Suarez. The estuary of Madagascar's largest river, the Betsiboka, forms the harbour, which faces south. The town was strongly garrisoned and could only be approached from the sea directly. Moreover, following the fierce battles around Antsirane, it was assumed that the landing would be resisted. To achieve surprise, therefore, Festing split 29 Brigade into two. The 2nd South Lancashires and No. 5 Commando, under his own command, would land directly at the port on Green Beach at 5.10 am on 10 September, and thus engage the enemy's full attention; 1st Royal Scots Fusiliers would be held in reserve. Meanwhile, 2nd Royal Welch Fusiliers and 2nd East Lancashires would form Stockforce – the second time a formation of this name had appeared – and would land 10 miles north of the town on Red Beach at 1.00 am, before moving southwards until they struck the main Majunga–Tananarive road. From there, Stockforce would attack the town from the landward side. The time lag was to allow Stockforce to close up to the town and then distract the enemy during the actual assault. Air support and naval gunfire was available on call. The men were to land with only light scales, carrying emergency rations of dried food. Stockwell was given some of the staff and signallers from 29 Brigade Headquarters and Force 121 in order to form a tactical headquarters; command of 2 RWF devolved once more on Gwydyr.

With its by now customary and expected efficiency, the naval task group dropped the landing force in exactly the right place at the right time, and just after 1.00 am on 10 September, Stockforce came ashore. The battalions found themselves straight away confronted by steep cliffs, but fortunately no enemy, and then difficult, scrub-covered country. The two battalions, however, pushed on, with the East Lancashires on the left, following the main axis and heading for the town's airfield, and the Royal Welch on the right, tasked to cut the main road into town and then lead the attack into Majunga. There was a good deal of confusion in the dark as the battalions struggled to find their bearings, but by 3.00 am, the advance was well under way. Just before 5.30 am, as it was growing light, the sky was suddenly filled with Swordfish and Martlet bombers from the fleet; the company commanders hastily put up the agreed recognition signal – red umbrellas!

What most of the attacking force later recalled with greatest clarity about this operation was neither the fighting nor the confusion, but the boiling heat and the clouds of mosquitoes which made every minute an absolute misery. The issued anti-mosquito cream, which came from Italy, was absolutely useless – in fact, it seemed to attract the pests – and was therefore generally used by the troops to smear on their weapons as protection from the humidity and dust.

Half an hour or so after first light the leading companies entered the town, and the Vichy commandant, Martin, made the surrender. However, getting word of this to his scattered troops was no easy matter and the shooting was only stopped when cars containing British and French officers, flying a white flag, toured the streets. At 8.30 am, Stockwell entered the Artillery Barracks and issued orders for the consolidation of the objective. The town had been captured at the cost to the British of only twelve dead; most of the French troops were captured and taken to Durban, where a few enrolled in the Free French forces, although in common with previous experience in Syria, the majority opted for repatriation to France.

With the town secure, Festing halted any further landings by 29 Brigade and its equipment, and switched all landing craft to 22 Brigade. 29 Brigade was re-embarked as rapidly as possible and this was completed by the morning of 13 September. Further operations to capture Tananarive – Operation Line – were left to the East African and South African brigades. Stockforce at this point was reabsorbed into 29 Brigade, and orders for the next phase of operations were issued. On the 14th, the naval task group with 29 Brigade embarked began the preliminary moves for Operation Jane, sailing around the northern tip of the island to the port of Tamatave, the officers and men filling the time studying maps and air photographs. After the success of Operation Stream, morale was high. It was assumed that the landing would be opposed, but on the 17th word came that the Vichy governor, M. Annet, had asked for an armistice, and there was uncertainty right up to the last moment as to whether or not the troops would be called on to fight. It was planned that the brigade would assault at three points: 2nd East Lancashires on Red Beach, north of the town; 2nd Royal Welch Fusiliers on White Beach in the centre of the town; and No. 5 Commando with 2nd South Lancashires onto the harbour moles from destroyers. 1st Royal Scots Fusiliers would again be held in reserve.

On the morning of 18 September, the transports and landing craft, escorted by *Illustrious*, the battleship HMS *Warspite*, three cruisers, and the attendant escorts, appeared off the east coast of Madagascar. Because of the uncertainty over the opposition, Festing decided to enter the harbour directly and demand the surrender of the garrison. A bombardment plan was also made should the French resist, a move which drew hearty approval from the troops: 'We were sick,' one recalled later, 'of hearing that men in our Brigade had been killed by the Vichy forces . . . we said, let's have no more of these face-saving but lethal demonstrations.' At 5.40 am the convoy entered the harbour and as the first wave of assaulting troops packed into the landing craft, a parley was conducted by radio from HMS *Birmingham* with the Vichy *Chef de Région*, M. Tenne. The French official stalled for time, at first refusing to parley without authority from the capital, then refusing to receive an embassy at all. He was informed that a party would be sent anyway in a launch under a white flag. At 7.30 am the launch approached the landing, but it was fired on and turned back with all speed. At 7.52 am the cruisers and destroyers opened fire on the shore batteries, and three minutes later the French bluff had been called: white sheets – makeshift flags of surrender – rose over the town.

Within an hour, troops of 29 Brigade were coming ashore both from landing craft and directly from destroyers. The men were expecting more treachery, but despite the casualties among the garrison caused by the shelling, the British were well received; some indeed were offered coffee and even breakfast! By the time that Festing himself came ashore at 10.00 am the town had been occupied and the extent of the *Chef de Région*'s bluff revealed – most of the garrison and almost all the guns of the harbour defences had already been withdrawn.

Later that day the brigade began to advance towards Tananarive and a linkup with 22 Brigade, with Stockwell's 2nd Royal Welch Fusiliers again in the lead on the axis of the main road, and the South Lancashires on the railway line; the immediate objective was the town of Brickaville. For the next twenty days, this advance continued in almost continuous rain, with the men carrying only fighting order and gas capes. The fusiliers found the first 4 miles of road particularly heavy going, as the withdrawing Vichy garrison had left behind a series of roadblocks, many of them almost 20 yards wide, constructed from cut-down trees and stumps; some included deep anti-tank ditches. In all, approximately fifty of these blocks were cleared by the Royal Welch Fusiliers alone during the next three days.

Next day, 19 September, Stockwell pushed his battalion on across the Fanarandrono River by a ferry at the village of Ivondro, with a reconnaissance force consisting of some motorcycles, carriers and Royal Engineers leading. C Company followed in lorries. At noon, the reconnaissance force came to the first of what was to be a series of bridge demolitions, all of which had to be rebuilt more or less to allow vehicle traffic to proceed, since the road and railway southwards towards Brickaville was carried by bridges across a succession of creeks, streams and rivers emptying into the sea. This first one took four-and-a-half hours to complete and by the time it was ready, dusk was falling and the carriers brought back word of the next demolition only one-and-a-half miles ahead.

Early next day, Stockwell issued modified orders for the advance: the reconnaissance force would scout ahead and report on the situation; each company was to be reinforced by engineers and gangs of locals, and each demolition in turn would be tackled by the leading company; as soon as it was passable, the rest of the battalion would move through, with the next company taking up the lead. Thus the work would be distributed and momentum maintained. By this means, seven demolitions of varying sizes were tackled during the 20th, but the work was heavy in the heat and humidity; it often required twenty men to cut and carry up large trees needed to carry the road. Festing came forward during the day, and expressed himself well pleased with progress despite the fact that, to add to the difficulties, heavy rain had now begun to fall and road conditions were very treacherous. Despite this, Gwydyr took a convoy of lorries back to Tamatave for fresh rations, while Stockwell and John Dickson mounted commandeered bicycles and set out on some personal reconnaissance. Dickson later estimated that they had covered almost 40 miles during the day.

Work on bridges continued throughout 21 and 22 September. During the morning of the 22nd, the Carrier Platoon, with the help of native labour, poled barges down the river to Brickaville, a trip so hot that Captain J.O. Williams complained that even the soles of his feet were sunburned. Stockwell and Dickson made the same journey that afternoon by motor launch, returning by motorcycle. Work continued as before on the 23rd and the battalion bivouacked on the road just short of Brickaville. The advance continued next day, with the eighteenth and final bridge demolition being completed. That evening, Stockforce was reformed, with 2nd Royal Welch Fusiliers, 1st Royal Scots Fusiliers and 2nd South Lancashires under Stockwell's command, while Festing kept No. 5 Commando and the East Lancashires; Gwydyr again took command of the 2nd Royal Welch Fusiliers. When the staff of Stockforce, drawn from Headquarters 29 Brigade, came up to join the force, 'their spotless appearance evok[ed] numerous pleasantries from the travel-stained Battalion.'

On the 25th, 2nd Royal Welch Fusiliers entered Brickaville, while a link-up was achieved between the South Lancashires and the South African armoured car squadron at Moramanga. The next day, Stockwell and Gwydyr went off southwards to try to make contact with the Vichy *Chef de Région* in Vatomandry, but here too demolitions made the route impassable. The troops, meanwhile, enjoyed a well-earned rest after their labours, before redeploying to cover the line of communication between Tamatave and Tananarive. This, as the War Diary pointed out, equated to an area equivalent to a triangle with its base drawn from Eastbourne to Torquay, and its apex at Leicester. Some of the areas occupied made a wonderful change: Manjakandriana, for example, home for a while to D Company 2nd Royal Welch Fusiliers, was high enough above sea level to have a European type of climate, with fruit and vegetables freely available. On the 29th, Stockforce again ceased to exist and two days later, a Victory parade was held in Tananarive, in which every unit of the force was represented. Stockwell himself went up for it with a representative party of the 2nd Royal Welch Fusiliers. The rest of the time was taken up with rounding up unco-operative Vichy officials in preparation for a handover of administration to the Free French. Despite this, relations with the locals were good.

Stockwell's photograph album contains pictures of a locomotive salvaged in Tamatave, and moved by raft to a point where a spur of the railway line could be built down to the water, in order for the locomotive to be dragged on to the line. Once there it seems that it was possible for it to get up steam and resume operations without undue difficulties.

*   *   *

Further operations to complete the securing of key points and harbours on the island were left to the East African and South African brigades, until on 8 November, eight weeks after the landing at Majunga, the Vichy administration asked for an armistice, following which it surrendered unconditionally. A Free French administration was thereafter installed and the leading Vichy officials interned in South Africa. It had been, as Rupert Croft-Cooke wrote, 'an ugly and bloody little battle and six monotonous months in a foul climate'. Battle casualties had been mercifully light, but the climate and the mosquitoes had taken a heavy toll – one battalion in 29 Brigade reported 200 cases of malaria at one time, and hospital admissions had been a drain on strength throughout the campaign. But it had been brought to a successful conclusion and the Japanese threat frustrated.

Only three days after the conclusion of operations in Madagascar, Operation Torch began in North Africa. With its conclusion came the end of Vichy as a government in any meaningful sense. Operation Ironclad and the subsequent campaign had been a model of good planning and security, and of operational and tactical excellence in execution. It would provide much for the planners of Operation Overlord to ponder – far more, in a positive sense, it might be argued, than the Dieppe operation. Certainly, a glance at some of the newspapers of the time shows that the operation had an enormous impact on morale and public opinion both in Britain and in the USA. It is not, however, a campaign which is now known about or studied, which is odd. This may be for two reasons. First, the Torch and Overlord operations overshadowed it, especially in terms of scale. Secondly, in the post-war political climate, it might not have been felt appropriate to rub in the fact that Britain and France, such close allies until 1940, had been at war. The co-operation during the Suez operation can only have reinforced this. And so Operation Ironclad was allowed to slip quietly into history's 'closed' files, which is a pity, for there is much in it with contemporary resonance.

For Hugh Stockwell, and indeed for the Royal Welch Fusiliers, it cemented a relationship with Festing, which was to endure throughout the War and beyond. Festing himself was awarded the DSO in recognition of his outstanding leadership; Stockwell, despite Sturges' efforts, received no recognition. But neither Stockwell nor the 2nd Royal Welch Fusiliers saw the final stages of the campaign. On 14 October, the battalion packed up and began the move back to Tamatave, where it was to re-embark and move on the 18th to Durban in South Africa – as a result of malaria and battle casualties, the whole of 29 Brigade had been declared unfit for further operations for three months. But Stockwell had other orders. He had commanded Stockforce on three occasions – once in Norway and twice in Madagascar; he had demonstrated repeatedly that he knew how to handle a brigade in action; and he got results. On 18 October, at the age of forty-one, he was promoted to the temporary rank of brigadier – he was still only a substantive major – and given command of a brigade in East Africa. It later became clear that Lieutenant General Platt had seen his worth and had had a hand in the matter; just as with the expedition to Norway, and the command of 2nd Royal Welch Fusiliers, Stockwell had been in the right place at the right time, and had made the most of the opportunities offered.

At Moramanja Station, Stockwell and his battalion parted, and Gwydyr-Jones once again resumed command, which he was to hold until February 1945 through the hardships and dangers of the campaign in Burma. For Hugh Stockwell, there was the excitement and fulfilment of promotion, but against that he had been only just over a year in command, during which he and his battalion had achieved a series of spectacular successes, bought with minimal casualties. Shared experience, especially where it involves hardship, danger, the loss of comrades is a powerful bond and it engenders deep feelings of mutual trust and affection. No surprise therefore that this parting was, in Stockwell's own words, 'a sad and gloomy day'.

Notes

1 Later Brigadier John Arthur Benson Dickson, born 4 May 1918, commissioned 27 January 1938, commanded 1 RWF 1959–1961, commanded 158 Infantry Brigade and retired 8 April 1964. Died 15 December 1979.

2 Later General Sir Michael Montgomerie Alston Roberts West GCB DSO▪ (1905–1978). *Who Was Who, 1971–1980*, p. 845.

3 Rear Admiral Edward F. Gueritz CB OBE DSC, born 1919. Gueritz knew Stockwell throughout his life and was later present at Suez in 1956.

4 Later Lieutenant General Sir Robert Grice Sturges KBE CB DSO (1891–1970). Entered the Navy in 1908 and transferred to the RMLI in 1912. He served throughout the First World War both ashore and in HM Ships. He had been GOC RM Division at Portsmouth, and commanded the occupation of Iceland in 1940. *Who Was Who, 1961–1970*, p. 1091.

5 Later Field Marshal Sir Francis Festing GCB KBE DSO (1902–1976). His biography by Lyall Wilkes is cited in Bibliography.

6 When Stockwell later commanded 29 Brigade in India and Burma, Brand would serve as his Brigade Major.

7 Later Admiral Sir Edward Neville Syfret GCB KBE (1889–1972). A South African by birth, he had joined the Royal Navy in 1904 and served throughout the First World War. He was later Vice Chief of Naval Staff 1943–1945 and C-in-C Home Fleet 1945–1948. *Who Was Who, 1971–1980*, p. 774.

8 Later General Sir William Platt GBE KCB DSO (1885–1975). *Who Was Who 1971–1980*, p. 630.

9 Later Admiral of the Fleet Sir James Fownes Somerville GCB GBE DSO (1882–1949). Somerville had returned to active service in 1940 having previously retired on health grounds. He became Flag Officer Force H at Gibraltar, and in July 1940 had commanded the operation to sink the Vichy French fleet at Oran. Later he took part in the defence of Malta and in the sinking of the *Bismark*. He became head of the British naval delegation in Washington in August 1944.

10 Later Admiral Sir William George Tennant KCB CBE MVO (1890–1963). He

had participated in the evacuation at Dunkirk in 1940, and later played a prominent part in the Normandy landings in 1944. *Who Was Who 1961–1970*, p. 1108.

11 Stream Line Jane – the sum of the three operations – was Sturges' nickname for Joan Stockwell. This has not been publicized before: HCS, when Commandant of Sandhurst after the War wrote to the authors of *The Red Dragon* saying 'I suggest you leave out the "Stream Line Jane" or reference to Mrs S – not that I mind, but I think it tends to distract from the structure of the book.' (Letter HCS–Graves dated 7 February 1948 in RWF Museum L/2655/187; also confirmed by Brian Cotton in RWF Museum L/2655/190(A), p. 11). This is an odd comment so perhaps Stockwell was sensitive about the obvious friendship between Sturges and Joan, and feared gossip.

Chapter Nine

Brigade Commander – East Africa, India and Arakan, 1942–1944

30 (East African) Infantry Brigade, a formation composed of units of the King's African Rifles, was based at Mariakani, about 50 miles north-east of Mombasa in Kenya where it was subordinated to the 12th (East African) Division. Here Stockwell joined the Brigade Headquarters on 2 November 1942. In the British Army, a brigadier is the most junior general officer, and a brigade the lowest level of organization that can be called a formation. Usually at this time, a brigade consisted of only its headquarters and administrative company, signals company and three or four infantry battalions. Thus the formation contained no capability above that already available within its battalions, and the commander's functions in combat were limited to planning and sequencing the operations of his units to achieve an effect greater than the sum of the parts. However, unless a brigade was allocated additional combat support units – artillery, engineers, military police, reconnaissance – and combat service support units – medical, maintenance, supply, transport – it could not operate independently outside the framework of a division as, for example, 29 Independent Infantry Brigade had done. Even when reinforced, a brigade commander could conduct only close operations in contact with the enemy – he had no ability to see anything beyond the range of the immediate contact battle, and if he had, he lacked the means to do anything about what he had seen. That said, brigades were small enough for the commander to know all his officers reasonably well, certainly down to company commanders, and many of the senior NCOs. In return, he would be easily recognized by the 2,500 or so soldiers.

East African soldiers differ in ethnicity and language from the men whom Stockwell had known so well in West Africa, however the King's African Rifles, which had been in existence as an African Corps since 1902, had a proven record of fighting prowess under hard conditions in both the First World War and in the recent campaign in Italian Somaliland. Military service had always been popular with the tribes, whose ability to operate in harsh conditions with limited supplies was of outstanding value. The men, generally known as Askaris, were tough and hardy, with simple needs and a wonderfully cheerful disposition. Like West Africans, they were loyal to a fault and, as they would repeatedly prove in Burma, phenomenally brave. Stockwell and the officers and men of the KAR took to each other straight away. 30 Brigade was in the process of being formed and trained, but out of the blue, a bombshell came from the GOC, General Platt:

My dear Hugh

A wire has come from India asking if you can be made available to command the 29th Brigade vice Frank Festing who has been selected for a Major General's command. I have a feeling that you would consider it low to accept this offer after I have brought you over here to command the 30th Brigade. I am, therefore, writing this line privately to you to tell you that you must not be influenced by any such thoughts. I shall be very sorry to lose you, but you have special experience to qualify you for command of the 29th Brigade, and as an old friend I feel I must advise you in your own future interests that you should say yes to this offer.

Stockwell would have been foolish indeed to turn down the offer of a British regular brigade on active service in a major theatre of war. He was, after all, still only a substantive Major, Acting Brigadier, and there was always the consideration about what might be his fate at the end of the War, assuming he survived. In the case of 29 Brigade there were, too, some additional special considerations. First, the brigade would be subordinated to the 36th Infantry Division, whose new GOC would be none other than the former commander of 29 Brigade, Francis Festing; this was the 'Major General's command' to which Platt had referred. Secondly, of course, he had served with the brigade on a highly successful series of operations, and knew many of the officers and men in its headquarters and units. Last, and very important, he would have under his command his old battalion, 2nd Royal Welch Fusiliers. Unsurprisingly he accepted straight away.

On 18 October 1942, 29 Independent Infantry Brigade sailed from Tamatave for Durban, and from thence to Pietermaritzburg. Every effort was made during the following weeks to ensure that as many men as possible went on leave, and a number of those who had no personal invitations were billeted in farms in the district. There were, however, strict rules on curfew when in camp, and a dim view was taken of those who had had too much to drink or were late back. One day, two defaulters in 2 RWF came up before Gwydyr. The first one had been an hour late for roll call at night; he got fourteen days. The second had not returned until first parade the next morning. Gwydyr asked for the man's explanation, and the fusilier replied, 'Well, sir, I did have rather a binge and was in such a state I thought it best to stay in a public convenience until morning, then freshen up in time for parade.' 'Just what I should have done, my dear,' said Gwydyr. 'You used your head. Case dismissed.'

In December the brigade embarked in troopships for its return to battle. The convoy crossed the line on 20 January and five days later Bombay was sighted on the port bow. The distant prospect of the vast city in the blazing sunshine was greeted with excited curiosity by most of the young soldiers, for whom this was their first sight, and smell, of India. Thus 29 Brigade, and Hugh Stockwell with it, moved inexorably towards an involvement in the war in Burma, an involvement which would last for almost three years in what was the largest and longest land campaign fought against Japan by any Allied army except the Chinese.

The next day the brigade moved by train to Pashan Camp, about 75 miles to the south-east of Bombay, in the cool hill station of Poona. Here it ceased to be 'independent', for it joined the newly formed 36th Infantry Division, along with 72 Infantry Brigade, under the command of Major General Francis Festing. Stockwell already knew most of the brigade headquarters staff. The Brigade Major was Major the Hon David Brand, a Territorial who had been commissioned into the Hertfordshires in 1939 and had been DAA&QMG in Madagascar. The DAA&QMG was now George Demetriadi of the Royal Welch Fusiliers. The units of the brigade had not changed since Madagascar.

Given a few weeks on his own in India awaiting the arrival of the brigade, Stockwell had time to study the methods which Slim in particular was pushing into the army, and which Wingate and his Chindits were attempting to prove. Slim placed great emphasis on physical fitness, military skills of all kinds, construction of field defences, the use of mules and all kinds of methods for improvisation. He also tried to train his subordinate commanders to hold their nerve – if surrounded, they should keep their ground and fight. He insisted on hard, realistic field training by day and by night – something that was not always in evidence in the training programmes in India. Slim also insisted on a review of planning procedures and methods for issuing orders, stressing the need for commanders to get forward and be seen among their subordinates. In this, like many of his generation, he was determined to avoid the charge of 'Chateau Generalship' which had been levelled at many senior commanders in the aftermath of the First World War, in which he had fought as a young regimental officer. But all this was really aimed at raising the morale of the men to a point where they believed in themselves and their own ability to beat the Japanese. His exposition of morale as being founded on three foundations – spiritual, intellectual and material – is still at the heart of the British Army's doctrine today.

By the time that 36th Division was formed, Slim's reforms had borne sufficient fruit for British strategy against Japan to begin the long process of change from the defensive to the offensive. Accordingly, 36th Division was built on 29 Brigade's expertise, and organized as an amphibious assault formation. With his research complete and his own mind cleared, Stockwell issued his first training instruction. 'I will,' wrote Stockwell, 'accept only the very best.' With Gwydyr's well-known eccentricities in such matters, this was going to be a hit-and-miss affair.

Stockwell arrived one morning to visit 2 RWF to find Commanding Officer's orders just finished. RSM Hubbard took him on one side and recounted what had happened. Gwydyr had tried the case and found the man guilty, and then pronounced sentence: 'Ten days, or three rounds in the ring with me.'

The fusilier had replied, 'I'll take the three rounds, sir.'

'I'm getting to be an old man now,' said Gwydyr, 'you had better take the ten days.'

A few days later Gwydyr was inspecting the battalion, and suddenly stopped in front of a fusilier. 'Your name, please?'

'Fusilier Thomas, sir.'

'Have you a sister?'

'Yes sir.'

'Does she like fish and chips?'

'Yes sir, with plenty of salt and vinegar.'

Turning to the company commander, Gwydyr said, 'See that this man is promoted Lance Corporal as from now.'

From February to April, the brigade embarked on a harsh regime of training and exercises. This was the means by which the ends set out in Stockwell's training directive would be achieved, and it was clear to everyone that it was a matter for the personal attention of all commanders. Stockwell himself was constantly visiting his unit and sub-unit commanders to watch and advise. Not that his presence seems to have been in any way resented as 'peering over the shoulder'. His considerable charm and twinkling sense of humour was always at work, and these, with his reputation, made him a much respected figure – and indeed it is no exaggeration to say much loved. Lieutenant Ray Simmons, who had served under Stockwell in 2 RWF in Madagascar, was appointed as Stockwell's personal liaison officer. He gave this assessment:

Apart from my father, Hughie Stockwell was the greatest man I have ever known. To be chosen as his liaison officer was a great privilege. The strange thing was that we were similar in looks and to a degree in temperament, and both our wives were called Joan! For him not having a son I always thought he took me on as an adopted son. In Poona I ran the brigade mess . . . and later in Burma during the fighting I was always at his side as a sort of bodyguard. He was well known by all the soldiers who thought the world of him; he commanded great respect and I cannot think of any officer, NCO or fusilier who did not hold him in the highest regard. He was completely fair with everyone in his battalion, brigade and [later] division, regardless of nationality or rank and he had a wonderful knack of getting on with people. But he was also very demanding and very hard on himself; he would not stand any nonsense, especially disobedience or disloyalty, and if he got his knife into you, life was not worth living.

The hard training regime continued through the middle of the year. During September, the brigade undertook its promised jungle training in a training area round Mahabaleshwar, a village about 1,000 feet above sea level. The distance from Poona was about 60 miles and the brigade carried out a four-stage route march at night, resting during the heat of the day. B Echelons – that is, the quartermasters, storemen, cooks and orderlies – preceded the column each day and selected the site for the next staging camp, so that by the time the troops arrived at each campsite a hot meal was ready, a bathing place chosen and haversack rations prepared for the next march. There was no accommodation for the officers and men except the surrounding woods – soon after arrival the air was filled with the sound of machetes being wielded vigorously and before long each man had made a brushwood bivouac and, in some cases, a trestle bed and wooden chair as well.

In October, the brigade was tested in combined operations for the first time since Madagascar. On 7 October, it began moving to Bombay for Exercise Otter, an ambitious assault landing exercise. The actual exercise took place on the 15th, during which an officer and three men of the South Lancashires were actual casualties – drowned in the heavy surf of the Indian Ocean. This was a moment when Stockwell as commander had to show a hard streak – it was wartime, and no matter how regrettable these deaths were, the test of combat would face the brigade before long. For the greater good, the exercise must continue – and continue it did. The troops and their vehicles pushed on ashore, and were not re-embarked until the following day.

By the 18th the brigade was back in Poona, where normal training resumed. Then, on 29 December, Festing, Stockwell and Aslett, Commander 72 Brigade, were summoned to Bombay for a conference, which took place on New Year's Day 1944 at the Headquarters of XXXIII Indian Corps. Something was brewing. On 2 January he was back in Poona, issuing orders for another brigade amphibious exercise, Porpoise, but on the 4th the exercise was postponed and they were again called to Bombay. After more conferring at XXXIII Corps, they flew on to see General Bill Slim at Headquarters Fourteenth Army at Comilla, almost 1,200 miles away, on 9 January. On the 11th, they went forward to the Headquarters of XV Indian Corps in the Arakan, under Lieutenant General Sir Philip Christison. On the 15th they were back in Bombay, and in Poona the following day.

All became clear on 24 January 1944, when Admiral Lord Louis Mountbatten, the Supreme Allied Commander South-East Asia, visited the brigades of 36th Division. According to the visit programme, Mountbatten spent less than fifteen minutes with each unit. At the end of his round of unit visits, Ray Simmons had to fall in the brigade in a hollow square so that Mountbatten could address the men from a soap box. Mountbatten arrived with Stockwell and Simmons recalled that the two seemed to have hit it off very quickly, something which was to stand Stockwell in good stead later. Mountbatten climbed up onto the soap box, pushed his cap to the back of his head and told the troops that they were shortly to take part in an amphibious operation against the Japanese – he was answered with a rousing cheer.

With the staff working overtime, the division was made ready in a matter of days and advance parties moved off to Chittagong on the other side of the Indian sub-continent. The object was the assault and capture of Akyab, a port on the Arakan coast, which was to be taken as part of an offensive by XV Indian Corps into the Arakan; originally, the object had been the Andaman Islands, but an operation on this scale became impossible when more than half the amphibious resources of the theatre were ordered back to Europe for operations at Anzio. Operation Bulldozer, as it was named, would remove the Japanese threat to Chittagong and provide bases for long-range bombing of the Japanese lines of communication. On the 28th, Stockwell addressed the whole brigade; and on the 29th/30th the troops moved by train to Bombay. Here, Exercise Porpoise was run, but refocused in order to familiarize the men with new amphibious craft – DUKWs and Alligators – afloat, on the beach and inland.

The brigade, with the divisional headquarters, then moved to Chittagong by ship on 7 February. But the operation against Akyab was off – Chiang Kai-shek, the generalissimo of the Chinese Armies, had made the landings on the Andaman Islands a condition for launching his troops against the Japanese in Yunnan. When this operation was scaled down, he refused further co-operation and this had a considerable knock-on effect on other planned operations. As a result all remaining amphibious craft were recalled to Europe, making any landings impossible. But instead of an amphibious assault, a sudden thrust by the Japanese farther north brought a more urgent role for the 36th Division.

Slim had determined on a limited offensive in the Arakan as the means of giving his troops the confidence to take on the Japanese in larger battles; accordingly he had fixed on a modest advance down the Mayu peninsula. The object of the campaign was to secure the small port of Maungdaw and then the road running from it, across the Mayu range, to Buthidaung in the valley of the Kalapanzin River. With this area secure, troops could be supplied by sea and east-west communication maintained using the road. The next step would be to use the peninsula as the springboard for a larger attack against Akyab and beyond. XV Indian Corps, consisting of 5th and 7th (Indian) Divisions, supported by tanks, and on its inland flank, 81st (West African) Division, had begun a drive southwards on 30 November 1943 with 5th Division to the west of the Mayu hills, and 7th Division to the east. At first the British advance went well. Maungdaw fell at the end of the first week in January 1944, but Razabil, a natural fortress on the Naaf River which had been strengthened by the Japanese, and which commanded the road south-ward, resisted all assaults until its defenders were methodically winkled out and killed, man by man.

The Japanese, however, had other plans, and the British advance merely accelerated them. In the bigger picture, the Japanese planned to remain on the defensive in Burma, but realized that the British were bound to attack them. Their plans, therefore, aimed at a spoiling attack towards the main British bases, Imphal and Kohima, the capture of which would have the added benefit of disrupting air supply to the Chinese. This attack, Operation U-Go, would be preceded by a subsidiary and essentially diversionary attack, Ha-Go, in the Arakan. Conventional wisdom says that the Japanese planned at the invasion of India, fuelled perhaps by the immediate post-war version of events published in Mountbatten's official report. Such publications will often tend to talk up the dangers, but the entirety of the evidence does not really support this view. That said, Mutaguchi was an extremely aggressive commander who advocated pressing on beyond Imphal using the INA to foment uprisings as a means of forcing the British to abandon the War. His superior, Kawabe, however, gave no authorization for any advance beyond the Imphal/Kohima objectives which, he said, would have to be cleared with Imperial Headquarters in Tokyo.

Even though it was expected by the British, Ha-Go still achieved surprise. The Japanese 55th Division under Lieutenant General Tadashi Hanaya had been divided into three parts. The main striking force of 112 Regiment under Colonel S. Tanahashi, who had been a formidable opponent in 1943, had slipped round the eastern flank of the 7th Division between it and the 81st (West African) Division; a second, smaller force under Colonel Kubo, had moved further east, blocked the minor road south from Goppe Bazar, then turned west and cut the main road to Maungdaw south of Bawli Bazar, isolating the 5th Division. The remainder of Hanaya's force conducted attacks on 5th and 7th Divisions from the south. The Japanese assumed that, having surrounded the 7th Division, it would, as the British had always done in the past, fight its way back along its lines of communication. It could thus be destroyed piecemeal as it tried to scramble clear. But despite being nearly overrun, and fighting desperately, the 5th and 7th Divisions held their ground and fought the attackers to a standstill. This was not at all what the Japanese had expected, and it upset their timetable and logistic arrangements (or lack of them) fatally. Tokyo Rose announced on the wireless that it was all over in Burma – in fact, as Slim later remarked, it was just starting. 26th Indian Division moved swiftly to recapture Taung Bazar and began to press on Sakurai's rear. At the same time, 5th Division, fending off the Japanese frontal attacks, counter-attacked up the Ngakyedauk Pass towards the 7th Division.

36th Division was released from Army reserve to Fourteenth Army on 8th February, and ordered to follow 26th Division, although at this stage it was not intended that a specialized assault division would be committed to any role except reserve. Stockwell himself has left no memoir of this period, and so the story has to be reconstructed from the war diary and some personal reminiscences of other veterans. Having completed its journey of more than a thousand miles across India, 29 Brigade left Chittagong on 11th February for the railhead at Dohazari, where the troops were transferred into lorries which

India, Burma, & China Theatre

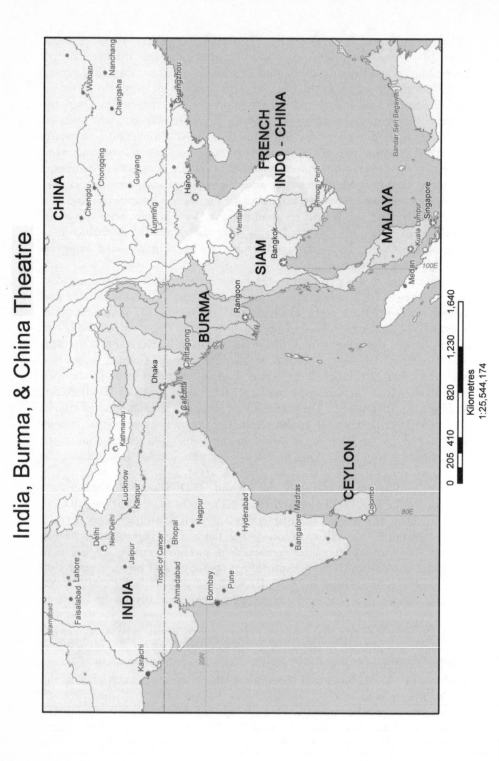

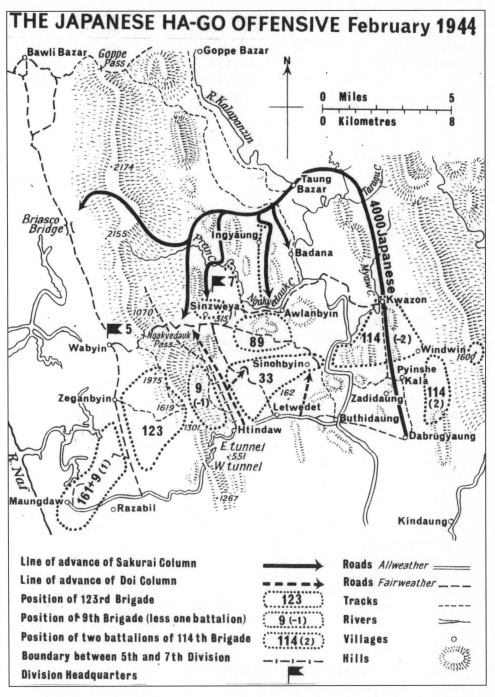

THE JAPANESE HA-GO OFFENSIVE February 1944

Bawli Bazar   *Goppe Pass*   oGoppe Bazar

N

| 0 | Miles | 5 |
| 0 | Kilometres | 8 |

R. Kalapanzin

2174

Briasco Bridge

2155

Taung Bazar

Prang C.

Ingyaung

Badana

Torau C.

4000 Japanese

Myaw C.

Kwazon

7

1070

Sinzweya

315

Ngakyedauk C.

Awlanbyin

5

Ngakyedauk Pass

Wabyin

89

114 (-2)

Windwin

1600

Sinohbyino

33

Pyinshe
Kala

9
(-1)

1975

Zeganbyino

1619

162

Letwedet

Zadidaung

114
(2)

1301

123

Htindaw

Buthidaung

Dabrugyaung

E. tunnel
551

W. tunnel

161+9 (1)

R. Naf

1267

Maungdawo

oRazabil

Kindaungo

Line of advance of Sakurai Column   Roads *Allweather*
Line of advance of Doi Column   Roads *Fairweather*
Position of 123rd Brigade   123   Tracks
Position of 9th Brigade (less one battalion)   9 (-1)   Rivers
Position of two battalions of 114th Brigade   114 (2)   Villages
Boundary between 5th and 7th Division   Hills
Division Headquarters

Source: *Report to the Combined Chiefs of Staff by the Supreme Allied Commander
South-East Asia 1943–1945* (HMSO, 1952).

107

carried them southwards through jungle country towards Bawli Bazar. The road must have been one of the worst in Burma and the discomfort of the journey was increased by wild rumours of Japanese progress. As the battalions drove over the wooden bridge at Bawli in the evening of the 12th they saw for the first time the long, jagged, inhospitable range of the Mayu hills, which for the next four months were to be their battlefield. Japanese aircraft were seen flying overhead and that night, almost for the last time in the campaign, dropped bombs – Allied air superiority, which had been building for some time, was by now assured and was to give the Allied ground forces their first taste of freedom of movement in the forthcoming campaign.

On the 14th, Stockwell briefed his commanding officers and the staff issued an operation order. In this, he described the Japanese positions: 143 Regiment and part of 144 Regiment were believed to be holding the general line Razabil to Buthidaung; part of 112 Regiment was located above Briasco Bridge; three other battalions were in depth, and one battalion was at Kyauktau. Festing's orders to Stockwell were for a limited operation only: 29 Brigade was to relieve 36 (Indian) Brigade of 26th (Indian) Division for offensive tasks to the east of the range, and in doing so, defend the bridge at Pruma Chaung, secure the Chota Maughnama Pass, patrol northwards as far as Panzai Bazar, and be prepared to counter-attack should the Japanese gain a lodgement in the pass.

On the 16th, Divisional Headquarters arrived at Bawli Bazar, and Festing and Stockwell went forward to reconnoitre. On the following day, the brigade began to deploy. The ascent was made in full marching order, stores being carried in the mule trains attached to each battalion, but before nightfall a point was reached beyond which the stores had to be manhandled. This was the first time the brigade had used mule trains and from now on these faithful animals were attached to each company almost permanently. Without their services no battles could have been fought and won in this difficult mountainous country.

By 20 February, firm battalion bases – boxes – were established, from which offensive patrols were sent out to look for signs of the enemy. The hills round the pass were full of Japanese parties, some holding positions and some on the move, for the stand of 7th Division had upset their plans and they were in some confusion, and very short of supplies.

As well as air resupply, rations for the companies of 29 Brigade positioned in the hills continued to be sent by mule, and the task of leading the mules developed into a highly organized drill. Drinking water, too, was loaded into special containers and the amount sent was carefully checked. Cigarettes, mail, ammunition, clothing and medical stores – even the leeks worn by the Royal Welch Fusiliers on St David's Day – were carried up on mules. Successful efforts were made by 2 RWF's Battalion Headquarters to send up a suitable St David's Day dinner to its companies in the Mayu hills; in fact, the excellence of the food provided far exceeded the facilities for eating it! Stockwell had been ordered to move the brigade that same evening towards Maungdaw to assume responsibility for the Ngakyedauk Pass, Mayu spine and its western slopes, but time was found for a 5.00 pm dinner in the 2 RWF administrative box, the only guests being Stockwell and George Demetriadi. The Reverend F.O. Bennett, who ate the leek in the usual ceremonial manner, toasted the Regiment from a goblet presented by Hughie Stockwell's uncle, C.I. Stockwell, which had been sent for specially, and which was carefully guarded until a favourable moment came for it to be returned to the rear party in India.

The Japanese by now had well and truly shot their bolt and, too late, were trying to pull back in small groups, covered by suicide detachments. Kubo's force was destroyed almost to the last man among the caves and cliffs of the Mayu range. Despite the desire not to use a specialized assault division in the line, the 36th Division's tasks were therefore modified: the division was to establish and maintain a firm base until monsoon positions could be taken up. The division was to hold Sinzweya, the Ngakyedauk Pass, the crest of the Mayu range between that Pass and the tunnels, Taung Bazar, Goppe Bazar and Pass, and Bawli. This would allow the 5th Division to be extracted and sent across to Assam, where signs of another, more serious, Japanese invasion were already brewing. 29 Brigade's role was to hold a firm line behind 5th Division to prevent Japanese infiltration through the mountain passes, using a system of defended boxes, from which patrols and counter-attacks could be launched. Brigade Headquarters set up its own box, for which 2 RWF was made responsible. At 1.30 am on 6 March the alarm was given, and shortly afterwards a party of about twenty Japanese penetrated as far as C Company of 2 RWF who opened fire and forced them to withdraw. At about the same time, another party penetrated the Brigade HQ area and had to be engaged by Stockwell himself, with David Brand, Ray Simmons and a scratch force. Brand, firing a Sten gun with great bravery, accounted for several of the twelve dead Japanese – accounts vary from three to six – and Stockwell himself undoubtedly killed several more of those found around the Brigade HQ, some of them only a few yards from his tent. The fact that the brigade commander had not shirked close combat went down very well with the troops. Gordon Milne recalled that:

> Whether the enemy knew they were heading into Brigade HQ or not we will never know. What we do know, however, is that the Brigadier and his Brigade Major put up a tremendous show, firing their Stens and lobbing grenades (while still in their night attire). The enemy I am certain must have had heavy casualties before they withdrew, which brings me to the first great quality of our Brigadier, a very fine soldier who could deal so calmly with dangerous situations.

Patrols during the next few days came across numbers of dead Japanese and also discovered the probable hiding place from which Brigade Headquarters had been attacked on the 6th. Spaces had been cut between the bamboos, the undergrowth was trodden down, and numerous Japanese tommy cookers were found in the area. In order fully to dominate the area, Stockwell issued new orders for patrolling:

All chaungs, paths and possible routes of infiltration within battalion areas will be constantly patrolled by recce patrols ... Should a recce patrol discover or hear enemy movement ... the battalion commander will order to the area strong fighting patrols to engage and harass the enemy ... In the event of any major concentration being discovered, I will arrange the necessary counter-attack and supporting fire programme.

What is revealing about this instruction is that Stockwell, while being explicit about what he required from the commanding officers, was not doing their jobs for them – there is nothing worse in any military organization than a senior officer who wants to do everyone's job except his own – but was clear about where his own responsibilities lay. As a principle, whenever two or more units, at whatever level, and supporting arms, are involved in any operation, it is the responsibility of the commander and staff at the next level up to command, control and co-ordinate that operation. Failure to do so invariably results in confusion at best, and friendly fire at worst.

So far, the defence of the Ngakyedauk Pass had cost 36th Division only 118 casualties all told. But the main route across the Mayu range, the 16-mile-long road that linked Maungdaw with Buthidaung, still remained in enemy hands. About halfway between the two villages, it passed through the range by two tunnels, which had once carried a light railway. The Japanese positions in the steep, jungle-clad hills covered the road continuously, but in three places they were particularly strong, amounting to fortresses. These were the tunnels themselves, and two buttresses, one on each side of the range, at Razabil and Letwedet. By 11 March, the two buttresses, which had been laboriously assaulted and cleared during the initial offensive, had been recaptured. The task of clearing the last stronghold, the tunnels, was given to 36th Division. 72 Brigade launched the attack on the western tunnel on 21 March after a heavy artillery preparation and two days later it was captured. On the 27th, 2 RWF was detached from Stockwell's command, and moved forward in transport to the Chaukmainywa area where the battalion was placed under command of 72 Brigade for the attack on the eastern tunnel, about a mile north-east of the western one. In the mêlée, a tank fired into one of the tunnels where ammunition was stored and it blew up in a series of tremendous explosions. In the confusion, the Welshmen rushed the tunnel and captured it.

A few days later, orders were issued for XV Corps to take up monsoon positions on the Buthidaung–Maungdaw road with 26th (Indian) Division holding the tunnels, 36th Division in the Wabyin area, and 7th Indian Division detached to fill the gap in Army Group reserve. During the first week of May 1944, the weather remained fine, but plans were being made for the 36th Division to be relieved of its static tasks by the 25th (Indian) Division, and return to India immediately after the monsoon broke – not least because the main Japanese offensive was expected soon on the Assam front.

* * *

On 10 May the advance parties moved in three-ton lorries from Wabyin to Tumbru on the road to Chittagong. On the 13th, Brigade Headquarters moved back to Kyaugyaung Transit Camp. On 4 June the handover was completed and next day the move back to India was begun. The division had lost another 119 men killed, wounded and missing since leaving the Ngakyedauk Pass. On the following day, 5 June, the troops marched in heavy rain to Kyaugyaung on the first stage of the journey. At the camp, the brigade paraded for Sir Philip Christison, who came to bid farewell to 29 Brigade and to thank them for their help. Early next morning the brigade began to embark in river transport for Tumbru; in Europe, it was D-Day.

29 Brigade drove through intermittent cloudbursts to Dohazari and on 9 June entrained for Sylhet. From there it had a long and tedious drive to the hill station of Shillong, in Assam, where the whole Division was to rest and refit. The Japanese, an ethnically and culturally homogenous force, had been smashed by a force that was anything but. 11th Army Group contained not just British brigades and divisions, but Chinese, East Africans, West Africans, and men from all the martial races of the Indian sub-continent – Gurkhas, Garwhalis, Mahrattas, Punjabis, Bengalis, Pathans, Sikhs, Afridis, to name but a few. This army has sometimes been spoken of as the sweepings of the Empire – as if it was some kind of rabble. It was not. Many of its formations were of extremely high quality. It is true that the asymmetries of culture produced many logistic difficulties – different rations, for example, for different religious groups – and the requirement for commanders to recognize differences, which produced strengths, and play to them, while compensating for potential weaknesses. It could be argued that the diversity of this army gave it strength, like a composite bow. The physical conditions it endured were far harder, for example, than anything encountered in North-West Europe, even in the winter of 1944–45. As John Masters remarked, Indians, Africans and Gurkhas provided the soul and backbone of the army – without them there would have been no army and no victory. Indeed these men were all volunteers, not conscripts, who came forward in large numbers at a time when British manpower was a declining resource, and proved themselves hardy fighters, careless of death, and unencumbered by the mentality of civilians in uniform that was sometimes found in European formations. Stockwell already knew the qualities of non-European troops from his service in West Africa, but to others, not least the Japanese, these must have come as quite a shock. That the army in general, and 29 Brigade and 36th Division in particular, had become as effective as they had in so short a time is a great tribute to the leadership, training, motivation and fighting qualities of the officers and men of all ranks. William Ritchie, the Commanding Officer of the Royal Scots Fusiliers, summed up the mood when he said of his battalion that it 'is now ready to take on the Japanese anywhere'.

111

Chapter Ten

Brigade Commander – Burma, 1944–1945

While 36th Division was refitting, the Japanese had launched their main offensive, Operation U-Go, on the Assam front – Operation Ha-Go in the Arakan had indeed been no more than a diversion. Once the Japanese offensive in Assam had been repulsed, Allied plans turned to breaking the enemy's hold on Burma. Set against the difficulties of terrain and weather, and an aggressive enemy, the Allies now enjoyed overall force ratios that were very favourable; and not only were the Allied armies now numerically superior, they were morally convinced they could win. Moreover, they held complete command of the air – from March to July 1944, the Japanese flew 1,750 sorties in Burma, against the Allies' 18,600. But ground offensive operations largely depended on the logistical art of the possible. On 3 June, Mountbatten received a directive from the Combined Chiefs of Staff which instructed him to expand the air link with China and exploit the development of a land route by constructing and exploiting the Ledo road.

Meanwhile, at Shillong, 29 Infantry Brigade was camped in the cool of the pine woods about 4,900 feet above sea level. 36th Division was substantially re-equipped with ordnance stores which had to come from as far away as Calcutta and Kohima, at a time when railway rolling stock was at a premium, and then brought on by road the 70 miles from the railhead.

On the last day of June, General Slim visited Shillong, where Stockwell had the pleasure of watching him decorate his old friend Clifford Burton, the Quartermaster of 2 RWF, with the MBE. Slim then spoke to all ranks down to corporal, where in an inspiring address he outlined the next task of 36th Division, and gave two reasons for choosing them. These were his confidence in Frankie Festing, its commander, and his respect for the outstanding performance of the division in the Arakan. British prestige, he said, had suffered, especially in India, from the exodus from Burma, and it could only be regained by the expulsion of the Japanese from Burma. No failure could be countenanced, and only the best troops would do. He went on to say that 'If in any doubt as to which of two courses to pursue, always choose the bolder.

I have disregarded this principle twice in my life and in both cases I was wrong.'

Slim's words on Gordon Milne made an impact: 'Those who were privileged to attend are never likely to forget it – they will probably never hear its equal. He partially lifted the veil and gave us a glimpse of the future.'

Slim was quite explicit about his intentions for Operation Capital: while the Fourteenth Army drove east and then south from Imphal, Stilwell's Chinese would advance south from Myitkyina. Meanwhile 36th Division would be moved to join Stilwell's command. Because the division was detached from Fourteenth Army, it usually receives only occasional mentions in British accounts of the campaign, or partial descriptions in regimental histories; its full story has never, arguably, been told. Stockwell himself left a memoir of this campaign in an album of photographs and notes compiled at the time, added to at various times later. These photographs in particular give a vivid impression of hardships and horrors of the war in Burma. In his notes, Stockwell gave his recollection of this time:

> After a break of three or four weeks at Shillong, whence we had moved from the Arakan for reorganisation and resuscitation, we moved up to Ledo in north-east Assam where we concentrated before flying in to Myitkyina at the beginning of August 1944. Here was the head of the railway line from Rangoon some 640 miles away to the south. 36th Division's task was to clear the Japanese out of northern Burma as far south as Mandalay and act as a flank guard to Fourteenth Army advancing from Imphal into the central plain of Burma directed on Mandalay and thereafter Rangoon. Also to keep in contact with the Chinese on our left flank, who were to operate down through Bhamo to Lashio, the head of a rail link from Mandalay. The division came under the operational command of the American General 'Vinegar Joe' Stilwell.

To carry out this task, Festing had to pare down the normal organization of the division. As he would have to rely on air supply, most of the division's heavy lift was left behind; his anti-tank platoons and batteries were re-equipped with mortars, and three Chinese batteries were also added to the division's order of battle. The reliance on air resupply was helped by the fact that a division in Burma, having been stripped of its heavy vehicles and guns, required only 120 tons of combat supplies each day, as against the Allied average in other theatres of 400 tons. 29 Brigade, for example, numbered only about 120 officers and 2,700 men.

Early in July, 72 Brigade was moved forward to Margherita, near Ledo in northern Assam. On 27 July, 29 Brigade and the Divisional Headquarters, feeling much refreshed and ready for any new experience, moved to Pandu, where they entrained for Margherita, arriving there on the 30th after a hot, cramped journey. After the cool of Shillong, Ledo was stifling and sticky – the first real taste of the Burmese climate. The camp too was a severe test of morale, being indescribably filthy, having been used for staging troops for some time. The tents leaked and the putrid smell of decaying vegetation was everywhere; leeches and snakes abounded. The men made valiant attempts to improve the deplorable living conditions, but many of the troops went down with malaria. It was an everyday occurrence for the bloated carcase of a buffalo or other animal to be seen – or rather smelt – floating down the River Brahmaputra.

Myitkyina fell on 3 August and a few days later Stockwell had an interview with Stilwell at Myitkyina. Stilwell, a man who hated the British like poison, and did all he could to ruin inter-Allied co-operation, was a man 'with a face like an ancient turtle and a tongue like whiplash. Even his best friend would find it hard to describe [him] as a very approachable type.' Stockwell described the occasion: 'Flushed with the anticipation of leading my brigade into north Burma I was ushered into his presence. Saluting, I inquired had he any special instructions? He replied "Sure, yes. Get to Rangoon, and now get out!"'

The move forward of 29 Brigade began on the 7th, led by the Royal Scots Fusiliers. It should have been completed by the 8th, however the monsoon was in full spate, and torrential rain and the haze caused by evaporation slowed things up; the last unit, 2 RWF, was not complete until the 14th. The journey by air took about an hour and lay over dense jungle country with occasional glimpses of the Ledo Road. At Myitkyina, the brigade killed its first Japanese in north Burma, ambushing some remnants of the garrison trying to escape down the line by night without arms or ammunition, and in a wretched state through sickness and malnutrition. From there, the troops marched to the rail-head for a move forward. This march was of 3 miles across paddy fields in which, in heavy rain and under artillery fire, the men were wading up to their waists, weighed down with mortars, wireless sets, batteries, ammunition and stores. In its forward concentration area at Sahmaw, which had been hard hit by air strikes, the men had their first experience of G 1098 stores and supplies dropped from the air by the USAAF. Stockwell himself remembered that: 'At Sahmaw I saw David Brand, the BM, on his knees by the dropping zone. I enquired tenderly what was the matter. He said "in the next few serials is Brigade HQ Box 230 – which is my valise and in it is a bottle of gin – I pray that it lands intact!"'

The railway corridor extends from Myitkyina in the north to Katha on the Irrawaddy in the south, a distance of about 145 miles. The first part, which runs through the Mu Valley, is cultivated and fairly open, broken by numerous banks and bunds, which made good fire positions for the Japanese. Later on the country is increasingly wooded, ending up in dense jungle. In addition to the railway, which at this time was fairly intact although some bridges had been blown and most of the engines and rolling stock wrecked, there was also a road, which at times followed the railway, but at some points diverged by up to a mile. This road however had fallen into disrepair during the Japanese occupation and in places had almost disappeared. It was discovered that on

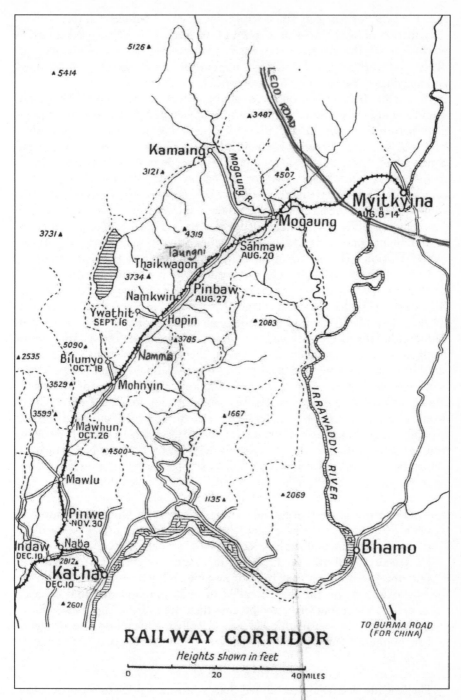

RAILWAY CORRIDOR

Heights shown in feet

0   20   40 MILES

Source: Lieutenant Commander P.K. Kemp and John Graves, *The Red Dragons: the Story of the Royal Welch Fusiliers 1919–1945* (Aldershot, 1960).

the railway a one-ton jeep, fitted with railway wheels, could pull three large, fully loaded railway trucks at a speed of 30 mph. This improvised solution worked so well that the absence of engines was not as serious as at first seemed likely. But every damaged bridge, no matter how small, meant the unloading and ferrying of a cargo until it was repaired.

72 Brigade had pushed on to Mogaung, where 29 Brigade following on found a sea of brown mud, through which all vehicles, guns and heavy equipment had to be manhandled. This took several days and was an exhausting business. A lot of corduroy road making was required to improve things, which added to the burden of labour as 29 Brigade moved along the railway to Onbaung, a few miles north of the enemy-held village of Pinbaw, the capture of which was essential in fulfilling the flank security task for Stilwell's Chinese. There followed a pause of two days, during which Stockwell and his commanding officers were able to fly over the forward enemy positions in small biplanes known as L5s, which were used for close artillery support, or in the occasional Dakota supply aircraft bringing Chinese troops forward.

The battalions of 72 Brigade had by now been reduced to around 350 combatants each, with most of the casualties caused by heat and sickness. 72 Brigade therefore halted at the village of Nansan Chaung, and on 22 August, 29 Brigade took up the lead in the first phase of the battle for Pinbaw. To support the advance, Stockwell was given a battery of four 105mm guns manned by Chinese gunners. In addition, there were American forward air support control parties attached to the brigade and battalion HQs. Once Stockwell had organized an air strike in support of one or more of his battalions, control of the aircraft could be left to the air support control party which would direct the aircraft by wireless. This intimate control of aircraft from the ground was probably as well orchestrated here as in any theatre of the War, and certainly compares very favourably with accounts from Normandy at about the same time. But it was not all as smooth as it might seem – multinational operations seldom are. Stockwell himself recalled that:

After organising a strike by the mortar battery on a Japanese position while I was up with the East Lancashires for a company attack, some of the bombs fell uncomfortably close, one in fact behind me about 20-30 yards away! Anyhow the company attack went in – cleared through the Japs and I went on my way back to Brigade HQ, passing the CO of the mortar battery on the way. I called in and complimented him on a successful shoot, but suggested he kept them well pitched up, as we did not want any own casualties. He replied 'velly many tanks – no damage I am hoping?' I said 'No.' He replied 'velly good – we kill two 72 Brigade yesterday.'

The Brigade War Diary recounted that 'a few days prior to the attack [on Pinbaw], 72 Brigade had captured a most loquacious prisoner of war.' This man reported that Pinbaw was defended by around 750 Japanese soldiers, with orders to hold until the end of the month. Stockwell's plan for the capture of Pinbaw was therefore in three phases. In the first phase, 1st Royal Scots Fusiliers were to advance down the axis of the railway to the chaung and rail crossing just north of Pinbaw in order to threaten the enemy's right flank, while the 2nd East Lancashires attacked and captured Ingyingon on the northern bank of the Nansan Chaung. The second phase would then begin with the East Lancashires forcing a bridgehead across the chaung; in the final phase, the 2nd Royal Welch Fusiliers could pass through this bridgehead and attack Pinbaw.

But no plan ever survives contact with the enemy. The attack went in at dawn on 25 August and by the early afternoon the East Lancashires had taken Ingyingon, but had been badly delayed by enemy opposition west of the road and had not yet forced the crossing of the chaung. Accordingly, Stockwell called up 2 RWF and told Gwydyr – who was now recovered from his wound and back in command – to attack across the chaung, capture Pinlon and take possession of two small features known as Blackcock and Woodcock, which dominated the village from the west. By 6.00 pm this had been accomplished with air support, and the brigade hastily dug in during the first hours of darkness.

At about 1.00 pm the next day, Stockwell gave orders to 2 RWF to capture and consolidate Pinbaw. The attack began about 3.00 pm with an artillery barrage. The country was very close, the Japanese fought fanatically, casualties were heavy on both sides and no progress was made. Stockwell therefore decided to break off the attack until the morning. During the night torrential rain fell and next day the attack was put off for four hours while the men in the forward positions, unable to light fires, waited impatiently. By this time the chaungs were in flood and communication with the forward companies was often a hazardous operation.

Stockwell again modified the plan, ordering Gwydyr to secure the bridgehead over the chaung, and then bringing forward the East Lancashires, who were relatively fresh, to pass through and take Pinbaw: 'The enemy's shouts of "come and get us", which had punctuated the night, brought their just rewards at dawn. At 0600, 2 RWF went into the attack. Approximately 20 Japs were defending a bridge. Those not killed quickly ran away.'

No sooner had 2 RWF consolidated than the Japanese counter-attacked fiercely, but the fusiliers held their ground and the Japanese were forced to withdraw. The rest of the day was spent in trying to force the position in a series of company attacks from the right flank of the village, but little progress was made. That night, Stockwell and his COs laid fresh plans and at dawn, the attack was renewed. It was soon apparent that the Japanese had had enough, and had withdrawn during the night, leaving only a few snipers, and no wonder – eighty-one air strikes had been put in on the village, and after the battle 101 enemy dead were found. Even Vinegar Joe was impressed, telegraphing to Festing on the 27th: 'In getting to your objective so promptly, congratulations to you and your men. Smart work. We are proud of you.'

Pinbaw itself was a collection of wooden houses on stilts, sitting above a lake of muck, slime, filth and stench. Most of the buildings were damaged, with as many holes in the floors as in the roofs. After a pause for resupply, the Royal Scots Fusiliers occupied Hopin on 11 September, where again there was a brief pause, extra heavy rain having washed away the bridge on the Nansan chaung, severing communications. Patrols still went out though, and these began to find horrific evidence of the weakness of the enemy's supply system, in the form of many Japanese soldiers lying dead, emaciated from starvation. On 14 September 1944 the brigade started out for Ywathit, some 20 miles further south. The monsoon was still in full spate and as a result the Namkwin chaung was flowing fast, but the troops waded across and hauled stores over by rubber dinghy – only to learn when across that, as a result of the heavy rain, the road would be closed the next day. A night of torrential rain was endured in hastily erected bivouacs. Next day the weather improved sufficiently to allow the advance party to set off for Ywathit, but the weather broke again and the main body did not arrive until the 16th. Here, work on a defensive perimeter began at once and the next day active patrolling was resumed, but few Japanese parties were located in the many mapped and unmapped villages.

Following new orders from General Dan Sultan, who had taken over Stilwell's responsibilities in Burma, 36th Division resumed its advance on 15 October. There was no information on whether the Japanese were a covering force or a main defensive position; moreover, the railway was badly damaged, the bridges were down and the road, which at Hopin diverged from the railway and did not rejoin it until it reached Mohnyin, was in poor shape. 36th Division was therefore faced with an advance to make and maintain contact with the enemy, and at the same time construct a road good enough to bring up heavy transport and guns. Lack of accurate intelligence is often cited as a failing in this theatre, and it is a good example of how improvisation, so effective elsewhere, could not make up for the paucity of resources in comparison with other theatres. Festing's plan therefore was for 72 Brigade to advance through Hopin on the railway axis and occupy positions just north of Mohnyin, while 29 Brigade was to advance down the axis of the road.

By first light on 18 October, Bilumyo, which was found to be clear of the enemy, had been reached – the Japanese had fled the previous night. Pinhe could be seen across the paddy fields and patrols were sent out to reconnoitre. Soon after 9.00 am next morning, 2 RWF entered Pinhe, reported it clear and sent a patrol on to Pintha. Gwydyr decided to mount an immediate attack with three companies. Artillery was not yet available, but an air strike was laid on and went in soon after 1.00 pm. For a time the advance was checked by enemy mortar and machine-gun fire. In the meantime the 2nd East Lancashires had driven the enemy from Mohnyin, and as a result the Japanese found Pintha untenable and withdrew. The brigade bedded down for the night and next morning pushed forward to Tegyigon, while a dropping zone for supplies was established in the Pintha area. This meant something more substantial to eat than the jungle packs which the men had lived on for the last four days.

On 22 October, Kadu was entered without opposition and the railway station was captured. On the 24th 2 RWF started down the railway to Mawhun, where it was known that the Japanese had massed a considerable number of guns. Unsurprisingly, next morning they were shelled for over an hour by Japanese 75mm guns.

On the 25th the advance continued and after a stiff fight Mawhun railway station was occupied the next day without opposition. 29 Brigade had now passed an important geographical landmark on the road to Mandalay: the main watershed had been crossed, and the chaungs all now flowed south instead of north. Just as important was the fact the troops were fighting along the grain of the country, and not across it. On 29 October, 2 RWF again led off along the railway, while the East Lancashires and the Royal Scots Fusiliers moved along the road. Mawhe was reported clear and shortly afterwards a company on a wide sweep into Okshitkon captured six cartloads of Japanese equipment, the drivers having fled on the patrol's approach. Meanwhile the other two battalions had met tough opposition advancing along the tortuous road, thickly bordered by jungle, and it seemed probable that they would not be able to reach their objective, a rail crossing over a chaung known as BM 492. Stockwell therefore ordered Gwydyr to swing across and take this objective from the flank. This was done – but only just: the northern side of the chaung was taken, and a small bridgehead secured on the south side. A Japanese counter-attack drove this detachment back, but the attack, which had severed the Japanese line of communication, had caused considerable confusion to the enemy. At dawn the next morning, the Japanese were found to have withdrawn from the whole area.

By 1 November 1944, Brigade and Divisional Headquarters were established near Henu, just north of Mawlu. This area had been occupied previously by the Chindits and was known as the White City Block. Here, the jungle gradually receded from the floor of the valley and the road and railway ran together along the eastern foothills. Next day the heavy baggage, including the men's large packs and blanket rolls, arrived, and that night – the first occasion since the move from Ywathit on 15 October – they enjoyed the luxury of a blanket. But at Mawlu, which the Chindits had occupied and heavily mined, the Japanese made a determined stand around the railway station and the bridge just to the south; the Royal Scots Fusiliers again faced a hard fight to get them out.

By this time, the newspapers had begun to report 36th Division's advance as the most rapid made by the Allies in Burma, stressing the close co-operation between different nationalities, the good supply system using, as conditions dictated, road, rail and air, and the excellent air support. There had been a price, though, in casualties, and on the survivors too. Photographs in

Stockwell's album show unmistakeably how tired and worn everyone was, and how thin; his notes too remark on how weary everyone was of the physical hardships, and the strain of fighting an unrelenting enemy like the Japanese. The mental strain is hard to quantify. A man's chances of survival, leaving aside the chance of mortar or artillery rounds, depended on: the shooting skills and nerve of the Japanese soldier who engaged him, often at very close range; his own ability to react, and carry out the standard battle drill; and the way he and his companions worked as a team. Tiredness, fear, dysentery and weather all had their effect too. Such things tend to erode the limited stock of courage which every man has, to a varying degree, and which, once used up, cannot be replaced. For leaders like Stockwell, the strain was therefore even more telling – anyone can be brave for five minutes and win the VC, but the man in charge, at any level, has to be brave all the time. The physical strain is much easier to comprehend: the average officer and soldier had to carry his weapon and ammunition, spare ammunition for the automatic weapons, two or three days rations, water, spare clothing, a shovel, steel helmet, and probably a share of heavy weapons or other equipment like radios and batteries, stretchers or mortar bombs. This had to be humped through the monsoon or hot weather, in and out of fighting, for months.

After the long spell of rapid progress, there now came a more serious hold-up. 72 Brigade was passed through 29 Brigade to continue the advance, but beyond Mawlu the jungle was much thicker and all movement off the beaten track proved difficult. 72 Brigade made good progress for a dozen miles, but after that enemy resistance stiffened and on the outskirts of Pinwe the advance was brought to a standstill in the bloodiest fighting so far. The Japanese, needing to extricate their forces withdrawing from the west before the main Fourteenth Army advance, had decided to make a firm stand at Pinwe. They occupied well-prepared and heavily fortified positions on either side of the Gyobin Chaung, where dense jungle put a stop to any determined outflanking movement. The frontal attack on these positions, which began on 10 November, was carefully planned with air and artillery support, but all possible lines of approach were kept under continuous fire by the enemy and at the end of fourteen days of heavy fighting little headway had been made.

The struggle for Pinwe continued for more than three weeks, with severe casualties on both sides. On 24 November, with 72 Brigade close to exhaustion, Festing decided to interchange the brigades: 29 Brigade had had a rest, with time even to write letters home, bathe in the chaungs, and let their kit catch up – just as well, as the nights were now quite chilly and sweaters were needed after dark. On 26 November, the regrouping was completed. But by now the fighting had decreased in intensity and Japanese resistance, after so long a hammering, especially from Allied heavy artillery and air strikes, was visibly weakening. 72 Brigade's attacks had all been mounted on a single battalion frontage; now Stockwell decided to commit two battalions in his first assault echelon – the Royal Scots Fusiliers and the Royal Welch – and then reinforce with the third, the East Lancashires. The road and railway were about 1,000 yards apart on the approach to Pinwe, but they converged at the station, which was dominated by high ground to the west.

On 27 November, patrols were sent out by all the battalions to feel their way down either side of the railway and several skirmishes with the enemy took place. Finally, on the 30th, St Andrew's Day, patrols of 1 RSF and 2 RWF, working their way on both sides of the railway line, passed numerous deserted bunkers and foxholes without drawing fire. The Royal Welch patrol approached Pinwe station where the patrol leader, with two men, went on until he reached the first seven railway trucks standing at the north end of the station. The place was deserted.

Just south of Indaw, on 16 December, 29 Brigade linked up with patrols of 19th (Indian) Division, which was advancing from the west. To the Royal Scots Fusiliers fell the honour of making the actual link-up, with the 1st/6th Gurkhas. The tasks allotted to 36th Division of clearing the railway corridor and linking up with Fourteenth Army were thus completed after five and a half months and nearly 200 miles, against stubborn opposition, and for the most part in the foulest weather conditions that South-East Asia could provide. Slim's confidence had been amply repaid.

Festing now received fresh orders from General Dan Sultan, who had relieved Stilwell. The division was to split: 26 and 72 Brigades were to cross the Irrawaddy at Katha and advance south towards Mongmit, while 29 Brigade, with 130th Field Regiment under command, was to move 40 miles south to Tigyaing, cross the river there, and then move along the east bank of the Irrawaddy towards Twingge. From here, 29 Brigade would link up with 19th (Indian) Division, which was astride the Irrawaddy between Thabeikkyn and Kyaukmyaung, facing two Japanese divisions; there was a chance that 29 Brigade, advancing from the north, would take the northern of these two divisions, the 15th, in the flank.

On 18 December, the brigade moved from Indaw to Kunbaung, and on the 23rd to Tigyaing, where Christmas was celebrated. There was not much leisure for this, as the Japanese had to be kept moving – and they took no heed of Christmas. However, Stockwell was determined that every man should have the best Christmas dinner that could be provided, and that each unit would have a whole day of rest in order to observe the military proprieties. The base supply organization was wound into gear by the divisional staff, and sent forward pigs, ducks, beer, tinned puddings – even crackers and paper hats! The USAAF came up trumps as usual and dropped the supplies in. Stockwell remembered that:

> From time to time my caravan caught up. It had been converted from an old wheeled ambulance. It was with me in the Arakan and made this trip. We reached Tigyaing on the Irrawaddy about 160 miles south of Myitkyina and enjoyed a short pause and Christmas before crossing the

river. Christmas dinner. Ducks – they were flown in live and dropped in panniers. The cooks then let them out as there were still 40 hours before they were due to be eaten. The scene was pandemonium as the company cooks tried to catch the ducks as they sailed around Tigyaing – a sight to behold!

Geoffry Foster's medical opinion as ADMS was that 'Any [man] who failed to achieve acute distension, flatulence and the headache, which, after all, seem to be the main object of Christmas Day in the Army, had only himself to blame.' In battalion areas, the chaplains held Christmas services. In the evening a Welsh choir, hastily reassembled by 2 RWF, sang carols: as Brian Cotton recalled, 'The men sang beautifully.' Stockwell contributed to the occasion by declaiming purple patches from *Henry V* and other plays of Shakespeare. He then moved on to do the rounds of the brigade. Gordon Milne remembered of his unit's campfire party:

> Who should be one of the leaders of the sing-song? Yes, the Brigadier, with a lovely rendering of 'Alouetta'. It took a lot to enter into that kind of atmosphere, and how few soldiers while on active service can say they had the honour of being entertained by their Brigadier? Certainly the Japanese would never have understood the relationship we had at that time, all ranks were in it <u>together</u>. Brigadier Stockwell was the very essence and spirit of a real comrade.

On Boxing Day, Stockwell sent the first patrol across the Irrawaddy, and learnt that the Japanese forces, with which it had lost touch, had crossed the river 30 miles to the south at Tagaung. On the 29th a patrol reached Tagaung and found that the last party of Japanese had set off southwards for Twingge two days before. The next couple of days were devoted to identifying a crossing site and preparing for an immediate river crossing followed by an advance down the east bank of the Irrawaddy to Twingge. The Irrawaddy, about half a mile wide and with a fast current, resembled 'a conveyor of driftwood and corpses, dirty, muddy, and generously dotted with semi-sunken ships in varying stages of dilapidation, and, owing to its filth, was . . . quite unfit for [swimming]'. The brigade crossed between 1 and 2 January 1945. Men and transport were ferried across on rafts built out of Japanese pontoons, Heath Robinson affairs made up of logs and canoes – indeed anything that would float. Stockwell himself recalled of the river that:

> It was about 900 yards wide with a four to six knot current . . . Getting about 900 mules across the river no easy task. We had to start them swimming with their own handlers in a boat alongside. Once under way and facing in the right direction the halter could be let go.

At about the same news had come in of the immediate award of the DSO to Gwydyr. Three rounds were fired by the divisional artillery at midnight on all recorded targets as a salute to this popular award; by the law of unintended consequences, this caused great excitement as the troops thought at first that the battle had begun again. After the War, Gwydyr had, like many others who achieved high rank in wartime, reverted to his previous rank of Lieutenant Colonel and was commanding the 1st Battalion of the Royal Welch Fusiliers in Germany. A keen brigadier, well aware that the War had interfered lamentably with training, had staged a brigade TEWT on the intricate subject of river crossing by all-arms formations, stressing the need for close co-ordination, detailed staff work and hands-on command. 'Now,' he said, 'Lieutenant Colonel Gwydyr-Jones was commanding at the crossing of the Irrawaddy. Do tell us how you did it.' 'My dear,' replied Gwydyr, 'I simply got into my canoe, and my man paddled me over.'

By 4 January the whole brigade had reached Tagaung. Shortly after midnight on the 6th torrential rain began to fall – a subsidiary monsoon had arrived – and three hours later the roads were treacherous. Rain continued all day and on the 7th the road was closed to motor transport: but a further 7 miles were covered the following day. By the 9th the brigade had reached the area of Pauktabin, where 2 RWF once more took up the lead. The brigade was now approaching the area where more serious enemy opposition was to be expected.

29 Brigade was now completely cut off from the rest of 36th Division, except by air supply, by the Shweli River, impassable roads, and by miles of scrub and jungle. Casualties and reinforcements had to be ferried in and out in single figures by light aircraft, so Stockwell could take no risks. On 10 and 11 January strong patrols, guided by friendly Kachin levies, pushed out south towards Twingge and south-east towards the Mongmit road. Gordon Milne recalled at about this time that:

> I was out on a small patrol going along a jungle path when who should come along but Brigadier Stockwell. Suddenly a dog who seemed to be attached to the Brigadier darted into the thicket. On further following up the dog's indication we produced a rather surprised Jap for whom the war was over. We <u>were</u> taking prisoners at that time. I have always marvelled at the superb intelligence of that dog, not only his loyalty to his master, but his ability to sense the near presence of the enemy. Who said that animals were dumb?

On the 11th, patrols found that points on the Twingge road, previously reported clear, were now strongly held by the enemy. Some vicious fighting erupted and carried on throughout the day with 2 RWF inflicting many casualties on the enemy, although making little progress. Stockwell accordingly ordered the brigade to concentrate at Pauktabin, as identification taken from dead Japanese gave the first information that the Japanese 31st Division was now engaged on this front.

All in all, it seemed that the Japanese were stretched, and fighting on a broader front; indeed as it later turned out, they were well aware of the threat to their flank and their communications posed by the advance of the 36th Division, and were regrouping. Stockwell therefore came up with a new brigade plan. The 1st Royal Scots Fusiliers were to secure the right flank and then push forward as far as Twingge; 2 RWF were to hold the central block in the Daungbon-Banwe area and patrol south towards the Twingge–Mongmit road, astride which there was a very strongly held Japanese bunker; and the 2nd East Lancashires were to advance down the eastern track from Pauktabin, via Tonkwe, to Kyaukpyu. This plan, however, miscarried. On 12 January, the Royal Scots Fusiliers passed through to continue the advance, while 2 RWF moved to occupy Daungbon, a small village 3 miles east of Myega, within range of Japanese foraging parties. When the 2nd East Lancashires set out for Kyaukpyu they ran into a strong enemy roadblock a mile and a half short of Tonkwe and were forced to withdraw. The brigade therefore remained in the Pauktabin area and the 2nd East Lancashires, keeping one company about 2 miles down the Tonkwe track, reverted to a protective role.

After their success on the Tonkwe track the Japanese became aggressive again and the following night raided Pauktabin. To counter this, Stockwell stepped up the patrolling programme and during the next few days both sides set a number of ambushes. There was still some doubt at this stage whether the brigade should continue south through Twingge to link up with 19th Division or, avoiding Twingge, advance east through Kyaukpyu to rejoin 36th Division in the Mongmit area. For the next fortnight, therefore, active local patrolling went on, and at the same time long-range patrols penetrated deeply to the south and south-east, especially near the bunker on the Twingge–Mongmit road near its junction with a track from Banwe. Eventually, the Japanese evacuated the bunker after a sequence of events remembered by Gordon Milne:

> So one sergeant and five fusiliers came out to escort our sergeant and three sappers out to the bunker to demolish it. When we got within striking distance we came under very heavy fire. Sadly we lost a fusilier. Our sergeant decided to stay put, but then ordered us back to our position again. The Welsh boys were back slightly before us but when we arrived at our starting point there was Gwydyr standing beside a tea urn handing out mugs of tea laced with rum. 'I'm so glad to see you boys back,' he said. 'Don't worry, tomorrow we'll clear them all out.' The Japs must have heard him, because on the very next patrol that went out not a trace of the enemy was to be seen. I'm quite convinced that the Japs, too, had heard about Gwydyr and gave him due respect!

On 14 January 2 RWF moved to Banwe and began constructing a fortified position. Over Banwe, 2 RWF flew a Union flag, which had originally been used in the assault on Tamatave in Madagascar. This brought several admonishments from the brigade staff, who regarded it as the prerogative of the Viceroy and the Commander-in-Chief. During the afternoon of the 14th, the position was attacked by the Japanese, who were forced back. A strong patrol was sent out from Daungbon on the 15th to open communication with the rest of the brigade; once achieved, keeping the road between Daungbon and Banwe open became a daily task and active patrolling was continued. On 17 January a patrol from Banwe set out to reconnoitre the south-east track. As the patrol pushed cautiously on down the track, it came across trees felled across the road at various points, all offering good cover to enemy pickets, but none of them were manned, until they came in sight of a section of Japanese near two bunkers, one either side of the road. This enemy position was the objective of many patrols during the next fortnight and tension remained high. Gwydyr, walking round 2 RWF's positions at stand-to with RSM Hubbard, came across a large cobra writhing on the path. 'You're a good shot, sir,' said the RSM, handing Gwydyr a .38 pistol. 'You kill it.' 'My dear, I don't care for it,' was the answer. Nevertheless, Gwydyr killed the snake with two shots and then called out hastily, 'Don't shoot, men – it's only your Commanding Officer.' Next day, Stockwell came over to talk to him and as they were talking, a sudden burst of Japanese fire whistled overhead. Gwydyr, quite unmoved, snorted, 'Piss-poor shot. Wouldn't have *him* in the battalion.'

At Twingge came some unexpected news:

We were in close contact with the Japs . . . following closely the line of the Irrawaddy on our right flank. Div HQ and 72 Brigade had swung inland to Myitson and Mongmit. From Twingge to Mongmit there was a lateral road about forty miles long, so 29 Brigade was very much isolated. From Mongmit the road ran south to Maymyo about eighty miles away; and the Twingge-Mongmit road was about 180 miles from Myitkyina. Here at Twingge in the middle of the night George Bastin brought me a signal to say I was to take over command of 82nd Division back in the Arakan forthwith.

Stockwell had to leave at a few hours' notice, and the command of 29 Brigade devolved on George Bastin. After so long an association, and so much shared hardship, it was a wrench to leave so many friends in his old battalion and his brigade, a brigade which he had made very much his own. His promotion came as little surprise to those of his subordinates who knew his qualities. Gordon Milne had this to say: 'We knew and never doubted that his qualities would be recognised, and that we would lose him by his receiving higher commands, but he had set the standards which kept right on till the end of the campaign.' Recognized he was: in April 1945 he was mentioned in despatches, and in September he was made CBE.

But for Stockwell himself it was, as the *Daily Express* reported on 4 March 1945: 'Major to Major General in five years.' The paper went on to extol the 'ex Commando's rise . . . another of the go-ahead Generals with a Commando background, and he becomes the fourth successive brigadier of the 29th Brigade of the 36th Division to be promoted'. It had indeed been a meteoric rise, although once again, Stockwell had had the luck to be in the right place at the right time – but he had continued to show that he had the ability to take on the tough jobs and get results.

Chapter Eleven

The 82nd (West African) Division, 1945–1946

The circumstances under which Hugh Stockwell was given the command of the 82nd (West African) Division were unusual, to say the least. On 20 December 1944, Mountbatten, the Supreme Allied Commander South-East Asia, had visited the division in the Arakan, accompanied by his new Chief of Staff, Lieutenant General Sir Frederick ('Boy') Browning. On arrival, Mountbatten's party had been driven around the divisional area by the GOC, Major General George Bruce, a tall and fiery Canadian, who saw himself in the mould of George Patton, for he flaunted a pair of ivory handled Colt revolvers. Bruce drove his guests across three chaungs – through which the vehicles had to be manhandled by their escort – and well beyond the forward line of his own troops. Mountbatten had already formed the opinion that Bruce was 'without exception the most dangerous and fiery driver I have ever driven with . . . Having practically thrown us out of the jeep when he was negotiating the first obstacle, we refused to sit in the jeep when he was negotiating subsequent ones.' Towards the end of the drive, Mountbatten 'began to wonder whether we should find the Japanese lines before our own, since warfare here is very open and fluid, and the Front is moving rapidly'. No harm was done, but Mountbatten privately told Christison, Commander XV Indian Corps, what had happened. At about the same time, US General Wedemeyer also paid Bruce a visit which nearly brought his career, and his life, to a premature close. Stockwell later recounted at a reunion dinner that Bruce:

> had a leaning to a Western approach to his responsibilities, and, taking [Wedemeyer] around his division in his Jeep, he threw his Stetson hat into the air, drew his pearl-handled revolver, and . . . proceeded to put six bullets through it, to the obvious enjoyment of the Africans nearby.

On Christmas Day, Christison himself, accompanied by Mountbatten's American Deputy Chief of Staff, Major General Horace H. Fuller, visited Bruce. Much the same happened again and Christison 'noticed he [Bruce] had been drinking'. Despite this, Bruce insisted on personally driving his guests around in a jeep, accompanied by an armed escort in another vehicle. Soon he was badly – and obviously – lost and shortly afterwards the party came under small-arms fire from Japanese positions. Christison took charge, ordering everyone out of the vehicles, and the senior officers conducted a fighting withdrawal through a paddy field. During this, General Fuller, who was aged fifty-eight, became separated from the rest of the party, and a counter-attack had to be launched to rescue him. When the group met up again with troops from the 82nd Division, Bruce, greatly excited, stood up and addressed them in Hausa saying that 'On this festive day, you will be pleased to hear that I, your General, have been engaged in hand-to-hand combat with the Japanese. We have come off victoriously.' Wild enthusiasm followed, partly because the Africans misunderstood the situation, and thought that General Fuller was a captive, about to be delivered up to them – for what purposes one dreads to think. Luckily, the confusion was at last sorted out, although Christison later wrote that Fuller 'was unconscious and supported between two Africans, his face a whitish-yellow . . . The American had had a coronary, and died later.'

Christison made further discrete enquiries, discovering that the brigade commanders had lost confidence in Bruce and no longer had any faith in his judgement. Christison sent for him, but Bruce 'sent a message that he could not come as he was ill. My DDMS ordered him into hospital. I consulted Leese and he agreed that he must be replaced.' It was put about that Bruce had been evacuated because of a foot disability, which Mountbatten's diary records as 'an in-growing toenail'. He was gone on 12 January 1945, the date on which Stockwell took command, around midday. The Corps Commander's judgement was immediately confirmed by Bruce himself. Christison wrote an adverse report on Bruce and when the report was taken to him in hospital by the Assistant Military Secretary of XV Corps, Bruce pulled one of his ivory-handled revolvers from under the sheets, pointed it at the officer, and shouted, 'Tear that up, or you're a dead man!'

When it came to finding a successor, Stockwell was almost self-selecting. He was well known to Christison from 36th Division's involvement in the Arakan, and there was no doubt about his capabilities. He was obviously held in the highest regard by Mountbatten and Slim; Mountbatten's diary records of him in connection with his relief of Bruce that 'I can hardly imagine a better Divisional Commander.' He had been in command of a fighting brigade for two years, much of it in combat – coming from Upper Burma he had, in his own words, 'the full measure of the enemy'. He was senior to the three brigade commanders in the 82nd Division and last but not least, he was an old West Africa hand, which would not be lost on the officers and men of the division. In the event, they were delighted to get one of their own as their GOC. As he himself remarked, the job 'fell on my plate like a ripe plum'.

The 82nd Division was one of two formations formed from the expanded RWAFF, the other, older, division being the 81st, commanded by Major

General Frederick Loftus-Tottenham, which fielded only two brigades. There were in addition ninety-seven other West African units in the SEAC theatre of operations ranging from an anti-aircraft artillery brigade, to corps and army troops. If the 11th (East African) Division is included, then the total number of African troops serving in Burma comes to 90,000, only marginally less than the British at 100,000. As Julian Thompson has remarked, if the soubriquet of 'Forgotten Army' belongs today to any contingent that fought in Burma, it must be the Africans. The 82nd Division had been formed in August 1942, and although it was the newest formation in theatre, two of its brigades – 1 and 2 (West African) – had seen service in Abyssinia and Somaliland. On arrival in India in the summer of 1944 the division was organized for its task, while the troops were rehearsed in air supply and other techniques, and made ready for combat. The 82nd Division order of battle was headed by the divisional reconnaissance regiment. Then came three brigades: 1 (West African) Infantry Brigade, made up of the 1st, 2nd and 3rd Battalions of the Nigeria Regiment and the 5th Auxiliary Group, under Brigadier F.W. (Frank) Clowes; 2 (West African) Infantry Brigade, made up of the 1st, 2nd and 3rd Battalions of the Gold Coast Regiment and the 6th Auxiliary Group, commanded by Brigadier E.W.D. Western, always known as 'Tank'; 4 (West African) Infantry Brigade comprised the 5th, 9th and 10th Battalions of the Nigeria Regiment, and the 2nd Auxiliary Group, commanded by Brigadier A.H.G. (Abdy) Ricketts. The total strength of the division was 762 officers, 198 British warrant officers, 1,405 British NCOs and men, and 25,307 African warrant officers, NCOs and men. Thus, with 2,365 Europeans, the peacetime average of about 10 per cent was maintained.

Slim had firm views on the organization of African divisions, as he made clear in *Defeat into Victory*. Visiting the 81st Division, he wrote that:

> Their discipline and smartness were impressive, and they were more at home in the jungle than any troops I had yet seen. They had neither animals nor vehicles with their fighting units, but were organised on a man-pack basis . . . I was at once struck by two things. First, by the horde of unarmed porters who were needed to carry supplies, ammunition, baggage, and the heavier weapons, and secondly by the large number of white men in a unit, fifty or sixty to a battalion. Accustomed as I was to Indian battalions in the field with usually only seven or eight Europeans, it struck me as an unnecessarily generous supply.

Slim was, as he admits, writing from the point of view of an Indian Army officer – a rather different culture and as ever, it is in culture that the real asymmetries of warfare lie: between oneself and one's allies, just as much as between oneself and the enemy. Stockwell, who knew the West African soldier more intimately, had rather different views. An excellent example of this is the use of carriers.

Every African carries some kind of load on his head; it was a natural place to put a load and many of them grew a special tuft of hair to act as a cushion. It was a commonplace sight to observe an African with his pack, haversack, water bottle, pair of boots, Bren gun, and slouch hat, perched in a neat pyramid on his head. Considerable weights were carried in this fashion; the charging engines for wireless sets weighed almost a hundredweight, and yet they were head-loaded up and down the hills day after day. Even the stretcher-bearers used to carry their patients head-high.

Brigadier Charles Swynnerton, who later succeeded Stockwell in command of the 82nd Division, remarked that the West African was 'the only soldier amongst all the different nationalities from which the British Army in Burma was drawn, who was capable of operating for months on end in the worst country in the world, without vehicles and mules and was alone able to carry all his warlike stores with him'. Nor should it be forgotten, when picturing 'hordes' of carriers, that in comparison even a light Indian infantry division required some 2,500 vehicles to supply and maintain it. The Auxiliary groups also carried out many tasks which in a standard infantry division would have to be borne by the fighting troops: they cleared dropping zones and air strips, collected and distributed air-dropped stores, loaded and unloaded aircraft, and assisted the engineers in constructing ramps and bridges.

Stockwell, although convinced that the high ratio of Europeans was necessary in an African formation, noted on his arrival that all was not as it should be. Captain F.K. Theobald, attached to the 82nd Division, thought 'The RWAFF suffered from NCOs being sent to the force by English battalions in order to get rid of them.' Stockwell himself went into this question in some detail after he had been with the division for several months, but in his memoir of the early days he supports Theobald's remarks, saying that:

I found it [82nd (WA) Division] rather a luxury organisation . . . There were an enormous number of somewhat indifferent British NCOs in the division. They were a hindrance. I sent them back as first-line reinforcements to British units in the Fourteenth Army. I made the Africans take over and things began to take shape. Once I had got rid of the indifferent BNCOs, formed the auxiliary groups, and once the officers understood what we were after, I think the division clicked into shape.

I sacked some COs. They weren't battle worthy. The colonial influence had softened their outlook. We were tough and hard in 29 Brigade, every officer had to be a crackerjack at his job; this lot were soft, with carriers and chop-boxes, gin etc. They hadn't got the stomach for the fight. If a CO hadn't got it, no-one else would, so away with him.

At the time Stockwell arrived to take command of the division, it was engaged in the Arakan, and he must have experienced a sense of déjà vu as the old familiar place names from the previous year's campaign came up once more. The 1944 campaign, in which Stockwell and 29 Infantry Brigade had taken part, had closed with the onset of the monsoon. But as a result of the frustrated Japanese invasions, the Allies had complete command of the sea and air. Losses had been made up, and Mountbatten and his subordinate commanders felt in a position to be able to use the mobility which command of the sea and air gave, to seize and maintain the initiative, and force the Japanese to fight, for a change, on ground of Allied choosing. The 1944-45 campaign in the Arakan was thus a series of combined operations commanded and controlled from a fully integrated, Combined HQ consisting of HQ Naval Force W (Rear Admiral Benjamin Martin), XV Corps (Christison) and 224 Group RAF (Air Commodore, later Air Vice-Marshal, the Earl of Bandon). The land force commander, therefore, could operate with the knowledge that air superiority gave control of the air flank; and the Eastern Fleet, with its three battleships, three fleet carriers, battle cruiser, eleven cruisers and thirty-two destroyers controlled the maritime flank in the Indian Ocean.

82nd Division formed part of Christison's XV Indian Corps, which was not part of Fourteenth Army, but came directly under 11th Army Group. Some explanation of what was in hand is therefore necessary in order to make sense of what follows. In the Arakan, a four-division corps was employed to protect the flank of Fourteenth Army, but a much smaller Japanese force opposed it. General Seizo Sakurai 's Twenty-Eighth Army, which was responsible for Arakan, deployed only a regiment of the 54th Infantry Division and part of the 55th Division there. General Sir George Giffard, GOC-in-C 11th Army Group and ALFSEA, had recognized that this was a very inefficient way of fighting. He believed that the best thing to do was push the Japanese back to a point at which they could no longer mount an offensive – preferably by seizing Akyab – then contain them with one division, and release the rest of the corps for operations on the main effort. To achieve the destruction of the Japanese in Arakan, Christison had four divisions — 25th and 26th (Indian), and 81st and 82nd (West African). He also had 3 Commando Brigade and 50 (Indian) Tank Brigade. Supporting the corps were 224 Group RAF, 12th Bombardment Group USAAF, one RAF transport squadron and a squadron of L5 light aircraft for liaison and casualty evacuation; and a naval task group equipped with landing craft which had only been left in Burma as they were too decrepit to make the journey to Europe.

Christison's plan had called for an advance towards Donbaik-Rathedaung-Myohaung by 25th (Indian) Division on the right, 82nd (West African) Division in the centre protecting the flanks and rear of 25th (Indian) Division during its advance, and 81st (West African) Division on the left; in concert, 3 Commando Brigade and 26th (Indian) Division would carry out amphibious operations against the flanks and rear of the enemy. The sea flank was to be secured by the Arakan Coastal Forces, and the whole operation would be supported by air bombardment and resupply. Christison's offensive had begun on 12 December 1944 and three days later the 82nd Division had taken over the village of Buthidaung, much fought over during the past two years. This opened a few miles of road from Maungdaw to Kalapanzin and using this, about 600 river craft of all kinds were moved through the Mayu hills and launched in the Kalapanzin River, to help with the advance. Concurrently, 26th Division, supplied from the sea, had occupied the tip of the Mayu peninsula on Boxing Day 1944 and was poised across the narrow channel to seize Akyab. The Japanese did not wait for a full-scale attack, but evacuated the place, which fell without a shot on 2 January 1945.

Loftus-Tottenham with the 81st Division had meanwhile contributed to the Japanese evacuation of Akyab, moving in a wide arc to the east through thickly forested mountain country and striking at Myohaung, the hub of Japanese communications, with the leading brigade, 4 (WA) Brigade, of 82nd Division, under his command. The strength of the defenders had been estimated at one battalion of 111 Infantry Regiment, with six guns, but Japanese officers later told 82nd Division that their strength had been a regiment of three battalions, supported by engineers and two batteries each of six guns. The attack had been planned for 10 January, but was deferred to the 15th. Stockwell accordingly issued his first Operational Instruction, in which he gave some characteristically direct guidance to his subordinates, such as 29 Infantry Brigade would have recognized, but which may have come as a shock, or perhaps a breath of fresh air, to the 82nd Division:

I wish all ranks to be inf[or]m[ed] of the importance of the task that lies ahead which I am confident will be quickly achieved if all ranks realise the necessity for the speed of their operations which demands a high degree of endurance and determination which I know the Div will prove to have.

On the 18th, Stockwell received his first short-notice directive from Christison, who modified this plan to try to prevent the Japanese escaping. Urgent orders directed the 82nd Division to move east from Hitzwe as soon as possible and, instead of relieving the 81st Division, it was to cut the Japanese line of communication in the Lemro valley 2 miles south of Myohaung, and then assist in the capture of the town. 1 (WA) Brigade, which had moved in accordance with the original instructions, was already through the Kanzauk Pass, with 2 (WA) Brigade following, both brigades moving as fast as they could. 1 (WA) Brigade crossed the Kaladan on 20 January, and moved on Myohaung from the north, i.e. the enemy's rear, a move the Japanese later stated caused them some surprise.

The Japanese therefore, caught between the two West African divisions, had no choice but to extricate themselves, which they managed to do after severe fighting, and on 24 January had pulled out of the ancient capital of Arakan. For the RWAFF, this was an historic day, with twelve of its battalions, representing all four West African territories, engaged in the conclusion of this action. It was the greatest concentration of force ever achieved by the

RWAFF, and is still celebrated as the main festival in the successor armies of Nigeria, Ghana, Sierra Leone and the Gambia – not that Christison ever gave them much credit.

The only Japanese withdrawal route for guns and vehicles was the road that ran along the Arakan coast, a few miles inland. This road met the new road from Prome, which came through the An Pass, at Taungup. Christison's intent for his operation, Romulus, was to trap the Japanese by interposing a force on the coast road, so severing the line of retreat – his landing craft gave him the ability to carry this out. Stockwell's part in Romulus was given to him on 24 January, just before Myohaung fell. Leaving the 81st Division to mop up in Myohaung, his division was to take 4 (WA) Brigade back under command and, supplied by air, pursue the Japanese 111th Regimental Group, often referred to as the Matsu Detachment. He was to follow the Hpontha–Kani track towards Kangaw and the Tanlwe and Yaw chaungs towards Kyweguseik – in other words, he was to be the hammer, and 25th (Indian) Division the anvil. However, Christison told him not to press too hard, because he did not want the Matsu Detachment to join up with Sakurai's main body before 25th Indian Division was behind them and astride their communications. To assist his resupply and supplement the division's carriers, Stockwell was given the Inland Water Transport (IWT) boat fleet, which was to be brought down as soon as possible.

The landing at Kangaw took place on 22 January. A beachhead was established, but fanatical Japanese counter-attacks supported by artillery came in almost non-stop until the 29th when the tide turned. The advance of the 82nd Division meanwhile began on 27 January, in weather that was dry and still reasonably cool – even cold at night. Stockwell organized the division into three columns: on his right, the Reconnaissance Regiment and the Anti-tank Regiment moved down the west bank of the Lemro River towards Minbya; in the centre, 4 (WA) Brigade moved down the river in boats towards Hpontha; 1 (WA) Brigade was on the left, also moving on Hpontha; and 2 (WA) Brigade, after a pause at Myohaung, was following up. Captain J. A Dunford described the advance thus:

> Wonderful thick jungle and bamboo covered the mountain ranges and the jeep track led over the mountains and down to the rivers and streams like a giant switchback at a fun fair. The track seemed endless, always another mountain barrier seemed to rise up in front of us to block our way. . .
>
> It was at this stage that we came onto 'air dropping' for our supplies. Nearly every day the little loads attached to their white parachutes would come floating down bringing us our rations and ammunition. Our 'chop' was excellent and nobody went short. Without air supplies the Division could not have continued for even 24 hours, yet we felt quite indifferent about the route that lay behind us and the possibility of the enemy popping up in our rear. Those responsible for air supplies

certainly did an excellent job of work and we occasionally enjoyed such delicacies as cold roast chicken and cake. Fresh eggs were also frequently supplied.

Minbya, and contact with 25th Division, was achieved on 29 January; Hpontha was reached the same day. A pause for resupply followed, during which Stockwell called a co-ordinating conference and issued new orders on 1 February. The advance kicked off again on 3 February. By 8 February, 74 Infantry Brigade of the 26th Division had pushed north-east and linked up with Tank Western's 2 (WA) Brigade in the Kani area, where Western passed temporarily under 26th Division's command, while 4 (WA) Brigade pushed on to Kaw. Caught between the two divisions, the enemy finally broke at Kangaw on 2 February, leaving more than 300 dead across the battlefield. During the first half of February the Japanese took to the hills, leaving behind them another 1,000 dead, sixteen guns and great quantities of vehicles and stores; only small parties stayed behind to delay the advancing Allied troops. Everywhere there were abandoned stores and equipment; the division retrieved some British Bren guns, and also some Japanese machine guns, which were turned on their former owners. However, the Japanese had succeeded in getting the bulk of their troops away, and all their heavy guns. Japanese booby traps were also found, of which two types were much in evidence. One was a bomb disguised as a tin of Libby's canned strawberries, the other explosives faked to look like a lump of coal. Since neither of these items was supplied in the rations, they failed to have the desired effect. The capture of the islands of Ramree and Chedubra followed, which were vital as forward air bases for the supply of Fourteenth Army pressing on into southern Burma. It was a triumph of joint and combined operations, the more so when one considers the shaky state of the landing craft, and the fact that the best-trained amphibious force – 29 Independent Brigade – was away fighting as a standard infantry brigade. What has become clear subsequently, however, is that the premise on which Romulus was based was mistaken. The Japanese defence in Arakan was not designed primarily in order to allow the extraction of their troops from Myohaung, but to prevent what they – equally mistakenly – saw as a British attempt to break through from the coast into the Irrawaddy Valley through the Arakan Yomas.

Whatever the conceptual basis had been, by the end of this operation, the Japanese garrison of the Arakan was in a bad way, having suffered crippling losses; but it was still capable of putting up a fight. The remnants of the 54th Division were in two well-separated groups: one, made up of the 154th Regimental Group around Kangaw, blocking the road east over the An Pass; and the other, made up of the 121st Regimental Group, 40 miles to the south at Taungup, covering the road to Prome. Its task was to protect the rear of the Fifteenth Army in the Irrawaddy Valley, where the Japanese expected to fight the decisive battle of 1945 – again, a clear indication that they feared an attack from the Arakan coast in this direction, in concert with other moves from the north. To the west and north, the Matsu Detachment was to act as a covering force in the Kaladan area, and impose as much delay as possible. The 55th Division had moved east and was centred on the Prome–Henzada area, from where it could move either north against Fourteenth Army, or west.

With these dispositions in mind, but misunderstanding the logic that lay behind them, Leese, who succeeded Giffard, gave Christison new orders. These directed him as a first priority to develop Akyab and Ramree as bases for the air supply of Fourteenth Army. Slim, although grateful for this, also urged that Christison's other tasks should be pursued, in order to prevent the Japanese from shifting forces – especially the 55th Division – against him. These tasks were all expressed in terms of geographical objectives, rather than destruction of the enemy. They were the clearance of north and central Arakan; the securing of a bridgehead at Taungup; and the opening of the Taungup–Prome road, if possible before the monsoon, to provide a land supply route. In addition, Slim urged that Christison should push hard against the An Pass as well as up the Taungup road.

With this in mind Christison decided that a subsequent advance would be developed down the coast road, in order to destroy the Japanese at Taungup. This would open the way for an advance to Prome. The destruction of the Japanese at An and the seizure of the Pass fell to Stockwell, who was ordered to push his division, less 2 (WA) Brigade, south-eastwards from Kaw and up the Dalet Chaung to approach the pass from the north-west. This was to be followed by the landing of a brigade of the 25th Division 30 miles south of Kangaw and 12 miles west of An. From there it was to advance to link up with 82nd Division, surrounding the enemy and completing their destruction. Once this was complete, Stockwell was to advance southwards towards Taungup, leaving the An Pass guarded by the detached brigade of the 25th Division. A further refinement was introduced when it was decided that the 25th Division would establish a bridgehead in the Ruywa area through which 2 (WA) Brigade would be passed to rejoin the 82nd Division, and 22 (East African) Brigade would be passed through another bridgehead in the Letpan area once it had been secured by the 26th Division, come under Stockwell's command, and attack An from the south.

Stockwell later said of this time that his main priority was to:

> instil a sense of urgency, by putting a pin under the tail of the brigadiers, and getting around myself all the time. I was pretty tired after two-and-a-half years of fighting, so I made sure I got maximum rest at night. I would be up with the battle all day, and then issue some orders to the staff in the evening, so that by my own personal presence, I could instil a bit of vim into the thing.

The An operation opened on 4 February. The route of the advance was through the Arakan Yomas, the thickest, most mountainous, and most difficult country in the region. This was very different country from the orchard bush or even tropical forest of Nigeria and the Gold Coast in which many of the soldiers were quite at home, although it must be borne in mind that many others were from the northern districts of Sierra Leone, Gold Coast or Nigeria, which are semi-arid, savannah country. Even though African troops had great powers of observation and hearing, and an instinct for danger in close country, this kind of warfare was slow and bloody. The leading battalions were constantly in contact with the enemy. Every ridgeline and chaung crossing had to be fought for, against an enemy who would not surrender even when wounded or disarmed; and who was well dug in with bunkers capable of withstanding anything except a direct hit from a 250lb bomb, and that could only be approached along a razor-backed ridge. Small wonder that on some days less than a mile of ground could be made. Stockwell himself wrote:

> On February 10th the leading troops of 10 N.R. bumped trouble near Kyaukpandu, a village some two miles south of Kaw and about a quarter of the way to Kyweguseik. Soon after, the two forward companies were counter-attacked while digging in. Eight more enemy attacks were made during the night but, after severe fighting, were beaten off . . . There were fierce hand-to-hand struggles on a ridge top, but after sustained fighting the attack had to be called off owing to mounting casualties.

Add to this fanatical opposition the fact that every pound of food and every round of ammunition had to be carried by the auxiliaries on the head from the drop zones, and one can dimly picture the nature of the fighting. Captain Danford again:

> Life now consisted of moving forward by day and forming a defensive perimeter at night. Nearby would be an air strip prepared by our own sappers or 'Aux' group. From here we would collect our supplies before moving forward again. Our long slow-moving lines of men, heavily laden with equipment and stores, winding in and out of the jungle and across open paddy fields, seemed very vulnerable.

Morale may have been good, but Stockwell was still finding it necessary to instil urgency, and bear down on slackness and inefficiency, which he hated and which he knew could cost lives when facing an enemy as determined and competent as the Japanese. On 6 February he sent out a signal to the commanders of all subordinate formations and divisional troops units, saying:

> This division is not alert in the field. All load parties must be escorted by vigilant escorts. All weapons must be carried ready for instant action. At every halt sentries must be posted . . . the Jap is everywhere . . . Disciplinary action to be taken by all commanders seeing any signs of slackness.

He had at least now a personal staff officer in the shape of an ADC to take on routine jobs like copying down signals, organizing his programme, transport, administration and so on: Lieutenant Ray Simmons, who had served with him in 2 RWF in Madagascar, and in HQ 29 Infantry Brigade on the Railway Corridor, was at that time in hospital recovering from jaundice. Simmons recalled that:

> A chap came in and said 'there's a message for you. General Stockwell has got command of the 82nd Division and wants you as his ADC.' I said straight away 'I'm off tomorrow,' to which the doctor replied 'Oh no you're not!' I said 'just you try and stop me!' and I caught the first flight the next day down to join HQ 36th Division, and they shipped me on to the 82nd.

Ray Simmons duly arrived, despite doctor's orders, on 8th February.

On the 15th, 4 (WA) Brigade at last got into a position overlooking the Japanese communications on the Yaw Chaung, but was not able to make anything of this, for Stockwell had had to redirect the brigade across the hills towards Dalet, following 1 (WA) Brigade. By the 24th, the leading battalions had closed up to the Dalet Chaung, clearing away some determined opposition. That night, using only rubber boats and parachute cord strung across the watercourse, the chaung was crossed just below Kweshi. The crossing operation continued over the next two days, but the Japanese soon became aware of what was going on and 82 Reconnaissance Regiment reported a good deal of movement northwards up the chaung from Tamandu, in order to try to contain the bridgehead.

So by 27 February, all Christison's moves except the attack on Letpan were under way, although Japanese resistance was now increasing, and progress had slowed both in the Dalet area and between Ruywa and Tamandu. In particular, 2(WA) Brigade had been brought to a halt at the foot of a precipitous ridge west of Sabagyi, and had been ordered to turn north and make for the road between An and Letmauk. By the first week of March, most of the 25th Division had been brought down in follow-up landings and, despite fierce Japanese counter-attacks, operations to encircle the force at An were progressing. But just when things seemed to be going well, events elsewhere caused the operation to be called off. As the country around An was the worst type of jungle-covered hill country, with no roads, the troops could only be supplied by air. At the same time, the Meiktila-Mandalay battle was in full swing and its success too depended on air supply. Faced with a decision on priorities, Leese decided in favour of Slim. Christison was ordered to contain the maximum number of Japanese troops with his attack on An, and by making a landing at Taungup from which to attack Prome, but without any air supply.

Christison tried to push ahead with the landing 35 miles north of Taungup, but this advance was soon held up by strong Japanese blocking positions.

Outflanking these was not possible without air supply and forcing them frontally would be far too costly. At the operational level, Leese had made the right decision, but it meant an immediate halt to operations at An, and the modification of others. On 1 March, Christison gave Stockwell and Wood, the GOC 25th (Indian) Division, new orders. Wood was to capture Tamandu by 4 March to allow a Forward Maintenance Area (FMA) to be opened there, as a means of substituting for air supply. Stockwell's orders were more complex. He was to leave 1 (WA) Brigade and 82 Reconnaissance Regiment at Dalet, to move on Letmauk from the north down what the Africans called Happy Valley; he was to take 4 (WA) Brigade and his divisional troops down the west bank of the Dalet Chaung to its mouth, and then along the coast road to Tamandu, from where he was to attack Letmauk from the south, establish a road block between Letmauk and An, and fix the garrison of An by active patrolling. Christison also warned Leese that without the support of the IWT fleet, he would not be able to undertake any operations towards Taungup.

Stockwell moved fast to put the plan into effect. By 3 March, Clowes had 1 (WA) Brigade concentrated at Dalet, ready to move on Letmauk. On the 4th, 74 Brigade of 25th Division entered Tamandu after a hard fight. On the 6th, Western with 2 (WA) Brigade cut the Letmauk–An road, but was forced back by a Japanese counter-attack to high ground just west of the road around Point 1269 and Point 1106; between the 6th and the 8th, at least sixty Japanese were confirmed killed in this fighting. On the 7th, Stockwell himself, with the balance of the division, arrived at Tamandu after a long forced march of 24 miles on rough jungle roads and tracks. His intention was to move into a frontal attack up the Tamandu–Letmauk–An road as soon as the FMA was up and running. After a preliminary operation to clear the Japanese outposts on the hills overlooking Tamandu from the east, the attack began the next day, 8 March. It was apparent almost straight away, however, that this was going to be a lengthy affair. The road was no more than a series of river cross-ings so routes had to be found across the razor-backed ridges and tracks had to be cut and graded. Then there was the enemy; the Japanese had shown great skill as well as their customary ferocity in pushing Western's brigade back; and the end of air supply had a bad effect on the troops' morale. As the Official History puts it: 'They took it to mean that something had gone wrong . . . West African troops had previously shown that any setback quickly affected their morale and fighting value.' The view from the ground shows, however, that things were not quite that simple:

Changing climatic conditions were now affecting our tactics. The useful and comforting morning mists of the winter no longer existed to cover awkward attacks or the risky passage of chaungs, defiles, or open ground . . . [the troops] could only be maintained by exertions which only the troops of the R.W.A.F.F. are capable of; their food and water was passed from hand to hand, or rather head to head, and initially took 36 hours to reach the forward troops. Casualties, trying to come back by the same

138

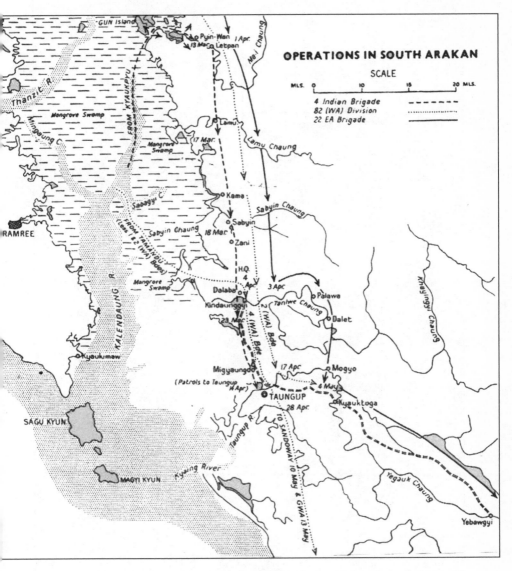

Source: Colonel A. Hayward and Brigadier F.A.S. Clarke, *The History of The Royal West African Frontier Force* (Aldershot, 1964).

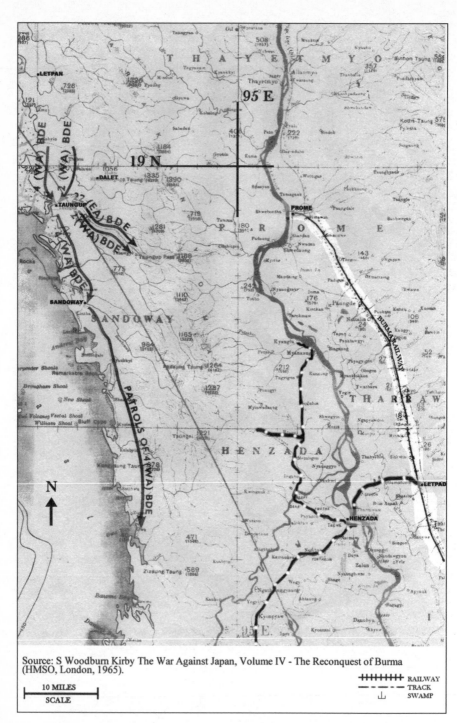

Source: S Woodburn Kirby The War Against Japan, Volume IV - The Reconquest of Burma (HMSO, London, 1965).

RAILWAY
TRACK
SWAMP

10 MILES
SCALE

82nd (WEST AFRICAN) DIVISION MOVES, MAY–JULY 1945.

route, in some cases took just as long. Many parties of carriers and runners were left marooned here and there during the night . . .

. . . we had not received new clothing and most of us were in rags. The jungle rivers, streams and mountains had wrought havoc on us and we were far more battered-looking than the Japs we saw . . . the green drill was in some cases hanging in festoons down our backs.

Casualties had been heavy amongst both Africans and Europeans, among them the commanding officers of the 5th and 10th Nigeria Regiments who had both been killed on 1 March. The new Commanding Officer of 10 NR was none other than Hughie's cousin, N.C. (Nigel) Stockwell. On 9 March, Christison again issued revised instructions. The role of XV Corps was further modified to that of driving the Japanese northern group to the east of An and holding it there until the monsoon; establishing a bridgehead at Letpan; cutting the Taungup–Tamandu road; and exploiting south to the Tanlwe Chaung to try to prevent further Japanese troop redeployments into central Burma. To ease the supply situation, two brigades of the 26th Division would be sent back to India. Stockwell's part in this plan was very much on the corps main effort, and to make the point, he was given the guns of the 6th Medium Regiment RA with 5.5-inch howitzers and a squadron of medium tanks of the 19th Lancers, both from the corps troops. He was to take over the Tamandu area from 25th Division, which would withdraw to Akyab, take on the task of driving the Japanese east of An, and then use 22 (EA) Brigade, which would again come under his command, to hold them there until the monsoon. Having carried out these tasks, he was to move against the Japanese force at Taungup, destroying or containing it until 15 May. At that point, 22 (EA) Brigade would move to Letpan, and 82nd Division would withdraw to Chittagong.

Operations against An made little progress over the next week – on the contrary, the Japanese delivered a series of fierce counter-attacks, and the Africans were very tired: 'Every yard of ground was contested by gun, mortar and machine-gun fire.' 4 (WA) Brigade, supported by 6th Medium Regiment RA and a troop of tanks, advanced from Tamandu on 12 March and next day met the Japanese near Shaukchon. Clearing this position took until the evening of the 14th, and the brigade did not reach Letmauk until the 17th. Concurrently, 1 (WA) Brigade had found it impossible to reach Letmauk from the north, so Clowes had swung them round to the Tamandu–Letmauk road and the brigade arrived in Letmauk on the 20th, behind 4 (WA) Brigade. While 1 (WA) Brigade was moving into Letmauk, 22 (EA) Brigade was disembarking down at Tamandu. With four brigades, supported by guns and tanks, Stockwell now planned to move 1 and 4 (WA) Brigades directly on An, linking up at last on the way with 2 (WA) Brigade which was still at Point 1269 on limited air supply. This plan began to unfold relatively smoothly, and it must have seemed to Christison that his object of tying the Japanese down was about to be achieved – especially as 4 (Indian) Brigade of 26th Division had landed at Letpan on the 13th, and was doing

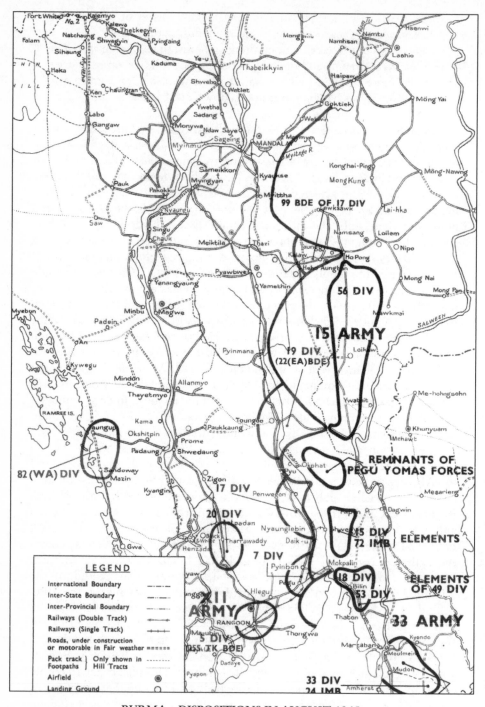

BURMA – DISPOSITIONS IN AUGUST 1945

Source: S. Woodburn Kirby, *The War Against Japan, Volume IV – The Reconquest of Burma* (HMSO, London, 1965).

well. However, the rate of advance of Stockwell's division had fallen well short of what had been envisaged, with the result that the Japanese felt confident enough to keep control of both the roads from the coast to the Irrawaddy with a reduced garrison, concentrate behind their blocking positions with what was left of the 55th Division, and send these troops against Slim.

Christison felt that it was more important than ever to stop this and issued orders on 21 March. Stockwell was instructed to contain the Japanese force west of the An Pass for as long as possible. In order to increase pressure on the Japanese at Taungup, he was ordered to detach 22 (EA) Brigade by road to Letpan at once, where it would come under command of 26th Division, and to follow it with one of his West African brigades not later than 15 April. He was also to hold the balance of his division in the An area ready to move to Chittagong as soon as shipping became available. His detached brigade would follow later, at which point Tamandu FMA would be closed. 4 (Indian) Brigade had meanwhile continued to advance southwards, and by the end of March had reached a point just short of the Taungup Chaung; a new FMA had been set up at Kindaunggyi, and 22 (EA) Brigade had concentrated at Letpan. Around An, Clowes, supported by the medium guns and tanks, had managed to link up with 2 (WA) Brigade and relieved it in place.

Further operations were now affected by Mountbatten's decision to launch Operation Dracula, the amphibious assault on Rangoon, which would take place in early May, and which required the 26th Division as the assault force. This again led to a change in orders for Stockwell and his division. First he was to move his headquarters down to the Tanlwe Chaung-Taungup area and take over command of all troops on the mainland, including 4 (Indian) Brigade, by 5 April; then he was to bring down 2 (WA) Brigade from Tamandu to join him no later than 15 April, followed by 4 (WA) Brigade and the divisional troops. The men and light equipment were to be moved by sea, and vehicles and heavy stores by road. Once concentrated, the division was to relieve Lomax's 26th Division in place, hold the Taungup area, protect the FMA at Kindaunggyi, and exploit towards Yebawgyi on the Prome road. He was told that he could rely on sixty tons per day air supply, and sixty tons by sea. 1 (WA) Brigade, reinforced with the Reconnaissance Regiment, a light battery, two mortar batteries and the Anti-tank Regiment, was to be detached to corps control, to guard the FMA at Tamandu and continue the holding operation against the enemy at An.

Stockwell disposed four brigades in the Letpan area. Facing him, he assessed the Japanese force to consist of only part of the 121st Regiment, and some divisional and lines-of-communication units. His intention was to cut their line of retreat out of Arakan by sending 22 (EA) Brigade, supplied by air, east-wards along the Tanlwe Chaung, establish a base at Palawa, and from there, attack south to sever the Taungup–Prome road. Once this was achieved, 2 (WA) Brigade would advance from Taungup to destroy the Japanese, who would be trapped between the two brigades. While the preliminary moves to effect this plan were in progress, 4 (Indian) Brigade reached the Taungup Chaung, and its patrols penetrated the town and the surrounding country. On 17 April, it was relieved by 4 (WA) Brigade and withdrawn to take part in Operation Dracula.

Brigadier R.F. Johnstone, with 22 (EA) Brigade, reached Palawa on the 15th and turned south, meeting enemy resistance as he did so. On 26 April he was about 10 miles east of Taungup near the Prome road, and on the same day 2 (WA) Brigade pushed the Japanese out of their positions 4 miles north-east of the town. The following night, 4 (WA) Brigade moved onto the high ground south-east of Taungup and on the 29th occupied the town. However, Stockwell's hopes of trapping the Japanese main body were frustrated as 2 (WA) and 22 (EA) Brigades met near Mogyo next day without meeting any Japanese – the enemy had slipped out over the hills that night.

At about this time, perhaps feeling sensitive about comments on the inability of the division to make rapid progress in the close Arakan country, and amplifying his remarks when taking over as GOC, Stockwell issued a sharp directive to all British officers and NCOs in the division. From time to time he had heard reports that officers or NCOs evacuated sick or wounded had, in idle conversation, made detrimental remarks about the capabilities of African soldiers in battle. To him, this was no help in prosecuting the war effort, no help in fostering good relations in a multinational force, and showed 'a gross form of disloyalty to every one of our Senior Commanders'. It also showed that those who spoke thus were:

> not leaders and therefore are not fit to hold the rank they do and draw the pay they do, and give the example that . . . it is our duty to show. I would stress to you that it is entirely my business to decide what tasks are carried out and the capabilities of the formations I have the honour to command. I can assure you that as long as the division exists I shall do all in my power to make it an efficient fighting machine, and for that I expect and demand your complete cooperation, full energy and determination . . . I myself consider that it takes a great deal of moral courage to set the African the example he deserves or give him that leadership which is so necessary.

This was strong stuff indeed, and to some extent supports what Slim had said, especially about the inadvisability of drafting in British officers and NCOs willy-nilly to colonial formations, rather than taking well-motivated volunteers. Captain Bill Edwards remembered that:

> I commanded 2 Platoon, A Company, 1 GCR. Our original British CSM went sick with trench foot, and the CQMS went down with malaria. I considered these were self-inflicted wounds. Mepacrine was very effective. Their places were taken up within the company. I lost my British sergeant who became CQMS, which meant that I had to lead every

Hugh Stockwell's father, also Hugh
Stockwell, in the uniform of the
Highland Light Infantry, about 1905.
(Stockwell Family Papers)

2. A young Hughie Stockwell in India with his
mother, Gertrude Emily Forrest.
(Stockwell Family Papers)

Hughie Stockwell with his father and mother about 1910.   *(Stockwell Family Papers)*

4. The Red Dragons conce
party, 1924. The group
includes Hughie Stockw
Bill Moody, Frederick
Shove, Mrs Moody, Mrs
W.B. Garnett and Winni
Pringle.
(Stockwell Family Pap

5. Hughie Stockwell mount
on The Monk, about 1926.
(Stockwell Family Pape

6. 2nd Battalion The Royal Welch Fusiliers on Parade at Pembroke Dock, St David's
Day, 1924. The battalion was probably only half its established strength at this time
(Royal Welch Fusiliers Archive

7. The 4th Battalion Nigeria Regiment Polo Team, 1931: Ladas Hassell, Sydney Mason, Harold Combe and Hughie Stockwell. *(Stockwell Family Papers)*

8. Hughie Stockwell and friend, with native beaters, prepare for a shooting trip in Nigeria, 1932. *(Stockwell Family Papers)*

9. The marriage of Hughie Stockwell and Joan Garrard, 9 December 1931, at Bramley, Hampshire.

(Stockwell Family Papers

10. Hugh Stockwell and Barney Griffin with a group of soldiers in the uniform of the RWAFF, Nigeria 1931. *(Stockwell Family Papers)*

11. Stockforce moves from Pothus to Rognan, Norway, 27 May 1940.
(by permission of the Imperial War Museum)

12. Men of Stockforce embarked in a Puffer, Norway, 28-29 May 1940.

(by permission of the Imperial War Museum)

13. Troops of 29 Infantry Brigade land at Majunga, Madagascar, in Operation Stream, 10 September 1942.

(by permission of the Imperial War Museum)

14. Men of 2 RWF ferry a locomotive in Madagascar during the advance on Brickaville, September 1942. *(by permission of the Imperial War Museum)*

15. 'My dear, a long, hot, bath...' Gwydyr Jones, Frankie Festing and Hughie Stockwell in the railway corridor, Burma, October 1944.

(Trustees of the Liddell Hart Centre, King's College London)

16. Hughie Stockwell giving orders to the 29 Infantry Brigade command group near Pinwe, Burma, 26 November 1944. Standing, from left: Dick Caldwell (Brigade staff), unknown, Paul Longden (Brigade staff), Archie Haddon (DAA&QMG), Rowland Marriot (Brigade Intelligence Officer), Colin Oakes (Liason Officer), Kenneth Wright (Liason Officer), unknown, unknown, Gwydyr Jones (2 RWF), Roy Bonner (Liason Officer), unknown, Hugh Stockwell. Sitting, from left: unknown, unknown, William Ritchie (1 RSF), Tony Legard (Fd Coy RE). Standing to right of map: Tom Eccles (2 East Lancs), George Bastin (Deputy Brigade Commander), Paul Walker (36th Division HQ LO).

(Trustees of the Liddell Hart Centre, King's College London)

17. Pinwe falls to 29 Infantry Brigade, Burma, 30 October 1944.
(Trustees of the Liddell Hart Centre, King's College London)

18. The assault on the Arakan Beaches, Burma, 1945.
(by permission of the Imperial War Museum)

19. Soldiers of 1 (WA) Infantry
Brigade fording the Dalet
Chaung in the Arakan,
Burma, February 1945.
*(Trustees of the Liddell Hart
Centre, King's College London)*

20. A group of Jewish Hanagah
soldiers in Haifa, 1948.
*(by permission of the Imperial War
Museum)*

21. Stockwell views fighting in Haifa from an observation post, Palestine, 1948.
(Royal Welch Fusiliers Archive)

22. Hughie Stockwell when Commandant of the RMA Sandhurst with FM Montgomery, outside the Royal Memorial Chapel, 27 October 1950.
(Stockwell Family Papers)

24. Stockwell's command group with General André Beaufre, Port Said,
6 November 1956. *(Stockwell Family Papers)*

25. 3 Commando Brigade RM assaults Port Said by
helicopter on 5 November 1956, the first such
operational use of helicopters.
(by permission of the Imperial War Museum)

26. 3 Para and 3 Commando Brigade link up outside Port Said, 5 November 1956.

(by permission of the Imperial War Museum)

27. Stockwell as Colonel of The Royal Welch Fusiliers and DSACEUR inspects 1 RWF at Iserlohn, Germany, in 1963.
(Royal Welch Fusiliers Archive)

28. Working on the Caen flight at Devizes on the Kennet and Avon Canal, 1970 with Admiral Bill O'Brien and Dudley.
(Kennet and Avon Canal Trust)

29. Hughie, Dudley and Joan cross the K&A Canal to Railway Cottage, Christmas 1975.

(Stockwell Family Papers)

patrol thereafter. I found African ORs to be very dependable and could look after themselves better in the jungle than British ORs. I only became louse-infested on two occasions and that was when I was with British troops.

On 1 May, Headquarters XV Corps was made solely responsible for Dracula, and Stockwell's division came under the direct command of HQ ALFSEA. So ended what became known as the Battle of the Arakan Beaches – not that there were any beaches worthy of the name. Considering that it had only ever been a subsidiary operation, the early objectives were successfully achieved and the whole operation was as good an example of combined operations as could be imagined, given the available resources. But the secondary objective, preventing Japanese reinforcements from reaching central Burma, had failed. As John Hamilton put it: 'Gen Christison never did succeed in trapping any Japanese in Arakan, despite . . . landings, at Ru-ywa and at Letpan. . . XV Corps resembled a frustrated bulldog whose teeth never actually met in the seat of the absconding burglar's trousers.' That said, Slim himself remarked that 'In actual fact, the enemy reinforcement thus set free did not amount to as much as I feared at the time.' A combination of the reassignment of air supply, and the withdrawal of 25th and 26th Divisions, probably meant that this objective was unachievable. However, the Official History is guardedly contemptuous about the role of 82nd Division: '54th [Japanese] Division could have been hard hit had 82nd (W.A.) Division's advance not been so hesitant.' Easy to say, but the men on the ground faced an enemy in terrain ideally suited for defence, and through which it could take eight hours to cover 500 yards in thick bamboo without even the enemy taking a hand – conditions which were markedly different from those in central Burma; nor was it ever suggested that British or Indian troops could have done better. Moreover this assessment fails to give due weight to three important operational consequences of the campaign: first, the seizure and operation of the airfields at Akyab and Ramree, without which supply of the Fourteenth Army would have been diminished; secondly, the Japanese had been so distracted and indeed dislocated by the fighting in the Arakan, that they were unable to influence the mounting of Operation Dracula against Rangoon; and lastly, by the end of the campaign the Japanese in the Arakan had been destroyed as a coherent force and the remnants driven out, allowing the transfer of the bulk of XV Corps elsewhere.

When questioned about his tactics after the War, the GOC of the Japanese 54th Division revealed the underlying mutual misconception of the opposing sides in the Arakan, saying that: '54 Div's role was to annihilate the British forces on the waterline and not let them into the hinterland at all.' In this context, Stockwell's own summary stressed this, and shows that although at the operational level of command all the objectives were not achieved – in that the Japanese were not *pinned down* as had been intended – tactical successes meant that in some respects, the achievement actually exceeded appearances:

The Japanese Commander almost invariably disposed his forces with the object of defeating the British landings on the waterline. In his own words he 'kept close to the coast'. This tendency was common to most Japanese coastal defence practice. While it fulfilled the principle of offensive action, it partially sacrificed those of mobility and security. As a consequence the overland hooks of 82 (W.A.) Div. went far to disorganize his defence on at least three occasions.

The first occasion was near Myohaung, when the possibility of a coastal attack in the rear had been foreseen by the construction of strong defences at Kangaw. The landward flank had, however, been left open by the failure to hold the Kanzauk Pass.

The second occasion was the arrival of 1 and 4 Bdes. at Dalet. At this time the main Japanese force was stubbornly resisting the landings both at Myebon and Kangaw, and so little provision had been made for flank protection that the Dalet thrust was met, not by a mobile reserve, but by pulling out 154 R. from the Kangaw battle.

The third occasion was the establishment of 2 Bde.'s road block on the An road. At this time the Japanese Commander had once again disposed the bulk of his striking force at strategic points on the coast from Dalet to the mouth of the An Chaung, a total of some 70 miles, and against a superior force. One would have considered that under such circumstances it would have been imperative to hold a reserve in the area of An. However, there does not appear to have been any such reserve, and the force which was used to attack 2 Bde. was 111 R, which was withdrawn from its positions on the coast.

So perhaps with adequate resources at the theatre level, more could have been achieved. As it was, hard decisions on resources and priorities had to be taken, and the consequences accepted. Maybe the last word lies with the enemy. The Japanese already knew the worth of the African soldier. After the second Chindit operation, their view had been that:

> The enemy soldiers are not from Britain, but from Africa. Because of their beliefs they are not afraid to die, so even if their comrades have fallen they keep on advancing as if nothing had happened. They have an excellent physique and are very brave, so fighting against these soldiers is very troublesome.

To confirm that this was still the case, Japanese casualties inflicted by the 82nd Division up to 14 May were: known killed 1,018, believed killed 414, known wounded 383, believed wounded 375; 40 prisoners were taken. Captured equipment included 10 artillery guns and mortars, 30 machine guns, 260 small arms and large quantities of ammunition. In return, the units and formations of the 82nd Division had marched up to 428 miles during the campaign, and endured the heaviest battle casualties in XV Corps: 2,085 of the corps' 5,093 killed, wounded and missing fell in Stockwell's division – proof that they had borne the brunt of battle in the Arakan.

In May 1945, the Allied victory over Germany was at last achieved and was celebrated on the 8th of that month. Twelfth Army was formed under Stopford on 28 May and took over all operations in Burma from Fourteenth Army, except for the Arakan civil division. With the Arakan now clear of Japanese troops, XV Indian Corps was also returned to India, however Stockwell and the 82nd Division, while under operational control of IV Indian Corps, was placed under the direct command of C-in-C ALFSEA.

Ray Simmons recalled a conference called by Stopford, at which all divisional and corps commanders were present, to discuss future moves:

> Stopford said 'Well, we're going to attack Rangoon. Hughie, what do you think about how we should go about it?' General Stockwell had thought about this before, and said straight out 'Put 81st and 82nd Divisions on the Army's right flank, send Merrill's Marauders down the spine, and put 17th and 26th Divisions on the left. Start one hour before dawn and we'll be in Rangoon by the end of the day.' Stopford said 'Gentlemen, that, in essence, is my plan!'

While 26th Indian Division carried out its dramatic and successful amphibious assault south of Rangoon on 4 May, Stockwell was given the rather unexciting task of remaining in the Arakan in the division's current positions until the end of the monsoon. He was given administrative responsibility for the area between the Dalet Chaung and Gwa, and also told to patrol east of the Taungup–Prome road in order to establish contact with IV Indian Corps, which had taken over responsibility for all troops of XXXIII Indian Corps when it was disbanded on 28 May. These mundane-sounding tasks contained, however, several implied responsibilities. First, the Japanese were still present in some strength in southern Burma and, although much reduced in capability, were still dangerous. 82nd Division's position therefore had to be held to secure the right flank IV Corps during the closing stages of operations; the supply route through Akyab also remained essential, and had to be protected. Stockwell wrote to his subordinates stressing the importance of explaining carefully to the Africans what was happening: 'I must stress the importance of an all-out effort at this period to assist the overall picture for the clearance of the enemy from Burma. Every Japanese killed or contained in the area carries a real dividend.' Secondly, Gwa was almost 50 miles south of the division's present positions, which meant that a long stretch of coastline and hinterland would have to be covered by active, long-range patrolling in order to ensure that it was clear of the enemy; in fact, the area was occupied by the leading elements of the division between 10 and 13 May. Lastly, security would have to be provided for the return of a civil administration; here the threat came not so much from the Japanese, but from closer to home – a well-organised Burmese resistance movement, with Communist sympathies, had sprung up during the Japanese occupation.

The division settled into monsoon accommodation, and the tempo of operations slowed immediately. Stockwell decided to take advantage of the operational pause to go home on leave; he had, after all, not seen his family since leaving for Madagascar in early 1942. He made use of a scheme called LILOP, or leave in lieu of Python – Python being the demobilization scheme for the Army which had begun once the defeat of Germany was certain, and which was causing Slim and Mountbatten to protest that future planned operations in Malaya and against Japan were not sustainable at the planned rates of release. Before he went, he called a conference on 12 May of all brigade commanders, divisional troops commanders, senior staff and commanding officers of battalions. There were several reasons for this conference: first, Stockwell wanted to take stock of the campaign, and glean as much from the collective experience of the division as possible; secondly, he wanted to be sure that the right arrangements for training, welfare, morale and discipline were in place in order to keep the division fully occupied; thirdly to review the arrangements for the divisional leave scheme; and last, to give orders for the setting up of a divisional school, which would be established to train an expected intake of 250 British officers and NCOs. Given Stockwell's earlier remarks about the need for Europeans to understand their role, the setting up of this school is not surprising – although in the event, these reinforcements never arrived.

On 23 May Stockwell handed over temporary command of the division to Charles Swynnerton, and, preceded by a warning telegram, flew home. From the airfield he made his way to North Wales by train, where Joan and the girls were there to meet him at the station. Since being told he was on his way home, Polly, a bloodthirsty child, had been working up to ask her father a question of great moment. Scarcely before greetings had been exchanged, she burst out with 'Daddy, how many Japs have you killed?' Stockwell's response was indicative of someone who had been away at war for so long that he had got out of the habit of parenthood. Instead of making light of it, or exaggerating hugely for the benefit of a childish imagination, he drew himself up and said, 'It is not the business of generals to go around killing enemy soldiers.' Polly was massively disappointed and withdrew hurt.

On 6 July, Stockwell returned to Burma and immediately began a round of visits. The divisional intelligence summary for 23 June to 6 July, published for his return, reported extensive patrolling and more clashes with groups of Japanese soldiers, as well as the frequent use of air strikes. As a result, the area east of the Prome–Rangoon road was reported as generally clear. Some Japanese soldiers had surrendered, carrying with them leaflets that had been dropped by air; one soldier from the 54th Division was interrogated and was described as voluble and fairly reliable. He 'wound up his story with an impassioned harangue on the Japanese spirit (*Yamato Damahii*) concluding with a demand for immediate death. The effect of these fine sentiments was somewhat spoilt by his next request, one for a supply of toilet paper.'

Stockwell had arrived back just as the remaining Japanese forces in Burma began the preliminary moves for their long-expected attempt to break across the Pegu Yomas into Siam, which began on 19 July. ALFSEA had good intelligence on this move and Mountbatten considered it 'imperative that 4 Corps should be kept up to strength'. Given the high level of concern which Mountbatten had signalled to London over the effect of Python on his troop levels, and the fact that Stockwell and his division were not only underemployed, but only partly subject to Python, it seems odd that the division – a full-strength, experienced formation – was not shifted to the Sittang front, as was 7th Indian Division. Why not? The Politically Correct might jump to the conclusion of racism, but this just does not hold up in a multicultural force like Twelfth Army. The most likely explanation is that such a move was too far in the time available, given the very limited road and air transport, and shipping, that was available – the division would have to have been moved north by sea to Chittagong and from thence by air or road to Mandalay, before moving south and ending up just a hundred miles or so east of where it had started after a journey of around a thousand miles. The chances were that the action would be over before the division got into position – so best to leave it where it was. However, at the very least, the division might have exploited eastwards from the coast to harass the Japanese rear – the Japanese had after all withdrawn the same way – providing of course that sufficient air supply was available. But not even that was permitted. There is one further factor that might help to explain the situation: Indian Army pride. The Japanese had humiliated the Indian Army during the early days of the war in Burma, and rubbed salt into the wound by forming the INA. So therefore the Indian Army must deal with the destruction of the Japanese. Indian Army officers, whether British or Indian, were known to resent greatly the presence of the only two wholly British divisions in Burma – 2nd and 36th Infantry Divisions – and the same resentment may well have been applied to the African divisions. Left in the Arakan chasing dacoits – bandits – whose activities were already increasing, the 82nd Division could only look on.

Then, on 5 August, Stockwell was summoned to a meeting at Headquarters Twelfth Army. On 11 August, Stockwell himself summoned a divisional conference to discuss the move of the division from its present locations to join the main body of Twelfth Army in central Burma, as a precursor to operations in Malaya. It was planned that the division would move to a concentration area around Tharrawaddy, due east of Gwa, by 1 November. Preparations began at once, with a high priority given to repairing the roads.

In the midst of these plans came the momentous news of the dropping of the first atomic bomb on the Japanese city of Hiroshima on 6 August, with the second one being dropped on Nagasaki on 9 August. Conventional air raids continued on Japanese cities until the 14th when, after the personal intervention of the Emperor, the Japanese government accepted the Allied demand for unconditional surrender. For many it was a shock, for others a reprieve, for everyone a surprise and a relief.

Negotiations on the cessation of hostilities and the Japanese surrender in Burma began on 12 August, but fighting continued right up until the last moment. A signal suspending operations was issued at 5.55 pm on 15 August, and peace proclamation parades, with holidays wherever possible, were held; in the 82nd Division, this took place on Kindaunggyi airstrip. Further orders were issued to the Japanese on 20 August. Between the 15th and the 20th, the Japanese blew up quantities of ammunition and stores. Of course, it was some days before word reached the lower echelons, and several negotiations broke down between 20 and 24 August. Final orders were therefore not issued to the Japanese until 11, 12 and 13 September, following which the British progressively reoccupied all Burma, and civil government began to return.

Stockwell and Ricketts were able to fly to Singapore for the Japanese surrender ceremony on 12 September. This immensely satisfying event took place at the Municipal Building where enormous crowds had gathered. Inside, the flags of all the Allied nations were hung in the hall, and a ceremonial guard of Chinese irregulars under British officers was drawn up. At each of the eight pillars stood an armed sentry representing the nationalities that had fought for the Allied cause. In the centre of the main audience room two long tables had been arranged, six feet apart. Mountbatten, Slim and their most senior subordinates and representatives of the American, Netherlands, Australian and Chinese forces, occupied one. The other was reserved for the Japanese delegation. Behind them were the 400 or so spectators, Stockwell among them. Two galleries were filled with the press, and everyone watched and listened intently as Mountbatten made his formal address, inspected the Japanese credentials, and read the Instrument of Surrender. Mountbatten recalled his impression of the Japanese delegation:

> With the exception of Numata, who looked almost human, I have never seen six more villainous, depraved or brutal faces in my life. I shudder to think what it would have been like to be in their power. When they got off their chairs and shambled out, they looked like a bunch of gorillas with great baggy breeches and knuckles almost trailing on the ground.

Despite the surrender, planning for the move of the division continued. Operational Instruction No. 11 was issued on 14 September, but the move was suspended because of the non-availability of shipping to ferry the division's transport and heavy equipment. Stockwell suggested moving to a concentration area between Akyab and Chittagong, an eminently sensible suggestion given that the Japanese surrender had entirely negated the reasons for making the original move, and the most likely future for 82nd Division was disbandment, followed by embarkation on the coast and a move back to West Africa. A good deal of what soldiers refer to as 'greatcoats on, great-coats off' went on, but the upshot was that the original move was ordered to go ahead, and approved by HQ ALFSEA, pending the availability of shipping.

On 1 October, 82nd Division left ALFSEA command and came under the command of HQ Twelfth Army. On 12 October, further orders were issued for the move to central Burma. Stockwell at this point gave orders for the troops to be trained for internal security duties and gave his brigadiers respon-sibility for their own IS areas. This was prompted by rumours of an uprising; Aung San had concluded an agreement with Mountbatten at Kandy under which the Burmese Liberation Army (BLA) would disarm, but 4,000 men would be retained as the basis of a Burmese Army. This process was going well, but even so, the minorities feared the intentions of the BLA. No rising took place, but the post-independence history of Burma seems to show that these fears were not altogether unfounded.

It was not until the end of December that orders for the move were finally received, and it was mid-December before the process was complete. The rationale for the move was also made clear: 82nd Division was to close in on Rangoon, both for ease of administration and to be near the main port of embarkation, for the men of the RWAFF were by now due for repatriation. First in, first out, is the general rule in the Army, and the highest priority there-fore went to the 81st Division – the 82nd had no alternative but to sit tight until transport was available. The scale of the repatriation problem should not be underestimated. The British Empire had to move several million men from and to many different parts of the world: Canada; Australia and New Zealand; South, East and West Africa; India; garrisons for Singapore, Borneo, Malaya and Hong Kong; occupation troops for Japan; and British troops home for demobilization. There were also large numbers of internees and prisoners – both friendly and enemy – to be moved. All this with limited air and sea trans-port, a good deal of which was needed to feed the populations of various war-torn parts of the world, or maintain the existing forces.

In general the soldiers took it well, but it was a question of keeping the men occupied. The British officers and NCOs did what they could, organizing courses to give the men skills for their return to civil life as well as military training, sports competitions, drill and ceremonial. The latter remained as popular as ever, although Captain F.W.E. Fursdon of the Gold Coast Company of West African Engineers recalled that mishaps could occur:

> I will never forget one afternoon parade disintegrating after an unwary bush cat had been foolish enough to cross the edge of the parade ground. Five minutes later the company was back on parade again, in perfect formation, whilst the unfortunate cat was being boiled in the huge 40-gallon cauldron in the cookhouse – fur and all.

The appearance of game was one of the few events that could break the discipline of a West African unit. The author recalls a battalion at Port Loko in Northern Sierra Leone in 2000, drawn up ready for a very senior visitor, break ranks and chase after a squirrel which was ill-advised enough to appear in front of the parade. When order had been restored, the senior visitor asked the soldier who had caught the animal what he was going to do with it. The man's face cracked in a huge grin, and he replied, 'Sah! Gan eat 'em!'

John Hamilton remarked that:

One cannot help but wonder what would have happened if British troops, after more than a year in jungle, had been stuck for nine months or more in bamboo huts on a featureless, hot and dusty plain remote from anything more closely resembling civilisation than the railway-men's club at the nearest junction and no amusement beyond out of door film shows. But GHQ India almost completely got away with it. The Africans in those days were not used even to film shows; they made their own amusements; they were fond of card games. Within limited hours they could visit the nearest village.

Demobilization – Python – applied of course to the Europeans in the division, with the Rhodesians being given a high priority. Stockwell's ADC, Simmons, finished his war service in October 1945, and was replaced by Captain R.L.J.B. (Richard) Neville of the Oxfordshire and Buckinghamshire Light Infantry, who assumed the appointment on 6 October 1945. John Dickson of the Royal Welch Fusiliers kept up the Regimental presence, however, when he joined the division as its GSO2 on 1 July 1945; he had of course been Stockwell's Brigade Major in 29 Infantry Brigade, and doubtless Stockwell had arranged the move. Rapid changes among the administrative staff of the division can scarcely have made Stockwell's task easier as he lobbied hard, with some success, for the welfare of his men. He was instrumental in getting some small but important concessions, taken perhaps for granted by white officers and men, for the African soldiers who had shared equally in the dangers and hardships of the war. Leese's despatches noted that:

West African morale was good . . . Repatriation and home leave became the main topic of interest of the West African troops, but a clear statement of policy on the subject was still awaited when I relinquished command. The increases in expatriation allowance, and the extension of the free postal concession to West Africans, were appreciated.

Pay and allowances had become something of an issue among African troops in the rear areas when serving alongside Europeans. Until the outbreak of war, the colonial government had been responsible for all administration, and when this was taken over by the British War Office, African pay, at one shilling per day, was half that of a British private soldier. Some soldiers felt that they should receive the same pay for enduring the same conditions – although as one contemporary source pointed out, the African soldier was far better off than his civilian counterpart doing agricultural or other work at home.

Orders for embarkation were received in February, although the first moves were not to begin until May; it would be September before the process was complete. Brigades were to be grouped with divisional troops units on a colony basis, for ease of repatriation. However, all formations would disband in Burma before embarkation, and troops would revert to RWAFF command. First out would be 1 (WA) Brigade, then 2 Brigade, and finally 4 Brigade along with the Divisional HQ and any unbrigaded units.

Stockwell himself was ordered home after almost four years abroad, and sixteen months as divisional commander. Before he left, he made another exhaustive tour of all the units of the division from 1 February to 16 March 1946, wishing to see personally – and be seen by – as many men of the division as possible. Typical of this tour was the parade with representative companies from all units of 2 (WA) Brigade in Rangoon under Frank Clowes. After inspecting the parade, Stockwell made a speech in English, which was translated into Hausa, the main purpose of which was to pass on a message from Mountbatten:

> This parade today marks not only an occasion on which I have been proud to present medal ribbons, but it represents others of you who have won medals, and it marks your prowess in battle.
>
> I have received a signal from Admiral Lord Louis Mountbatten, our Supreme Commander . . . 'I want to say goodbye to your men of 82 (WA) Division now that you are returning to your homes, and to thank them for the part they played in bringing about the enemy's final surrender. Your splendid advance down the Arakan was only one of many contributions you made to the victory.
>
> The part you played will not be forgotten. You have made the name of your Division known throughout the world, and history books will tell how men of Nigeria, the Gold Coast, Sierra Leone and Gambia travelled far from their homes and helped beat the Japanese, the jungle, and the monsoon.'

Stockwell himself later wrote of his time with the division that it was:

> an experience never to be forgotten. The staunch determination of the African soldier in face of not only a fanatical and determined enemy, but also terrain in which no self-respecting soldier would ever seek battle, carried us through . . .
>
> They fought splendidly and stood up to much privation and hardship.

They never turned their heads at any task I asked of them – cheerful – resolute – and truly men, their shining bodies and enduring friendship remain with me always.

His achievements in command of the division had been recognized by a mention in despatches – his fourth – in May 1945, and in June 1946 he was made a Companion of the Bath, to add to his DSO and CBE. Not surprisingly, though, after such a long spell in the jungle, he also took home a bad dose of malaria, which stayed with him for the rest of his life.

At 4.15 am in the dark of the early morning on 16 June 1946, Hughie Stockwell was driven down to the seaplane jetty in Rangoon. Waiting to see him off were his brigade commanders, commanding officers and a large group of officers and men of all ranks. His car drew up and the General jumped out, as was his way, shaking hands and exchanging a few last words with members of the waiting group. Then, he inspected a guard of honour of 100 men of the Nigeria Regiment, turned out in the Zouave full dress of the RWAFF, before making his short, but heartfelt, final address:

> Our ways must part, and with that I wish you all good-bye and good luck. I shall always remember your loyalty, your cheerfulness and your splendid spirit through all the difficult, exciting, and happy times we have had together. You are all my friends and I shall look forward to meeting you again wherever you may be . . .
>
> Sai wata rana.

Then as he stepped aboard the launch that was to take him to the dimly seen shape of the Imperial Airways flying boat moored in the harbour, formality gave way as the guard broke ranks, surged down to the edge of the jetty and gave three rousing cheers. As he boarded the Sunderland flying boat which was to take him home, Stockwell was given the Hausa farewell, not from the lone bugler which had been his lot in 1935, but from the massed buglers of the Nigeria Regiment – a fitting tribute to one who had commanded an African division in war.

Chapter Twelve

The 44th (Home Counties) Division, 1946–1947

Hughie Stockwell had been lucky throughout the War and was lucky again now. While still only a temporary Major General, acting Brigadier and substantive Colonel, he did not share the fate of many of his contemporaries and drop back several ranks as the Army contracted. Instead he held on to his temporary rank and was given another command, the 44th (Home Counties) Division, located in south-east England. The division formed part of Eastern Command and the GOC-in-C was none other than Lieutenant General Sir Oliver Leese, who had been C-in-C ALFSEA, and therefore Stockwell's superior in Burma, and who had moreover been a previous commander of 29 Independent Infantry Brigade.

Stockwell arrived home from Burma on 14 June and therefore only had two weeks before taking up command. What must have been something of a shock, even after the rigours of war, was the state of the country. Stockwell had returned to a Britain in which most of the major city centres had been bombed to rubble, half a million homes destroyed and another quarter of a million severely damaged; and where acute rationing was still in force. Most people were not actually hungry, since bread and potatoes were not rationed, and those in country areas, like Joan and the girls up in North Wales, could supplement rations by growing vegetables and keeping pigs or fowls; but they were run down by years of shortages and overwork, and by a very dull diet indeed. Sweets and chocolate were still strictly rationed, and tropical fruits were almost unknown. People looked pale and thin, down at heel and very shabby, for new clothes were obtainable, but rarely except on the black market. This was in a Britain whose huge empire had been triumphantly restored, but whose balance of payments was crippled; a Britain which controlled some of the most valuable raw materials on the face of the earth, but in which, in February 1947, the Foreign Secretary had to walk up several flights of stairs to a cabinet meeting because the lifts had been immobilized by a power cut. The price of victory must have seemed a high one.

* * *

155

Stockwell's new headquarters was to be co-located with the headquarters of a new military district, Home Counties District, which took the place of the old pre-war Home Counties Area. The district was already in existence and Stockwell was to take command as GOC on 3 July 1946. The division would not be fully resurrected until 1 January 1947, at which point he was to take command of both the division and the district. In general terms, the whole scheme was very close to the situation of 53rd (Welsh) Division and the Welsh Area in which Stockwell had served as Brigade Major of 158 (Royal Welch) Infantry Brigade before the War. The headquarters, which until 1939 had been at Woolwich, was now established at Risborough Barracks in Shorncliffe, just outside Folkestone in Kent. The territory of the District covered the counties of Surrey, Kent and Sussex, less the metropolitan areas of Surrey and Kent, and a small part of Surrey near Guildford that belonged to London District. It was divided between two subordinate sub-districts, one based in Dover, which covered Kent; and the other based in Brighton, covering Surrey and Sussex.

The discomforts of life in post-war Britain were, however, mitigated by the excitement of a move. Stockwell of course had already had his Python leave, but even so, moving the family down from North Wales was likely to take a little longer than the two weeks he was now given; in the end he did not assume command until the 19th. Joan and the girls were uprooted from the farm in North Wales and moved hurriedly down to Dover. While the GOC was also Deputy Warden of the Cinque Ports, and Deputy Constable of Dover Castle, the Lord Warden and Admiral of the Cinque Ports was none other than the former Prime Minister, Winston Churchill, who was installed, with Stockwell in attendance, on 14 August 1947. Afterwards he took lunch at Dover Castle with the Stockwells, for although the Deputy Wardenship had become a ceremonial position, it carried with it a beautiful residence in the Castle, in the shape of the Constable's Tower. The girls had a fine time exploring the Castle – Anabel was small enough to get into the suits of armour in the dining room – and were able to keep their ponies in the Castle stables. But the speed of the move may explain in part the disappearance of Stockwell's wartime letters home – Joan had to pack and get out of the farm quickly, and so anything not essential was tipped on the bonfire.

The 44th Division was to be composed entirely of units from the TA, which was reconstituted on 1 January 1947, although recruiting did not begin until 1 April. The framework of units was to be provided by volunteer officers and senior NCOs with war service, and regular Permanent Staff Instructors (PSIs) and HQ staffs, augmented by volunteers, and built up from 1950 onwards by National Servicemen. Under the National Service Act, men would pass into TA units for three and a half years of compulsory part-time service following their service with regular units. The 44th Division, although containing its complement of divisional troops, had only two of the old pre-war 44th Division brigades: 131 (Surrey), based at Surbiton in south-west London, and

133 (Sussex and Kent), based in Tunbridge Wells. The division's third brigade, located in London District, was 47 (London) Infantry Brigade. Interestingly, two of Stockwell's subordinate commanders were by some margin his seniors in age and experience, and another was a contemporary. This was a considerable test of Stockwell's ability to get on with others, but he seems to have passed it comfortably enough.

The immediate post-war years were thus a period of preparation for the influx of National Servicemen carrying out their reserve service. Initial recruiting was very slow indeed. 4th Buffs, for example, recorded only thirty-eight men enlisted in the first year, exactly matching the number of TA officers, permanent staff, and civilian clerks engaged to supervise them:

> There were two deterrents to enlistment. One, inevitably, was the aftermath of war, which not only left former territorials with quite enough experience of soldiering to quench the desire for more, but also prolonged the call-up of men who might otherwise have become volunteers. The other was the plan to make the Territorial Army a part-conscript force, in violation of a long and proud tradition of voluntary service.

There were tensions too, due to the split of responsibilities between the County Reserve Associations and the chain of command, and the clash of volunteer ethos with National Service. One Territorial summed things up rather harshly:

> The serving blokes in the brass and hardware frankly didn't understand us. They wanted to open from 10 to 4, so why the devil we couldn't be on tap during the same hours was an anathema. They didn't realise that we were with some anxiety trying to catch up on our jobs on which our bread and butter depended; nor that the brigade could not be paraded tomorrow morning for inspection by the new Brigadier, who got quite stuffy when told that was really impossible.

It was the work of the District, though, rather than the TA division, which absorbed most of Stockwell's energies. The Port of Dover, for example, was a main centre for the flow of leave and duty personnel, and families, moving between Britain and the new British Army of the Rhine. Then there was the need to reorganize and regroup the wartime system of Primary Training Centres (PTCs), where soldiers received basic training; Infantry Training Centres (ITCs), where soldiers were given more advanced combat training; and Primary Training Wings (PTWs), for non-infantry soldiers. These were now needed to deal with the continued flow of National Servicemen into the Army. Within the District there were also a large number of static installations, ranges, depots, schools and training establishments, including the School of Musketry at Hythe, and it must have afforded Stockwell a measure of wry amusement to exercise command over a place in which he had enjoyed so many high jinks as a young subaltern.

Domestically, life centred on the Constable's Tower, and there was an early surprise: Hughie's father, a widower now since 1944, had retired from the Police Force and sold the family home at Shrub End. He appeared at the Castle with his worldly possessions in a suitcase, and stayed for some time – Neville Bosanquet remembered him there at dinner in late 1946. From then on, Hughie senior adopted an itinerant lifestyle, staying with whichever of his five children would have him. Any inheritance Hughie Stockwell might have had therefore disappeared; so too did any letters which he had written to his parents, which, along with the hasty move from North Wales, explains the complete lack of wartime correspondence from his time in the Far East.

After only a year in Dover, and with the rebuilding of the TA division only just begun, Stockwell was unexpectedly given another command. This was to be the 6th Airborne Division – Stockwell's third divisional command – on active service in Palestine. It would appear that this appointment had been made at the personal behest of the CIGS, Field Marshal Montgomery. On becoming CIGS, Monty had decided, among other things, that senior officers needed training in command, and that a broad tactical doctrine needed to be evolved for the post-war army. He tackled both problems in a series of exercises at the Staff College, Camberley, attended by all general officers in the Army. Professor Nick Bosanquet recalled that at a family wedding in Colchester in 1980, Stockwell remembered one of these exercises, which dealt with amphibious warfare. Looking down the list of major generals, Monty had seen that Stockwell had commanded a West African division: 'Bow and arrow soldier is he? Let's see what he can do.' Of course, there were few generals with as good a grasp of amphibious operations as Stockwell – and Monty remembered. When a replacement for the GOC 6th Airborne Division was required, Monty put the finger on Stockwell, who had become one of his protégés.

Stockwell gave up command of the 44th Division on 25 July 1947 and spent the next month settling the family in to Acrise House, an official residence next to the nearby training area above Hythe, and the girls into school. Joan and the girls stayed at Acrise alone until Joan bought a house at 129 Elgin Terrace, Notting Hill Gate, in West London, in partnership with her sister Hazel. This was a shrewd move, although living together caused a good deal of friction. From there, Polly went to art school, and Anabel to St Paul's Girls' School. Stockwell himself went off to Palestine in August, back to doing what he did best – field command.

Chapter Thirteen

The Evacuation of Palestine, 1947–1948

It was a hot day and in the dusty haze of northern Palestine, the young soldier sweated out his spell of sentry duty. He would soon be due for Python, and when he came off duty that evening, another day could be ticked off his chuff-chart. Hearing a sound behind him he half turned, and then stiffened automatically as he saw that it was his CO – having a look round no doubt before lunch. The CO looked unusually glum, thought the sentry, as the Old Man took his pipe from his mouth, coughed, and stared gloomily at him.

'How long have you been in Palestine?' he enquired.

'Getting on for two years now, sir,' was the soldier's nervous reply.

'Do you read the newspaper?'

'Off and on, sir.'

The CO stared out across the perimeter wire to where a Jewish herdsman was leading his cattle through the noon haze. He turned back to the sentry and said, 'Do you know why we are here?'

'No, sir,' came the reply with more than usual emphasis.

'Do you know the difference between an Arab and a Jew?'

This caused some deep thought for a while. 'It's not very easy sometimes, sir.' The sentry looked with reproachful embarrassment at his CO, who started to relight his pipe.

'Do you know what Ramadan is?'

The sentry looked crestfallen and shuffled his feet. 'It's when the wogs don't work during the day, isn't it, sir?'

A brief explanation of the significance of the Muslim holy month followed as the sentry tried to look enlightened. Having thus unburdened himself, the CO turned away to go across to the Mess for lunch, and the sentry heaved a silent sigh of relief. But as he turned, the CO paused and said, 'I suppose you know who Shertok is?'[1]

The sentry's face lit up – he was on to a winner. 'Shertok?' he replied. 'Yes, sir, he's the Camp Education Officer.'

*   *   *

159

The young sentry was probably typical of many thousands of his fellows stationed throughout the Middle East in the years following the end of the Second World War. In those years, British power was still dominant here, and its hub was the great military base of the Suez Canal Zone, the largest armed camp in the world and the centre of a network of other bases spreading out to Malta, Cyprus, Libya, Transjordan, Iraq, Aden, the Persian Gulf states – and Palestine.

Since 1944 British forces had been trying to hold down an increasing campaign of terror by Jewish nationalists, people who had clearly learned their trade from the Nazis, and who proceeded to put what they had learned into practice against first the British, and then the Palestinian population. This terror was waged chiefly by two terrorist organizations: *Irgun Zwai Le'umi*, or IZL, which translates as the National Military Organization; and *Lachemey Heruth Israel*, or Hebrew Fighters for the Freedom of Israel, more generally known as the Stern Gang. This gang, led at first by Joseph Stern until he was killed in 1942, and then by Nathan Friedman-Yellin, consisted of about fifty extremists who had broken away from IZL and during the War had actively co-operated with the Italians and Germans in conducting operations against the British. Between them, these two organizations accounted for perhaps 12,000 of the then population of about half a million Jews. Their activities were officially condemned by the Jewish Agency, but even its own security organization, Hagana,[2] became involved at times with confrontation. On 3 November 1945, Foreign Secretary Ernest Bevin, exasperated by the legacy of the Balfour Declaration and exhortations from US President Truman, announced that only 13,000 Jews would be allowed to enter Palestine from Europe, and that the Royal Navy would intercept any attempting to do so illegally. Then as now, there were multitudes anxious to flee their old homes for the chance of a new start – and plenty of criminals ready to make money by charging desperate people exorbitant sums. The ships used were often rusting hulks which were barely seaworthy, and which were crammed with people in appalling conditions of filth and hardship. On the *San Miguel*, for example, there were nine people for every six cubic feet of passenger space. Many of those intercepted ended up in internment camps, causing much anti-British feeling among Jews all over the world. Incidents such as the interception of the ship *President Warfield* (renamed the *Exodus* by its Jewish owners), and the return of its 4,000 passengers to Germany in July 1947 added fuel to the fire. What seems never to have occurred to any leading Jew at the time was the fact that the incumbent Arab citizens of Palestine might have any rights at all.

The troops in Palestine in 1947 consisted of three fighting divisions: the 1st Infantry, 1st Armoured and the 6th Airborne, as well as a number of non-divisional units, and Empire troops from Africa. The country was divided into three military areas: 215 Area in the north, with its HQ at Haifa, covering the Galilee, the Jordan valley, Acre, Safad, Nazareth, Beisan and Tiberias; 21

Area in the south, covering the districts of Lydda, Gaza, Jaffa, Tel Aviv and Samaria; and 156 Sub-Area which covered Jerusalem. Area HQs controlled all static units, installations and infrastructure, leaving the field formations free to conduct internal security operations. Also in the country were units of two Arab formations: the Transjordan Frontier Force, and the Arab Legion. The Transjordan Frontier Force included the Cavalry Regiment, 1st Mechanised Regiment, Mobile Guard Squadron, and a range of support and logistic units. In 1947, it had fifty-four British officers, and twenty-nine WOs and NCOs on its establishment. The Arab Legion, by contrast, owed its allegiance to King Abdullah of Transjordan. As well as a headquarters and training organization, it included 2,000 gendarmes, 2,700 men in the three regiments of its mechanized brigade, and 3,300 men in the infantry companies of its two garrison groups – which were troops asked for by the British Army, and not required by Transjordan. After independence and the Jordanian-British Treaty of 1946, Abdullah had placed the greater part of the Legion at the disposal of the British government for garrison duties in Palestine, and it was mostly deployed guarding oil installations, pipelines, camps and dumps.

After inconclusive talks with the Jewish leader, David Ben-Gurion, on the establishment of the Jewish and Palestinian states, it was decided in February 1947 to pull out the garrison and surrender the Mandate to the United Nations, with the promise of an evacuation by May 1948. The best that could be hoped for now was a dignified withdrawal – but even this was to be denied. A UN Committee of Study, UNSCOP, was convened under the leadership of Count Folke Bernadotte to examine the problem in May, and this was in progress when Hughie Stockwell arrived to take command of the 6th Airborne Division from Major General Eric Bols on 19 August. As already intimated, this was his third appointment as a divisional commander, and all three were very different. This command, as well as being operational, was likely to be sensitive given the situation; the military was but one – albeit important – element in the new theatre of operations, but for the first time in his career, Stockwell was exposed to the political dimension.

The 6th Airborne Division had moved north from Tel Aviv in January 1947 to take over from the 1st Infantry Division. The north of Palestine was in sharp contrast to the settled agriculture of the south; for the most part it was hilly terrain, with spectacular views over the Jordan Valley and the Sea of Galilee. Cattle, sheep and goats grazed the sparse vegetation but there was little arable farming. It was not wholly bleak, as Sir Henry Gurney, the British Chief Secretary in Palestine, noted in his diary:

20th March 1948. Palestine light is of incredible clarity. It is brittle rather than glaring; translucent like spring water. In March and April [after the rains] among the hills of Samaria, Galilee and Transjordan, the wild flowers sprinkle the rocky and pale green landscape with red, yellow and blue. Sometimes the red anemones cover a whole hillside, and the blue lupins shine for miles like great splashes of ultramarine paint spilt among the young grass.

Haifa, the main city of the north with a population of around 150,000, of which around two-thirds were Jews, was also the chief port of Palestine and was home to extensive oil facilities belonging to Consolidated Refineries Ltd, as well as storage and pumping installations belonging to Shell, the Iraq Petroleum Company, and others. The Divisional HQ, with the staff under the direction of the GSO1, Lieutenant Colonel Michael Dewar, was located in the Carmelite Monastery of Stella Maris on the western spur of Mount Carmel, near Haifa. One of its three subordinate formations, 2 Parachute Brigade, commanded in August 1947 by Brigadier Hugh Bellamy, had been returned to England. The other two brigades and the divisional troops units remained in Palestine, with 1 Parachute Brigade under Brigadier J.P. O'Brien Twohig in Haifa, 3 Parachute Brigade under Brigadier F.D. (Francis) Rome in Galilee, an ad-hoc formation called Craforce (2nd East Surreys, 3rd King's Own Hussars and 1st King's Dragoon Guards) – so called because it was commanded by the CRA of the division, Brigadier Cyril Colquhoun – looking after the main oil pipeline and an internment camp at Atlit, and the divisional artillery units deployed throughout the area. Units of the Arab Legion included the 1st Mechanised Regiment, with HQ Squadron, one armoured car squadron, and three mechanized squadrons, all on pipeline control – static guard and patrol – and No. 1 Garrison Group, made up of five Garrison Companies and one Security Company distributed on static guard duties in and around Haifa, and at vulnerable Jewish settlements.

As it happened, Stockwell's arrival coincided with a thoroughgoing revision of the command arrangements in Palestine. From 15 August, the districts and sub-districts ceased to report directly to HQ Palestine, and came under the direct command of divisional commanders, whose boundaries were adjusted to coincide with the districts. All administrative units, installations and supernumerary police units were likewise transferred to the divisions. Stockwell was allocated Haifa city and port, the whole of Haifa district, and the Galilee. In addition to his own division, he was also given authority over the Commander Transjordan Frontier Force and his HQ, which would be moved into Galilee and 'be available, under GOC 6 AB Div, to take direct command of TJFF units operating on the frontiers, and of any British units allocated to him'. The relationship with the Palestine Police was an interesting one. Although the police, who were the one exception to the rule that Jews and Arabs could not work together, carried out distinct functions and were largely under expatriate British officers, they were under the command of the divisional commanders for all operations, a fact acknowledged by the Inspector General, Colonel Nicol Gray in July 1947.[3] This had the advantage of giving Stockwell a unified command although in giving the military authority over the civil power, it acknowledged that the security situation had broken

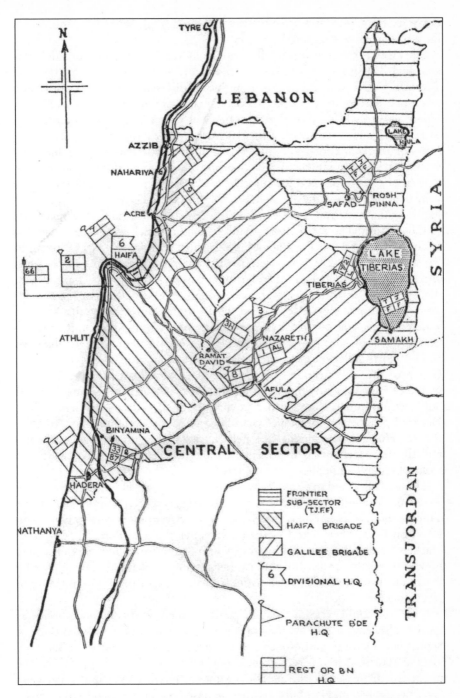

**DIVISIONAL LAYOUT IN NORTHERN PALESTINE,
NOVEMBER, 1947.**

Source: Major R.D. Wilson MBE MC, *Cordon and Search. With the 6th Airborne
Division in Palestine* (Aldershot, 1949).

down irretrievably – but since the British were leaving anyway, a short-term fix was all that was required.

Stockwell's orders gave him 'the task of maintaining law and order and safeguarding British interests in the North Sector, in conjunction with the civil authorities'. He thus faced two completely different problems: preserving peace on the frontiers of Galilee, and keeping Haifa in running order. He had barely arrived when a directive from the War Office came in instructing him to reduce 2 and 3 Parachute Brigades into a single brigade and carry out a series of amalgamations to reduce the number of parachute battalions. This would leave him in January 1948 with only one parachute infantry brigade in Palestine. To compensate for these losses, a number of non-brigaded units were to be attached to the division. Once he had settled in, therefore, Stockwell had to make some rapid adjustments to the deployment and responsibilities of the division. The main effort would be Haifa, which would be controlled by the bulk of O'Brien Twohig's 1 Para Brigade, reinforced by 40 Commando Royal Marines from Cyprus, to look after the port, three Army major units and three minor units from the divisional troops. Twohig was charged with the internal security of the city, the protection of oil installations, the prevention of breakouts from Acre prison – a constant source of trouble – and a watch over the coast to arrest illegal immigrants. Within his area, the protection of the important port facilities and some oil installations were allocated to HQ North Palestine District, which was reinforced by a No. 1 Garrison Group of the Arab Legion. To take the place of 3 Para Brigade, Craforce would be reinforced and made responsible for the security of the East Frontier Sub-Section, and law and order in the adjoining districts of Galilee. The Nazareth Sub-Section of Galilee was allocated to the Commanding Officer of the 3rd Hussars, Lieutenant Colonel Charles Peel, with his own regiment, and the 1st Mechanised Regiment of the Arab Legion, led by Lieutenant Colonel Hugh Goldie, under command.

The area allocated to Craforce was huge and rugged, and the troops to task were insufficient. Stockwell was accordingly given command of the Transjordan Frontier Force, and issued a directive, which was to come into effect on 6 October. The Commander of the Frontier Force, J.W. (Shan) Hackett,[4] was ordered to deploy forces into the Nazareth Sub-Section where he was to assume control of the frontier in Galilee, maintain law and order in conjunction with civil authorities and prevent illegal immigration and smuggling.

Stockwell could not, however, concentrate solely on matters in Palestine as he was also engaged in a series of correspondence with the War Office in September, October and November about the division's move to Germany after its tour in Palestine was complete. He was clearly not happy about the proposed dispersal of the division after its move to Germany between Schleswig-Holstein, Hamburg and Berlin, based on the advice he had received from Bellamy. There was, he felt, too much emphasis on the possible IS role of the division in Germany, and not enough on its training as a fighting formation. Rather than disperse, he preferred to concentrate at Hamburg, with a brigade at Lüneburg. There was also much correspondence about the difficulties of keeping parachute infantry brigades up to strength; Stockwell was in favour of taking men not yet qualified as parachutists, and trickling back through parachute training in Britain.

The strategic picture became clearer in September 1947 when UNSCOP advocated the end of the British Mandate and the creation of an independent Palestine partitioned into two states: one Arab and the other Jewish. In the ensuing vote in the UN General Assembly, no satisfactory agreement on partition could be reached and in the aftermath of the vote, the Arabs, determined to resist any partition of the country, increasingly took up arms. Politically, the British decided to take no responsibility for any action that implied implementation of partition, an attitude that Sir John Glubb, the Commander of the Arab Legion, summed up as 'well, if you don't like us, you can sort yourselves out as best you can.' This is perhaps unfair, since the British were certainly in a difficult position. Oil interests and the imperial lines of communication had to be secured, and anyway, the traditional stance of the Foreign Office had been pro-Arab. This engendered a feeling that the Palestinian Arabs were being abandoned to Zionism – a force that was in any case heartily disliked by most British officials.

Against a background of terrorist attacks, the security of oil installations in Haifa and the pipeline from Syria assumed high importance. Stockwell considered that sabotage was inevitable, but there seemed no proper answer to the question of who was responsible for the protection of oil installations. Was it the oil companies or the security forces? The two main pumping houses in Haifa were guarded by detachments of the Arab Legion, and there were nearly 400 police officers involved with oil installation security in various places. Stockwell felt that it was unsatisfactory to have the military accept partial responsibility in this way; accordingly he asked for guidance from the GOC over who must accept responsibility, and for what. He also stressed the need to survey all installations, and distinguish between points which were vital and needed military protection, and those which were, although important, not vital. In the meantime, on 10 September, there was an attack on the Haifa refinery, probably by local employees inside the site, and so Stockwell summoned the representatives of the oil companies on 15 September to discuss security. Although the companies were recruiting civilian guards, and co-operating with the police and the military, Stockwell felt that the military would have to be reduced, throwing more responsibilities on the already over-burdened police. He therefore urged the companies to compensate by setting up proper security teams with the right expertise, and to fund them properly, so that at the very least they would be able to establish credible perimeter security and control of access.

One significant destabilizing factor not mentioned in Stockwell's analysis was the continued illegal Jewish immigration from Europe. This had not, however, been forgotten. On 1 October, Stockwell called a conference in

Haifa, to co-ordinate the response to the expected arrival of two ships carrying about 4,000 illegals from central and Eastern Europe. These were the *Northlands*, carrying about 2,500 people, and the *Paducah*, an ex-US Navy gunboat with an American crew, carrying about 1,500. The conference was attended by Stockwell's subordinate commanders. Also present was Commander A.F. de Salis, the Senior Naval Officer, Palestine; Alfred Law, the District Commissioner; and representatives of the port authority and the civilian services. Standing Orders for actions to be taken when ships were intercepted already existed – in essence these boiled down to arresting Jews if they had landed, and taking them under escort to Haifa where they would be interned in a suitable camp and dealt with by the civil power. The difficulty with this was that the available vehicle lift would only carry 800 people at a time, rising to 1,200 on 7 October, so a series of shuttles would be necessary to take people to Atlit internment camp at Haifa, from whence they would be transferred to Cyprus. Captain Gordon Dinwiddie, who usually ran the divisional battle school, was told to get the camp prepared with security provided by the brigades, and with all administration handled by the Sub-District. An additional complication was then discovered: at the time that 4,000 illegal Jewish immigrants were being brought into Haifa, several thousand Muslim pilgrims would also be arriving to take ship for the Haj to Mecca. In the event the ships arrived on 3 October along with a third, the *Farida*. The arrival caused intense press interest but there was little trouble, although when the immigrants were interviewed it was found that the Russians were doing all they could to encourage Jewish immigration, presumably in the hope of further destabilizing the region, embarrassing the Western Allies, and extending their future influence in the region. When one considers that the population of, for example, Haifa, was around 150,000 in 1947, having been just under 40,000 in 1939, it must become obvious that the battle against illegal immigration was one that, despite the detaining of significant numbers, the British could not hope to win.[5] And it was not just people being smuggled in by the Jews, as Gurney noted in his diary:

> 24th March . . . This morning a problem came up in the shape of the 50 American armoured vehicles brought to Haifa from Philadelphia in the 'Flying Arrow' as agricultural tractors. All sorts of bribes have been offered to customs and Police to let these through for the Jews, but . . . they must go away again.

Stockwell himself was out of Palestine for much of November 1947. By the time he returned, plans for the British withdrawal had been published. With the knowledge that the Mandate would be ended on 15 May, and the British gone by 1 August 1948, the final six months of British rule were characterized by growing inter-communal violence both inside and outside Palestine. Violence or not, withdrawal was the order of the day, and the GOC's staff issued orders for the scheme of evacuation. These outlined the plan by which the Southern Sector would be the first to go and Haifa the last. Lieutenant General MacMillan, the GOC Palestine, had been closely consulted about the date of withdrawal and the reason why it was as late as August was the large numbers of personnel, and the huge quantity of military stores and equipment that had been built up, in the expectation that Palestine would continue as a British base. As well as the 70,000 troops and 5,000 British police officers, there was a great body of colonial administrators and their families, all needing to be moved either overland to Egypt, or by sea from Haifa. Then, in addition to equipment held by units, there were some 210,000 tons of stores, much of it held in and around Haifa. A single division – the 1st Infantry Division – would gradually assume command of the whole country and then close in on Haifa, which thus assumed a particular and vital importance both for Stockwell and for the whole of British Palestine generally.

January saw fighting between Jews and Arabs which brought some relief from attacks by Jews, whose armed groups switched most of their attention to the Arabs, but the frontier was the major problem area in December and January, especially where Craforce, soon to be without the support of the Frontier Force, was thinly spread over their large area of harsh, hilly terrain, dotted with settlements and villages living in mutual fear and hatred. Craforce had done its best to patrol villages, as much to show the flag as to deter violence, and thereby encourage the Arabs to stay and not flee. Gregory Blaxland wrote that:

> It was a task tinged with pathos, for it was a hollow form of reassurance that the troops brought, and the faith engendered in some Arab villages, after ponderous introductions and the ritualistic serving of mint-flavoured tea, sometimes made the visitors feel guilty of fraud. It was much harder to penetrate the cold suspicion encountered in the kibbutzes.

This is a fairly typical reaction, as Stockwell's ADC, Peter Cavendish,[6] also recalled:

> It took about six weeks from arrival to change the British Army's atti-tude from pro-Jew, in sympathy with what they had suffered under the Germans, to very much anti. They were devious, arrogant people with no sense of humour. The Arabs were also devious, but were courteous and had an immense sense of humour. Senior commanders tried to be fair minded – I remember Hughie saying 'You've got to try.' But it was hard.

At the other end of the spectrum, illegal immigration continued to be a problem. On Sunday, 30 December 1947, 1 Para Brigade supervised the con-trolled disembarkation of illegals from two large ships, the *Pan York* and the *Pan Crescent*, which between them carried a total of 14,546 people. On the same beaching at Nahariyya, 300 were screened, 131 detained and 1,800 released at once. On New Year's Day 1948 the *Archimede* sneaked in and beached at Nahariyya. By the time she was discovered, about 720 people had got ashore, of whom 131 were detained. Another 300 were screened – all were found to be central and east European Jews – and a further 1,800 were released immediately. The final official figures showed that between 1946 and 1948, forty-seven ships were intercepted, with a total of 65,307 illegals transferred to Cyprus or camps in Palestine. Immigration on this scale was beyond the ability of the security forces to control, and had already changed the ethnic balance of Palestine decisively in favour of the Jews.

Despite the impending handover, Stockwell – perhaps on the prompting of higher authority – wrote to all his subordinate commanders in early January 1948, to say that he was

> becoming somewhat concerned at the amount of unofficial contacts that appear to have been taking place by Commanders at all levels, with so-called representatives of 'Hagana', Jewish committees, and Arab executives . . . Both Arab and Jew are masters of the art of intrigue and . . . such contacts can only lead in the end to Commanders being caught on the wrong leg.

Stockwell went on to remind his subordinates that contacts below their level must have their approval, and that the only contacts he would permit to them would be of a wholly official nature. In the light of his subsequent contacts in Haifa, this was rather ironic; but that he had to issue such a reminder may have added to his irritation a couple of weeks later. Stockwell was away from the division in early February when a spat broke out with MacMillan's head-quarters. On the 5th, Rome, who was acting as divisional commander, signalled HQ Palestine, warning that there were indications of attacks on Jewish settlements along the north-eastern border with Syria by artillery and mortars, firing from across the border. Rome felt that the divisional artillery, which was certainly very limited, would not be able to counter this effectively and asked for air strikes. This brought a sharp response: air strikes were not authorized and Rome was not to become involved with the use of air power in any way – but the use of artillery or mortars, in other words a proportionate response, was authorized. This should have been the end of the matter, but on the 13th, MacMillan wrote personally to Stockwell on his return in some irritation, since Rome and others had continued to lobby for the use of aircraft. MacMillan said bluntly that such decisions lay with him, and that Stockwell must grip his subordinates. Stockwell characteristically wrote back at once, accepting responsibility and undertaking to make sure this kind of thing did not happen again. Although not one to stifle initiative, and always ready to protect his subordinates, this was clearly irritating and, coming on top of the earlier reminder on unofficial contacts, close to disloyalty – something Stockwell would not tolerate.

What had taken Stockwell away was the bitter news that 6th Airborne Division would not after all move to Germany, but as a result of reductions in the Army for reasons of economy, it would cease to exist on its withdrawal from Palestine. Stockwell had therefore left Palestine briefly from 6 to 10 February to be present at a meeting at the War Office to discuss the reduction. In general terms, the plan was to reduce the division to a single parachute brigade, including three parachute infantry battalions and supporting arms and services. Stockwell himself was on record as not liking the Brigade Group set-up, presumably because it weakened cohesion at divisional level, 'but this of course depends on how you are organising the divisional troops'.

The news caused great gloom in the division, as Major Tony Farrar-Hockley,[7] the DAQMG in the Divisional Headquarters, remembered. 'It was thought to be the beginning of the end for airborne troops.'

In 1993, Polly wrote a short satirical opera based loosely on her father's final days in Palestine. In it, she gives a sketch of family life at Acrise in Hughie's absence, guessing at his and her mother's views on the stresses of married life. Although fictional, it is revealing:

SCENE 3

General Hughie's home . . . His wife is sitting in a chair near a window, beyond which the rain is pouring down. She is reading a letter from her husband . . . The two girls enter squabbling. Lollipop [Polly], the older and the plainer, is wearing a kilt, a scruffy jersey, grey knee socks and worn and dirty pink satin ballet shoes. Bella [Anabel], the younger, is wearing jodhpurs, gumboots, a bowler hat and an equally scruffy jersey. Lollipop is tugging Bella's pigtail.

BELLA
Mummeeeeeeeeeeeeeee Lolly says
Tatters isn't a real horse,
Only a barrel inside an old carpet.
She is a pony isn't she Mummy?

LOLLIPOP
When I dance Cinderella
I'm not having that old rug pull my coach!

BELLA
Silly pink shoes!
You're too big to be a fairy!
Ya, ya, ya!

Lollipop thumps Bella and a fight ensues . . . .

[Earlier], General Hughie is musing:

Windswept hills . . . Family again . . .
The stench of ponies in the rain.
And my dear wife, always so loyal.
Those awful wars so spoil
Our married life.
Yes, how she does complain . . .
And the two girls, both, alas, so plain . . .
Do I really need them all again?
Hell, perish the thought!
. . . Though I'm so lucky with my plucky wife,
She tries to keep the fires alight.
It's good she's waiting there for me,
Her poor tired warrior from overseas.

While his division was run down the business of securing Haifa remained critically balanced. Official Communiqué No. 151 laid down that after the end of the Mandate there would still be some British troops in Haifa running an enclave to ensure the complete evacuation. Stockwell added some additional points to this, which were addressed to the population:

It is therefore our intention that Haifa should run and function as a normal city and that the citizens in it shall proceed normally about their lawful vocations.

Part of the Municipality will be a British Security Zone, in which no armed persons shall be allowed to move . . . Throughout the remainder of the municipality the British will have free access and passage at all times and will enjoy the amenities of the city.

In fact, Rome had already begun to have misgivings. He had taken over 1 Para Brigade in Haifa from O'Brien Twohig in early 1948 on the withdrawal and disbandment of his own 3 Para Brigade. In a report to Stockwell in late February he said that the expected Arab invasion which would follow the departure of the British was now likely to occur anytime from mid-March onwards. The general IS situation, especially in Haifa, was therefore likely to deteriorate; the Jews were well aware of this situation. Because of the run-down in troop levels, he urged that the Haifa enclave be established immediately with an appropriate garrison of up to two infantry brigades. Stockwell clearly heeded this advice, and equally clearly he had some reservations of his own about the plan. He therefore wrote to MacMillan on 1 March 1948, asking that while the handover arrangements from 1 Para Brigade to 1 Guards Brigade of the 1st Division were settled, the Guards should keep the 3rd Hussars until 30 May, an additional month.

Certainly, all was not well in Haifa. The situation had deteriorated steadily after the UN vote; there had been inter-communal sniping at first, and gradually all-out gun battles had developed. By late February, both sides had brought in mortars and heavy machine guns, as witnessed by a succession of large finds of weapons, ammunition, explosives and mortar bombs in the city throughout the early months of the year. During March and early April 1948, the Arab Liberation Army was strengthened in Haifa by reinforcements of several hundred Iraqis and Syrians, a few European mercenaries, and some ex-Transjordan Frontier Force men who had infiltrated through the thin screen provided by Craforce. The Arab command was divided between Yunis Nafa'a, a Lebanese (or by some accounts a Palestinian), and Amim Bey Ezzadin, an ex-Frontier Force major of Syrian origin. Most of these men were infiltrated into the suq, from where on the night of 12/13 April, the ALA went over to the offensive, with the aim of severing the main Jewish thoroughfare in the city.

For their part, the Jews were not prepared to wait until the British withdrew, to end the Arab threat. They also received considerable reinforcements to counter this from the Palmach, Hagana and IZL and although they were less aggressive, here more than elsewhere, later evidence suggests that they were content to build up their forces in preparation for the implementation of their Plan D – that was, to secure all areas allocated to the Jewish state under the proposed UN partition resolution, along with isolated Jewish settlements outside them, and to secure corridors leading to them. This, for the first time, was going to require Jewish forces to capture and clear Arab villages, towns and cities, and was possible to contemplate because of a secret deal with King Abdullah, under which Abdullah would be able to claim the Arab areas as defined by the UN resolution. But once the Jews began to flex their muscles and scent success, they rapidly lost any feeling of restraint imposed by this agreement.

Throughout this period, Stockwell conducted affairs in Haifa in almost total independence; his superiors in Palestine, Egypt and London, dislocated and distracted by other events, were not in touch with developments. Neither Gurney's diary nor General Cunningham's papers during his time as High Commissioner contain anything of substance concerning Haifa; indeed Gurney's diary also notes the fragile state of communications: '20th April: Mail from London has now ceased, and we only get telegrams . . . nearly all inland trunk telephone and telegraph lines are now broken down, and as a result the Police wireless net has handled 95,000 groups [of Morse cipher] in the last 48 hours.'

Stockwell repeatedly summoned Arab and Jewish liaison officers and urged them to restraint. As only one battalion of 1 Para Brigade – Lieutenant Colonel Theo Birkbeck's 2nd/3rd Parachute Battalion – was available to intervene in the struggle, demands for restraint had to be backed up by aggressive patrolling by the Staghound armoured cars of the 3rd Hussars, supported by infantry and anti-tank guns. Both sides said they would limit their actions out of respect for the British – but these were 'vague and useless promises'.

Stockwell's ability to deal with the deterioration in the situation was made harder by the increasing tempo of withdrawal. On 3 April, Main Headquarters 6th Airborne Division closed, and Stockwell, with his tactical HQ only, became GOC North Sector, co-located with the HQs of North Palestine District and 1 Guards Brigade. On 6 April, 1 Para Brigade passed control of Haifa to 1 Guards Brigade, under Brigadier George Johnson, and on the 16th it had begun to embark on the troopship *Empress of Scotland*. 1 Guards Brigade was now responsible for Haifa, Acre and the main roads leading north and north-east; Craforce, until its withdrawal, was responsible for all routes from Jenin to Haifa, and the co-ordination of the withdrawal of all British government officials and police from eastern Galilee.

At the same time, Safad continued to be a focus of increasing tension between Jews and Arabs. In January, an intelligence report suggested that 800 Arab irregulars had entered the town from Lebanon; the police had asked for reinforcements, and Craforce obliged; for several months, a half-company of the Irish Guards, supported by armoured cars, had preserved a fragile peace. In early April, the Hagana began to infiltrate the town and tension again increased. The CO of the Irish Guards, Lieutenant Colonel David Gordon-Watson, sent Stockwell a written appreciation of the situation after a visit to his men there, which was a remarkably accurate summary of what was unfolding. He wrote that the commander on the spot 'does not have enough force to intervene in likely battle', or even stop it happening. The favoured course of action would be to arrange a truce for evacuation of Hagana, and a complete evacuation of Jews from the Eim Zeitim district: 'the issue is EITHER, the Hagana leave, OR British troops hand Safad town over to the representative municipal control [i.e. the Arabs].'

Dan Kurzman, who had been able to interview all the main protagonists, now dead, wrote an account of what followed in Safad in his book *Genesis 1948*. Kurzman says that on 12 April, Stockwell took tea with the Arabs of Safad. The tea party took place at the home of a Safad notable, Mohammed Yusef al-Khadra and produced astonished Arab smiles, for Stockwell viewed an Arab military victory in Safad as an absolute certainty. True, Safad was supposed to go to the Jews under the United Nations partition plan, but they numbered only about 1,500, compared to 12,000 Arabs, and could not possibly win a battle. Ultimately, he felt, those stubborn Jews would ask the British to arrange things peacefully – and Safad would go to the Arabs. He offered to turn over key strongholds to the Arabs when the British withdrew from Safad. 'You understand, of course,' he said, 'you are not to attack the Jews until the British withdraw – on April the 16th.' 'Of course,' replied Colonel Adib Shishekli, the Syrian commander of the small unit of ALA men based in Safad. Stockwell then posed other conditions for British co-operation: the Arabs would have to permit British intervention in the fighting if the Jews requested it; and they must treat the Jews humanely when they captured the town. 'Of course, of course,' Shishekli promised. Stockwell was satisfied as he left.

172

Two days later, on 14 April, Charles Peel marched into the Central Hotel to interview the Jewish leaders of the town. Meir Maivar, owner of the hotel, who had served in the British Army during the Second World War, led them. 'Really,' said Peel, 'Hagana should leave the town and let the citizens here – Jews and Arabs – reach a peaceful agreement of their own.' When the Jewish leaders refused, Peel continued, 'Well then, I suggest that you let us evacuate the women and children at least, because I predict a very unhappy fate for you.'

Maivar scowled. Things did indeed look bad. The British would certainly hand over the medieval citadel to the Arabs when they left. From there, the Arabs could fire into the Jewish quarter on the lower slopes of the hill, while other Arabs attacked from the adjacent Arab quarter. Moreover, this hill was surrounded by other Arab-held heights, including one to the north, opposite Mount Canaan, crowned by a British Taggart fort, a modern, reinforced-concrete bunker complex that the Arabs would also control. Together with the police station, these strongholds dominated the whole of Safad, including the road approaches. Indeed, the town was already under siege, and Jewish morale was low. Most of the inhabitants were ultra-orthodox shopkeepers or scholars, people with almost no understanding of or sympathy for the aims of Zionism. Furthermore, this was one of the few towns in Palestine where the Jews were, in fact, less intellectually able and less motivated than the Arabs, who dominated the professions. They were not, Maivar knew, fighting men. Indeed, many citizens were asking for an agreement with their Arab neighbours, or failing that, to be evacuated.

Despite all this, Maivar and his few fighters knew they would have to hold Safad – it was *the* key strategic town in northern Galilee. The town sprawled at the base of the upper, or eastern, Galilean finger, wedged between Syria to the east and Lebanon to the west. Since Jewish settlements within the finger were hopelessly trapped in a valley dominated by Arab hilltop villages, Safad might be all that stood in the way of an Arab sweep through the whole northern part of the country. Maivar scanned the rugged, brown mountains and gave Peel his answer: 'Everybody stays!' Peel rose to go. 'You do understand, don't you, that it will take only about two hours for the Arabs to clean you out?'

On 15 April about 1,000 Arabs prepared to assault the Jewish quarter and were only prevented from doing so by the intervention of the 3rd Hussars. That night, further Arab reinforcements arrived, moving the situation beyond the ability of Peel to control. Stockwell, as he had intended, gave the order for all troops to withdraw from the town. On 16 April, Peel was able to put his prediction to the test, leading his troops out of Safad to the shock and consternation of the Jews, who had expected them to stay at least two weeks longer. It was the first surrender of British-occupied territory.

The British withdrawal was followed by a furious battle, which did not go the way everyone had thought it would. After fourteen hours of shelling and close-quarter battle, an uneasy quiet settled over Safad – the Jews had held out after all. The next day, a unit of Palmach soldiers infiltrated through the Arab blockade to be welcomed hysterically. Other Jewish forces followed, breaking the Arab grip on the region. Fighting went on until 10 May, but by the end every Arab had left Safad, leaving the tiny Jewish population to enjoy their triumph in the deserted streets and empty houses.

The handover of Safad was soon followed by dramatic events in Haifa. Dan Kurzman, again, was able to interview most of the chief participants of the events in Haifa. He put together an interesting account of events there, and Stockwell's part in them, from the Jewish point of view. Although a partial view, it is largely corroborated by other accounts in the Israel State Archives, which for the Mandate period are fortunately in English. At 11.30 am on 20 April, he says, Stockwell called Amim Ezzadin to his headquarters, and handed him a note. Ezzadin sat reading it at Stockwell's desk and as he did so, his hand began to tremble slightly. The note said that British troops had started to evacuate the positions they had occupied along a line roughly separating the Jewish and Arab zones in the city, and that they would henceforth occupy only the port of Haifa and a few other points necessary to ensure a safe troop withdrawal from Palestine. 'In the last two weeks,' the note read, 'clashes between Arabs and Jews have increased to a great extent . . . I have no desire whatsoever to involve my troops or members of the police in these clashes.'

When he had finished reading, Kurzman says, Ezzadin looked up and said firmly: 'We do not accept your decision. The British Army must accept the responsibility for the well-being of the inhabitants . . . I don't see any chance of holding out against the Jewish forces. We protest this arbitrary division of the city, which amounts to turning over Arab Haifa to the Jews.' Stockwell replied dryly, 'These are my instructions and I'm not prepared to change them.' No written instructions remain in Stockwell's papers, but it is easy to guess where they had come from: once the British left, Haifa would certainly fall to a Jewish state; moreover the British withdrawal would be far more difficult to conduct if fighting continued in the city. Politically, therefore, it made sense to let the Jews have a free hand. But Stockwell could well understand Ezzadin's discomfort. Hagana would clearly have the advantage in a free battle for Haifa, given that they overlooked the sea and dominated the approaches to the city. The Arabs, largely bunched at the foot of the hill, were in a situation similar to that in Tiberias.

Furthermore, Arab morale in Haifa, so high after Arab workers at the oil refinery had killed forty-one Jewish workers in December 1947, had plummeted when the first Arab military commander, Mohammed Hamad al-Huneiti – a former Arab Legionnaire – was killed in mid-March in a Jewish ambush of an arms convoy he was leading from Lebanon. Huneiti, a forceful commander, had brought order out of the customary chaos of Arab leadership and had organized a capable defence. But with his death, new disputes led to the flight of most moderate Arab leaders and many of the rich Lebanese businessmen.

Kurzman, however, suggests that there was more to the matter than at first

174

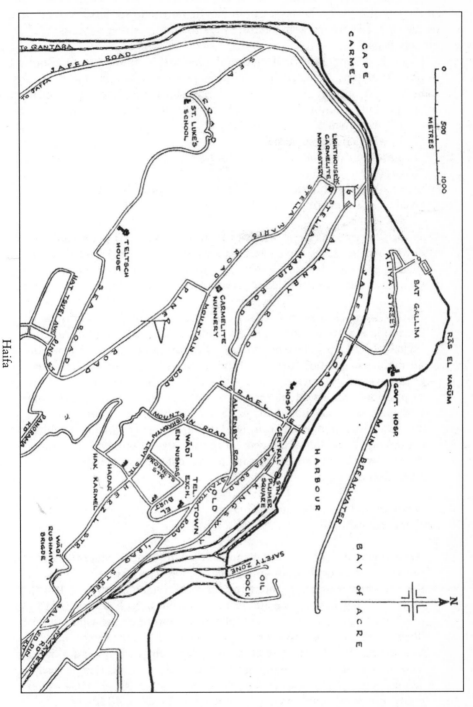

Haifa
Source: Yoav Gelber, *Palestine 1948* (Sussex, 2001).

seems apparent. Aba Hushi, who represented the Histradut,[8] and Harry Beilim of the Jewish Agency, he says, had in fact first come to see Stockwell as early as the end of February with a daring plan to end the street fighting that had already begun.

Hushi had apparently said, 'General, we wish to speak to you about an important matter, a matter that will perhaps seem to you madness . . . You must understand that the Jews will not give up Haifa, and a prolongation of the present situation may bring on a confrontation between the Hagana and the British Army.'

'Well, what do you suggest?'

'You should hand the city over to us.'

'*What?*'

'After all, in the end the city will be part of the Jewish State.'

'Well . . . Give me time to think about it.'

Over the next eight days the tempo of battle continued to mount, and finally, after four meetings, Stockwell had his answer ready – on 18 April, Maundy Thursday, two days before the meeting with Ezzadin. In the official account, Stockwell set out the rationale for his subsequent actions on the fighting thus:

> During these clashes, my forces deployed in Haifa were continually becoming involved in attempting to quieten the battles, and during the night of 17/18 April the troops, chiefly the armoured cars, were in action all night using 2-pounder and PIAT fire, with varying results. Their efforts were only partially successful and casualties were rising . . . my dispositions, made with all the forces at my disposal, were isolated and in themselves weak should any major assault be made by either side . . . The town itself and its environs is a large area to cover and the problem continually confronting me was (a) the security of our evacuation and (b) the amount of force necessary to prevent these increasing Jewish-Arab clashes.

To Ezzadin and his colleagues, Kurzman records that Stockwell set out the situation in this way:

> 'Gentlemen,' he had said, 'after consulting with General MacMillan I've thought a great deal about your offer . . . and I'm ready to accept . . . But my chief concern is about the lines of evacuation for the British army.' 'We'll help you keep and secure those lines,' replied Hushi. 'How much time will you need to complete the capture of the whole city?' 'Between twenty-four and forty-eight hours.' 'You are pretentious and headstrong, Mr Hushi,' said Stockwell. 'With the division and a half I have at my command, I wouldn't be able to do it in less than a week.' 'Would you care to wager? Say, for a bottle of whisky?' Hushi then wrote in a notebook: 'Stockwell – one week; I – 24 to 48 hours.'

But it has been alleged that Stockwell was also motivated by other, more personal, considerations. On 18 February 1993, *The Times* carried an article which claimed that 'General Hugh Stockwell . . . had become a late convert to their [i.e. the Jews'] cause after a stormy love affair with the beautiful wife of a junior officer.' This lady was dubbed 'Miriam' in Polly's opera, and Polly characterized Miriam in one fictional scene as 'a most luscious Jewess in her mid thirties . . . dressed to kill'. She painted a picture of infatuation by a Stockwell who was plainly captivated by a passionate and exciting woman, who presented so stark a contrast to his cold, complaining wife back at home. This, although dramatically appealing, is very far from the truth.

Major, later Major General, Dare Wilson says that 'I was on his staff as G1/G2 Ops in Palestine and saw much of him . . . this is the first reference to a liaison of this nature I have read or heard of.' More importantly Stockwell's ADC, Captain – later Major General – Peter Cavendish, followed Stockwell around closely at all times and knew exactly what was going on. He was also responsible for Stockwell's personal security – the General was by this time Number 3 on the Stern Gang's assassination list, after the High Commissioner and General MacMillan. He had this to say when interviewed:

> Either I or the security section escorted him at all times,[9] and we never let him out of our sight. At night he would sometimes say 'Right, let's go out on the town: boy, [that was me] go to bed!' Hughie would then go to a nightclub just outside the perimeter with one of the drivers, shadowed by one of the staff officers, or Lance-Corporal Medland, his orderly from the Parachute Regiment, and me – I had to stay out of sight, and when we got back home, sneak in and pretend to be asleep. One woman appeared repeatedly, and had obviously been deliberately set on him by the Jews. This was Peta Woolfe-Rebuck, wife (or so it was said) of the Hagana liaison officer to the British, Peter Woolfe-Rebuck.[10] Intelligence was certain that this was a put-up job, and Hughie was well aware of it. He allowed the woman to pay court, and indeed let her pay for an awful lot of meals and drinks: he in fact took both her and the Hagana for a ride. As to the talk of an affair, there was absolutely nothing in it. He could not have hidden it, I would have known. And in fact, the Jews' attempts to get at him like this were if anything counterproductive. He was concerned to treat everyone equally and if the situation had been reversed he would have offered the same deal to the Arabs. The Woolfe-Rebucks persuaded him that the Jews were a bunch of shits.

The Hagana or Sherdut Yedist were certainly trying to catch Stockwell in a honey trap to blackmail, and thus manipulate him – but they failed. This did not stop them from trying to generate rumours of an affair, which could have had the same effect as the deed itself. But we need not be detained any further by this newspaper report. The only reason that it has been included is that, an allegation of this seriousness having been made in a reputable English newspaper, it has to be refuted. There are perfectly logical and militarily sensible explanations for why Stockwell took the course he did: his position was isolated, and there was no possibility of reinforcement. British intelligence had consistently reported that Hagana was better organized, trained and equipped than its Arab opponents, and was likely to succeed in combat; and he was in no doubt about the requirement to hold open Haifa as an evacuation port and head of the Iraq oil pipeline. Moreover, contacts with Hagana were nothing new, as Naomi Shepherd has noted:

> Contacts between Jewish and RAF Intelligence began in 1937. Arab documents detailing the identity and plans of the [Arab] rebels captured during British raids were handed over to the Hagana, while the Jewish Agency, which had its own Arab informers, provided information on the internal discussions of the Arab Executive and Arab Higher Committee.

Then in January 1948, liaison was set up between Hagana and the Palestine Police in Jerusalem and Haifa, and it was even agreed that there would be no more searches for arms other than for caches that had been used in attacks on the British. In this context, Stockwell's actions become far more understandable.

On 19 April, Good Friday, Hushi and Harry Beilim again asked to see Stockwell. He agreed to receive them, but Cyril Marriott, the Political Adviser to GOC Palestine, and Law, the District Officer, were also present. Probably in view of the fact that there were two witnesses present, Hushi made no reference to earlier meetings, but took the line that in their view, the Jewish position was no longer tenable in Haifa, that they would mount an attack on the area of Mount Carmel to secure their situation; he had been sent from Tel Aviv to command it. The Jewish quarter was in fact on the lower slopes of the mountain, and overlooked the Arab suq, or old town, and was separated from it by the Wadi Rushmiya. Stockwell told Hushi that this would be most unwise, and that it could well result in direct combat with the British – not least because his own HQ was still in the monastic buildings on the mountain. But this was the trigger for the handover: Stockwell decided that a major clash was imminent, and this was the time to reveal at least some of his intentions to the higher command, but without implicating anyone else in any deal. He would, he said, 'retain my present dispositions in Eastern Galilee and re-deploy my forces in Haifa, whereby I could secure certain routes and areas vital to me and safeguard as far as possible my troops'. The re-deployment was set to begin on the 21st, as Stockwell's men pulled out of Tiberias.

Thus the meeting with Ezzadin on the 20th. But as Ezzadin was now about to leave Stockwell's office, the General, according to Kurzman, said that, of course, the Jews were only just being given the same news. Deeply depressed, Ezzadin, without informing Haifa's other Arab leaders, took a boat for Beirut en route for Damascus, in order to summon help. Soon afterwards, Nafa'a also left, leaving the Arabs with no military command at a critical time.

In Tiberias, on the night of 18 April, Hagana troops attacked uphill from the old city, and downhill from the new city, cutting Arab Tiberias in two. The Arabs were in deep trouble. King Abdullah of Transjordan had sent thirty lorries to Tiberias to evacuate women and children: hence the question of whether the men remain – and face almost certain death. Early in the afternoon of the 19th the lorries arrived and were soon filled with women and children. The men then climbed in of their own accord, and within the hour, the ethnic cleansing of Tiberias was accomplished.

The British might regret it, but they could not be sentimental. For Stockwell, the main effort had to be to secure those routes and areas around Haifa essential to the scheme of withdrawal – principally the convent of Mount Carmel itself, which commanded the main road, the Divisional HQ and Peninsula Barracks, the Port, Harbour Street, the Police Barracks, Haifa airfield, the railway station and the workshops complex, and the major oil installations. All other positions were abandoned. Stockwell himself, when interviewed later for a BBC TV programme, laid out his logic thus:

> My prime responsibility then came about to secure a tidy, organised, withdrawal of all forces in the northern sector, out of Palestine. I had a look at this problem and I eventually decided the only safe way to do this was to secure the area that I, personally, wanted to hold . . . in the whole of the northern sector it became impossible [to maintain law and order] as we had fewer and fewer soldiers, we'd been fully stretched as it was . . . we were having an enormous number of casualties as I thought, totally unnecessary for the British soldier, achieving absolutely nothing, and after I re-deployed and secured the routes, I had no more casualties but it left the Jews and Arabs face to face.

Miss S.P. Emery, an English schoolteacher in Haifa, reported personally something of Stockwell's reasoning in a letter to her mother:

> 14th March 1948 . . . today we had Major General Stockwell, GOC Northern Palestine, and his number 1 Colonel, Dewar, and Captain Peter Cavendish, ADC, and the Bishop, all to lunch.[11] We wanted his advice about guarding our building when we leave it. We had hoped that General Stockwell would quarter soldiers or police here, but he says it is too vulnerable. However he is going to instruct the Army section which is just opposite to us, that they are on no account to allow the Jews to occupy the building.

Stockwell's assurance to Miss Emery was important, for as the British redeployed, they were indeed shadowed by Hagana men. On the 22nd, Stockwell issued further orders to the effect that in future, troops were not to move out of their positions at night, but return fire at snipers only. Attempts to quell fighting or disorder could be resumed only at first light; but the implicit assumption is clear: security of the withdrawal route and the avoidance of casualties were now more important than stopping inter-communal violence. Dorothy Blanche Morgan, writing to the Anglican Bishop in Jerusalem, reported that despite Stockwell's assurances to Miss Emery, 'the British Army (Brigade of Guards) are now in Miss Emery's school, and apparently sharing it with the Hagana . . . all eating straw like the ox.'

The Jewish fighters in Haifa had not waited for Ezzadin to reach Damascus. While the British re-deployed, the fighting in Haifa continued to escalate, with 400 well-armed Jews engaged against 2,000 Arabs. Spearheaded by students of the Technion Institute, the Jews were preparing to take over all Haifa at the very moment when Ezzadin was being told of the British withdrawal. Indeed, when the evacuation had begun the previous night, it had caught Hagana, and even many British officials themselves, by surprise. The Hagana plan, known as Operation Misparayim (Scissors), was to cut Arab Haifa into three parts in a three-pronged attack beginning after dark, with forces from Mount Carmel to hook up with troops driving from the Jewish-held commercial centre near the port. But at about 1.00 pm on 20 April, only about an hour after Ezzadin had left Stockwell's headquarters, Mordechai Makleff, commander of the operation, sent a company to occupy Nejidah House, a large concrete office building that controlled the Rashmiyah Bridge, over which all eastbound traffic from Haifa had to pass. By thus drawing Arab defenders to the eastern edge of town, the other Jewish forces could more easily smash into the rest of the Arab force. The occupation of the building did indeed draw a violent Arab response, and many of these Jews died. The survivors were finally rescued when armoured cars reached the building the following night. But shortly after midnight, while the Arabs were concentrating on the besieged house, Makleff struck with devastating force into the main Arab areas, taking house after house, partly with fire, and partly with loudspeakers demanding surrender. By 7.00 am on 21 April, the Jews had made considerable progress, but the Arabs were still far from knocked out, and the Jewish commanders were certain the Arabs would fight to the end.

Thus, it was with disbelief mingled with relief, that Makleff and the other Jewish leaders received a message from Stockwell asking what Hagana's conditions for peace might be. Fighting to the end may well have been the original Arab intention, but for one thing, the military commanders had left the town, and for another, Kurzman suggests that Stockwell apparently asked for Jewish terms even before the Arabs requested them. For when he realized, to his amazement, that he would inevitably lose a bottle of whisky anyway, he saw no reason for letting the battle be prolonged; and in any case, London might order him to intervene to secure the withdrawal route before the Jewish victory was decisive.

Actually, members of a hastily formed Arab Emergency Committee, most of whom were Christian and favoured co-operation with the Jews – some,

Kurzman says, were even ready to accept partition – had tried unsuccessfully to reach Stockwell soon after the fighting started. Finally, at about 9.00 pm, after the Bank Manager, Farid Sa'ad, who was a committee member, had made innumerable telephone calls, Marriott had rung back to say that Stockwell would see him at 10.30 am the following morning, 21 April. This was more than three hours after Stockwell had asked the Jews for their surrender terms, and it may be that Kurzman's conspiracy theory has another angle: that Stockwell had learned privately of the Arab approach, and had fended them off until such time as he could judge the likely Jewish reaction on the wise principle that a man in his position should never ask a question without being pretty sure he knew the answer.

The Arab deputation, led by Sheik Abdul Rahman Murad, included Farid Sa'ad; Victor Khayat, a property owner; Elias Khousa, a lawyer; Amis Nasr, Secretary of the Chamber of Commerce; and Georges Muammar, a Lebanese lawyer. Farid Sa'ad and others insisted with much agitation that it was the duty of the British as the Mandated power to take over the city again and permit the 400 or so Arab reinforcements waiting at Haifa's barricaded borders to enter. Stockwell gave them a cool stare and refused, exclaiming: 'I am not prepared to sacrifice the lives of British soldiers in this situation. My only suggestion to you is to begin negotiations with the Jews for a truce.' Despite some pressure to the contrary from Law and Marriott, who were concerned for the Arabs situation and of course not privy to the wager, Stockwell issued immediate orders that no reinforcements for either side were to pass through British-held territory. In desperation, Murad asked what the truce conditions were. Stockwell hurried to another office where Mordechai Makleff was waiting for him. 'Here are our terms,' Makleff said, handing him a sheet of paper. Stockwell scanned it quickly and, returning to the Arabs, slowly read out eleven conditions to them. Principally, they were to agree to Hagana control over the whole city; the surrender of all weapons to the British, who would hold them until the Mandate expired and then pass them over to the Jews; the dismantling of all roadblocks and free movement throughout the city; the expulsion of all foreign troops from Palestine within twenty-four hours, and the handing over of all mercenaries; and an immediate curfew in the Arab quarters. On the other hand, those Arabs who remained in their homes would have equal rights and duties as Jews.

By this time, word had come that the Hagana forces had linked up in the centre of the city, splitting the Arab area into three parts. The Jews had lost only eighteen men killed and the Arabs about 100 dead and 200 wounded in the operation thus far. Stockwell then looked quizzically at the Arabs – the conditions were fair, he felt, in view of the magnitude of the Hagana victory. But the committee members, though more moderate toward Zionism than most Arabs, were not yet prepared to risk the wrath of the less moderate. They agreed to meet at the Town Hall with a reply at 4.00 pm that afternoon.

With the situation disintegrating by the minute, Elias Khousa went to the Syrian Consulate and via the Consul sent an urgent radio message to Syrian

President Shukri el-Khouatly and his Prime Minister, Khaled el-Azam, informing them of the Jewish demands and requesting instructions. But despite further reminders in the next three hours, no reply came. The committee, deeply split on whether to accept or reject the truce terms, could only agree to stall, and try to force some compromise amendments. When the members arrived at the Town Hall as agreed, they saw for the first time in days Haifa's Jewish civilian leaders, with whom they had long been close friends: Gutil Levin, Head of the Jewish Community; Beilim and Avazi of the Jewish Agency; Major Daniel Motke from the Hagana command; Jacob Solomon and Elias Lipshizt, lawyers; Daniel Killenbaum from Histradut; and Peter Woolfe-Rebuck. Jews and Arabs embraced one another and took coffee together while they waited for Stockwell and Marriott to arrive. At last the meeting opened and Shabbatai Levi, the Jewish Mayor of Haifa, whom the British had made a CBE, stated dramatically that the Jews did not want a single Arab inhabitant of Haifa to leave. Arabs and Jews, he said, must continue to live peacefully together as they had in the past. The Arabs would remain equal citizens in every way. But the Arabs continued to stonewall, until Stockwell snapped impatiently: 'If you don't sign this truce I shall not be responsible if three or four hundred more [Arabs] are killed by tomorrow.'

'What are you trying to do?' asked Victor Khayat. "We know Shabbatai Levi, Jacob Solomon, and all these people. We are old friends.'

Stockwell replied stiffly, 'If you are old friends, I understand that I can withdraw and that my services are no longer required.'

The Arabs then asked for an adjournment of an hour and a half to consider the revised terms, during which time they would appeal once more for help from Damascus. It does seem, however, that perhaps under pressure from Law and Marriott, Stockwell made it clear to the Jews that he would prevent an attack on the suq, which would undoubtedly result in heavy civilian casualties. Moreover it is clear from the Israel State Archives that he also modified the wording of the Jews' original conditions to the extent that although accepting their demands, and accepting Hagana liaison officers with his units, he insisted that they be implemented by his own troops – presumably to demonstrate that it was the British, and not Hagana, who were still in charge in Haifa.

The Arabs, unable to obtain advice from Syria, were split between the Muslims and Christians. The Christians in the end refused to accept any surrender pact, apparently because of earlier instructions from Damascus that they were to be killed if they consented. The Committee could do no more therefore than instruct the delegates 'to act according to their best judgement'. Stockwell in his official report seems to confirm this when he wrote that the Arabs insisted they had no direct authority to sign, and even if they did, they could not control the foreign fighters. They therefore returned at 7.30 pm. Grimmer now, they rejected the terms flatly as 'degrading', having decided not to risk being branded as 'traitors' for submitting to the Jews. And indeed, seen from the Arab point of view, the Jews' terms for a ceasefire were in fact a demand for complete capitulation. Even so, Stockwell was furious. 'You have made a foolish decision,' he said. 'Think it over, as you'll regret it afterwards. You must accept the conditions of the Jews. They are fair enough. Don't permit life to be destroyed senselessly. After all, it was you who began the fighting, and the Jews have won.'

The Arab population seems to have shared that view, for many among the Arab population were now fleeing in panic: in addition to those fleeing by land, almost 10,000 people fled to the harbour, where every available craft was mustered to ferry them to Acre. Stockwell was unwilling to intervene at this point, and therefore the delegation said they could only ask the General to supply transport for these people and their household effects and let them go to the Arab countries. Actually, they knew the British could not supply adequate transportation, and hoped that their intransigence would force Stockwell to push Hagana out of the Arab quarters so that the refugees could return. Stockwell then turned to Makleff.

'What is your reply?'

'It is their own business,' Makleff answered, 'and they must decide on it alone. But I am determined to take over the city by force if necessary.'

Shabbatai Levi, tears in his eyes, then pleaded with his Arab friends to agree to the terms and urge their people to stay. But the Arabs rose slowly and walked out. Silently, they drove home through streets heaving with refugees and the few belongings they could carry.

Next day, the 23rd, the Arabs wrote to Stockwell confirming their position, and admitting that the exodus of their people was voluntary but stating that 'the request for transport was to the greatest extent prompted by your refusal to take any action to protect the lives and property of those residents.' In response, Stockwell did agree to provide protection for refugee convoys leaving the town, which prompted the Arab Committee to begin establishing local boards to organize the evacuation. This rather gives the lie to post-war attempts by Khousa and others to blame the British for the flight of the Arabs. As Naomi Shepherd has written: 'The flight of most of the Arab population during the 1948 war, following the defection of its leadership, ensured Jewish control of a far larger area of Palestine than had been envisaged in the various partition plans.'

Even so, forty thousand people, four-fifths of Haifa's Arab population, fled their homes. Dorothy Blanche Morgan wrote that: 'When the battle was over on the morning of 22nd April, refugees poured out of the Arab area and we had crowds from the Wady Hisnas on this compound . . . for the first few days we had over 400 people (Arabs and Armenians) . . . many have now left (mostly to Lebanon).' Only about 4,000, nearly all Christians, remained. Their departure was followed by 'disgraceful looting' by Hagana, which Stockwell's troops had to stop. Stockwell, interviewed later, wrote thus of the panic:

[The Arabs] were left disorganised, with no particular direction, whereas the Jews were highly organised, knew exactly what they wanted to do, and they had the organisation to do it, so when they were left face to face, then it was clap hands for Daddy, and . . . the Jews went at it like a ton of bricks . . .

I used to go down to the Suq which is the main Arab quarter in Haifa, and I used to go round the cafes and talk to them, and they were very worried. They all said that they would cut the throats of the Jews if they came anywhere near them but of course it was the last thing they were able to do . . .

When people panic it grows like a bush fire, I don't know why. They see some people pushing off, packing their kit, and they think they had better go too. Mind you it wasn't absolutely sudden . . . the fear of the Jews had been building up for a considerable amount of time, and they realised the strength of the Jews and they were worried of course that the Jews would overrun the houses, and burn them and kill their children and wives and destroy their houses . . .

Stockwell's men were left to try to curb looting, look after the wounded, and protect fleeing refugees. Stockwell, having handed over a bottle of malt whisky to the winners of one of history's most extraordinary wagers, gave orders that the exits from the city were to be firmly held, and the Jews prevented from exploiting their success by advancing beyond the city. He supplemented the redeployment orders with North Sector Operational Instruction No. 1, on 27 April, in which he laid down his intentions for the forthcoming handover period now that Haifa was under Jewish control:

To ensure the security of our forces in the Haifa enclave.
To dominate the town of Haifa.
To sit astride all routes leading into Haifa, so as to be able to deny the use of these routes, if necessary, to the Jews.
To keep open the road communications to Ramat David airfield and Nazareth.
To be prepared to ensure the security, from Jenin to Haifa, of all military convoys proceeding from Jerusalem to Haifa.

At the same time, he reported to MacMillan that he regretted in the circumstances being unable to maintain peace and order, and accepted full responsibility for all his actions. Rather disingenuously, to say the least, he also reported that the Jews were 'astonished at the speed and success of their operation'. His tactics had been extremely risky, and not at all in keeping with overt instructions to remain impartial. But with hindsight, there seems little else he could have done to prevent further loss of life, especially given the lack of any political will to do other than withdraw in reasonable order, and given what is now known about the collusion between King Abdullah and the Jews, which had fuelled the Jews' attacks in the first place. Marriott came in strongly on this point in Stockwell's support, writing in his despatch on the events that:

I feel that I have now been here long enough to express my opinion on what led to the Battle of Haifa – as the clash of 21st/22nd April has become known locally. When I wrote my despatch No 1, I already suspected that it was the complete break-down of the Civil Administration which had put the military authority in the position which I described.[12] I am now convinced that the Civil Administration has, for at least two months, been more interested in the liquidation of their own affairs and with the detail of winding up their own offices than with the maintenance of law and order, and in the circumstances, of close liaison with the Military Authority . . . It was therefore with indignation that I heard a British civilian, to whom I remarked that I had not yet discovered what the Civil Administration did or knew, criticise General Stockwell saying that it was felt that he had let the civil power down. The plaint was that he should have told the Arabs, when they adopted increasingly offensive tactics against the Jews in the first fortnight of April, that they must stop and that he would protect them from Jewish aggression. This should surely have been the province of the Civil Power who could have invoked Military aid if necessary.

Reading between the lines of this despatch, it may be that at some point, Stockwell took Marriott into his confidence. MacMillan, who must have been party to at least some of what had taken place, was in no doubt that Stockwell had done the right thing. In his final report he wrote of the battle in Haifa 'on its conclusion [British troops] were of immense assistance in getting the town running again and evacuating Arab refugees. All areas vital to our evacuation programme were safeguarded throughout the fighting.' In any case, wider events now took over. At the end of April, David Ben-Gurion proposed a ceasefire over the withdrawal period, to which Cunningham managed to get the Arab League and the ALA to agree on 6 May. The British therefore had a welcome breathing space before their departure.

Stockwell was by now very close to the end of his time in Palestine, and he would lose his command after only ten months as the 6th Airborne Division was to be disbanded. He had to be found another appointment and he was somewhat surprised – but also relieved – to receive a signal on 24 April, informing him that he was to take up the appointment of Commandant at the Royal Military Academy Sandhurst. He was required for this prestigious appointment on 20 May – only five days after the expiry of the Mandate in Palestine and less than one month ahead – but this was subsequently amended to 7 June. In the interim, Stockwell stuck with the planned move to Aldershot.

The British Mandate ended at midnight on 14 May 1948, and on 15th, Stockwell boarded an aircraft for Britain – with the odd sensation that his life was repeating the events surrounding his departure from Burma and the disbandment of the 82nd (West African) Division in 1946. At the same time, most of the remaining divisional troops embarked on the troopship *Empress of Australia* and sailed for home, although one unit, 1st Airborne Squadron Royal Engineers, remained until the departure of the last British soldiers on 30 June, a month earlier than had been originally announced. According to *The Times* report of Stockwell's romance with Miriam, however, there was one final irony:

> According to legend, as the British forces evacuated, leaving Arabs and Jews to fight over Palestine, they deliberately left behind three tanks for the Zionist forces on the orders of General Hugh Stockwell . . .
> Aside from the immediate military ramifications of this unusual farewell present . . . the gesture was symbolic of the future course of relationships among Israel's ruling elite. The Jewish state's political and military leaders have since shown scant regard for the Old Testament's seventh commandment.

Again, however, there is no evidence that this is true. What is true is that the evacuation of Haifa was a reversal of the previous British policy of building up a base in Palestine, and that the huge task of evacuating military stores was not accomplished. £70,000 worth of ammunition was dumped in the sea, vehicles were sold to Jews and Arabs alike, ammunition dumps were raided by both sides, and around 100,000 tons of general stores were simply abandoned. If three British armoured vehicles did find their way into Jewish hands, it is far more likely to be the result of all this confusion, rather than an act of deliberate conspiracy by an officer who could, had he wished or been obliged to do so, have provided rather more than a miserable three vehicles.

For the British, Palestine was a salutary lesson. The Army had been pushed into a campaign ill prepared for an insurgency, and military successes during 1947 – such as Operation Agatha in Tel Aviv – had failed to translate into wider success when it became clear that the government had neither the will nor the authority to continue governing Palestine. Maurice Tugwell summed things up thus when interviewed by David Charteris: 'The Jews had the highest quality of terrorists that the British Army faced in the post-war period, so the Army probably set its standards by them, and it did them good . . . what was learned was applied much better elsewhere.'

Hughie Stockwell came out of the Palestine campaign with his reputation further enhanced, and his tally of honours increased. He was mentioned in despatches for the period 27 March 1947 to 26 September 1947. In addition, and most unusually for a Major General, he was knighted for his actions in the period 27 March 1948 to 30 June 1948. Knighthoods are usually reserved for officers in the rank of Lieutenant General, and it is therefore a measure of the importance of his work in Haifa that he received this remarkable distinction. At Buckingham Palace on the auspicious date of Tuesday, 1 March 1949, he was invested by King George VI as a Knight of the British Empire. His private feelings were not particularly exalted, for the whole campaign had left a nasty taste. Polly remembers that he said that it was the worst campaign in which he ever served; in all the others there was only one enemy, whereas in this there were two. He also remarked that the worst mistake he ever made in his military career was not to hang Menachim Begin when he had the chance to do so – although when this was is not clear – but had not done so because, unlike Begin and his associates, 'I do not murder men in cold blood.'

Notes

1 Moshe Shertok was the leader of the Jewish Agency's political department and had been a leading Zionist for years. Born in 1894 he was educated in Istanbul and fought in the Turkish Army in the First World War. He carried out numerous Zionist missions during the inter-war years, and during the Second World War was active in recruiting Jews into the Allied forces. See Peretz, Cornfield, *Palestine Personalia* (Tel Aviv, 1947).

2 Hagana was formed in the 1920s during anti-Jewish riots. It was organized and equipped on conventional lines, although part-time, and many of its members had served in the Allied armies. Within Hagana there was a small professional elite formation known as Palmach, organized into small commandos.

3 Colonel William Nichol Gray CMG DSO KPM FRICS late Royal Marines (1908–1988). Inspector General in Palestine 1946–1948, where he did much to improve the morale, efficiency and equipment of the force. Police Commissioner in Malaya 1948–1952. *Who Was Who*, Vol VIII.

4 Later General Sir John Winthrop Hackett GCB CBE DSO■ MC DL BLitt MA (1910–1998) had commanded a cavalry squadron in Palestine in 1938. He was Commander 4 Para Brigade at Arnhem. He was CO 8th (Midland Counties) Parachute Battalion until he went on LILOP, and thereafter was appointed as Commander Transjordan Frontier Force. Later GOC 7th Armoured Division 1956–1958, DCIGS 1963–1964, C-in-C BAOR 1966 and Principal of King's College London 1968–1975. *Who's Who*, 1997.

5 Recent figures suggest that 40,000 Jews entered Palestine between 1945 and 1948, while another 51,000 in thirty-five ships were intercepted and interned. See Naomi Shepherd, *Ploughing Sand: British Rule in Palestine* (London, 1999), p. 222.

6 Later Major General Peter Boucher Cavendish CB CBE, born 1925, commissioned 1945 into the 3rd Hussars, subsequently 14th/20th Hussars. He became Stockwell's ADC on 3 January 1948, having been commanding a squadron in Haifa. He retired in 1981 (*Army List*).

7 Later General Sir Anthony Farrar-Hockley GBE KCB DSO MC BLitt. He had served throughout the Second World War in the 6th (Royal Welch) Parachute Battalion, before returning to the Glosters. He was captured in Korea, later commanded the 4th Armoured Division and NATO's AFNORTH. He also maintained a highly successful career in writing and broadcasting. See his entry in *Who's Who, 2003*, for full details.

8 The Jewish Labour Movement in Palestine. Actually much more than a trade union, it was the sponsor of the Kibbutz movement and its objectives,

synonymous with Zionism, were those of the creation of an independent, secular, Jewish state. Its leader was David Ben-Gurion, and it became the basis of the Israeli Labour Party.

9   When moving around the city, Stockwell, a staff officer and the ADC travelled in a staff car driven by Cpl Powell, or Driver Hill, with two outriders on motor-cycles, an escort jeep back and front, a radio jeep, and an armoured car; there is plenty of photographic evidence of this in Cavendish's collection and the Stockwell family albums.

10   Woolfe-Rebuck attempted to ingratiate himself by claiming to be English, and to have been educated at Winchester. Peter Cavendish, who was a Wykehamist, questioned him closely and was highly suspicious; he then checked with the college, which had no record of him at all. Clearly he was an imposter. Interview with Major General Peter Cavendish, 26 June 2003.

11   Miss Emery was, apart from his own units, one of the few people that Stockwell would go and visit – usually people were summoned to see him. Another exception was Brigadier Hector MacNeil, a retired officer who ran a pig farm north of Haifa, and whose business would clearly fold when the British left!

12   It is a fact that as early as January 1948, a deal had been struck with the Jews whereby British Civil Administrators were withdrawn to cordoned-off areas in Jerusalem and Haifa, where they could be protected by the military, leaving the Jews a free hand elsewhere. On 31 January, the Government of Palestine had broadcast its intention to implement Operation Polly – the evacuation of all non-essential civilians, and Operation Cantonment, the move into secure areas. Stockwell was required to provide military accommodation and administration for 500 of these people.

Chapter Fourteen

The Commandant, 1948–1950

There is a story of two Sandhurst cadets who, having had a better-than-average run ashore in London on a Friday night, had managed to miss the last train back to Camberley. The milk train would get them in too late for breakfast roll call, and they decided to try hitch-hiking down the A30. After a time, a large and splendid Lagonda motor had pulled up. In the front was a driver, and in the back, an alert-looking, smartly dressed, middle-aged gentleman with fair hair turning to grey, and a neatly trimmed moustache. Even sitting down, it was obvious that he kept himself very fit and he looked as if the clothes he had had at nineteen would still fit him. The two accepted the invitation to 'hop in', and it was quickly established that the car was going right past the Sandhurst main entrance. After a pleasant drive and a friendly chat, the two were quite at their ease. As they approached their destination, however, they realized that they were very, very late, and that entering by conventional means would result in a difficult time with their company commander next morning, and that a burglarious entry would have to be effected. 'Don't worry,' said their host, 'I'll drop you off, and all you'll have to do then is get back to your rooms somehow.' The two, deeply grateful, did just that.

Next morning, being Saturday, was the Adjutant's drill parade. All three Colleges were formed up on Old Building square, and who should turn up to inspect the parade but the Commandant himself. As he passed by the first of the two miscreants of the previous night (for it had been he in the car) he paused, winked, and whispered 'Glad you made it!' It was an episode that, although typical, passed rapidly into legend.

Stockwell had received a letter from the Deputy Military Secretary in Headquarters Middle East on 26 April telling him that he would be required to take up the appointment of Commandant at Sandhurst 'immediately on arrival in the UK'. In the event, he negotiated a takeover date of 7 June, and an arrival date of 25 June, giving him time to move the family to Camberley before assuming command. He took over from Major General F.R.G. Matthews, a former GOC 53rd (Welsh) Division, who had been appointed

GOC Land Forces Hong Kong. Until 31 July, Stockwell was also still GOC 6th Airborne Division, concerned with the run-down of the division, and the career management of the officers and NCOs. Indeed according to Peter Cavendish, this aspect took up much of his time until the end of 1949.

Stockwell and his family took up residence in the splendour of Government House, the neo-classical pile hidden in the trees on the far side of the barrack square from the Old Buildings. Matthews had had the task of establishing a new Sandhurst. The RMC had ceased to function in 1939, and during the Second World War Sandhurst had operated as an Officer Cadet Training Unit (OCTU) for the Royal Armoured Corps. It never re-opened. Instead, a new establishment was formed: the Royal Military Academy Sandhurst. The new Sandhurst took the place of both the RMC and 'the Shop' – the former RMA Woolwich. For the first time, the training of all regular officer cadets would be in one establishment (National Service and Short Service Commissioned officers were trained at Mons Officer Cadet School in Aldershot). Instead of gentleman cadets there were now officer cadets, enlisted into the Army, and no longer paying fees, but drawing pay. Sandhurst was to produce a different type of officer for a modern Army.

The training regime for the eighteen-month course at Sandhurst centred on the function of an officer to command and lead his men both in barracks and in battle. It also included military subjects, in order to equip the officer with the same skills as his NCOs and men, and technical and liberal studies to complete his education. Its aim was 'to produce a young officer with a sound education in appropriate military and academic subjects, with a wide interest in the current problems of world affairs, and the enthusiasm to continue to increase his knowledge by his own initiative'. Although the best of the two pre-war predecessors was to be preserved, there was to be no return to the standards of those times; as Stockwell himself remarked, 'the trouble with some of the pre-war standards was that they were rotten.' From the beginning, however, sports and games were important, and included rugby, soccer, cricket, rowing and cross-country running. Clubs were also formed to pursue climbing, sailing, flying, motoring, music, parachuting, fly-fishing, rifle shooting, the beagles and the drag hunt. Stockwell himself obviously relished the opportunity to return to his old pastimes: his appointments diary records him attending committee meetings of the drag hunt and the beagles – as well as inquiring about grazing for ponies, and taking a close interest in the piggeries! He also had decided ideas on the style of the place. Peter Cavendish recalled that:

> When Hughie took over from Matthews, we drove over from Aldershot at about 3 o'clock, had a chat, went to tea at Government House, and then went back to Aldershot. On the way back in the car, Hughie said 'Right, now we're in charge of Sandhurst. Boy (he always called me 'boy'), we've got to think how we make it spark. They're a dull lot at

the moment, and officers are supposed to have drive, initiative, and get-up-and-go!

He was right, it was dull – but it had been brilliantly organized. Stockwell's headquarters was housed in one wing of the Old Buildings, and a full staff supported him. A chief instructor and an adjutant assisted each college commander, while a major commanded each company, with four or five other officers and the same number of NCOs. One thing which was held in common with the old RMC was the quality of these officers and NCOs: none but the best were accepted, and in the aftermath of the War, most had combat experience. Ian Moody, who was Stockwell's godson, and a cadet at this time destined (like his father) for the Royal Welch Fusiliers, remembered some of them:

> Lord Cathcart, the Academy Adjutant was, as was to be expected, always immaculately turned out but was not as fearsome as he superficially appeared. He worked very well with cadets, JUOs and SUOs, involving them appropriately in disciplinary and other matters. RSM Brand I remember for his girth, voice, and way of marching. RSM Lord was initially RSM of New College, before taking over from Brand as Academy RSM. He was a great character, always upright and scrupulously fair. Whilst preparing us for passing off the square, he constantly reminded us that Winston Churchill had failed to pass off twice, and we were likely to follow that way: no wonder – what a terrifying experience it was to have an individual drill test in front of the Adjutant. I was in Ypres Company, and my Company Sergeant Major was [J.M.] Rioch, the Army hammer and shot champion. He could lift a 350cc motorbike over the tailboard of a three-ton lorry without assistance.

Stockwell had arrived just before the end of the summer term, and it was he, therefore, rather than Matthews, who was present at the first passing-out parade on 14 July 1948. At this parade, at which the first 278 cadets who had entered the Academy in 1947 were commissioned, the King himself took the salute. The King had arrived in good time and gone to Government House to make his final preparations, where he was looked after by the Stockwell family. Stockwell then left ahead of the King, and was at Queen Victoria's statue with the Lord Lieutenant of Berkshire, and Emanuel Shinwell who was then Secretary of State for War, when the King drove up at exactly 11.37 am. There were to be formal introductions there, which Shinwell insisted on making in Stockwell's stead. Peter Cavendish was on hand:

> Shinwell made the formal introductions, and when they got to Hughie he said 'and may I introduce General Stockwell, Your Majesty?' The King replied 'Oh yes, that's all right, we've met already.' Shinwell was very miffed, but Mrs Shinwell laughed like a drain.

Ian Moody, who was on parade as a cadet, remembered:

> As Hughie and the King came up King's Walk towards the square, the
> heavens opened and it began to pour with rain. In no time at all we were
> soaked. We were wearing battledress – the Academy had not yet gone
> into blues – and the white Blanco on our belts, rifle slings, and even our
> gorget patches began to run into our uniforms. There was a canopy set
> up, from which the King could take the salute and watch the parade; but
> instead of standing under it, he took two paces forward and stood like
> us in the rain. That moment lifted everything, and he got the most
> tremendous parade.

After the parade it was back to Government House, and then to New Building
for lunch, which had been rehearsed to death and closely timed. When
pudding came, it was seen to be tinned fruit salad and the King said that he
would not have his, but while everyone else was eating he *would* have another
glass of whisky. Stockwell and the others bent to their pudding only to find
that the cherries, which were supposed to have been stoned, had not been, and
had therefore to be swallowed! The 'boy' was duly chastised later.

While he was drinking his whisky the King asked what the parade was
called, and was told it was simply called the Passing-Out Parade. 'Why not
call it the King's Parade?' said His Majesty, 'and call the Champion Company
the King's Company.' Charles Earle, the Adjutant, and a Grenadier, was
sitting within earshot, and was silently mortified – for there is of course only
one King's Company in the Army. But he had a bright idea, and at an oppor-
tune moment whispered to Stockwell that perhaps it might be 'Sovereign's'
instead of 'King's'. Some discussion followed, and it was agreed that the
Commandant would signal Buckingham Palace with the suggestion, and offer
a draft reply. Shinwell again tried to intervene, but was told by the King,
'Don't worry, I've arranged it all with the Commandant!' So it was. Charles
Earle drafted the signals, and the following day, Stockwell received a formal
message from the King, congratulating everyone on the standard of the parade
and saying:

> Now that the officer cadets for all branches of the Army are united in
> one establishment, I wish that this parade should in future be known as
> 'The Sovereign's Parade' and that the Champion Company should
> become 'The Sovereign's Company'.

The first Summer Ball, a magnificent affair attended by over 3,000 people,
followed that first passing-out parade. This Ball was to replace the old RMC
June Ball – but the numbers were huge and space was limited. Two extra dance
floors had to be put down, one in a marquee over the tennis courts, and one
outside lit by coloured lanterns. Sitting-out tables were in the gym, in tents, in
the squash courts – indeed anywhere they could be fitted. There was music by

the pipes and drums of the Scots Guards, by the RMAS Dance Band and Rumba Band, by Tommy Kinsman and by Edmundo Ross. It was a wild affair, which went on beyond the programmed end at 4.00 am, not least because young people in post-war Britain were not used to alcohol in any quantity and, with little available, everyone had brought a bottle or two. The result was a great deal of mixing of drinks, with predictable results. Ian Moody recalled that

> there was a great deal of drunkenness and bad behaviour . . . Large numbers of cadets were placed under close arrest, and first parade next day was an absolute shambles. Hughie was livid and at the beginning of the next term addressed the Academy. I remember one notable passage: 'If you want a woman, go elsewhere, and do not behave so disgracefully as some did at the end of last term.' Things were better controlled after that.

Now that he was back in Britain, Stockwell found himself engaged in Regimental affairs for the first time in years. He was not Colonel of the Regiment – that post was held by his old mentor Eric Skaife, who had assumed the Colonelcy on 10 February 1948 – but with the retirement of Lieutenant General Sir William Holmes, he found himself the senior serving officer of the Royal Welch Fusiliers. His first regimental engagement was a sad one. With the evacuation of India complete, the British infantry had been halved in size. The reduction had been achieved by disbanding the Second Battalions of all line regiments and this meant farewell to Stockwell's old battalion, 2 RWF. When the news of disbandment came, the battalion was serving in Malaya, where it had been reduced to a small cadre of six officers and twenty-three men. This draft had been brought home in March and stationed at the depot in Wrexham. At the end of June, Skaife received a letter from the King's Private Secretary saying that the King, who was Colonel-in-Chief, wished to receive a representative detachment from the 2nd Battalion at Buckingham Palace to mark its disbandment. The party met at Wellington Barracks on the morning of 15 July and shortly after noon moved to the Palace. Here Brigadier Skaife, General Sir Charles Dobell, Gwydyr, Jimmy Rice-Evans and Stockwell were all received in the banqueting room, after which the King went out onto the terrace where he met and talked to the whole party both formally and in-formally, and a group photograph was taken. The proceedings concluded at 12.55 pm and the whole party went to lunch together at the Criterion Restaurant in Piccadilly. The next day, the Second Battalion passed into history.

Over time Stockwell's style, and his enormous personal presence provided, as he had intended, the injection of example and leadership for the cadets; and just as importantly, for the officers and men on the staff. He showed few signs, however, of becoming a grown-up and took to riding around the Academy

193

not on a horse, but on an airborne folding motorcycle which he had seen ('Boy, get me one of those') – with a two-star plate on the front. The thing needed repairs about once each week, having been crashed by the Commandant, or one of the family. His habit of accelerating across the square while tooting his horn was his way of getting his own back for all those hours as a junior at the RMC on drill-sergeants' parades, and was more of the stuff of legend. It certainly endeared him to the cadets, while doing little for the blood pressure of the drill staff. David Russell, later his ADC in Malaya, remembered a different aspect:

> It was a hot day and I was on the parade ground in front of the Old Building standing amongst some 300 others and I was about to faint. He [HCS] looked at the parade from a distance and said 'there's a cadet in the centre rank who is about to fall over, someone should catch him.' And he walked on to his office. If that is not perception then I do not know what is and, for him, as I discovered later, when I became his ADC in Malaya, this was not unusual – very little missed his knowing eye.

Stockwell also did his best to keep up with old comrades-in-arms. He attended the annual reunions of Burma veterans and the Parachute Regimental dinner each year; and he was present at the Burma Campaign service of thanksgiving and remembrance on Thursday, 11 May 1950 in Westminster Abbey, at which all the nations which had contributed to the Allied victory were represented.

At the end of 1950, after what had been a welcome period of respite from operations, Stockwell was called back to active duty once again as a divisional commander, charged with re-raising the 3rd Infantry Division. His valedictory notice in *The Wish Stream* noted his popularity and achievements in settling the Academy so quickly into its new regime; and also that he was still the only Major General to have completed a full parachute-training course! It went on to pay tribute to Joan, although the editor had no need to, and clearly would not have done so had the tribute not been deserved:

> We should also like to take this opportunity of thanking Lady Stockwell for all she has done in RMAS life and for playing such a very important part in helping to weld all members of the staff and their families into one community.

Chapter Fifteen

Canal Zone: The 3rd Infantry Division, 1951–1952

The 3rd Infantry Division had been disbanded in Palestine in 1947, during Stockwell's tenure in command of 6th Airborne Division. Its disbandment was the result of the post-war reduction of forces and commitments in peacetime by a government faced with the huge economic pressures already referred to. However, by 1950, the threat from Soviet Communism was plain to see. Further afield, the Communist Malayan Races' Liberation Army had unleashed a murderous insurrection in 1948, and in June 1950 war broke out in Korea. By August 1950 British soldiers were engaged in two Far Eastern theatres and were on an operational footing in West Germany. Overall, with subsequent commitments in Kenya, West Africa, South Arabia, Eritrea and the Persian Gulf, the 1950s were to see the largest deployments of military forces in Britain's peacetime history. A Defence White Paper in 1950 there-fore set out the means of meeting future contingencies through the creation of a strategic reserve in the United Kingdom, consisting of a regular armoured division, infantry division, and parachute brigade. National Service was also restored to two years to provide the manpower.

Commanding four different divisions must be close to, if not actually, a record in British military history. Hughie Stockwell had already disbanded two divisions, and re-formed a third. He was therefore well aware of the task at hand. As with 44th Division, Stockwell would also be responsible for a district, in this case East Anglian District, the headquarters elements and troops of which were already in place and functioning.[1] The District covered the counties of Norfolk, Suffolk, Cambridgeshire, Huntingdonshire, Bedfordshire, Hertfordshire, and Essex. The 3rd Division began to re-form in early 1951 with Divisional Headquarters at Colchester along with 19 Infantry Brigade also at Colchester, 32 Guards Brigade in London District, and 39 Infantry Brigade at Dover, under Brigadier John Tweedie, who had commanded New College at Sandhurst during Stockwell's tenure as Commandant. Stockwell's immediate superior was the GOC-in-C Eastern

Command, Lieutenant General Sir Gerald Templer, whom Stockwell had last known as GSO 2 of 53rd (Welsh) Division, when he himself was Brigade Major of 158 (Royal Welch) Infantry Brigade. Both had come far since then, but the old rapport was still strong. Templer's biographer records that towards the end of 1950, Templer had suddenly announced his intention of visiting Sandhurst. 'What's he up to?' the Academy Adjutant had asked Tony Aylmer, Templer's ADC. 'He's got nothing to do with Sandhurst. It's not in Eastern Command. Is he going to do something with the Commandant?' Indeed he was; Hughie's legendary charm was unabated, and the two men clearly got along very well despite Templer's reputation as a difficult customer. Noel Annan, for example, described him as 'a ruthless, incisive, dynamic commander, biting or disarming as occasion demanded. His smile was ferocious: like a wolf.'

The re-formed 3rd Division was, like every other formation of the Army at the time, made up mainly of National Servicemen, whom the 3rd Division history summed up as:

> the ever cheerful, lowly paid, quick-witted youngsters to whom the country owes such a debt. While Britain endeavoured to administer and garrison worldwide commitments far beyond the scope of the pre-war regular army, these young men in battledress, jungle-green and khaki-drill defied the Chinese masses on the Imjin, defeated guerrillas in Malaya and Kenya, and dealt resolutely with mob violence and bombing in Middle Eastern town and village.

Stockwell assumed command on 1 January 1951, the date on which, on paper, the division became active. The Stockwells were given the old GOC's residence, Roman Hill House, just outside Colchester. Polly remembered this as 'a very pretty Regency villa with a nice garden and paddocks for our ponies'. Many of Hughie's memories from childhood, youth and early manhood were of Colchester – and his father had only retired from the post of Chief Constable four years before. Returning brought an odd mixture of sensations: comforting, because of old familiarity – the place had not changed greatly; and alarming for the same reason, as the majority of the Victorian barracks were still in a largely Victorian condition. Despite Montgomery's efforts over conditions of service when he was CIGS, money was short and the officers and men lived in pretty basic accommodation.

Stockwell was instructed to have his new division fully trained by the end of 1951, and he called a Divisional Discussion with his key staff and subordinates on 22 February 1951. His original notes are still preserved, and these set out his thoughts and priorities:

> I want to report the division 'fit for war' by the end of the present collective training season, and at all times to have it so organised that after a

very short period of concentrated effort it can take its place in the field. By that I mean –

Each part of the division must be fully capable of playing its own role and all the integral parts of the division so knitted together that they can function in battle as one unit.

To prepare 'steady order' for the division and so exercise the whole in various battle drills, that they become automatic and by an intensive short period of training the various techniques can be applied.

It must be realised that the division is the fighting unit of the British Army.

Stockwell then goes on to stress his priorities for physical fitness and basic military skills, before turning to collective training and battle drills:

Every unit and sub-unit must be trained to move across country by night, reach a pre-arranged objective, and be able to locate themselves at any time. Road moves must be practised . . . my aim is to be able to move the division by night over a considerable distance and be deployed before dawn. Such movement will be constantly practised.

Not surprisingly, therefore, the whole year was spent in arduous field training. Sir Anthony Tritton, Stockwell's ADC, remembered that this put a good deal of pressure on the divisional staff, and there were several GSO1s before Stockwell settled on Lieutenant Colonel John Willoughby. An intuitive commander like Stockwell, who moreover operated on the Montgomery model – spending as little time in his headquarters as possible – needed a staff that was rock-solid. Under Willoughby, the staff was working efficiently by the time that major divisional exercises were tackled. Of course, with a superior like Templer, nothing could be left to chance, no matter how well he and Stockwell got on personally. Templer spent much of his time with Stockwell, and in visiting the units. Templer would not tolerate anything approaching slackness – any officer who got things badly wrong was unlikely to receive a second chance if Templer was on hand to see it. Not even a car accident during one of the divisional exercises at Stanford in May 1951 put Templer off; Stockwell heard of the accident and dropped in to the hospital at Baldock where he found his chief with a fractured leg and two broken ribs. Even while the bones were being set, Templer would think and talk of nothing but the conduct of the exercise.

Templer was soon back at work, and visiting hard. Another frequent visitor was Montgomery, who had commanded 3rd Division in 1940 and despite being Deputy SACEUR in Paris, he could not leave his old command alone. He and Templer would often share a car journey back to London, and confer on Stockwell's progress. Stockwell recalled a sequence of events, which clearly resulted from one of these car journeys. In January 1951:

We had hardly formed up when Monty rang me from Paris and briefly what he said was, 'Ah – I am very glad to hear you have got command of the 3rd Division; now when I commanded it, it was a very good Division! I should like to meet all the Commanding officers.' I replied, 'What about a date in early April?' 'What!' he said, 'Next week, please.' At that time, the battalions were scattered all over the UK. Anyhow, he came and we had a dinner in the 19 Brigade mess and he addressed all the COs for fifty minutes! He also said he wanted to see me in his room. 'What do you think is the most difficult manoeuvre a division can do?' 'I don't know', I replied. 'Well, I'll tell you' he said. 'Move the division fifty miles by night and be dug in at dawn ready to receive the enemy.' This advice was reflected at a divisional conference held on 22 February, and as a result we took part in Exercise Hammer and Tongs, set by Gerald Templer as a divisional test exercise.

There was in fact quite a long delay between the divisional conference and the exercise:

The basis was an advance to Stanford to meet the enemy, but by September we had got to know every lane and road in East Anglia, so we had practically only to clap our hands and the boys were off. To cut a long story short, by dawn I was in a slit trench at Divisional Tactical HQ near Stanford when Gerald Templer turned up. 'What the hell do you think you are doing?' he asked. I said, 'What's wrong?' He replied, 'You are here and dug in before the bloody enemy has been positioned!' I reckon that was the best test of our nine months' training.

The division went on to take part in Exercise Surprise Packet which began on 1 October at Stanford, from where the division moved south to carry out an assault river crossing of the Thames near Pangbourne, with the newly re-formed 6th Armoured Division, then preparing for service in Germany. An exercise in Britain on this scale, employing four infantry brigades and three armoured regiments, had never been held in peacetime before; arguably, it has never been seen since.

But even before the end of the year the strategic reserve was to be required, for trouble was brewing in Egypt, a country which would occupy much of Stockwell's attention for the next few years. Under the Anglo-Egyptian Treaty of 1936, the British garrison was supposed to withdraw to the Suez Canal Zone, with the task of 'ensuring in cooperation with the Egyptian forces the defence of the Canal'. Egypt was to provide the new barracks, but had not done so, and there was a great unwillingness to leave the great centre of command and control for the bleak wasteland of the Canal Zone. The Canal Zone covered an area 90 miles long from north to south and 60 miles east to west, with the canal as its eastern boundary. It contained dozens of camps, supply depots, RAF stations and other installations, the biggest of which was

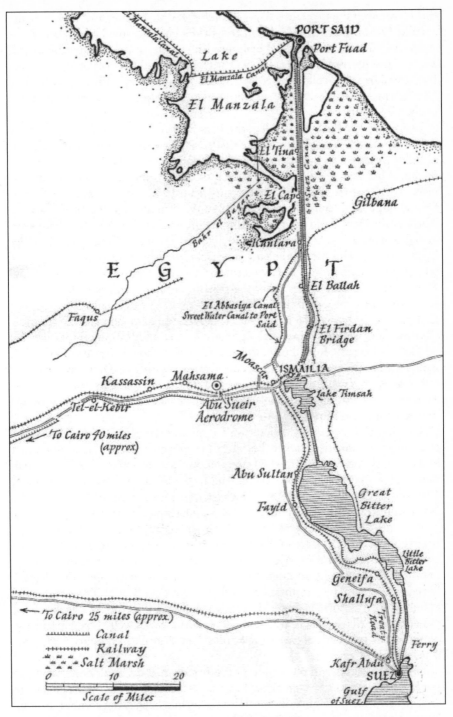

THE SUEZ CANAL ZONE

Source: Kennet Love, *Suez – The Twice-Fought War* (London, 1969).

the 15 square mile ordnance depot at Tel-el-Kebir. During and just after the Second World War, when it was the world's largest armed camp, the Zone supported fifteen infantry and armoured divisions, sixty-five air squadrons, and the Mediterranean fleet. In 1951 it employed 80,000 Egyptian civilians. By the end of 1946, following considerable civil unrest in Cairo, GHQ Middle East had moved to a camp site, primitive in its condition, on the western shores of the Great Bitter Lake.

In August 1951, Dr Mossadeq, the President of Iran, seized control of the Anglo-Iranian Oil Company and expelled all British employees. No British military riposte was forthcoming and, encouraged by this, Mustapha Nahas Pasha, who was now Prime Minister of Egypt following the murder of Nokrashy, tabled decrees abrogating the 1936 treaty and the Sudan Condominium agreement of 1899. They were made law on 15 October – Abrogation Day – and serious rioting again followed in Ismailia and other Canal towns; Ismailia and Port Said had to be cleared and garrisoned by British troops. This meant the end of normal life for service families, many of which were sent home. But General Sir George ('Bobby') Erskine, GOC Troops Egypt, made it clear that the British had no intention of leaving and requested reinforcements. Foreign Secretary Anthony Eden supported Erskine. On 2 October 16 Para Brigade moved to Fayid, and HQ 1st Infantry Division flew in from Tripoli during the first week of November, followed by 32 Guards Brigade. In addition, the government decided to mount Operation Roller further to reinforce the Mediterranean with 3rd Division. Exercise Surprise Packet was still in progress, and it was not until its conclusion, at Templer's request, that the C-in-C Middle East asked Stockwell how soon his division could get moving.

The first to move under Operation Roller was 19 Brigade. Within a week of completing Surprise Packet they were landing from RAF Hastings aircraft in Tripoli. Altogether it was the fastest build-up ever achieved by the British Army up to that point, in peacetime, and it involved the move of 6,000 men, 170 tons of equipment and 330 vehicles by air in ten days. In November the Navy shipped out the remainder of the 3rd Division to Cyprus.

With his division complete in the Mediterranean, Stockwell was ordered to prepare for Operation Rodeo Flail – a contingency plan for an amphibious landing at Alexandria, with the aim of rescuing British nationals. This would be carried out in conjunction with Operation Rodeo Bernard, a thrust by 1st Infantry Division from the Canal Zone to Cairo. Planning for the former reached an advanced stage, including beach reconnaissance by the Royal Marines at Alexandria. Stockwell took part in the planning for this with Naval Task Force 56 at Tobruk in January 1952, but it was never effected.

On 17 November 1951 a new phase began in the Canal Zone with the appearance of *Bulak Nizam*, or the Egyptian Auxiliary Police. These men were well armed and, although not especially brave, had been given combat training before being sent against the British. They mounted several attacks in Ismailia and Suez, inflicting some casualties but taking many more themselves. The contest reached a head with a protracted battle in Ismailia in January 1952 between 3 Infantry Brigade and *Bulak Nizam* in which forty Egyptians died and another sixty-five were wounded. The reaction to these casualties came on 26 November – Black Saturday – when serious rioting, orchestrated by underworld mobs with the connivance of the Egyptian government and directed at British lives and property, broke out in Cairo. Fortunately King Farouk ordered the Egyptian Army to clear the streets and calm the situation. This it did in short order. Eden, as a result, was later of the firm opinion that the Egyptian authorities had been prompted to act only by the belief that 'we had the forces and the conviction that we were prepared to use them.' But tension in Egypt eased immediately and both Rodeo Operations were suspended.

Nevertheless there remained a massive security threat in the Canal Zone. After the evacuation of Palestine, the Canal Zone had been divided into two brigade sectors. In February 1952, following the events of Black Saturday, Stockwell with his headquarters, 32 and 39 Infantry Brigades moved in from Cyprus to assume responsibility for the northern sector of the Zone, known as Canal North, which comprised the area from Port Said to Ismailia, and included both towns. 19 Brigade moved from Libya to Cyprus, and 3 Commando Brigade Royal Marines was temporarily taken under command but was later replaced by 16 Parachute Brigade.

Stockwell deployed the division with 32 Guards Brigade at El Ballah and Port Said, 39 Brigade at Tel-el-Kebir, and 16 Parachute Brigade at Ismailia. The task was to secure the numerous military installations, depots and barracks of the sprawling Middle Eastern base against organized theft and sabotage by professional Egyptian gangs that were reputedly advised and trained by German experts. These duties consumed a vast amount of manpower. *The Border Magazine*, for example, described the duties at Tel-el-Kebir thus:

> The manning of TEK Garrison with its sixteen searchlights and gates took 100 NCOs and men in 48-hour shifts at one time, and virtually all training ceased. In addition a body of sixteen men in eight pairs lay in ambush at night against light-fingered but broad-shouldered gentry crawling under the wire. Many a round has been fired and hit its human mark, whom we are assured are paid £1 a night to steal by the arch spiv thieves.

The easing of tension brought some slight improvement to domestic conditions, but the Egyptians remained unco-operative and few domestic servants returned. Conditions in most military camps were primitive since most had few permanent installations or facilities for off-duty hours – and outside, there was nothing but sand:

The patience and good temper of the British soldier is legendary, but conditions in the Canal Zone during the division's 2¾-year tour stretched these qualities to the limit. Guards and duties took up 80% of a unit's time, and when off duty the soldiers' home was an EPIP (Egyptian Pattern, Indian Produced) tent pitched on a hot, dusty patch of desert. If he was lucky his cookhouse and NAAFI canteen were in temporary corrugated iron buildings, redolent of DDT fly spray and dominated in the summer by the creak of antiquated electric *Punka* fans that stirred the stuffy, overheated atmosphere. His meals, cooked on spluttering oil-burning stoves, would have made today's diploma-bearing . . . cook shudder.

Despite occupation duties, the division still had to be kept ready for war. On 26 March 1952, Stockwell called the divisional staff and his brigade commanders in to give them his views on where the division stood:

Sweat saves blood, but brains save sweat and blood. I want to feel that we all study our profession and try to absorb the military art into our system. We have had nearly a year here now in which we have put in some very excellent training and during which I consider you have all given of your best. I feel that we have certainly made many strides and learnt a lot, but we still make many stupid mistakes and I think this is because we are not thinking quite hard enough or we are not quite sure of what we are after.

Stockwell handed over his command on 2 May 1952 and left for home just as his old divisional commander from Burma days, Frankie Festing, arrived as GOC Troops Egypt. Much as he would have wanted to renew the old partnership, he was required by another former superior, Sir Gerald Templer, for an operational appointment in Malaya.

The Occupation of the Canal Zone ended finally with a new Anglo-Egyptian Agreement signed by Gamal Abdul Nasser, who had deposed King Farouk in July 1952, and British Foreign Secretary Anthony Nutting in 1954. The words of Lieutenant Colonel Robert Senior to his battalion, the 1st Bedfordshire and Hertfordshire, summarize the life and achievements of 3rd Division during the years in Egypt:

There is no excitement to look back on, of battle in Korea, or jungle fighting in Malaya or Kenya, but rather of arduous and monotonous duties in sand, flies and heat, with living conditions and amenities much to be desired. Such tasks called for greater fortitude, high morale and strong discipline; these you displayed and maintained in the highest degree throughout.

No wonder that nearly fifty years on, there was an active campaign to secure the award of the General Service Medal for service in the Canal Zone, which at last ended in success in the summer of 2003.

Notes
1 The Division was freed from district responsibilities in May 1951.

Chapter Sixteen

Malaya, 1952–1954

7th January 1952

Dear Prime Minister

I send you this note by Gerald Templer. Robertson having declined to face the problem of Malaya, Templer is now easily the best man for the job. He is a very great personal friend of mine.

I have had a long talk with him. He is quite clear as to what is wanted; all he needs now is good men, really good men, who can be relied on to get on with the job under his direction.

If you will see he gets the men he wants, he will deliver the goods; of that I am sure.

Yours ever
Monty[1]

The campaign in Malaya is usually held up as a textbook example of counter-insurgency – in contrast to Palestine. This success is presented as having been built on two things: British expertise in imperial policing; and the development of the concepts and techniques of limited war. As a result, Malaya became a touchstone for British expertise in counter-insurgency, particularly after the publication of Sir Robert Thompson's best-selling book *Defeating Communist Insurgency* in 1966, six years after the Malayan Emergency had officially ended, and ten years after it was dead in all but name.

At the close of the Second World War, the States of Malaya consisted of three British possessions: the Straits Settlements, Penang and Malacca; and nine princely states under British protection. The development of rubber and tin had made it perhaps the richest possession in the Empire and had encouraged a high level of immigration from India and China. Its population of five million was divided between two-and-a-half million Malays, two million Chinese, half a million Indians – mostly Tamils - and around 1,200 Europeans.

The Japanese conquest in 1942 had hit Malaya hard, and particularly affected the Chinese. Their country had been at war with Japan for years, and fear of the invaders drove many out of the towns and cities, and into the bush, where they became squatters. On the jungle fringes they established shacks and grew vegetables – but they had no legal right to the land they farmed. The Japanese invasion brought the Malayan Communist Party (MCP) and its military wing, the Malayan Peoples' Anti-Japanese Army (MPAJA), to prominence as the main agent of resistance. By the end of the War, the MCP could boast 37,000 members, while the MPAJA was 10,000 strong and well armed. Not surprisingly, it was also almost exclusively Chinese. By contrast, the Malay police had unwillingly collaborated with the Japanese, and this provided a source of tension. The returning British received a generally warm reception, partly because the British were regarded as a stabilizing influence on the mixed population; partly because of the brutality of the Japanese occupation; and partly because the British stated their intention of granting independence as soon as possible after an initial period of stabilization. In December 1945 the MPAJA was disbanded. Although 6,000 of its soldiers handed in their weapons, the remaining 4,000 did not, and most MPAJA units went underground – and waited. The liberation was followed by the imposition of a Malayan Union – a hugely unpopular creation – and unrest soon followed. There was near famine, strikes and demonstrations by trades unions grew, and although the colony was not at this point affected by Communist insurgency, a general strike was called on 15 February 1946. Intelligence sources warned repeatedly that direct action was close.

On 1 February 1948 the Federation of Malaya was created, to take the place of the Malayan Union. This consisted of all the Malay states, but Singapore remained separate. At the same time the MCP, inspired by the triumph of Mao-Tse-Tung, and led by a 26-year-old Chinese, Chin Peng, who was an experienced guerrilla who had fought the Japanese and been awarded the OBE by the British, launched its campaign. Its volunteers were organized into ten regiments each of 1,000 men. These regiments formed the Malayan Races Liberation Army (MRLA), which for the first stage of the war was to operate as independent platoons from the jungles which covered four-fifths of Malaya.

Malaya was well suited to guerrilla warfare. The peninsula was 700 miles long and 200 miles wide at its widest point. A mountain range ran down the peninsula in a great arc from the Thai border to the east coast. The climate was tropical with heavy rainfall and high humidity to add to the severe terrain. The MRLA – or CTs (Communist terrorists) as they became known – operated from the jungle, while the Min Yuen, plain clothes workers who supplied the fighters with food, clothing, men, weapons, ammunition and information, operated among the population. The third leg of the organization was the Lie Ton, or assassination squads.

*   *   *

205

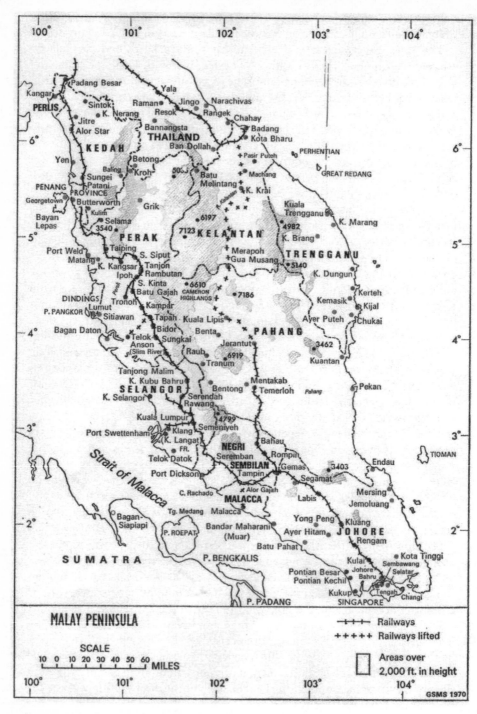

Source: *Philip's University Atlas* (London, 1973).

206

In October 1948, Sir Henry Gurney, who had been Chief Secretary in Palestine at the time when Stockwell had commanded 6th Airborne Division, was sworn in as High Commissioner following the death in an air crash of his predecessor, Sir Edward Gent. Gurney immediately realized the political nature of the war, and therefore that the path to independence must be followed. He also laid down that terrorism was a criminal, not a political act and that therefore the police should lead with the military in support where police capabilities were inadequate. He followed this up by taking additional powers to register squatters and issue identity cards, and to deport detainees who were not British citizens. Gurney's were the first steps towards the co-ordination of operations which until then had been lacking, particularly in intelligence.

In April 1950 Lieutenant General Sir Harold Briggs was recalled from retirement and appointed Director of Operations, in order – in theory – to co-ordinate every aspect of the campaign. Briggs had an immediate impact and within two weeks he had proposed to Gurney the plan that became the basic blueprint for success in Malaya. This plan, which showed that the lessons of Palestine had indeed been heeded – and quickly – began a new policy of moving scattered squatter settlements and establishing protected villages. Briggs also established an integrated committee structure from the State War Council down to districts, to bring together the efforts of the military, police and civil authorities in fighting the Communists. Joint military-police operations rooms were established in every district, and the civil administration was strengthened. The co-ordination of intelligence gathering, collation, analysis and dissemination was a high priority, since many police records had been destroyed during the Japanese occupation, and the database had to be rebuilt from scratch. Co-ordination of intelligence had never been strong in Palestine, and Nicol Gray, who had been Inspector General in Palestine during Stockwell's tour of duty there, had in particular been accused of failing to use Special Branch properly. Therefore, the roles and functions of the police and military were strictly defined: the police would have primacy in fulfilling their normal functions in the towns and villages, with the military providing a framework across the country to help the police where they could not cope, provide a striking force and dominate the jungle areas around settlements.

In June 1951, Briggs began a strict policy of controlling food. This was a key aspect of the campaign, aimed at making the insurgents spend more time on keeping themselves alive than on carrying out operations. Before this could take hold, however, the insurgents increased terrorist activity and on 7 October 1951 they killed Gurney in an ambush. Briggs retired soon after, worn out and ill. He was dead within the year.

After the General Election of 1951, which had brought the Conservatives to power in Britain, Sir Oliver Lyttleton became Colonial Secretary. He already knew Malaya and began to take a close personal interest in it. One of his first moves after a visit there was to dismiss Gray. In 1952, General Sir Gerald Templer was appointed to succeed Gurney, and to take over the post of Director of Operations. Templer was by all accounts a hard man, not only to his subordinates but also to his enemies, and the friends of his enemies. He earned much criticism for the Tanjong Malim incident early in his time in Malaya, but it gained the respect of the local population and it seemed to work. It also underlined the extent of Templer's powers. He was familiar with the technique of collective punishment from his time in Palestine during the Arab revolt; it existed in most British colonies, but usually it needed the authority of the Colonial Secretary. Not here.

Templer also took quite literally the promise to provide the best men to get the job done. In March 1953, Lieutenant General Sir William (Bill) Oliver was posted in as Chief of Staff. Templer did, however, require a civil deputy, and this post went to Mr (later Sir) Donald MacGillivray. The GOC Malaya was Major General Roy Urquhart, the hero of Arnhem, who had commanded 16th Airborne Division (TA) in Britain, while Stockwell had commanded the 6th in Palestine. One recent work suggests that when Stockwell was summoned from the Canal Zone to command the fighting troops as GOC Malaya – he was what we would now call the Land Component Commander – he 'replaced Roy Urquhart . . . in circumstances that caused some disquiet both at that time and afterwards'. The same source also suggests in a footnote that Templer was not always good at choosing subordinates and surrounded himself with syco-phants. This is a serious misreading of the situation. Urquhart's biographer, John Baynes, points out that the problem – if problem it was – was one of personalities. Templer was a live wire, a tease, something of a bully, and never still. Urquhart by contrast was cool, calm, quietly courteous and measured in his approach. He had got along well with Briggs, but felt ill at ease personally with Templer. After two years in the climate of Malaya, he was also tired and probably rather stale. He had, however, played a key role in devising the Briggs Plan, which Templer did not alter – nor did he move him on early. Templer wrote to Lyttleton on 7 May 1952 that: 'Roy Urquhart leaves 1 June and Hughie Stockwell (my choice) arrives. Urquhart has been very good but has developed too sedentary a mind.' Stockwell certainly was Templer's personal choice. He lobbied Slim, the CIGS, hard, and Slim had accordingly signalled C-in-C MELF:

> In view of reorganisation in Malaya and developments in Indo-China, it has become necessary to put an exceptional man in command of Malaya. By far the most suitable for this is Stockwell and I have reluctantly, knowing the importance of your theatre, decided he must go to Malaya.

C-in-C MELF had agreed at once, and Templer had replied: 'Delighted about Stockwell. Please give grateful thanks to the Chief of the Imperial General Staff.' But to suggest that because he was wanted for this job, Hughie Stockwell was by nature or necessity some kind of toadie is ludicrous. It is true that Stockwell was one of Templer's inner circle, and that in character he had much more in common than did Urquhart. But Templer was a difficult superior, a hard taskmaster who rewarded anything less than success with the sack, and no one would voluntarily have sought to become his subordinate unless they were absolutely confident in their own abilities. In any case, Stockwell was a natural choice, quite apart from the fact that Templer knew and trusted him – quite a different thing from considering him a yes-man. As one officer put it:

Stockwell . . . was a welcome breath of fresh air after Urquhart . . . Templer was at times difficult but what do you expect if you appoint someone to the top job with the aim of stirring things up a bit because that was needed? A few feathers always get ruffled. Stockwell was no lap dog and we all got on perfectly well with Templer's office. He was the boss after all.

Stockwell moreover had a proven record in combat operations throughout the Second World War. He knew the jungle and the techniques required in it. He knew how to command colonial troops as well as British units, and get the best out of each. He knew something of Communist guerrillas, too, having dealt with the Burmese Liberation Army in 1945. And most recently he had commanded in a failed internal security operation – in Palestine – where he had been exposed to the political complexities of the civil-military interface, and the art of the possible in such circumstances. 'Once he [Templer] had Hugh Stockwell as GOC Malaya he was reasonably happy.' Stockwell himself said of Templer that 'if he thought there was something, or somebody, wrong, he would tell me and leave me to sort it out.' Last but not least, Hughie Stockwell was a charming man, who could get along with anyone. In a war which, by its nature, had to be prosecuted by committee, and in which a great diversity of services and agencies were involved, charm, tact and diplomacy were indispensable qualities.

The Stockwells arrived on 6 June 1952, having had a month to sort out their affairs in England. The girls did not go with them: Polly was now at the Chelsea School of Art, living in Elgin Crescent, and having a wonderful time free from parental control; Anabel, still a schoolgirl, was a boarder at St Paul's. Neither of them set foot in Malaya and at holiday times they either went to relatives, or to a house that Joan had rented when she had given up the farm at Criccieth. This was Erw Suran, a cottage on the cliffs above Tremadoc which belonged to another regimental family, the Livingstone-Learmonths. The house was basic, and had no electricity, but the girls loved it. Joan eventually bought the property, for she had a stronger feeling for Wales and its people than her husband did – probably the result of her long stay at Criccieth during his absence. Stockwell's feeling was more for the Regiment.

The first four days in Malaya were spent in taking over the job from

Urquhart, and meeting all the principal military and civil authorities with whom he would have to deal. A big party for Urquhart followed, at the Senior Officers' Mess, and on the following night, the Urquharts and the Stockwells dined with the Templers at King's House. The handover was completed on 11 June when Urquhart left for Singapore and then home. The Stockwells moved in to Flagstaff House in Kuala Lumpur, a graceful colonial house which, when the Stockwells arrived, was decorated in subdued tones. Joan, who had become more and more unconventional, and less and less inclined to the role of army wife, had the place redecorated in strong colours, and brought in quantities of banana trees and other large plants in enormous pots. The house had fine gardens, adjoining quarters for the Malay staff, and a bungalow for the ADC. In Anthony Tritton's place came David Russell, a 12th Lancer who was already serving in Malaya with his regiment – and who had been among the first on the scene after the death of Gurney. Russell had been a cadet at Sandhurst during Stockwell's time as Commandant, and rapidly established a close rapport with both the General and Joan. Russell went everywhere with the Stockwells and became more of a Military Assistant than an ADC.

Stockwell's headquarters was in the barracks outside Kuala Lumpur town, and was run by the Brigadier General Staff (BGS) – effectively the Chief of Staff – Brigadier Rupert Brazier-Creagh. Brazier-Creagh was an experienced and capable staff officer – a perfect foil to Stockwell. His chief intelligence officer was Major (later Major General) Griff Caldwell, a shrewd, clever Sapper whom Stockwell trusted implicitly. Stockwell told Russell early on: 'If Caldwell wants me, you get me – at any time of the day or night.' With the headquarters in good hands, Stockwell could get on with what he preferred above all: visiting units in the field.

The organization of troops in Malaya was somewhat haphazard, and Stockwell immediately began a rationalization, establishing two districts in North and South Malaya as the structure in which the existing British and Gurkha brigades would operate. He had, however, no authority over the RAF, but fortunately he established an excellent working relationship with the AOC, Air Vice-Marshal George Mills, and from January 1953, Air Vice-Marshal Wallace Kyle. AHQ Malaya was located at Changi in Singapore, rather remote from the rest of the military and civil command structure, and in early 1954, Kyle moved up to Kuala Lumpur. This allowed ever closer co-ordination of air operations with ground forces, and by early 1954, the RAF was undertaking a wide range of operations using both fixed wing and rotary aircraft: troop lift, casualty evacuation, air resupply, offensive air support, visual and photographic reconnaissance, spraying of MRLA crops, artillery fire direction, target marking, communications and psychological operations. The last included leaflet dropping, loud hailing and aerial broadcast missions.

Stockwell set out his views on the Army's contribution in a series of speeches which were as much a mind-clearing exercise for Stockwell himself as they were a statement of what he intended his subordinates to do. A paper on 'The

Army in the Cold War' summarized Stockwell's views on how the Army would play its part in defeating the insurgency in the broader strategic context of the Briggs Plan as developed by Templer. The title is the clue to his thinking: the Cold War is a war against Communism, which occasionally breaks out into a shooting match – this is one such outbreak. One must therefore understand the enemy and his political and cultural motivation – then address his defeat through a strategic solution in which military force is only a part. This is clear thinking for someone who had never received a formal training or education in the higher levels of military operations and strategy, and it set the scene for much of the way in which operations under Stockwell developed in Malaya.

In a follow-up piece, he pointed out that the Army had two roles: first, training and preparation for general war; and secondly, aid to the civil power. He concentrated on the second role, since this was the current problem, but acknowledged that it was degrading the Army's ability to do the first. Much of what he wrote was clearly influenced by events and experiences in Palestine – for example, Hackett's paper on lessons from Palestine. He was from the first very clear about the importance of intelligence, whether from Special Branch, local sources or from operations; indeed there is clearly a place in his theories for operations designed solely to produce intelligence: stir up a wasps' nest, watch what pops out, track it, and it may lead you to the targets for a whole series of new operations. What he felt would be wasteful would be to become bogged down as a garrison force, or be fixed by routine framework patrolling, which was activity based rather than intelligence based. More flexibility was required to prevent this: 'To have flexibility we must create reserves in each area so that the Army can tackle its main task, which is the destruction of the enemy in their jungle habitat.' Despite the apparent tactical successes enjoyed by the CTs up to this point, Stockwell clearly felt that their position overall was far from strong, and that it was he, not they, who held the operational initiative. But even so, he knew that he 'must finish the contest because it saps our soldiers and soaks up money and could become a running sore. We must return ourselves to training for war and not be bogged down in IS. We have got to raise a Federation Army.'

The next stage in the war was, therefore, more specialized operations against specific targets isolated by penetration. Deep jungle penetration was Stockwell's preferred line as opposed to close operations. As a point of military doctrine it is interesting to see this discussion being held, using this terminology, since it is usually considered that the delineation of the battlefield into deep and close did not begin until the development of the American techniques of Follow-on Forces Attack in the mid 1980s. Yet here is a debate that can instantly be recognized and understood today. For Stockwell it was the deep battle that mattered, which took the fight to the enemy in their jungle fastness, and which was the only real way of bringing them to battle in a war in which there was no linear front. The Jungle Warfare School at Kota Tinggi in Johore was established for just this purpose. The only alternative was to lure the enemy out and then engage them on ground – not necessarily geographical ground – of his choosing. This course of action he had to develop faster than the MRLA could develop their Maoist model, and he chose to do so in specific target areas in south-west Kelantan, south-east Kelantan, north-west Pahang, south-east Pahang, Belum Valley, North Kedah, and the towns.

One example of this sort of operation was Hammer, a battalion-level operation by the Somerset Light Infantry with the local police, backed up by a good head of Special Branch and a sound MIO. This began in August 1952 and from the start it was run as a long-term, intelligence-driven operation, aimed at disrupting the CT supply organization in the Kuala Langat forest reserve (North) area of Selangor. By disrupting the organization, it was hoped to prevent food – and in particular, rice – getting to them; by this means the Security Forces would force the CTs to fight for food, thereby expending time and effort on their own survival, rather than on the insurgency – or else surrender. The target area was a complete district, and the operation was under the control of the Civil Administrative Officer, who combined all military and civil forces and agencies in a single effort. All known enemy agents were arrested, and Briggs's strict food control measures were imposed, including the removal of surplus rice, a reduced ration issue of cooked ration to villages, convoying of commercial traffic, and control of road movement. The operation was supported by an intensive, and recognizably modern, information plan to get the local people to co-operate and understand why the operation was being carried out. One illustration was Operation Dictum, mounted by Hugh Green, the DG Information Services, in south Selangor in February 1953. This operation included speeches by local politicians, articles in newspapers, information sheets, and wireless broadcasts. The material used and the stories run included showing up CT atrocities, being honest about mistakes, and highlighting successes including social programmes. This was firepower of a new kind: not kinetic, to be sure, but psychological. There were two distinct target audiences for the effect of this sort of fire: first, the civil population of all ethnic groups; and secondly, the CTs themselves. As intelligence developed, Hammer was extended to include more overt military measures like forest sweeps and bombardment of suspected enemy positions. By February 1953, thirty-five of the seventy known CTs in the area had been eliminated by death or capture, while forty-one supply dumps and fifty-five camp sites had been identified and destroyed. The interrogation of prisoners revealed that CT morale had been badly affected, and further information later that month resulted in a main insurgent camp being located and attacked, with the resulting elimination of a complete CT platoon.

Hammer produced some important lessons in itself – sweeps were not effective, for example. But it was clear that these operations had to be long term, and they would tend to proceed in cycles of success and lull; therefore fast and effective exploitation of opportunities was important. Command had to be decentralized, and the use of helicopters was becoming a force multiplier for troop deployment, recovery and supply. As early as April 1952, a paper by the Command Planning Staff had recognized that technical innovation, as well as tactical innovation, was possible here, in supporting deep penetration and the offensive handling of troops. Certainly, these helicopters represented a big technological step forward from Stockwell's Burma days, which he was quick to grasp. The RAF had ten Westland S-51 helicopters, but their reliability had been poor. In October 1952 the US agreed to release ten Sikorsky S-55s for Malaya, provided that Royal Navy pilots operated them. Troop trials were begun at once: 'My aim is for further tactical mobility using the S-55 and the SAS,' Stockwell wrote, and later: 'You will know that the ten Naval S-55s have completely revolutionised the conduct of operations in Malaya, but more are needed and I would suggest that, if possible, the RAF should be persuaded to provide Malaya with more than ten.'

The air supply figures alone for both rotary and fixed-wing reflect this philosophy: by November 1953, the total drop was 848,112lb, the equivalent of 184 Valetta aircraft loads – the biggest monthly total during the Emergency to date, and a total since the Emergency started of 15,397,228lb.

Hammer, and other operations like it, made a rapid and demonstrable contribution to the business of seizing the initiative. It is of note that as early as September 1952, Templer began to feel that morale had been restored, and that the strategic and operational initiative was passing to the British. This was evident not from any one point, but from the whole series of Stockwell's successful intelligence-driven operations which inflicted such heavy attrition on the insurgents. The MRLA response was to conduct a reorganization into smaller cells, or independent platoons, which would be harder to follow, and to change tactics to hit-and-run attacks. Aggressive patrolling also forced them to move many larger camps over the Thai border, thus increasing the time taken to mount an attack.

Food control was clearly biting, and the insurgents, Stockwell felt, were being forced to change tactics. Better tactics and shooting at low level could, he thought, double the kill rate by the Security Forces in ambushes, and if that were to happen, the war on the ground was as good as won. Stockwell picked up on this rapidly: his headquarters regularly issued Operational Memoranda detailing lessons learned from the analysis of past operations, for the troops on the ground. The feeling that a corner had been turned is clear in an Appreciation of the Situation produced by Templer's staff in October 1952 and sent to the CIGS. In it, very satisfactory progress is reported, but the tone is almost embarrassingly obsequious to Templer himself – Briggs is given credit for the plan, but every advance, every success, is ascribed personally to Templer: 'The most important single factor has been the appointment of General Templer as High Commissioner and Director of Operations.' No one else gets a mention, and it is obvious that the cult of Templer has begun early. From that time on, it is difficult to find any book that credits anyone other than Templer himself for progress in Malaya – and yet clearly it was a team effort.

One of Templer's unbending rules was the co-ordination of intelligence: if the use of intelligence by the Army compromised Special Branch penetration of the MRLA, then Special Branch requirements would take priority. For the long haul, Templer was undoubtedly right, and Caldwell agreed. Stockwell, if he felt annoyed at times, just got on with the job.

An occasional source of friction was the role of the Combined Emergency Planning Staff, or CEPS. This consisted of a team led by the GSO1, Lieutenant Colonel Napier Crookenden,[2] an airman, a police officer, and a civil servant. Their task was twofold: first to develop operational plans based on intelligence garnered by Special Branch and by Caldwell; secondly, recalling the example of Montgomery's liaison officers, to act as a directed telescope for Templer. At Templer's direction, this team would go off to a particular state or district, tour the area, talk to the military, police, Special Branch and civil authorities, and make an assessment. They were regarded, quite rightly, as Templer's spies and had not specific instructions been issued that they were to be assisted, there would certainly have been resistance to their activities.

Back in Kuala Lumpur, the team's assessment would be turned into a report with recommendations covering all aspects of the Emergency regulations: resettlement, food control, the police, the co-ordination of intelligence, the direction of military operations. This report had first to be submitted to Stockwell, who would discuss it with the local military commander concerned, and any disagreement with its findings had to be resolved or fully outlined in a written response. There were quite often disagreements, for Crookenden was an outspoken officer and used the authority of his chief without compunction; he was fortunate, perhaps, not to have incurred powerful enemies in so doing. Although Caldwell was quite comfortable with the process – 'they did not really get in the way very much' – Stockwell did not always like the process, and said so, but Templer would brook no interference with it. And his was, of course, the final say.

Generally, and despite friction over the role of the CEPS, Templer left the conduct of operations to Stockwell, but occasionally he insisted on a major change in operational activity. His first one was to depart from Briggs's plan to roll the CTs up from the south, and go for the places where terrorists were weakest through the exploitation of good intelligence, and then work outwards from cleared areas. To put this into effect, in November 1952, during Operation Hammer, Templer made some important changes in the military command structure. 17th Gurkha Division had been formed with two brigades under the command of Major General Lance Perowne in July, to cover the south of Malaya. Following this, Stockwell was appointed as Commander of the Federation Army concurrently with his role as GOC Malaya – an important step in integrating British, Commonwealth and indigenous forces. To have one Major General sitting on top of another would have been odd indeed, but Templer already had a strategy. On 11 November 1952 he had written to Sir John Harding, the CIGS, that:

Charles Keightley and I had a long go a few days ago on a wide variety of subjects. One of these was Hughie Stockwell. As you may know, I personally asked Bill Slim to post him here in succession to Roy Urquhart ... I need hardly tell you that he has enthused new life into all the troops, and his tremendous enthusiasm has made its effect felt throughout the whole country. He really is doing a magnificent job of work. Charles has written to you recommending that Hughie be promoted to Lt Gen in his present appointment. There is no doubt about it that the responsibilities which he is shouldering should carry that rank ... I realise very well that this is all tied up with the number of Lt Generals which we are allowed by the Treasury.

The Military Secretary minuted CIGS on 19 November to advise that all lieutenant generals' vacancies were filled, but that Stockwell might be promoted on a temporary basis and then made substantive as a vacancy occurred. Harding therefore replied on these lines, agreeing a grant of temporary rank, but adding that the primary reason for allowing the promotion was:

not to compensate Hughie. I have got him definitely marked down in my mind for a Lieut-General's job as soon as he becomes available but I have definitely set my face against taking him away from Malaya until he has been there at least two years, because I know full well what a bad effect all round constant changes of command . . . have.

On 12 May 1953, therefore, the Army Council granted Stockwell the temporary rank of Lieutenant General.

Underpinning the formation of the Federation Division was Stockwell's role as commander of the Federation Army. In this context, one of his most urgent priorities was the development of the Federation Regiment, created on 20 March 1952, and later the Federation Armoured Car Regiment. In due course, signals, engineer and service units followed. These were multi-racial regiments, in contrast to the already-extant Malay Regiment. Recruiting and training soldiers were relatively easy, and in the short term, the model of the RWAFF or the TJFF was available; Stockwell was of course completely at home with this method of raising and operating colonial troops. Templer, however, had other ideas: to introduce as many Malayan officers, of all races, as rapidly as possible. Such a methodology goes to the heart of the moral component of fighting power in a force, by concentrating on putting in place a reliable, incorrupt and apolitical leadership. This tried and trusted method has recently been used in Sierra Leone, Afghanistan and Iraq.[3] In Malaya, it was to be achieved partly by sending promising young men to Sandhurst, and partly by training them in country. Stockwell, having overseen the commissioning of Africans in the 82nd (WA) Division, had no difficulties in principle with this, and he and Templer sat together on the first selection

215

board. There were 179 candidates, of whom they chose six Chinese, three of mixed race, and one Malay: most Malays preferred to serve in the Malay Regiment, and Stockwell had to persuade two other candidates to transfer from the Malay Regiment in order to achieve the right ethnic mix.

The strength of the Federation Regiment by late 1953 included a total of 127 British officers and 38 British NCOs and men, and 51 Malayan officers and 5,601 NCOs and men. Stockwell was determined to press ahead with the expansion of the Federation Army, but leadership of the right quality remained a problem. Several of his speeches expound this theme; in one, undated, entitled 'The Army and the People', he explains to an audience of Malayans that:

> the Army is merely part of the people. All the soldiers in an Army are just part of the people . . . The Malay Regiment is open to Malays and the Federation Regiment is open to all races in Malaya . . . But when one builds up an army quickly one must have the leaders, the officers and the NCOs, and it is the training of these leaders which takes the time . . . until these officers are trained, we will have to rely on British officers. In the end, we hope all these Regiments will be commanded and officered by Malayan officers.

The model in use during this transition looks rather more like that of the old Indian Army than the RWAFF with its 10 per cent of Europeans, but there are some parallels, making it something of a hybrid, reflecting Stockwell's own experience in the slow process of training and commissioning Africans.

The Federation Military College, now located at Sungei Besi near Kuala Lumpur, was a success from the start. The College ran two wings: a boys' wing run on English public school lines; and a cadet wing, modelled on Sandhurst. This College has turned out to be a major contributor to the growth of the Malaysian Army as a constitutional force; the influence of Stockwell, as a former Commandant of Sandhurst, is clear to see. His contribution to the successful formation of the Federation Army was recognized by his appointment in December 1957 as Colonel of the Malay Regiment.

One important means of improving civil-military integration was the structure of State and District War Executive Committees. To improve these further, a series of two-day courses was run to make sure that members understood the dynamics, could exchange ideas and share views, could study past operations, and could practise joint planning. Stockwell frequently addressed these courses, and used this to push his message. 'One of the troubles which the Federation has to overcome is its division into eleven entities,' he would remark, and one of the good things about the committees and the courses was that they encouraged everyone to think federally. He pointed out a factor still distinctly recognizable today: 'Joint planning even on an inter-service level is never easy – we have been brought up in our own way of thinking and our own traditions', but what must be developed is 'the ability to direct the maximum effort against the enemy by the integration of the civil and military resources available . . . Where co-operation and understanding are good, we have had first-class results.' He also stressed that the economic situation of even a rich country like Malaya could not indefinitely bear the cost of the insurgency, and money spent on security would be better devoted to social programmes, so 'make the people realise that, by ending the Emergency, their lot will be improved. Do all you can to build up the Home Guard so that it can take over the jobs of the Specials . . . Press on with all the things that are going to make the Chinese in the new villages feel settled . . . Show the people that we stand for justice, and make them respect us by a fair and firm attitude. Stamp out corruption and petty jealousy.'

There was of course time for relaxation. Malaya offered plenty of distractions in terms of sports, be that game shooting, riding, polo, tennis or fishing. Joan would have liked more freedom to explore than the security situation allowed. She got out and about whenever she could, and kept pets, including a monkey, to divert her. Hughie and Joan were able to take some trips together: a Sunderland flying boat took them to Pangkor Island with its dazzling, deserted beach and comfortable rest house. On one visit here, Joan bought a sea otter, which, named Angelina, afterwards lived in the bathroom adjoining Stockwell's study in Flagstaff House – but of course the animal kept getting out. On one occasion, the broadcaster Chester Wilmott, who was staying, was roped in to an otter-hunt for the escaped beast, which was found chewing a stack of confidential reports on brigadiers and major generals left by the Military Secretary for Stockwell's attention!

Stockwell and Templer continued to get on well, and the Templers and the Stockwells went on short holidays together to the hill stations of Penang, even though Templer himself did not much care for holidays. During the week, a quiet evening dinner with the Templers, followed by badminton in the Stockwell's drawing room with Peggie Templer and Joan Stockwell holding up the net, or else corridor cricket, was a regular fixture. Joan and Peggie Templer, however, were not nearly so much at ease with each other, for Joan was everything that Peggie was not, and Peggie undoubtedly thought her a difficult woman. Their relationship can probably best be described as guarded. Midway through their time in Malaya, Joan went back to England for an extended visit, leaving Stockwell to look after himself, ably assisted by David Russell:

So he entertained those people he wanted to entertain, rather than those he felt he had to. 'Right David,' he would say, 'go and get the piano.' So I had to get the staff out and have the piano carried over from my bungalow. I would then play, accompanying whatever songs the company wanted.

217

There were other breaks too from operations. On 18 October 1952, Stockwell succeeded Eric Skaife as Colonel of the Royal Welch Fusiliers. This was a period when the old Cardwell system returned to its full flowering: the Regimental Depot had re-opened at Wrexham, and taken in its first draft of recruits on 3 January 1952. National Service was running at two years in the Regular Army followed by two years in the TA; the 1st and 4th Battalions were thus fully manned. Moreover, regular recruiting for the Royal Welch Fusiliers was so good that when, as a result of the requirement for more troops in Malaya and Korea, eight regular second battalions were ordered to be re-raised, 2 RWF was among them. On the day before the funeral of King George VI in February 1952, Lieutenant Colonel 'Winky' Benyon, then serving with the 1st Battalion South Wales Borderers in Eritrea, was told that he had been selected to raise and train the new battalion. In due course, after Stockwell's time, the battalion served for two years in Malaya. Stockwell was of course delighted to have been chosen, and even more delighted by the return of his old battalion to the order of battle. However the demands of operations were his first priority, and anyway, the distance from home was huge. Together, these factors made it impossible for him effectively to discharge his duties. While he remained in Malaya, Major General Sir Maurice Dowse – with whom Stockwell had served in 2 RWF in Germany in the 1920s – was appointed as Deputy Colonel.

David Russell, who lived and worked closely with the Stockwells for an extended period, later wrote his impressions of Stockwell himself at this time, saying later that:

Very little missed his knowing eye when he visited the wide cross-section of units we regularly saw. For me this was a marvellous three-year period with the General and his family and it had a profound influence on my life. During this time I willingly fell under the Stockwell spell. His tolerance was unbounded. I double-booked him for appointments, stranded the GOC's car in an alleyway . . . and we still remained great friends. In Malaya, it was the sheer style and elegance he brought to everyday life and his ability to talk and get through to all age groups. He was an important man, yet modest, a soldier's soldier who would talk to anyone but knew all the loneliness and responsibility of high command. And through all this he had a personality that engendered love and admiration amongst all those who knew him.

. . . Against his own high standards of hard work and professionalism, his sense of fun was boundless and all who knew him from rulers of lands to the straightforward working soldier found it hard not to fall for his combination of integrity and charm. He was one of those rare people who was equally at home in the Palace or in the Corporals' Mess . . . if [Joan] sometimes took a less than traditional course as a senior Army officer's wife, that made him chuckle and brought out the well-known General Hughie twinkle.

In November 1953 it was settled that Templer would be relieved in the autumn of 1954 to become C-in-C British Army of the Rhine, and Commander Northern Army Group – although as things turned out he never took up this appointment. However Templer had made his mind up that he wanted Stockwell to continue as his subordinate, and therefore that he should become GOC I (British) Corps, in Germany. Stockwell was therefore warned to leave Malaya in April 1954, to be relieved by Lieutenant General Geoffrey Bourne.

Stockwell's contribution to the ending of the insurgency can be judged from the facts. By the time he departed, terrorist incidents had declined from 600 per month in 1951 to 100 in 1954, and surrenders increased. Intelligence summaries recorded CT dead as 374 during 1948; 618 during 1949; rising to 1,107 during 1952. September 1953 brought in the declaration of the first White Area, in Malacca, in which all emergency regulations were lifted. In January 1954 White Areas were extended to include the coastal area of Trengganu, parts of Kedah in February, and parts of Negri Sembilan in March. The plan for 1955 produced by Bourne has Hughie Stockwell's metaphorical fingerprints all over it, signifying that Bourne had no intention of upsetting what was a winning strategy. Moreover, a report produced by Bourne soon after he had taken over made several interesting points, among which were that: 'The general level of cooperation amongst the many services and departments . . . is excellent.' He refers to the Briggs-Templer-Stockwell approach as a 'steady squeeze', and says that 'No one here, including Templer and Stockwell, offered me any ideas of ending the Emergency in less than years. Everyone admits it is going to be a long haul.' And so it was: the Emergency did not formally end until 1962. Taking this one step further, and looking at what was achieved in the light of the experiences of Stockwell and others earlier in Palestine, one can say that a truly strategic approach was taken, with the military playing its proper part alongside other lines of activity. The difficulty faced by Templer and Stockwell – and many others – was in defining and attacking what would now be called the enemy's centre of gravity; that is, the aspect of the enemy's power which, if destroyed, defeated or neutralized, will bring about his downfall, while defining and defending their own. In such a campaign, the enemy's centre of gravity is likely to be something nebulous like a set of social conditions, or a political goal; while one's own may be the legitimacy and authority of the government, or its will to continue the struggle. The Templer/Stockwell combination effectively addressed this difficulty by removing the insurgents' ability to conduct military operations demonstrably, while at the same time addressing the political and social causes of insurgency: what David Charteris has called 'a "two-front" war: a "strategic" battle for legitimacy and a "tactical battle for control"'. His terminology is wrongly applied, but his meaning is clear. The contrast with Palestine is obvious.

The handover between Stockwell and Geoffrey Bourne actually took place on 6 April 1954, and on the 7th, Templer gave a dinner in Kuala Lumpur to say goodbye to the Stockwells and to welcome Bourne. The Stockwells departed the following day for a week in Bangkok, after which they flew back to England. Once again, Stockwell's achievements met with significant official recognition. Although he was already a KBE, he was made a Knight Commander of the Order of the Bath (KCB) in the 1954 Birthday Honours. Urquhart's biographer has compared Stockwell's award with the lack of any recognition for Urquhart – certainly Urquhart was treated shabbily. He was not the last military officer to have successfully carried great responsibility, only to receive disloyalty from those at home. But this does not detract from Stockwell's achievements – Urquhart did not exercise the extent of operational command that Stockwell did, and although he helped put in place a winning plan, he was not there to execute it.

Notes

1 Letter from Montgomery (CIGS) to Churchill.
2 Later Lieutenant General Sir Napier Crookenden KCB DSO OBE DL (1915–2002), commanded 9th Parachute Battalion 1944–1946. He later commanded 16 Para Brigade 1960–1961 and was GOC-in-C Western Command 1969–1972. *Who's Who*, 2002, p. 493.
3 The author was Commander British Forces and Military Adviser to the Government in Sierra Leone, 2000–2001; Deputy Commanding General, New Iraqi Army in 2003; and GOC British Forces Iraq, 2004–2005.

Chapter Seventeen

Corps Commander, 1954–1956

At the close of the Second World War, I (British) Corps had been one of three corps occupying the British sector of Germany. By early 1946, the other two corps, VIII and XXX, had been disbanded leaving I Corps, transformed into a district, in charge of the various tasks of occupation and reconstruction. On 1 June 1947 it too was disbanded. The rising threat of Communism made it clear that the Rhine Army had to be transformed from an army of occupation to one which could play its part in deterring Soviet aggression, or, should deterrence fail, in fighting a Soviet invasion of the West. The corps was reformed on 18 June 1951 – the first time that the corps level of command had existed in peacetime as a standing force. Thus the re-establishment of I Corps was a major statement of British commitment to a continental strategy, and the Corps Commander was bound to be to some extent a political choice as much as a military one, a safe pair of hands in every way.

Stockwell had served several corps commanders in Burma and India, and understood this level of command perfectly well. He had, however, no experience of armoured or mechanized operations, and needed a good staff with the right expertise. He was fortunate, therefore, to have Brigadier Ken Darling as his BGS,[1] Brigadier Guy Jameson as AQMG and Colonel John Sleeman as the Colonel GS. Mark Henniker, who had commanded a brigade under Stockwell in Malaya, was the CCRE, and John Rendall was the CCRA. Stockwell also took with him David Russell, his ADC, who stayed for the first six months before handing over to Hugo Meynell of the 12th Lancers; Richard Sinnett joined him from 1 RWF in 1955 as his Military Assistant.

Stockwell took over command on 15 October 1954, with the substantive rank of Lieutenant General, from Lieutenant General Sir James Cassells. During 1953, the Headquarters moved to renovated pre-war German barracks, Ripon Barracks, in the University City of Bielefeld in North Rhine-Westphalia. The Stockwells – Hughie, Joan, and 16-year-old Anabel, moved into the Corps Commander's residence, Hoberge House, which lay on a wooded ridge a few minutes drive to the south-west of Ripon Barracks. Polly did not join the family, for not only was she working as an artist at

Taormina in Sicily, but she was now a married woman. In 1953 she had married John Hope, whom she had met at art school, at St Peter's, Vere Street, W1. After a fashionable London wedding and a reception at The Architectural Press in Queen Anne's Gate, by courtesy of her uncle by marriage, de Cronin Hastings, the two had gone off to Italy on honeymoon and simply stayed there. This suited Polly and John pretty well: Polly had no desire to live with her parents; and John and the General were never quite on the same wavelength.

Hoberge House was leased from the owner of the Steinhagen gin distillery which was nearby, and as well as housing the family, there was an annexe for the ADC. Richard Sinnett described it as being:

> right up in the hills in a lovely bit of wooded country. It is a lovely place and is looking very spick and span just now as the Princess Royal is coming to stay in early April . . . There is a very nice Germanic cellar, with a small bar. Next door is a room large enough to show films.

On one of her visits, Polly painted the cellar in bright colours, and added a large mural of a naked girl in a bathtub.

The Corps was subordinated to the Commander Northern Army Group, a British officer who doubled as C-in-C BAOR, based at Rheindahlen on the Dutch-German border. During the whole of Stockwell's tenure as Corps Commander, this appointment was held by the former GOC 6th Airborne Division, General Sir Richard ('Windy') Gale.[2] Gale's Brigadier General Staff – effectively his chief of staff – was John Tweedie, who had been a college commander at Sandhurst under Stockwell, and later one of his brigade commanders in the 3rd Infantry Division. A very useful friend at court, therefore. It was Stockwell's first visit to Germany since his time with the first BAOR, twenty-four years before. In 1954, the Corps had under command four divisions: 2nd Infantry Division, commanded by Major General Basil Coad, based at Hilden; 6th Armoured Division, commanded by Major General Roddy McLeod at Lubbecke; 7th Armoured Division, commanded by Major General Ken Cooper, and later Stockwell's old friend from Palestine, Shan Hackett, at Verden; and 11th Armoured Division, commanded by Major General John Anderson, at Herford. There was also a Canadian Divisional HQ, the 2nd Infantry, with one brigade group – 2 Infantry Brigade – based around Soest in the Sauerland. This spread of garrisons meant that Stockwell had to spend a good deal of time travelling in order to visit units and formations in barracks and in the field. He and the divisional commanders had a Mercedes 300B – their top model at the time – which Mercedes had given as a goodwill gesture – no doubt with advertising in mind. Stockwell was driven by Sgt Hill of the RASC, who had been with him since Palestine. Once, when making an inspection of a divisional headquarters, the staff car broke down. Being the man he was, Stockwell overcame this lack of transport immediately, by flagging down a NAAFI wagon that happened to be passing. The divisional commander meanwhile was waiting on the barrack square with a guard of honour, and when the tea wagon hove into view was heard to shout, 'Get that blasted vehicle off the square!' No sooner were the words out of his mouth than Stockwell appeared from the cab; the poor divisional commander's feelings can only be imagined.

There was also a special train, which belonged to the C-in-C, and was made available by Gale, with proper working, sleeping and dining accommodation; this was especially useful as a base during exercises, or on long trips so that work could continue during what would otherwise be dead time. Stockwell's enthusiasm for helicopters also continued unabated. Although still a novelty, light battlefield helicopters were now becoming available for command and liaison. Stockwell was allocated a five-seater Westland WS-51 Dragonfly – later replaced by a Widgeon. Richard Sinnett wrote in a letter during one exercise that:

> The helicopter has been the biggest boon of the exercise. Instead of bumping along dusty tracks we merely hop across to where we want to go in a fraction of the time, and land right beside the people we want to visit. Our helicopter is a British one and takes three people apart from the crew.

The corps battle plan was based on the then NATO strategy of the trip-wire: that is, a relatively thin screen of conventional forces deployed on the inner German border to give warning and then delay, before a full-scale American nuclear response was launched. Until 1954, training followed an annual cycle made necessary by the regular drafts of National Servicemen, and a steady progression from individual to company, battalion, brigade and divisional exercises, with corps or army CPXs thrown in. Tactics and techniques were, like the formations and the equipment, still recognizably those of the North-west European campaign. All this was about to change and Stockwell was to be the man who changed it. In 1952, a trial firing of a nuclear shell had taken place from an American 280mm gun, demonstrating the feasibility of using low-yield tactical warheads on the battlefield. Almost immediately, an opinion began to emerge that this heralded a different context of battle from that of the unwieldy – and lacking in real combat power – divisions of the Corps. Moving fast and often, in agile, all-arms groupings, rather than digging in and waiting, would be the best protection in such a battle. During 1955, therefore, the principal exercises centred on an experimental infantry division, formed on 2nd Division, composed of mixed infantry brigade groups, and a Light Armoured Division, based on the 7th Division. In the Infantry Division, each brigade group would have an armoured regiment of Centurion tanks, two or three infantry battalions, and integral combat and service support. The Armoured Division had only four regiments of tanks, a mechanized infantry battalion mounted in APCs, one field artillery regiment, and an engineer squadron – not really a division at all, which was by no means an unqualified success and pleased no one.

Richard Sinnett recorded the sequence of exercises, and the preparations for them by the 2nd Infantry Division in his letters and diaries, as did the Regimental Journal. New equipment was taken on from September 1954 onwards. The troops were issued with the Belgian Fabrique Nationale (FN) rifle of 7.62mm calibre, the Energa anti-tank rifle grenade, the 17-pounder anti-tank gun, the American 3.5-inch rocket launcher, and a range of vehicles including the Austin Champ, a new model of the Bedford 3-ton lorry, and the Humber 1-ton APC, the infamous 'Pig' as it became known:

> We have all new range vehicles and feel we look very modern.
>
> Our vehicles – 80 all told – are all brand new post war models, including Austin Champs – the jeep's successor. They are certainly very impressive, being complete with breathing tubes for going under 5 foot of water – it will take more than rivers to stop us now!

Exercises Rebirth and Two Keys were held in September 1954, followed by Exercise Battle Royal, in which a total of 130,000 British, Canadian, Dutch and Belgian troops took part, supported by 870 tanks and 400 heavy guns, in an exercise area covering 4,500 square miles. The concept of the exercise, devised by Gale, was that the aggressor would be channelled into certain lines of advance by tactical atomic strikes, and then counter-attacked by armour and parachute troops:

> A degree of realism was introduced by mock tactical explosions of nuclear weapons from which great pillars of smoke went up in the sky.
>
> The farmers, of course, had their moans, which were often justified as there was heavy damage to crops. Compensation was always met, but compensation for a spoilt crop is no real substitute.

Even though the war had been over for ten years, there was clearly still a problem with displaced persons and refugees. Responsibility for this problem had originally lain with Control Commission for Germany (CCG), and then with the Federal German government. However, senior British officers' wives seem to have played a significant part in organizing such things as welfare, recreation, and employment. Richard Sinnett recorded in March 1955 that:

> Lady S is coming with us to Hamburg as she is a big noise in the D.P. Organisation and is travelling round to meet some of her lieutenants . . .
>
> We have been having a pretty hectic time these last few days culminating in the Displaced Persons meeting which took place today. Lady Templer is the queen bee and has been staying at Hoberge for the last three days.

Now that he was back nearer home, Stockwell could take up the Colonelcy of the Regiment, and he clearly made great efforts to catch up on his duties. Regimental Headquarters was running in Wrexham, handling day-to-day matters under the direction of the Regimental Secretary, D.I. Owen. The big regimental event of 1954 was the presentation of new Colours to its three battalions, made necessary by the re-raising of the 2nd Battalion, and the great age of all three stands of Colours then in service: those of 1 RWF had been in service since 1880, and those of 2 RWF since 1859. It was the old Regimental Colour that Stockwell himself had carried on parade on St David's Day at Pembroke Dock thirty years before. The Queen, who had become Colonel-in-Chief following the death of her father, King George VI, agreed to present the Colours, which symbolized the very essence of the Regiment's ethos and traditions, at what would be a Regimental parade and the first time that the two regular battalions had met since Poona, when Stockwell had commanded 29 Independent Infantry Brigade. The ceremony was fixed for 23 July, and the venue was Wroughton airfield. Winkie Benyon, commanding 2 RWF, remembered that:

It was a hectic period, but great fun. We rehearsed on the airfield, we rehearsed the wet weather programme in the gymnasium; the Colour parties rehearsed . . . the bands rehearsed, and all other manner of minor duties rehearsed their role for the great day. Finally on 21st July the Colonel of the Regiment accompanied by his deputy Maj-Gen Sir Maurice Dowse took the dress rehearsal. There were a few minor changes but by and large we were ready.

The weather forecast for 23rd July was indifferent, but locally it was thought that things would be manageable. Stockwell ordered the full programme to go ahead. The parade was so large that a double line of guards was formed in front of the saluting dais and the great mass of spectators who had come from all over England and Wales – and other parts of the world – to see the great event. Another crowd met the Queen's train at Swindon station, and Stockwell was warned of her arrival and progress over the Chief Constable's radio. At 11.30 am, Stockwell met the Queen at Wroughton Military Hospital. On behalf of the Regiment, he presented her with a regimental brooch, a red dragon in rubies and diamonds set in platinum. A few minutes later, wearing the brooch, the Queen moved by car with Stockwell to the parade ground. Winkie Benyon recalled that:

Suddenly it seemed there on the saluting base, dressed all in white, was the slight figure of – The Colonel-in-Chief. The Royal Salute crashed out and I must confess that I felt proud indeed as I reported to Her Majesty, 'Your Royal Welch Fusiliers are present and ready for your inspection. There are 101 officers and 1,006 Other Ranks on parade.'

225

The Queen inspected the parade from the back of a Land Rover, and then the old colours of the 1st and 4th Battalions were trooped through the ranks for the last time. Carrying the Regimental Colour of the 1st Battalion was Second Lieutenant W.P. (Bill) Roache, later famous as a television actor. The Queen then presented new Colours to each battalion, and addressed the officers and men on parade in words which Stockwell himself probably helped to compose:

> I was very proud to become colonel-in-chief of The Royal Welch Fusiliers in succession to my father, and I have already been able to see parts of all three battalions of the Regiment. Now – by a fortunate chance – they are all able to join in a regimental Parade. I am sorry that it could not take place in the Principality; but this morning this airfield will, for many, be Welsh territory.
>
> The Royal Welch Fusiliers have a strong tradition of family loyalty. Sons follow their fathers into the Regiment, and the serving members of it greatly value the continuing interest and association of its veterans . . .
>
> Thus, watched critically but affectionately by old members of the Regiment, surrounded by many friends and supported by the good wishes of all who live in Wales, you may properly feel proud as you give your first salute to these new Colours.

The final parts of the parade completed, the Queen inspected the ranks of the Comrades, and took lunch with Stockwell and the officers. When the Queen left, her route was lined by hundreds of fusiliers and families. Stockwell spotted poet and writer Siegfried Sassoon, who had served in the Regiment during the First World War, in the crowd, and made a point of presenting him to the Queen. The memorable day was concluded with celebration dinners for all the men – Stockwell made a point of visiting every dining room – a cocktail party and a dance.

Back with the Corps, in April 1955 Stockwell went to Paris for Monty's CPX V, one of a series of so-called command post exercises which the Field Marshal ran as DSACEUR, following the precedent he had created as CIGS. These exercises had begun in April 1952, as a remedy for what Monty believed to be a low standard of generalship among the commanders of the Continental Armies. These CPXs were designed to be the precursors to field manoeuvres and in those years, they were NATO's only real attempt to exercise its higher command and communications in peacetime. Richard Sinnett described the exercise, from 25 to 28 April, in a letter:

> The array of brass at the exercise was quite staggering. We rubbed shoulders with it all at lunch each day, which everyone had in the cafeteria near the exercise hall. All the NATO countries sent their top men. Both the CIGS and General Templer, who takes over soon, were there. Mountbatten represented the Navy . . . Monty's handling of such a high-

powered gathering was nothing short of masterly. By no means all of his audience were on his side, in fact a notable few are dead against him – nothing short of jealousy in our opinion. Our playlet, in which General Hughie gave out his orders for an attack to his divisional commanders, went off very well, and as far as we could see all the people that mattered were suitably impressed.

In the summer of 1955, the exercise programme of late 1954 led on to a series of trials exercises for new organization, equipment and tactics, known collectively as Chameleon. These began soon after the celebration of St David's Day, which Stockwell attended at 1 RWF's barracks, and went on until September. 1 RWF's experience was typical:

> One Officer has worked out that in the last 273 days he has spent 104 nights out of his quarters on training. The result is a very different battalion from the one that was on exercise Two Keys a year ago. . . .
> To impress the Divisional Commander B Company jumped off their Centurions at speeds of up to 25 mph at Borkenbirge . . . At Soltau we almost fried on the backs of those same Centurions during a very dusty heatwave.

Stockwell had the task of directing the exercises, which he did from a Corps HQ in the field. Richard Sinnett, who by now was Stockwell's MA, recalled that 'We have . . . travelled many hundreds of miles in the last ten days as the general as director tries to see as much as possible. We are swamped by the big brass who are spectating. It is nothing to have two or three four-star generals at our HQ.'

More widely, as a result of all this effort, Gale and Stockwell came to certain conclusions. First, that the proposed employment of tactical nuclear weapons was feasible. Secondly, that armoured formations, rather than airborne troops, were the most suitable counter-attack formations. Thirdly, that the corps level of command had to be exercised with troops on the ground – large-scale exercises are often the least interesting for troops, but without large bodies of men and equipment deployed, the frictions of movement and logistics, of getting orders into the hand of the recipient in a timely manner, and the mechanics of planning and conducting a battle from small, mobile, tactical headquarters could not properly be realized. And last, that integration of ground and air forces was essential.

The Secretary of State for War's report, largely compiled by the HQ BAOR staff, concluded that 'hard-hitting, self contained groups' would be the norm in the future and that 'Battles of the future will be fought as battles of all-arms fighting as a team . . . armour is now to be integrated in the infantry brigade.' A genuine step forward in capability was in sight, therefore. The process of reshaping the corps got under way in 1956. The 11th Armoured Division disappeared, and was converted into 4th Infantry Division. It and the 2nd

Division were re-shaped with three brigade groups, each of three infantry battalions and an armoured regiment. 6th and 7th Armoured Divisions were stripped out to provide the units for the two infantry divisions, and became essentially large brigades of four armoured regiments, a motorized infantry battalion, armoured reconnaissance regiment and reduced combat and service support troops. Stockwell however did not see the changes in the corps come to fruition. In August 1956, another unexpected, short-notice, operational command demanded his attention, and he rapidly handed over command of I Corps to Lieutenant General Sir Harold Pyman – President Nasser of Egypt had nationalized the Suez Canal Company.

Notes
1 Later General Sir Kenneth Thomas Darling GBE KCB DSO (born 1921), GOC Cyprus during the latter stages of the EOKA campaign 1958–1960, C-in-C AFNORTH 1967–1969. *Who's Who*, 1971, p. 773.
2 General Sir Richard Nelson Gale GCB KBE DSO MC ADC (Gen) (1896–1982). *Who Was Who, 1981–1990*, p. 274.

Chapter Eighteen

Suez, 1956

Under the terms of the Anglo-Egyptian agreement of 1954, British troops evacuated the Suez Canal Zone in June 1956. Six weeks later, on 26 July, President Gamal Abdel Nasser nationalized the Suez Canal Company. When the news came through, Anthony Eden was dining at 10 Downing Street with King Feisal of Iraq, his son the Crown Prince Abdul-Illah, and Prime Minister Nuri Sa'id. Nuri said to Eden, 'You have only one course of action open and that is to hit, hit now, and hit hard. Otherwise it will be too late. If he [Nasser] is left alone, he will finish all of us.' As the Iraqis left, they passed by a bust of Disraeli. 'That's the old Jew who got you into all this trouble,' said Nuri.

The Stockwell family, meanwhile, had been looking forward to the Bank Holiday when the news broke, but apart from a conventional feeling of irritation that Britain's prestige had been dented in the Middle East, the event made no immediate impact, as he later recalled: 'Little did I realise that within a few days, it would plunge us all into a great adventure – an adventure which, so far as I was concerned, was to bring me many rewarding experiences, but also much frustration and disappointment.'

High-level planning for a military option against Nasser began almost immediately. However the first concern of General Templer, the CIGS, was, as his biographer recorded: 'to have a good, forceful commander to lead the troops if they were going to be used; and he felt strongly that this commander should be intimately concerned from the outset with the planning of the operation. He sent Bill Oliver to Germany to collect Hugh Stockwell.'

On 31 July, therefore, Stockwell received a telegram from the War Office telling him to meet General Sir William Oliver, Vice-Chief of the Imperial General Staff, who was flying across from Britain. Oliver arrived at RAF Gutersloh, then the nearest air station to Bielefeld and the usual terminus for duty flights, at 6.00 pm that evening. Stockwell turned up as instructed and collected Oliver. The VCIGS then told him that he was to command any land operations that might be mounted against Egypt, in what was likely to be a joint and combined undertaking with the French. 'We gathered General Oliver into a party we were throwing that evening at Hoberge and I had the greatest difficulty in keeping the news to myself, and passing off his visit as a normal routine outing.'

As so often before, Stockwell was an obvious choice for this difficult and dangerous task. Templer and Mountbatten – both hugely influential figures who had held vice-regal powers – knew and trusted him; he had a proven record in amphibious operations with 2 RWF and 29 Independent Brigade; he had also commanded an airborne division. He had served in the Middle East before, in Palestine, and in the Canal Zone, the latter in command of one of the strategic reserve formations; and he had had the experience of a rapid deployment in 1951. This last operation had also given him an intimate knowledge not only of the ways and means at hand, but also of the mounting bases, and the terrain over which the force would have to fight. Finally, of course, he spoke good French. The one factor that might have told against him, that he had fought against the French in Madagascar, was clearly outweighed by the rest.

Stockwell and Oliver flew to London the next morning, where Templer briefed him in a busy War Office personally, amid preparations for a forth-coming tripartite conference involving Britain, France and Egypt, and the military activity which would follow any political decisions made there. Stockwell was ordered to hand over his present command, but take such of the corps staff as he needed to form another headquarters, II (BR) Corps, which was to establish a planning cell in London as quickly as possible. Stockwell was then briefed by the Joint Planning Staff on their outline plans for the reoccupation of the Suez Canal Zone, which were based on a re-entry operation through Port Said. His Directive from the British and French Chiefs of Staff instructed him 'to be prepared to mount joint [i.e. multinational] operations against Egypt to restore the Suez Canal to International control by armed force'.[1]

Stockwell returned to Germany on 2 August to collect the key members of the corps staff, to form HQ II Corps, led by Ken Darling as BGS. The party then flew back once more to London on Sunday, 4 August to begin setting up II Corps and the initial operational planning. August Bank Holiday Monday was spent by the staff in being introduced to the old underground wartime HQ beneath the Thames, the Montagu House Annex of the War Office. This was, in Stockwell's own account, a maze of small offices and passages on three floors:

It was an unattractive place to work, you never knew if it was wet or dry, day or night. There was nothing cosy here, nor could the place be properly cleaned. No Mrs Mop on her knees scrubbing the passages with whom one could have a cheerful word as one jumped over her bucket, nor was she there to descend on your office sharp at 5.00 pm to clean you out and send you on your way home; it was all too secret. However, since it was both isolated and secure, we amused ourselves by getting a military policeman to man a blackboard on which he recorded whether it was light or dark, sunny or raining outside.

Stockwell's French deputy, General Beaufre's account was similarly un-complimentary: 'One . . . penetrated into a shelter at the far end of a garden and, going down a rather insalubrious staircase, reached the underground offices . . . they consisted of a series of tiny rooms, lit by electricity and with fresh air pumped in through air ducts as in a ship's cabin.' These working conditions inevitably added to the stress under which commanders and staffs operated.

The corps staff were soon joined by the maritime and air components. The maritime commander was Vice Admiral Sir Maxwell Richmond, the Flag Officer Second-in-Command of the Mediterranean Fleet, who retired in October 1956 and was replaced by Vice-Admiral Sir Robin Durnford-Slater. Air Marshal Denis Barnett, AOC No. 205 Group, Middle East Air Force, commanded the air component. Durnford-Slater in particular selected indi-viduals from the Mediterranean Command to join the HQ, and a number of faces well known to Stockwell appeared, among them Commander Teddy Gueritz from Madagascar days. The core of the air staff was drawn from officers on the Imperial Defence College course, headed by Air Commodore Thomas Prickett as their Chief of Staff. As it happened, Darling, Prickett and Charles Mills, the Naval Chief of Staff, all knew each other and this helped to integrate the staff quickly. In theory, command would shift between Air, Maritime and Land Task Force commanders according to the phase of the operation; however in practice Stockwell was primus inter pares, and led the development and implementation of the plan. It took some time, however, before proper security clearances were issued and those officers permitted to know the details of the operation were designated under the codename Terrapin.

The Anglo-French force had a simple allocation of national commanders, owing to a French willingness to let the British take the lead; France in theory subordinated her armed forces to the British, indicating that she had also sub-ordinated her strategy. As later events showed, this was at best only partially true. At the operational and component levels the arrangements were very simple: the British commanded and the French provided deputies. With their national hats on, these deputies commanded the French elements of the Anglo-French force. This was a straightforward arrangement while national political objectives remained closely aligned, but there were considerable difficulties later when national opinions concerning the timing and withdrawal of the Anglo-French Force diverged – but by then it hardly mattered. Stockwell's deputy was Major General André Beaufre, GOC 2nd Mechanised Infantry Division in Algeria. 'By and large we got on well together,' said Stockwell. 'At any rate we remained friends. He spoke perfect English, which certainly helped my indifferent French.' Beaufre for his part described Stockwell as 'tall, elegant, with a small white swept-back moustache, lively, and intelligent but nervy and as volatile as a "continental"' – not the usual picture that emerges of Stockwell, but if he was volatile and nervy, this is hardly surprising: the political pressures, lack of clear direction, uncertainties over time and place, enormous logistic difficulties, and poor working conditions all contributed to a highly stressful environment for those with great responsibility. Richard Worsley recalled a different impression of Stockwell at this time:

> He was extraordinarily wise, and very shrewd. He was no intellectual, but he thought things through and his judgement was absolutely sound. He understood the role and place of the staff and although he always led the appreciation process he was a very good listener. He handled people wonderfully well, no matter what service or nationality they belonged to: quite simply, we all loved him. And he was tremendously good with the rank and file, who always remembered him and knew exactly who he was. He was, no doubt, a great leader and a great commander.

Beaufre remarked rather cattily that:

> The choice of the leading personalities had clearly been made with an eye to co-operation with our Anglo-Saxon allies. . . We [the French], however, had already submitted a memorandum containing our accept-ance of the inter-allied command organisation proposed by the British. This memorandum, which was to weigh so heavily on subsequent developments, had apparently been accepted without discussion, being regarded as the natural corollary to British 'leadership'. . .
>   From the outset, therefore, we were under a British umbrella and we had accepted an 'integrated' system of command. This was a difficult start, I thought.

Nevertheless, the combined staffs at once began work on the joint planners' paper, which directed the force commanders to be prepared to mount joint and combined operations against Egypt in order to restore the Suez Canal to international control. D-Day was provisionally set for 15 September.

The British land forces allotted for the operation were: 3rd Infantry Division from the United Kingdom; 10th Armoured Division, a cadre division based in Libya; 16 Parachute Brigade; and 3 Commando Brigade Royal Marines. French land forces consisted of the 7th Mobile Mechanised Division, and the 10th Airborne Division of the Foreign Legion. It was a powerful land force, in theory well capable of defeating the Egyptian Army in battle, but things were not all that they seemed. Major General J.B. (Jack) Churcher, GOC 3rd Infantry Division, recalled that on 1 August 1956 the division was ordered to mobilize:

The mobilisation of the Division was a complicated business. We only had five infantry battalions out of nine, therefore four had to be brought in from outside. Our armoured regiment, the Greys, were removed from our command, the 1st and 6th Royal Tank Regiments were put under command, both of them on Salisbury Plain. 1st RTR had not fired its main armament for two years, I discovered, and I therefore refused to allow it to embark until it had done so . . . The drawing of all the mobilisation equipment went reasonably well, but this was the first time anybody had mobilised since the end of the war, there were some sticky moments.

Under Nasser, the Egyptian Army had developed into a comparatively well-equipped force, with improved morale and fighting power. With a strength of about 75,000 infantrymen, much of its equipment was Soviet supplied, and included anything up to 300 modern, well-gunned, and fast main battle tanks. The Army was deployed on two fronts: the bulk of its formations were in the Sinai facing Israel, while the 2nd Infantry Division with an armoured brigade was protecting Port Said and Alexandria. The operational reserve, consisting mainly of armoured troops, was held for the defence of Cairo.

The outline plan given by the joint planners was to blockade Egypt by sea, combined with air action to destroy or neutralize the Egyptian Air Force. This was considered essential, and would be followed, if necessary, by an assault on the northern end of the Suez Canal. There was to be a diversionary operation against Alexandria by concentrating 10th (British) Armoured Division on the Libyan/Egyptian border. Follow-up operations included an advance down the Canal. However, because of the confused strategic ends identified earlier, there was never any clear identification of the centre of gravity of either side in this operation: on the Egyptian side, was the object the capital – and thus Nasser? Was it the Egyptian Army? An assault on Port Said and the Canal Zone might secure the Canal, but would do little to bring down the Egyptian government; while an attack on Alexandria and onwards to Cairo was closer to the seat of the government, but far removed from the scene of the crisis, Suez.

What was the required political end state? As ever it is notoriously difficult unequivocally to establish this in the shifting patterns of strategic relationships in 1956. But British Foreign Office papers express the political objectives fairly clearly: to destroy the Egyptian Army, and thereby to bring down Nasser's government and install a compliant successor; to regain control of the Suez Canal, and then withdraw to the Canal Zone pending establishment of an International Authority. Compare this with the aim set to the military planners at the beginning of August, which gives an explicit indication of the Suez Canal requirement, but no mention of the desire to bring about what we would now call regime change. Thus the aim for the original Operation Musketeer plan was simply to restore the Suez Canal to international control by armed force.

*   *   *

These conundrums quickly became clear to Stockwell and his team, who realized that there were in fact two alternative courses of action. The first was to land at Port Said and focus on the Canal; the second, to land at Alexandria as had been planned when Stockwell was in the Canal Zone in 1952, and focus on the destruction of the Egyptian Army and as a consequence, both regime change and control of the Canal. They came rapidly to the conclusion that Port Said was unsatisfactory as a lodgement from which to develop military operations – the nearest suitable airfield was at Abu Seir, 50 miles south and close to one of the possible concentration areas for Egyptian armoured formations. The beaches were shallow and shelving, and the unloading facilities were limited. Moreover:

> Port Said is like a cork in a bottle with a very long neck: we would have to extract the cork and squeeze down the part that joins Port Said to the rest of Egypt; two parallel roads, the railway and the Sweet Water Canal all run down this causeway alongside the Canal proper. Demolitions along this route would have caused us no end of bother. Port Said, at its southern end, was joined to the causeway by two bridges over a link canal leading to Lake Manzala – only one of which was strong enough to take our Centurion tanks. These, too, could well be destroyed and we would again be faced with having to have bridging equipment well forward in the seaborne assault should we fail to capture these bridges intact. The Sweet Water Canal, which carries all the fresh water to the town, whose population was 170,000, could, too, easily be damaged. This would pose a considerable problem of fresh water supply not only to the civilian population but also for the troops ashore.

Alexandria, on the other hand, offered a suitable airfield that could be captured and consolidated quickly. It had excellent port and harbour facilities, and good beaches immediately to the west over which the assault force could rapidly begin building up a bridgehead. Although coastal defences were believed to be stronger here than at Port Said, the Egyptian forces in the area were fewer, and it would be more difficult for the Egyptians to move re-inforcements rapidly from the Sinai. Finally, there were good exit routes to the south, and the desert road that ran towards Cairo and the Pyramids led to where intelligence sources believed the main part of the Egyptian Army to be concentrated. Foreign Secretary Macmillan and Templer both agreed strongly with this analysis; Beaufre too agreed with the thrust of the argument, and true to form, pointed out that: 'We are in this operation with you because you are carrying it out; should you not do it, however, we would go it alone. It is therefore essential that, within our combined objectives, there should be French objectives.'

Stockwell and his colleagues established at an early stage eight principles in formulating their plans for Operation Musketeer, which were focused on military objectives:

We could not afford to lose. At no stage could we accept risks that might set us back.

We had to ground and destroy the Egyptian Air Force. The Air Marshal wanted 36 hours for the job and we therefore planned to launch the assault 48 hours after the first air strike.

The port and harbour had to be taken by a direct assault by the Royal Marines, supported by the power of the Allied navies.

We had to secure our exits to the south, using both British and French parachute landings to secure the short causeways, which led to the south.

The French assaults across the beaches had to link up quickly with these airborne landings. They had to establish bridgeheads for the follow-up.

We had to get these follow-up forces ashore quickly, so that the British 3rd Division, the British 10th Armoured Division, and the French Light Armoured Division would get to grips with the Egyptian Army and destroy it as soon as possible.

We had to be ready by Sept 15.

We would not enter Cairo.

The team believed that, with the Egyptian Air Force grounded and the Egyptian Army defeated and in disarray, the assault force would be able to move quickly and easily to the occupation of the Suez Canal Zone. There could conceivably be some trouble in crossing over the Delta, but nothing that disturbed them unduly. Alexandria would be established as the main operating base and the force could switch to an advanced base at Port Said later. At no time did the team consider the occupation of the whole of Egypt, or the overthrow of Nasser, or the capture of Cairo:

> We considered our approach would give us the quickest and surest military success; this would then leave us free to occupy the Suez Canal Zone and so restore it to international control. Any thought of occupying Egypt or taking over Cairo would have been out of the question. The forces required for such a job were beyond the capacity of what I had in my order of battle.

In this indirect approach to the objective, there is more than a hint of the experience of Madagascar: land away from the enemy's main strength, establish a base, drive inland and seize the objective from behind – and, moreover, leave the bulk of the land mass of the country untouched.

By 6 August, the team had completed an appreciation and made a plan, and there were combined staff talks with the French on the 7th, although the actual plan was not revealed: this did not go down well with Beaufre who wrote that: 'I imagined that a plan had been drawn up, but there was only an outline known as "Appreciation of the Situation".' Much of Beaufre's ill humour is readily explainable and understandable; Stockwell's own report admits that:

> Until certain measures had been agreed by the ANGLO FRENCH governments, the Task Force Commanders were forced to mislead the FRENCH Commanders and planners as to what the actual current plan was.
> At one particular meeting, the Land Task Force Commander spent over two hours explaining to General BEAUFRE, the FRENCH Land Task Force Commander, the merits of a plan aimed at landing at PORT SAID, while, in fact, the current plan and the one recommended by the Joint Task Force Commanders was the ALEXANDRIA operation.

The meeting referred to was held early on 8 August and the problem resulted from the fears of the Egypt Committee that, because French security was believed to be bad, information would get to the Egyptians from the French Embassy in Cairo as well as to Israel. Ken Darling recalled that Stockwell told him that the Alexandria plan could not be briefed to the French, and that:

> The best I could do when the joint meeting started was to pass round a note, surreptitiously saying no surprise was to be shown at whatever General Stockwell said . . . General Stockwell then gave a brilliant exposition which left the impression that our plans were to land at Port Said rather than Alexandria.

On Thursday, 9 August, Stockwell and his colleagues emerged to present the appreciation and plan to the Chiefs of Staff in the high-ceilinged, wood-panelled conference room of the War Office on Whitehall. Mountbatten was in the chair and the room was filled with upwards of 200 staff officers of all three Services:

> This was an important moment for us task force commanders. We were presenting a new plan, different from that which the Joint Planners had produced, and which up to now had been the basis of the military precautions that were being taken. We had to convince the Chiefs of Staff. We had to prove the validity of our choice of Alexandria, not Port Said, as our point of assault.

Admiral Richmond outlined the naval plans. He described the fire support to the assault by the Royal Marines on the harbour; the close in-shore fire support by destroyers; the support for the beach landings; and the employment of aircraft from the Fleet Air Arm as close support for the parachute troops. Air Marshal Barnett gave the air plan. Heavy bomber attacks on the Egyptian airfields by night, and fighter sweeps by day, would ground and immobilize the Egyptian Air Force. He estimated that 36 hours were needed to complete the task. Using the available British and French transport aircraft, the air forces could deliver 940 British parachute troops, and 960 French troops, to secure the causeways vital to the breakout southwards.

> I outlined the tasks of the Royal Marines, once ashore, to clear the port and harbour area; the tasks of the French sea assault to establish their bridgeheads ashore and their link-up with the airborne landings; the tasks of the follow-up forces in their advance to bring the Egyptian Army to battle. There was no inter-Service rivalry. Each of us was to hold the overall command of the operation when our own Service was in the ascendant: the Admiral during the naval phase, the Air Marshal during the air phase and myself during the land phase. The Marines once ashore, the parachutists once landed and the French over the beaches, all then came under my command. We reckoned on two days for the air phase, one day to establish ourselves ashore, two days to get at the Egyptian Army and perhaps three days more to get on to the Canal. By day five we would be at grips with the battle and by day eight we would have begun to line up along the Canal.

This plan certainly has Stockwell's fingerprints on it, but it also bears a remarkable resemblance to the Overlord plan: establish air supremacy, drop in airborne troops, link up by seaborne landing under the cover of the guns of the fleet, drive inland and build up logistics. The French view had been rather different: a short air bombardment and a drive on Cairo. But to Stockwell's relief, the Chiefs of Staff accepted the plan in principle, and the detailed planning was authorized. At the same time, a staff exercise of some magnitude – Operation Poker – was in progress to get forces on the move, and eventually deliver them off Egypt from widely dispersed locations. This was necessary since there was no one port within reach capable of handling the volume of sea traffic involved. The 3rd Infantry Division was concentrating on Salisbury Plain and the 10th Armoured Division was preparing to move from Libya. The Royal Marine Brigade had to concentrate in Malta, where its Headquarters was located, by bringing two of its three Commandos back from Cyprus. 16 Para Brigade was to bring its remaining battalion, combat support and combat service support troops from Britain and concentrate in Cyprus. These moves began as early as 12 August. The bulk of the French troops were in Algeria and all needed retraining. Just as important as the men and vehicles was the logistic support: there was insufficient food, fuel, aircraft bombs and ammunition of all natures stockpiled in either Cyprus or Malta, and this meant that additional stocks would have to be moved from Europe, creating more competition with movement assets. Only two serviceable Landing Ships Tank could be found, a figure that was raised to twelve by the time the operation was launched. As a further complication, Stockwell himself exercised no direct command authority over the assigned troops during this period: units in the Middle East and Cyprus were commanded and administered by GHQ MELF, while units in Britain and Germany were handled directly from the War Office through the Command concerned.

Moving the troops was not the only problem – there were also specialized preparations required. The two battalions of the Parachute Regiment in Cyprus engaged in anti-terrorist operations had to be relieved and taken to England to be given refresher training, since they had not jumped for over a year. They then had to be re-concentrated in Cyprus. Two of the Royal Marine Commandos were likewise engaged and had to be taken to Malta for amphibious training, which they had not done for ten months. Then RAF Transport Command had to be prepared and retrained to drop the parachutists; the landing craft for the Royal Marines had to be taken out of mothballs and moved to Malta; a new armoured brigade had to be formed for the 3rd Division, and the opportunity for some combined arms collective training organized.

Of course, everyone wanted new or additional equipment. The required LSTs to move tanks had been sold off at the end of the Second World War, and had to be recovered from Messrs Bustards, who were using them for the Irish pig trade! There was no waterproofing equipment for vehicles, which had to be found in stores depots and issued. Neither the parachute battalions nor the commandos had any anti-tank guns. Every officer and man had to be made battle-worthy, and the joint and combined headquarters had to be meshed together to develop an efficient command, staff and communications system. There was no headquarters ship, and no hospital ship. There was less and less time to put all this right. Given that this operation was taking place only twelve years after the greatest amphibious operation in history – the Normandy landings – the decay in capability is astonishing.

There was also one major procedural problem, already referred to: from where was this vast operation to be mounted in something approaching security? Cyprus had very limited harbour facilities; the only port, Famagusta, was already working to capacity to keep the forces on the island supported. Its airfields at Nicosia and Akrotiri would have to be strengthened and the runways extended. Moreover the work would have to be finished quickly if the timetable was to be met. As it was, the RAF had to develop and restore an old wartime airstrip at Tymbou, which caused a few old-fashioned looks from the pilots. But Malta, with its crowded towns and villages, small fields and rugged terrain was not the place in which to train or concentrate a large number of troops; it was, moreover, 900 miles away. It was decided that the only sensible course of action was to mount the airborne operation from Cyprus; the French therefore took over Tymbou. The sea assault would have to come from Malta and Algiers, with the follow-up from the United

Kingdom, Algiers and Libya. One important implication of this was that although the air planners were sure that 48 hours would be more than enough to complete the suppression of enemy air defences and the destruction of the Egyptian Air Force, they would have to develop enough target sets to maintain operations for the full four days needed for the assault forces to be convoyed to the Egyptian coast:

> The underground headquarters were not conducive to continuous high-pressure work and tempers flared from time to time; but it let off steam. On 24th August we accompanied the Chiefs of Staff to Downing Street, to present our plans to the Prime Minister and his colleagues, and to obtain their approval.
>
> We had been over to the Cabinet Office in advance to set up our maps. This was an exciting and stirring moment for me, not having been in 10 Downing Street before. Sir Anthony Eden gave us every encouragement, asking questions to clarify a point. He seemed confident and gay and with his natural charm thanked us and quickly gave his approval in principle to our ideas. While I am sure he must have been having a difficult time politically, he instilled me with confidence and I left much encouraged that our efforts so far had borne fruit.
>
> Though the many delays and changes of plan that were to follow caused much disturbance in our military hearts, little did I realise at the time the relentless political pressures that the Prime Minister was being subjected to right up to the moment that Musketeer was launched.

With political approval obtained, the staff could now produce an operation order, and this was issued on that same day, 24 August. General Sir Charles Keightley, Commander-in-Chief Middle East, had been appointed as Supreme Commander on 11 August, with the French Vice Admiral Pierre Barjot, C-in-C French Mediterranean Fleet, as his deputy. When the plan was discussed that day, Barjot sprang a surprise by suggesting that while the British attacked Alexandria, they should attack Port Said. Even Beaufre was caught out to an extent, and although he could not openly disagree, suggested that the Port Said operation might be examined as an alternative, contingency plan. Keightley and Stockwell, who had greeted Barjot's intervention 'with pained surprise', agreed to undertake a study.

The appointment of a Supreme Commander left the Task Force commanders free to get on with their preparations and to concentrate on fighting the battle, but still left some loose ends. Keightley, the theatre commander, was in Cyprus, distant from the action, with good strategic communications back to London and Paris, but poor tactical communications forward. Prickett recalled, for example, that Keightley had no impact whatsoever on business at his level. But at least Stockwell was now able to start getting around and visiting his assigned forces.

I flew to Algeria [on 2nd September] and stayed with General Beaufre and saw the Foreign Legion Division and the 7th Light Armoured Division. Both were fully battle-worthy. The former were much beribboned and had been at it for years in Indo-China and Algeria; they were a tonic to meet. They were led by General [Jacques] Massu, a tough and determined commander. I was certainly glad he was on our side!

I went on to Cyprus and saw FM Harding, who liked our ideas, although it was difficult for him having to cough up some of his best troops. The Parachute Brigade was getting ready and the airfields were being lengthened and strengthened for the many aircraft that were to be deployed there. I went on to Malta to see Admiral Grantham, the C-in-C Mediterranean. I was back in London by 4th September.

This last date cannot be quite right, for on 5th September, Beaufre and Stockwell were on board the HQ ship, HMS *Tyne,* off Malta taking part in an assault landing exercise. Stockwell in fact returned to London on the 8th.

When Stockwell got back, he found that it was no longer possible to begin the operation on 15 September: six days were needed to sail the assault forces from Malta, ten days for the forces from the United Kingdom, and six to seven days for the French from Algeria. The troops also had to be moved to the sea and air ports of embarkation. The last safe moment for a decision had, therefore, already passed. Later, the required moves were compressed into a period of ten days, but on 4 September, the operation was postponed by four days until 19 September. On the 6th, it was put off again for a further seven days to 26 September. By 8 September, the bulk of the striking force was in place and ready for Musketeer; the parachute battalions had been flown back to England, had done their training jumps at Imber DZ on Salisbury Plain, and were back in Cyprus. The 6th Royal Tank Regiment, now detached from 3rd Infantry Division, was positioned in Malta, ready to join the sea assault in support of the Royal Marine Brigade. The French parachutists were at Tymbou in Cyprus. But the planners estimated that the operation could not be held in suspense for longer than twenty-one days, because of the many and varied administrative problems building up. This meant that 6 October was the latest date for D-Day. Because of this, an idea was floated by the French at a meeting between Eden and Prime Minister Guy Mollet on 10 September, that an economic blockade backed by air and naval action only, aimed at destroying the Egyptian Army from the air, would suffice. Ground troops could then land in limited numbers, facing little or no opposition. It was thought that such a plan would be more flexible, would allow the timing of the operation with diplomatic activity, could be mounted more quickly and could be held for longer, and most importantly to avoid what were likely to be unacceptable casualties and collateral damage in and around Alexandria. The landing force objective was to be at Port Said, followed by the occupation of the canal and then a drive on Cairo as a subsequent operation.

There had without doubt been political second thoughts about the original

Musketeer plan, despite Eden's exasperation with what he considered as an over-cautious approach by the military; but Templer's caution was largely on logistic grounds, which suggested that if an attack on Alexandria did not lead to the end of organized Egyptian military resistance and the overthrow of Nasser within two months then 'it will be necessary to pause for approximately two months to enable logistical build-up to support a second phase.' Templer was also cautious because of the likely bill for troops that an occupation of Egypt – the logical conclusion of Musketeer – would bring: 'To hold it will take eight divisions and 500 Military Government officers,' he remarked. Keightley was also in no doubt that a change of plan was required; Stockwell and the other force commanders therefore had no option but to work up a new plan, known as Musketeer Revise. Stockwell, who was described at this point as being 'discouraged and on edge', had considerable reservations, as did Barnett. He wrote later that:

I must not leave the impression that our first strategic scheme was any flash in the pan. It had, after all, been recommended by the Chiefs of Staff and accepted by the Prime Minister . . . Once I was confident it was going ahead I flew out to Algeria to see . . . Beaufre. I also went on to Cyprus . . . It wasn't until I got back from Cyprus that I learned of the change of plan.

Beaufre too remarked that at the time Stockwell took the revision of the plan, in which so much had been invested, very badly:

I found Stockwell downcast and on edge. He was visibly discouraged and fulminated continuously about 'politicians'. He even added: 'You should be happy; it's your plan' . . . During this phase General Stockwell for the first time showed the characteristics which he was to display during the operation – highly strung, mercurial, irritable and then suddenly courtesy itself.

On the twentieth anniversary of the operation in 1976, Stockwell was interviewed by Frank Gillard in the *Listener*. When asked if the original intention had been to occupy all of Egypt, Stockwell replied interestingly, 'It looked like it, yes, from what we were planning.' No wonder Templer had taken fright. When asked therefore that while an invasion through Alexandria would look like war on Egypt, an action through Port Said could be presented as police action, Stockwell accepted the point.

The Revise plan was given a fresh aim, which in today's terminology was more a statement of intent rather than an aim. This was 'to create by sustained air offensive and by psychological warfare a situation whereby the Egyptian will to resist is broken and we can secure the Canal Zone, with a view to establishing international control and administration of the canal'. There was no mention of regime change, but otherwise a similar statement of political objective. It was a return to the Joint Planners' first concept of operations, a concept that Stockwell and the other Joint Task Force commanders had already discarded:

I believe that the weight and size of our assault against Alexandria, the fact that it wasn't directed immediately against the Suez Canal, and the difficulty of holding the operation indefinitely, together with the political discussions, which had so far prevented Musketeer being launched, all contributed to this change of heart. So the Alexandria operation was scrubbed and locked away, and we had to start all over again . . . Musketeer Revise, was planned in three phases:-

Phase I: The neutralisation of the Egyptian Air Force.

Phase II: Combined with a psychological warfare programme, a continued air offensive to disrupt the Egyptian economy, morale and armed forces.

Phase III: The domination of the Canal Zone and its occupation by land, sea and air forces as might be necessary.

The plan was to be such that it could be held till the end of October. No specific timings were given for Phase II, but in its original form, it was believed that Phases I and II would last between ten and fourteen days. In particular, Phase II was something quite new, involving the destruction of Cairo Radio, a carefully prepared programme of broadcasts from Cyprus, and then – and very ambitiously given the available technology – attacks on point targets of military value.

For myself, I was always convinced that we should have to put in an assault from the air and sea with land forces. I did not believe that a prolonged air offensive could win the day. Experience indicates that it tends to harden resistance, and I had my doubts as to the value, as a weapon, of psychological warfare. Anyhow, with modifications and variations the final operation was launched within the framework of Musketeer Revise.

A reduced order of battle was required for the assault on Port Said, so some units were stood down. There were also logistic adjustments required: ships had been lying alongside loaded with their vehicles and stores for over a month; their batteries were deteriorating, and maintenance all round was urgent. Some ships ought to have been unloaded, but with the uncertainty of when the fleet was to sail, this could not be done. As a result, for example, the Officers' Mess truck of the Life Guards was carried into Port Said, even though the Regiment had been dropped out of the order of battle, but 'At least this valuable vehicle got itself well up in the assault!' Reservists were also beginning to get restless. These men had been called up in early August; they were divorced from their families, homes and their civilian jobs. They had, said Stockwell, 'done splendidly, fitted into the pattern quickly, and were a great asset throughout the force,' but without action they were being thrown back on to routine domestic chores to keep them busy, and this brought boredom and discontent in its wake.

Planning continued through September, as Stockwell recalled:

Phrases such as 'police action' or an 'intervention' began creeping into our deliberations. These to us were divergences. We were clear that we would, if we were to go into action, use all the means at our disposal to win and win quickly. After all, one's soldiers had to be given every chance to do their job with the minimum of damage to themselves, and any other approach would be both risky and unnecessary.

The Revise plan was ready in draft by 17 September, and from 24 to 27 September Stockwell again visited Cyprus and Malta for discussions with Keightley and Grantham; and to visit units in both places. Meanwhile, the second London Conference, begun on 19 September, had rumbled to an indefinite conclusion; there was again no unanimity between the eighteen nations involved – the Egyptians did not take part – and Soviet opposition in the United Nations Security Council. On 6 October the Task Force commanders received instructions to prepare a Winter Plan for Musketeer, which might have to be held indefinitely. They were to hold the Task Forces together, at the same time devise some means of relaxation from the current state of readiness, but still be ready to launch the operation at ten days' notice. As Stockwell remarked, 'A somewhat dampening effect now began to pervade the air in the underground headquarters. After two months of excitement and anticipation of action it was something of a reaction.' The order for the Winter Plan was issued on 12 October, the fourth successive plan that had been prepared in little over four weeks, each one with a mass of detail and supporting instructions.

But now, Stockwell began to detect an air of mystery and intrigue among the French. He assumed that it must be connected with their supply of arms and equipment to the Israelis, and it had no appreciable effect on military planning: 'We had no inkling yet that the Israelis were also planning operations against Egypt and at no time throughout Musketeer did we have any contact with them, nor did their eventual action influence us in any way in our planning.' But by 15 October the Winter Plan was dead, and orders were issued to get ready to mount Musketeer Revise.

We were back in the act again. As it was, we had planned a naval and communication exercise [Exercise Boathook] together with a loading exercise for the Amphibious Force in Malta for the last week in October, so that the Fleet was assembling there. My own plans were to get out there and see it. HMS *Tyne*, our headquarters ship, was there too.

By 20 October events began to move quickly, and the staffs were completing work on the final details of Musketeer Revise. Stockwell decided to break Phase III of the plan into three stages: Stage One was to be a landing by the assault forces. Here he had, he felt, two alternatives: first, in the event of no opposition, or only light opposition, he could push the assault forces quickly through the town and on down the causeway; secondly if there was determined opposition, the assault forces would clear the town, and second echelon forces would then be passed through, and drive on down the causeway. Stage Two would be a build-up of forces in Port Said, the capture of Abu Seir airfield to the south-west of the causeway, and the opening of the Canal as far as Ismailia. Stage Three would be the occupation of the whole Canal. With one modification this plan was the basis on which Musketeer was finally launched. 45,000 British troops, with 12,000 vehicles, 300 aircraft and 100 warships were involved, along with 34,000 French troops, with 9,000 vehicles, 200 aircraft and 30 ships.

Once the order to launch the operation was given, hostilities were to open with an air offensive. At the same time, the assault fleets from Malta and Algeria were to sail, as would the follow-up forces from the United Kingdom and Algeria. The air offensive had to be sustained throughout the six-day transit of the fleet, and until such time as the amphibious forces were in position off Port Said.

The assault would be a combination of parachute landings by both British and French brigades, and a landing across the beach, with naval gunfire support, and close air support provided by the Fleet Air Arm. The second echelon of the assault would be a British parachute battalion brought in by sea, which was to advance south down the causeway.

The final Operation Order, Number 4, a full and detailed document covering all the timings, loading of craft, detailed tasks for all the units and both the air and sea support programme, was issued on 24 October. On the 26th, Stockwell and Ken Darling flew to Villacoubay, near Paris, to meet Beaufre:

By now, I had sensed in London that the French were more aware of Israeli intentions than we were and that they were getting their end of Musketeer jacked up ready to go, while we were still busy getting ready for Exercise Boathook. I think, therefore, that Beaufre was anxious to see me to convey the sense of urgency. Though I didn't discover all that was afoot, it became clear to me as a result of our talks that the Israelis were about to launch an attack on Egypt. General Beaufre never, in fact, said as much. But from the urgency he expressed for us to get cracking it was clear that the French knew what was cooking. We tied up our communication arrangements and agreed to meet in Malta.

There had indeed been a secret deal, as is well known, and Stockwell was probably the first British commander to be told the bones of the deal. Doubtless Beaufre enjoyed the chance to pay back the earlier British deception over Port Said. Ken Darling recalled that:

> There were two or three rather dilapidated wartime huts . . . There were one or two odd gendarmes standing about, sucking their teeth . . . Meanwhile I and the other officers of General Stockwell's staff sort of hung about kicking our heels. Eventually [Stockwell] came out of the hut and took me to one side and told me what he had learnt from General Beaufre, which was in a nutshell that it was likely that the Israelis were going to attack Egypt and we would undoubtedly get involved.

Stockwell said in his interview with Frank Gillard for the *Spectator* in 1976 that:

> It was in early October that we sensed there was anything like that going on, and, in point of fact, it wasn't until I saw General Beaufre at Villacoublay on the 26 October that I really knew for the first time that the Israelis were in on the act . . . in early October . . . the French, I think, were fully aware of exactly what was going to happen. But it was never disclosed to the joint task force commanders.

He later added that:

> Cairo was never our objective. I cannot help wondering now what other plans we, the humble soldiers, might have made, had we ever been told, or been allowed to share in, the secret deal the French in particular were cooking up with the Israelis. Certainly, had I known my left flank was secure, while we advanced down the canal, then the French . . . could have attacked through Alex while the British went down the canal to Port Said. It would have meant we could have accepted much more readily the possibility of the roads south being blown up . . . I would not have had to worry about being cut off. We could have accepted much greater risks with our parachute forces.
>
> I myself never had much, if any, contact with the many and varied politicians and diplomats . . . I was too busy.

The secret deal at Sèvres was a final attempt to provide a casus belli with at least the appearance of legitimacy: an Israeli attack, Operation Kadesh, was to be made on 29 October, following which Britain and France could intervene, with the supposed intention of separating the combatants and creating a demilitarized zone of 10 miles each side of the Canal. The political and intellectual acrobatics needed to justify this were considerable: 'We were all flummoxed,' said Prickett, 'because Musketeer had been developed on the basis of seizing the Suez Canal. It was now to be implemented to separate forces – something it had never been intended to do and really needed a new plan. It was thus obviously bogus from the start.' The Israelis were never part of the unified command structure, as the illusion had to be maintained that the Anglo-French adventure was a stabilizing force to be committed on the sole ground that it was a reaction to the Israeli attack in the Sinai. Some, but not all, of this was clear by the time that Stockwell and Darling flew on to Malta, where they arrived at about 8.00 pm on the 26th.[2]

On arrival in Malta, Stockwell and Darling went immediately to see Admiral Grantham, who was receiving information from London. The Vice-Quartermaster General, Lieutenant General Sir John Cowley, wrote that:

> At 5.30 pm on Friday, 26th October 1956, the C.I.G.S., Field Marshal Sir Gerald Templer, a splendid but not the most patient of men, who had remained remarkably calm throughout this difficult period, sent for me and said: 'The Prime Minister has decided that the landing at Port Said must take place as soon as possible, but he has said that no-one is yet to be told.' Those were Templer's actual words, but I knew him well enough to realise what he intended me to do.
>
> I returned to my office and telephoned the Director of Movements, Major General Robbie Ewbank, and said to him: 'I am not allowed to tell you this, but if I should state that the Port Said Operation is on and the troops waiting in Malta and North Africa must be alerted and embarked and sail as soon as possible to the Eastern Mediterranean, what would you do?' His immediate reply, which I remember distinctly, was 'I would assume that you had gone off your head.' 'You have every right to assume that,' I replied, 'and on that assumption I want you to collect all the ships available as soon as you can so that the troops . . . can be loaded without delay and sail for the Eastern Mediterranean.' Luckily, the Senior Officials of the Ministry of Shipping (as it was then called) were still in their offices and they got down to work immediately.

As a result of the information that Stockwell had brought, and the information that Grantham had received from London, it was decided to hold a conference at once. It was quickly determined at this conference that Exercise Boathook would be used to mount the assault as soon as the order to go was received. As Stockwell later remarked, 'Many officers and other ranks left UK ostensibly to take part in [Exercise Boathook] and the social life attached thereto only to find themselves in the real thing, slightly inadequately and inappropriately equipped.' Vice Admiral Sir Manley ('Lofty') Power, C-in-C Home Command and the flag officer in command of the aircraft carriers, had *Albion, Bulwark* and *Ark Royal* lying off Malta and said at once that he would sail with them to his operational area first thing in the morning, which he did. At the same time, loading of the transports started. Stockwell was also told by signal that French troops had embarked at Algiers: 'They were itching to be off. I think they thought that the Israeli attack might prejudice the planned Allied operations.'

The Israelis launched their attack on 29 October. The Anglo-French ultimatum was issued on the 30th, and was due to expire on the 31st. This demanded that Israel and Egypt should each stand back 10 miles from their own side of the Canal, or in the event of their refusal the Allies would invade Egypt to enforce these terms. The Israelis accepted the terms while Egypt refused them, even though Nasser agreed to a ceasefire. Musketeer was ordered, and in the circumstances it was directed solely against Egypt.

But the plan now contained fundamental problems that were inevitable given the foundations of quicksand that had been laid for the operational commanders. The casus belli for military intervention had not been made clear: that used to start the operation was the Israeli attack on Egypt, but the planners were working instead on a plan that had a much more deliberate build-up of force. The results of this were significant: first, the operational plan was not based upon a need to separate Egyptian and Israeli forces quickly. This, to much embarrassment all round, meant that the British were not able to insert a force between the Israelis and the Egyptians. The warring parties agreed to the ceasefire on 2 November, before the insertion of an Anglo-French airborne force could be achieved, which would at the earliest be on 5 November. The ostensible reason for intervening was thus removed, and whatever legitimacy the French and British might have gained for their military intervention was significantly undermined. Secondly, it meant that the only legitimate purpose for the military operation would be the imposition and monitoring of a cease-fire, and that was clearly not in accordance with the Anglo-French objective of seizing the Canal to restore it to international control.

Be that as it may, the military had orders to proceed at best speed. By what Stockwell described as a shrewd bit of anticipation, the assault fleet from Malta had sailed at 10.00 pm on 30 October, which meant that it would be off Port Said by late evening on 5 November, and the assault could go in at first light on the 6th. The British and French commanders met on the 30th and 31st to refine their plans. Back in Britain, by 7.00 am on 1 November, troop trains were pulling out of Dover and Colchester for Southampton and that evening the troopships *Empire Fowey, Empire Ken, Dilwara* and *Asturia* sailed into the channel with 3rd Infantry Division (less 1 Guards Brigade) on board. A day ahead of them steamed the transports carrying their vehicles and the tanks of 1st RTR.

Stockwell himself had sailed for Cyprus in HMS *Tyne* on 30 October with the whole of the operational headquarters staff on board. By the time that the headquarters were established there, only one day's steaming from the Egyptian coast, the air offensive was in full swing. Generally this went according to plan and was planned closely with the French, and, through them, the Israelis by daily telephone conferences. One episode confirms this: the Egyptians had moved their heavy bombers to Luxor, out of range of Cyprus-based aircraft, and so Prickett asked the French to have these attacked by the Israelis. This they duly did, although it was always assumed in London that the RAF had done the job. 'I did not disillusion them,' Prickett recalled. Air photographs brought in for Air Marshal Barnett's attention confirmed the accuracy of bombing attacks against the airfields. These attacks began at night, but were soon followed up by daylight raids and fighter sweeps designed rapidly to neutralize the Egyptian Air Force. Barnett was certain that he could achieve this while minimizing death, injury and damage to the civilian population, their buildings and houses. But on orders from the Cabinet Office, the size of bombs used had twice been reduced, down to 250lb, in order to minimize damage. There were also protests from the Americans, who were using Cairo West to evacuate their nationals. Stockwell himself, his views no doubt coloured by fighting the Japanese in Burma, thought little of this, remarking that avoiding casualties: 'wasn't so easy. For if an enemy fights, you cannot be all that choosy when you have a job to do and your own neck is in danger.' British forces were being sent into action by their political masters with serious limitations on the fire support available to the assault troops; that this could have happened with Service chiefs of the stature of Templer and Mountbatten is surprising. Moreover the psychological operations phase was hardly implemented at all: no resources were allocated to public information or media broadcasting, and the lack of smart munitions made it impossible for the RAF to put Cairo Radio out of action early on.

Stockwell's headquarters in Cyprus was located at Akrotiri, but Beaufre was 50 miles away – two hours by road or half an hour's flight – at Tymbou: not a happy situation and one which led to complications and dislocations during the working up of contingency plans:

> In Cyprus we Task Force Commanders were continually under pressure, chiefly I think on French instigation, to accelerate the next phase of Musketeer. They felt that we should be able to cash in on the Israelis' rapid advance and successes in Sinai. On reflection, had we known of the Israeli intentions and planned our operations accordingly, and had we sailed the assault forces in anticipation of their attack sooner, maybe we could have got in quicker and got farther down the Canal than we did . . . But as we couldn't sail the sea assault from Malta in anticipation of Musketeer, our timings were controlled by the six days' sailing time. There was no alternative.

This pressure led to a series of contingency plans being evolved. The first of these was Omelette, a quick occupation of Port Said by airborne troops against negligible opposition, and Omelette II, an opposed parachute landing, which was Beaufre's brainchild. Then there was Simplex, a parachute descent on Gamil airfield by both the British and French parachutists to seize the airfield and probe towards the town, co-ordinated with the seaborne assault. Last, there was Telescope, which was essentially a reworking of Simplex, aimed at securing both Gamil airfield and the crossings of the interior basin; and Telescope Modified, again the work of Beaufre, a similar parachute operation with only French troops. The French pushed hard for Omelette, which accorded with their agenda as expressed some time before by Barjot; but Stockwell refused absolutely, and settled for Telescope as being an acceptable risk. Stockwell's account again:

> The night before we sailed [it was shortly before dawn on the 4th] Mr. Head, the Minister of Defence, and the CIGS, Sir Gerald Templer, flew into Cyprus to tie up the last bits and pieces. We had clear instructions to keep damage in Port Said to a minimum. This would be to our eventual advantage and we had to be careful over casualties, particularly to the civilian population. This wasn't so easy, as if an enemy fights you cannot be all that choosy when you have a job to do and your own neck is in danger. I thought the CIGS felt as if he would have liked to join in.

The arrival of Templer and Head had followed meetings with the French General Staff in London on 2nd and 3rd, at which the French urged that the operation be speeded up in order to minimise the delay between the start of the bombing and the landing. When asked if things could be speeded up, Stockwell answered, 'We can't move until we're ready. We are ready now with the paratroops, but we can't put them in without support.' In fact, Major (later General Sir) Anthony Farrar-Hockley, then DAA&QMG, recalled that until forty-eight hours before the assault, the bulk of the brigade was still engaged in IS operations against EOKA in the hills of Cyprus, and had only just assembled in time. It was agreed therefore that the operation would commence the next day, with the parachute insertion twenty-four hours in advance of the arrival of the seaborne assault force. The troops were to push hard to secure the Canal, but there would be no move on Cairo.

HMS *Tyne* sailed from Cyprus for the Egyptian coast at 4.00 pm on 4 November. On board was the corps staff, reinforced by an air cell with a Group Captain Operations, detached from the main air staff that remained in Cyprus. A maritime air cell controlled all close-support ground- attack aircraft – which were carrier-based naval aircraft anyway – and the helicopters. Beaufre, unhappy with the ship's limited communications fit and with the arrangements for his staff, had transferred to the French ship *Gustave-Zédé*, leaving his second-in-command, General de la Boisse, as liaison officer. From elsewhere, the assault force was now closing in on Port Said: the Cyprus convoy with the immediate follow-on parachute battalions; the Malta convoy with HQ 3 Commando Brigade under Brigadier R.W. Madoc, 40 and 42 Commandos and the 6th Royal Tanks; the Algiers convoy with French troops; the United Kingdom convoy; the battleship *Jean Bart*, with the destroyers and

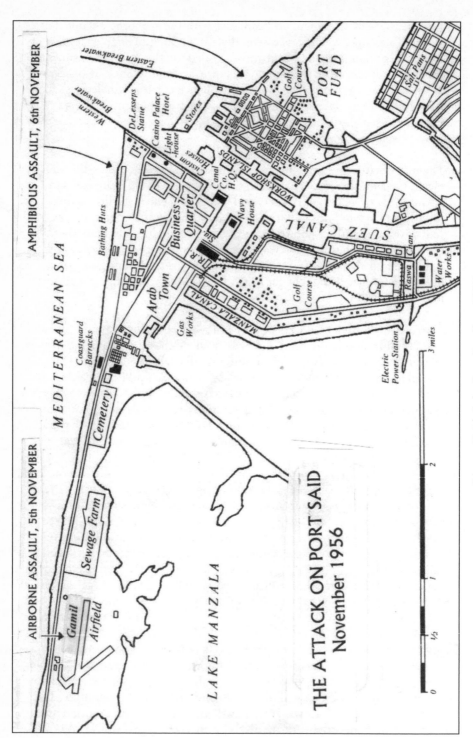

THE ATTACK ON PORT SAID
November 1956

AIRBORNE ASSAULT, 5th NOVEMBER

AMPHIBIOUS ASSAULT, 6th NOVEMBER

MEDITERRANEAN SEA

Gamil Airfield

Sewage Farm

Cemetery

Coastguard Barracks

Bathing Huts

Western Breakwater

Eastern Breakwater

DeLesseps Statue

Casino Palace Hotel

Light-house

Stores

Custom Houses

Canal Co. H.Q.

Navy House

Business Quarter

Arab Town

Gas Works

LAKE MANZALA

MANZALA CANAL

Golf Course

PORT FUAD

Golf Course

WORKSHOP ISLANDS

SUEZ CANAL

Salt Pans

Raswa Chan.

Water Works

Electric Power Station

0   ½   1   2   3 miles

Source: Keith Lyle, *Suez* (London, 1989).

cruisers that would provide naval gunfire support; HMS *Theseus* and *Ocean* carrying 45 Commando and the helicopters which would take the marines ashore. *Albion, Bulwark, Eagle* and two French carriers were already on station. As dawn broke on 5 November Stockwell was on the bridge while the leading aircraft of the stream carrying Lieutenant Colonel Paul Crook and his 3rd Parachute Battalion for the assault on Gamil flew overhead signalling 'G.M.' The yeoman of signals on the bridge quickly interpreted this as 'Good Morning!'

The British assault went in fifteen minutes before the French, and both were successful. Both had been directed onto small, confined dropping zones – particularly so the French – and both had to deal with some fierce resistance. The French paratroopers quickly captured the bridges: one was intact – a stroke of luck – the other blown. Stockwell's account continues:

> The whole gamut of battle was abroad: smoke, shelling, aircraft screaming overhead. Messages were coming into HMS *Tyne* from Brigadier Butler, the Commander of 16 Parachute Brigade, and from General [Jean] Gilles, the Commander of the French airborne assault. Gilles was flying above his troops in a transport, directing such supporting fire as they needed from the fighter aircraft who circled above awaiting orders to attack. This was a risky role, particularly as some half dozen of the Transport aircraft had been hit by the Egyptian AA fire, though without loss. Our communications worked well and I was in touch with General Keightley, General Beaufre in his headquarters ship, and Brigadier Butler ashore.

The 3rd Parachute Battalion was making good progress towards the town, dealing with any Egyptian resistance; Colonel Château-Jobert's *2ème Régiment Parachutiste Coloniale* had Port Said sealed off, and was in control of the area astride the Interior Basin. Stockwell asked Beaufre to mount a second French parachute assault on to the southern end of Port Fouad. This too was successful.

As early as 1.00 pm, French officers had been in contact by telephone with the Egyptian brigade commander, Colonel Hassan Rushdi, and at about 4.15 pm Rushdi opened negotiations for a ceasefire. At 4.30 pm, Butler arrived at Château-Jobert's headquarters, followed at about 5.00 pm by the Military Governor of Port Said, General El Mogih. Surrender terms were dictated to the Egyptians, and they were given until 9.30 pm to comply. The news of the surrender talks had been relayed by radio to Stockwell on the *Tyne* and Beaufre on the *Gustave-Zédé* at about 4.30 pm. Both had quickly dictated the terms of surrender, referred them to Keightley and Barjot for approval and had passed them to Butler and his French counterparts ashore. The shooting stopped and air attacks were put on hold. But at about 10.15 pm, before the ceasefire could be fully implemented, the local Egyptian commander had got through to Cairo and had been told to go on fighting. He was further told that

London and Paris were under attack from the Russians and that he would be well advised to be on the winning side! So the operation had to be restarted. Approval was given by Keightley to launch the amphibious assaults the next morning, though with continuing severe restrictions on supporting fire so as to keep damage and casualties to a minimum.

When the ceasefire had been called, revised orders were given to 3 Commando Brigade.[3] Instead of clearing the town, as had been the original intention, the brigade was ordered to move straight through and push on southwards down the causeway as quickly as possible. This order had to be reversed when the ceasefire was aborted. As night fell, Stockwell ordered the follow-on parachute battalion ashore to consolidate the position. He also ordered Butler to get one of his battalions – the 3rd as it turned out – to advance eastwards on the town from Gamil to support the link-up with the amphibious assault which would come in from Butler's right flank.

As dawn came up on 6 November, destroyers laid down saturation fire on the beaches to soften up any defences. 40 and 42 Commandos closed to the beaches in their Buffaloes, were quickly ashore and established a bridgehead. The Egyptian defenders had abandoned their positions and so opposition was negligible. Stockwell was therefore able to order the launch of 45 Commando by helicopter to increase the rate of build-up ashore.

As these moves began, Stockwell received a wireless message from Madoc, suggesting that there was a chance to achieve an unconditional surrender through the auspices of the Italian Consul. Characteristically, he decided to investigate personally, but said nothing to his Chief of Staff about where he was going:

> So with Air Marshal Barnett and General Beaufre I set off to go ashore. The Admiral escorted us in. As we were milling around off the town in the motor launch, looking for somewhere to land, we were smartened up by an Egyptian light machine gun, which put a series of bursts round us, one hitting the wooden bridge where we were standing. This brought the comment from the Admiral 'I don't think, General, they are quite ready to receive us yet!' Anyhow we quickly scrambled ashore. There was a good deal of misdirected shooting flying about, and tanks were rumbling down the streets, but we found our way to the Italian Consulate. After hanging around for some time for someone to turn up, we abandoned the idea. There seemed no prospect of concluding any negotiations.

Everywhere there were discarded Egyptian weapons and uniforms, clear evidence that the enemy had lost the will to fight, and that if the Allies pushed forward they could achieve all their objectives. Having located the headquarters of 3 Commando Brigade on the beach, the whole party piled into jeeps and made for the Italian Consulate to find General El Mogih. They arrived at about 9.00 am, and according to Richard Worsley, Stockwell's ADC:

Clambering over . . . prostrate bodies we eventually arrived in a better lit room where the Egyptian Governor was waiting for us, slumped in a chair. Stockwell tried to get him to issue some orders, but the unhappy man, who seemed completely exhausted, was entirely by himself with no means of doing anything. So we decided to abandon the idea of a cease-fire, which was clearly impossible.

Stockwell decided to remain ashore for a while, for he concluded that the first priority must be to clear the town. At 4.00 pm he was able to hold a conference at the Headquarters of 3 Commando Brigade and give out his orders for the next day's operations. In brief, these were for 16 Parachute Brigade to break out south from the causeway and move to the capture of Abu Seir airfield. The French under General Massu, with seaborne and airborne assaults, were to capture Ismailia. 3 Commando Brigade was to consolidate the town with the 3rd Parachute Battalion. Stockwell's own account takes up the story:

It was a tricky operation as everybody appeared to be armed and shooting indiscriminately. They had to shoot their way into every house and on to every roof, whence they could cover further advances down each street. It was important to link up with the French to the South of the town. 2 Para had disembarked and were lined up ready to go, they had to link up with a squadron of 6 RTR and then push off south down the causeway. There were strong pockets of resistance, in particular in the old Navy House building. This had to be subjected to an air strike to subdue it. It was latish by the time this battalion was linked up with its armour and ready to pass south of the French positions and it had therefore to advance in the dark. To accelerate this move every possible form of vehicle was gathered in to help.

It seems that Stockwell's ideas that the best place to bring the Egyptian Army to battle and destroy it – Alexandria – and the constricting effects on move-ment down the causeway from Port Said, were being proved to be right; and that the Egyptian defenders agreed with him.

Beaufre now departed to rejoin his launch and return to the *Gustave-Zédé*. Stockwell himself continued, in his own account:

I now had to get back to HMS *Tyne* to tie up the details of the air support. This didn't prove so easy. Darkness had fallen early and the helicopters had all flown home to roost. So with Brigadier Lacey, Dick Worsley, and Hugo Meynell (my ADC), we went down to the jetty where we managed to pick-up a landing craft with a cheerful Royal Marine coxswain who was ready to get us back to HMS *Tyne*. She was lying some four miles off to the north-west of the Canal, and he knew a short cut through the breakwater.

253

We set off, but no sooner were we through the breakwater than we ran into a heavy sea: the wind had whipped up the waves as they ran on to the shelving beaches. It was pitch dark. Then the pumps went out of action and the steering gear broke, and soon we were banging up and down with the sea spraying over us. It was impossible to find our way back through the breakwater and it seemed we had little hope of making *Tyne*. Dick Worsley exercised his somewhat limited knowledge of the Morse code with an Aldis lamp to attract someone's attention.

Worsley added to this:

I tried to get a helicopter sent to fetch us, but we did not have the procedures in place to do this. Nor did we have communications with *Tyne* . . . The landing craft had no life-jackets but General Hughie was sure everything would be alright. I did find an Aldis lamp in the stern and although the battery was running low I started flashing 'SOS' in Morse code. Suddenly I saw a light, and flashed at it, and the ship turned a searchlight onto us . . .

Stockwell's own account continues:

We altered course to try to keep the sea on our beam and to work our way north, parallel to the Canal, so that eventually we could get back into it and its quiet water. Suddenly we spotted a starboard light high up on our beam. Evidently some big ship, and it was almost stationary. The coxswain managed to manoeuvre us under its lee. A light was flashed on us and a hail from the bridge with an encouraging voice called 'Who are you? This is *Tyne*.' A stroke of luck indeed for a temporarily lost commander. It would have been an inglorious, moderate end to our adventure to be left wallowing about in the sea. Willing sailors soon hoisted us aboard. I found that the Admiral was a bit touchy about where I had been and what I had been up to.

Worsley remembered that things were even more dramatic than that:

Tyne let down a climbing net and all four of us scrambled up it. No sooner had we got off the landing craft than it sank without trace. When I got on board, Ken Darling gave me the most imperial rocket – but what could I have done? General Hughie had decided to go to where he felt he needed to be, indeed he would not have wanted to be anywhere else than with the leading brigades.

If Stockwell thought that this was the end of an exhausting day of adventure and drama, he was wrong, for the real shock was yet to come:

All I wanted at that moment was a whisky and soda. But Ken Darling appeared holding an urgent signal, so urgent that he insisted on my taking it before doing anything else. I looked at the slip of paper. It read 'Cease-fire at midnight'.

It was difficult at that moment for me to take in the words, let alone grasp the full impact of that brief signal. I was cold and tired and wet, yet also exhilarated after seeing my soldiers in action all day at Port Said. We were on the verge of complete success. Wednesday, November 7, would have found us well established on the Ismailia-Abu Seir line. By Thursday night we surely would have been down to Suez. Lives had been lost, but Britain had shown her worth. Now, just as we were reaping the reward of all the effort and the months of preparation, we were to be thwarted of our prize.

Trying to make the best of a bad job, Stockwell urged Butler to get as far down the Canal as he could by midnight. Butler did not need much urging and he was able to get as far as El Cap, about 3 miles short of El Quantara, where we would have been clear of the causeway. Anthony Farrar-Hockley recalled that:

Once we had linked up with the leading squadron of tanks, the column went steaming off with Butler in the lead, into the night. When the time came to halt we were nowhere near any sort of feature, so we just pushed on a bit further anyway to El Cap, where there was a bit of a ridge, and went into defensive positions. When dawn came up an LO from Force HQ arrived with strict instructions from Ken Darling that there was to be absolutely no forward movement.

And so in Stockwell's words:

That, for the moment, was that. It had been an exciting and successful battle and everyone had given of his best. The soldiers acquitted themselves quite splendidly. Considering the frustrations and delays in getting to grips with the job and the continually changing plans, orders and counter-orders, it was remarkable how well it all went . . .

. . . it was a military success. The cease-fire coming when we were all on the crest of the wave and in sight of achieving our military aim made stopping all the more galling. But . . . the whole Suez operation had been bedevilled from start to finish by the lack of a clear political aim.

A new plan had to be developed quickly for the new situation. Stockwell and Beaufre jointly agreed that there were three possibilities: holding the occupied area and defending it if attacked; re-embarking rapidly at short notice; and returning to the attack. Contingency plans were made for the last two possibilities by the staff; but the first was the most pressing problem.

Accordingly, the occupied area was divided between the two national contingents and garrisoned. As the occupying powers under the terms of the Fourth Geneva Convention, the British and French became responsible for law and order, public safety, the operation of utilities, the supply of food, water and fuel – in short, all the functions of the civil government.

It was not until 10 November that the troopships carrying the 3rd Infantry Division arrived off Port Said, having overtaken the slow-moving transports. After two days of uncertainty, 3rd Division was ordered to disembark on 12 November and relieve the Parachute and Marine Brigades. 19 Brigade under Brigadier E.H.W. Grimshaw took over responsibility for Port Said town, and 29 Brigade led by Brigadier Deakin took over the causeway running south, inclusive of El Cap. Still perpetuating the fiction of intervention, probably for the sake of face, Stockwell issued a signal to subordinate formations at 1.25 pm that day:

The Allied forces have carried out their allotted tasks brilliantly. It is a tribute to their accuracy and restraint that such results could be achieved with so few casualties on both sides. This has aroused the admiration of those at home. Our reason for intervention was to stop the war. When both sides had agreed to stop our purpose was achieved. For the first time there is now every possibility of a United [Nations] Police Force coming into being. It is our prompt action that has brought this immeasurably nearer.

A few days later, Stockwell wrote to Templer, obviously in reply to a letter from the CIGS, giving a summary of how he saw things at the time:

Thank you indeed for your letter. I was so glad to get it. Everyone is in fine fettle, morale is good – they are all working away like beavers and they are for the moment well occupied . . .

It all went very well and we so nearly pulled off a cease fire and surrender on the first night. I felt somehow that when they were shut in we should get some such reaction and thought we could not get to the telephone exchange but we did cut the wires; unfortunately there was a cable out to sea which went to Cairo via Alexandria which I did not know of and indeed had we known I doubt we could have done anything about it. So at the last moment they contacted Cairo and it all fell through. Had it come off then I would have pushed the Commandos down the road and we should certainly have been knocking at Ismailia by the time of the cease fire. I pushed 2 Para through the town irrespective of the battle going on to get them on tanks driving south as soon as I could, and we stopped dead on time. Had we pressed on we should have got irretrievably mixed up in another battle and it would have been a hell of a job to disengage.

Incidentally with the landings on Tuesday we had to go it pretty hard

256

and there was a hello bello of a shooting match all over the town that day. The Commandos fought well and were excellent at their street fighting. It is a very specialised game and I hope the School of Infantry tackle it at Warminster. Shoot your way up through the house to the roof and then have bren guns on the roof to cover the next bound.

The letter from Templer does not survive, but its tenor can be guessed at both from Stockwell's reply and from a manuscript note by Templer, giving his view that the operation was ruined by political indecision, for which the military would be held accountable. This fragment is all that survives of an account of Suez which Templer later told Stockwell he had written, but which has never come to light.

Stockwell also revealed his true feelings about Beaufre and the French, saying that:

The French are a bloody nuisance but we have them clobbered now. Beaufre

(a) Does not like being in a subordinate position. I have a daily conference at 3 p.m. to cover everything . . . but he only turns up when it suits him. He is as slippery as hell but when pressed he gets on with the job by and large.
(b) He never will take a military decision, he must colour it with his sympathy for the politicians. This is understandable for his superiors but it isn't his business. He ought to go as the French representative at UNO.

In the Canal Zone itself, 3rd Division's tasks at Port Said were to prevent action by the Egyptian Army, to maintain public order and to assist the restoration of normality and of utilities in the town. Stockwell wrote of this to Templer, saying that 'We struggle to restore Port Said. They are all frightened as hell. They don't know whether we are going to cut their throats, or Nasser . . . It is a lousy place anyway but we have the water and light working.'

In the event, the Egyptian Army observed the ceasefire correctly, although it did all it could to consolidate positions in Qantara and Ismailia so that any further advance south by the Allies would be costly. The major threat to security therefore was the Black Hand terrorist organization, well known to Stockwell and the British Army generally for its activities during the earlier occupation of the Canal Zone. The large quantities of arms that had been distributed to civilians by the Egyptian authorities, at the urging of the Soviet Ambassador, did not help. Worsley recalled that 'There were vast quantities of Soviet equipment captured, and evidence of Soviet influence uncovered. The operation certainly forestalled a Soviet move into the Middle East.'

Operations in Port Said followed a pattern familiar to British soldiers: street patrols, curfew, cordon and search, checking of vehicles and guard duties.

Major (later Major General) Eddie Fursdon, then DAA & QMG of 19 Brigade, described life in Port Said:

> In a remarkably short space of time our soldiers adjusted themselves to a life of constant patrol and guards. They learnt to be suspicious, cautious and extremely observant. I shall never forget watching one Royal Scots patrol working its way slowly along the wide street that separates Arab Town from Shanty Town. It was a patrol of seven, operating in the rough shape of a diamond. The rear Jock walked slowly backwards, his bren gun, slung from his shoulder, was held at the hip; slowly and continuously the barrel traversed the street, but I am sure it was his expression that made for the perfect behaviour of the crowd. His bonnet was back a little on his head; his young sunburnt face was set; it was quite clear to everyone, 'There will be no nonsense here'. There wasn't.

Stockwell himself received an early visit from the Governor of Port Said, Mohammed Riad, at his headquarters in the Canal Company offices. Riad he described as friendly and fond of the British, which encouraged him to make a point of getting out and about in the town, as was his wont, seeing the local conditions and visiting his troops:

> Immediately after our battle, Port Said – known to so many soldiers, sailors and airmen – a town of incident, bargaining, intrigue, guile, laughter and naughtiness – a first contact so often with the East, where Asia joins Africa, had a tragic, empty and suspicious air. Within hours heads began to appear, windows opened, a few of the more bold came out into the streets and it began to stir to life again. The instincts of trade, bargaining and good humour are felt deep in the heart of Port Said. Within days the streets were teeming. You see, this town had a population of 150,000, nearly all of whom had their being at the entrance to this turbulent canal.

Some witnesses describe Stockwell as driving himself around in a Land Rover, throwing sweets to the children and doing his best to tease the Soviet Consul by following him around. A guard had been put on the Consulate and the sergeant in charge had been ordered to photograph the Consul every time he went in or out, but in no way to hamper his movements. The Consul, by all accounts, became unaccountably shy of going out in public. Another officer who was about to go on leave offered to ring up Joan when he got home; Stockwell, who was enjoying a whisky and soda at the time, swung his legs up so that he was lying full length on a sofa, with his head on a cushion, and said, 'Oh yes, please – tell her I'm having a hell of a rough time!'

Stockwell himself remarked of this period that:

My early drives round the town brought friendly greetings and a truly remarkable welcome – remarkable because you can't fight a battle, however hard you try, without leaving the litter of battle around. Broken glass and shattered walls, bullet marks and shell holes, broken water mains and leaking sewage. It was here men fought for their lives. Remember over 5,000 were armed and fighting against us. Many impressed, few knowing why, some doped and all stirred by a handful of agitators . . . and yet as soon as it was over, or so it seemed, here was the hand of friendship . . . here were British soldiers, always gullible and always ready to spend their money on souvenirs.

Stockwell was also in regular touch with the Chiefs in London at this time and received nothing but praise for the way in which he had handled both the operation, and the aftermath. Templer, for example, writing on 5 December, said that 'Once again I take my hat off to you for what you've done in spite of all the difficulties with which you have had to compete.' A longer, follow-up letter from Templer, handwritten in green ink, and hinting at his own difficulties, came in on 14 December:

My dear Hughie

I think you will know how much you have been in my thoughts. I'm very sorry not to have written before now to say how <u>enormously</u> we have all admired your handling of this incredibly difficult operation.

As far as I can see, within the limitations imposed on you by London, not one single thing went wrong . . .

There will be plenty of witch-hunting ahead of us – both in the short term and by history; but no one will ever look for any witches in the forces in the Mediterranean.

It can't have been at all apparent to you but the Chiefs of Staff were trying to do their best for you. And I don't wonder. How you must have cursed us. I'm afraid the weight of world opinion was too much and the threats of economic and financial sanctions. Another 24 hours would pretty well have done the trick. Not entirely, maybe, but largely . . .

In all the spate of criticism in the press, there has not been <u>one word</u> directed against any of you out there. And that at least is satisfactory.

Take care of yourself. Thank you for the Russian rifle. If I could use it, I'd give my first attention to certain gentlemen in New York and London.

On 7 December, advance elements of the UN force under the Canadian General E.L.M. (Tommy) Burns began to arrive in Port Said. The end was in sight, but the later stages of the occupation were embittered by the kidnap and murder of Second Lieutenant Anthony Moorhouse. Stockwell has received criticism for not doing more to secure Moorhouse's release, but it is difficult to see what more he could have done. A report on the incident appears in his papers at King's College London. On 11 December, after Moorhouse's disappearance, Stockwell summoned Mohammed Riad, told him to find Moorhouse, and satisfy him that Moorhouse was being treated as a POW. This the Governor undertook to do. At the same time, Stockwell reported the kidnapping to Burns. On 12 December, Stockwell pressed Burns to do more and as there was a ceasefire that Burns was responsible for overseeing, asked for him to be exchanged. On the 14th, Burns claimed he had tried with the Egyptians, but that they had been obstructive.

On 3 December, Stockwell had received orders to re-embark by 18 December. The embarkation could be expected to last up to three weeks – it was Haifa all over again. The situation was made worse by the need to embark large numbers of Allied civilian nationals who had lost their livelihoods following Nasser's humiliating seizure of Allied industries, businesses and firms.

By 21 December, 6,000 UN troops had arrived mostly from Denmark and Sweden, and were interposed between the Allies and the Egyptians. The rearguard was formed by 19 Infantry Brigade, which completed its embarkation at 5.10 pm on the 22nd. Right up to the end, Stockwell kept trying to find Moorhouse – who by now was almost certainly dead – making a final effort on the 22nd before leaving – which he did directly before Grimshaw, the commander of the rearguard brigade. His mood on leaving was summed up in a letter to his subordinates:

> It will not be long now until we come to our final parting. Here was adventure, thrill, excitement and military success, such as soldiers had not tasted since they crossed the Rhine or sweated through the jungles to Rangoon. And, just as it was being unfolded, suddenly the task was over, and we are to be away and back home again. Ah well, success is a potent draught, and one sip is enough for any man. We have all tasted it this time. It is a rich and rare flavour, and we shall be thankful not to have had too much of it, with its heady after-effects.

Templer wrote again on 21 December welcoming Stockwell home: 'What a job you've done! And if it is any consolation to you, everyone knows it. You've been told to somersault backwards – and then forwards – and you've never been awkward, though I often thought I could hear at this distance the blueness of your oaths!' There were other impressive tributes: Mountbatten said on 22 January 1957 that 'Personally I feel that the Operation was a perfect example of three Service co-operation.' Monty, never one to dish out lavish praise, wrote on 3 January 1957 to say:

> My dear Hughie
>
> I would like to tell you how very much I admired the way in which you handled the 'conflict' in Egypt. It was a difficult job, the more so because

of political interference and infirmity of purpose. But you were calm and dignified throughout, and gave a good example of how to command in battle.

Stockwell himself always maintained that the operation had been justified and that militarily it was successful. Talking on Suez at the Royal Military College of Science, Shrivenham, on 23 September 1957, nearly a year after the event, he said that:

> I am very sure of one thing: the conception for the intervention in Egypt and the operation so far as it went was very right – it aimed at containing the [unreadable] manoeuvring of the Russians in the Middle East and certainly so far as one can see, the building up of Egypt and Nasser as a champion in that cause and eventually a united Arab world as a satellite of Russia.
>
> . . . it showed the world that we are always ready to fulfil our obligations under any treaty or alliance to which we subscribe.

Stockwell returned to England where II Corps was disbanded and reabsorbed back into I Corps, while he took a spell of leave prior to taking up his first appointment in London, as Military Secretary. The good opinion of Templer and others showed up in the Operational Honours and Awards list, when he was awarded a bar to his DSO. Templer himself wrote that 'If history deals faithfully with those in military command, the names of Generals Charles Keightley and Hugh Stockwell will go down as two men who carried out their task splendidly in the face of great political interference in military plans.'

Hughie Stockwell maintained to the end of his life that military operations were bedevilled throughout by a lack of any clear political direction. As he wrote in the *Listener:*[4]

> The tragedy, of course, from our point of view, was the ceasefire. Every soldier, sailor and airman, both French and British, had the adrenalin flowing in his veins. Then we were told to stop . . . so many had risked their lives, so many brave and courageous actions had taken place. Yet, in the event, there was little to show for it . . . All we wanted was 48 hours of air attack before loosing our assault, but the actual preliminaries lasted six days, thus bringing world opinion to bear at the United Nations.
>
> I think it was a military success, undoubtedly. We captured Port Said. We got as far down as we could before the ceasefire, we were all poised to break out, and the whole thing was a fine military operation. Whether it was a political disaster is not for me to say. We were there to fulfil political direction.

Notes

1 In 1956, multi-national operations were referred to as 'joint', and multi-service operations as 'combined'. This is distinct from modern use, in which multi-service operations are joint, and multi-national are combined. For the purpose of this chapter, the modern usage will be applied, except where quoting from personal accounts of official documents, in which case an explanation will be added.

2 There are occasional discrepancies in timings in various accounts, probably due to the fact that the British kept their watches on GMT. Timings in this account are all local time, two hours ahead of GMT.

3 As HQ 3rd Infantry Division was still in transit, the Corps HQ was transmitting orders directly to the brigade level of command. In the case of the Marine and Parachute brigades, used to operating independently and scaled with larger staffs than an infantry or armoured brigade, this was not a problem. This corps-brigade relationship did not occur again until the Kosovo operation in 1999.

4 The BBC made a programme called *Suez 1956* on 25th November 1979. It was a three-hour play written by Ian Curtis. The article by HCS in the *Listener* was prompted by seeing the preview, at the invitation of the editor, Antony Howard (letter to HCS, 18 October 1979 in KCL/Stockwell/8/6/26).

Chapter Nineteen

Re-forming the Army, 1957–1960

For the first time since 1940, Hughie Stockwell was out of command. On 1 February 1957 he took up the appointment of Military Secretary to the Secretary of State for War. The Ministry of Defence as we now know it still did not exist, even though there was a Secretary of State for Defence with over-arching powers. Direction of the three Services remained with the Service Ministers, and under them, the professional heads. In the case of the Army, the Right Honourable John Hare headed the War Office, with Templer as Chief of the Imperial General Staff. The duties of the Military Secretary, then as now, revolved around the career management of the officers of the Army – or rather, seeing that suitably qualified officers filled the many and various jobs.

There is, therefore, an inescapable tension in this job between the aspirations of individuals, who hope that the MS's staff engages primarily in career management – finding jobs for people – and the requirements of the Service, whose senior officers demand that the MS engages in finding people for jobs. Stockwell himself was personally responsible for managing major generals and above; his staff, in two divisions, each led by a brigadier as Deputy MS, looked after lesser officers. Although Stockwell had no desire to serve in London, and there is no doubt that he found the whole experience very disagreeable, he was to bring to this job his enormous skills in dealing with people. Anthony Farrar-Hockley said of him in this post, 'He had to look after the interests of people in the Army. He knew about people and cared about them as individuals.' Another commentator remarked that 'He had a vivid personality, and a gift of forceful, incisive expression. His manner was of such engaging friendliness that all who met him found him irresistible.'

The Stockwells were of course in the fortunate position of having their own London house, and they duly moved in to Elgin Crescent, from which they made periodic trips to Erw Suran. Polly was abroad, and Anabel was still at school; Dudley, a basset hound bought on impulse in Harrods, maintained the tradition of pets. Hughie Stockwell might have been a great trainer of men, but he was the world's worst trainer of dogs. Dudley was a menace who was, like all hunting breeds, prone to wandering off and having to be recovered after much searching, shouting and bad temper. And when he was around, he was a constant menace to female visitors, the insides of whose skirts he found irresistible.

After all the separation of their life thus far, and the postings abroad, the Stockwells were delighted to settle down in London. In 1957 Anabel, aged seventeen, achieved her ambition and married a farmer – Harris Wright. The Wrights went to live at Blaise Farm near West Malling in Kent, first in a caravan, then in a cottage and eventually in the house that they built themselves. Their daughter Gigi was born in 1958 and their son Diccon followed three years later.

Under normal peacetime conditions, there are enough moving parts in the Military Secretary's job to make it highly demanding. At the time Stockwell took up the appointment, however, the situation was about to become anything but normal. The size and shape of the Army had been under scrutiny since 1955 when the then Defence Minister, Selwyn Lloyd, had imposed retrenchment in the Defence Estimates. Lloyd had tried to reduce National Service from two years to one, but Harding as CIGS, and then Templer, had successfully resisted this on the grounds of commitment levels. As a sign of things to come, however, a new pay code with revised terms for short service regular engagements was introduced to encourage regular service. Over the next two years, the pressure began to build for an end to National Service in peacetime. The Navy and the RAF had no wish to keep it, and the Army clung to it only because of the size of its commitments: its tradition was in professional, regular, service; training conscripts took time and manpower; and the cost of maintaining a large force – even at NS pay scales – meant that there was little left in the pot for much-needed modernization.

But commitments remained the sticking point. Assessments pointed to a requirement for 200,000 British troops worldwide, later revised under political pressure to 185,000. Against this, the most optimistic forecasts predicted that recruiting would not sustain an all-regular Army of more than 165,000. When, after Suez, Macmillan became Prime Minister, he appointed the tough and capable Duncan Sandys at Defence. Sandys believed firmly that conventional armies were now all but outmoded for modern war and that nuclear deterrence was the way of the future, despite the evidence which Suez had provided to the effect that war, under the umbrella of nuclear deterrence, was still possible. Not surprisingly, he was soon head to head with the Service Chiefs. Macmillan, desperate to reduce the drain on the economy which military commitments produced, instructed Sandys on 24 January 1957 – just a week before Stockwell took up his appointment – to undertake a complete review of defence: he was to review policy, deployments, organizations, funding, and even pay and conditions of service. At one stroke, the Service ministers and the chiefs were sidelined.

Sandys' work, the Defence White Paper of 1957, might have been expected to address some of the shortcomings in the Services that Suez had highlighted. But these problems were subordinated to the development of a nuclear deterrent independent of the USA, whose support, after Suez, seemed dubious; and a compensating reduction in other forces. Sandys aimed to reduce defence spending from £1,600 million to £1,420 million, end conscription, and compensate for reduced manpower with greater mobility, the use of staging posts like Aden and Gan rather than overseas bases, and tactical nuclear weapons. Of the three Services, the Army came off worst. Templer and the Army Council were unshaken in believing that an Army of 165,000 would never meet its commitments. There were some noisy exchanges between Templer and Sandys, but much as Templer disliked and distrusted Sandys both personally and professionally, Sandys had Macmillan's backing and, although the Army Council regarded the White Paper as a disaster, it had no real option but to accept it.

Most of the reductions would be through the ending of National Service, but there would be reductions too in the numbers of regular officers and NCOs. These were planned by Stockwell's department to be spread over a four-year period from 1958 to 1962, using annual quotas. As far as possible, these reductions would be voluntary, and accompanied by generous redundancy payments. Politically, it was recognized that the Army's problem was different from that of the other services – not only did it have to take account of its regimental and corps structure, but it needed to shed more than twice the number of personnel as the Royal Navy and RAF combined. The requirement, for example, for the first year, 1958/59, was for 1,380 officer volunteers, and 1,819 NCOs: a total of 3,199. The actual number applying for redundancy that year was 25,800. Clearly, Stockwell and his department had no difficulty in filling the vacancies; the hard work came in making sure that as far as possible, the Army kept the right people, in the right age and rank ranges, and with the right skills and qualifications for the new Regular Army. Not everyone who applied would therefore get redundancy, while some of those who wished to stay were nominated for redundancy whether they liked it or not.

An Army White Paper had to be produced between April and July 1957. It still remained to be seen whether recruiting would fill the ranks with regular soldiers, for the economy was picking up, jobs were plentiful in civilian life, and in the aftermath of National Service, Army life did not enjoy a particularly rosy image. But the high command of the Army, of which Stockwell was now a member, was faced with some difficult decisions. An Army of 165,000 was only two-thirds the size it had been before the Second World War. Not only would individuals be made redundant, but also entire formations would go; and so too would some of the famous regiments, especially in the infantry. In this, the Army Council's hands were already tied, for after the withdrawal from India, all the second battalions of infantry regiments had been cut. A few were added back (including 2 RWF) on the basis of regular recruiting, to cope with commitments in Korea and Malaya. A bolder solution might have been to stick with Cardwell's principles, review the changing recruiting potential of regimental districts, and disband whole regiments accordingly. But now, after the few remaining second battalions had been disbanded, the Army Council was faced with sixty-four single battalion regiments, from which forty-nine battalions would survive, along with three battalions in the Parachute Regiment, and eight battalions of Guards.

For many people, including many senior officers, the experience of the Second World War led them to the conclusion that under the pressure of a war of national survival – such as might face NATO countries in the event of a Soviet attack – the regimental system of the British Army had broken down, and that a corps of infantry was the answer. For many others, however, the regimental system was the basis of the fighting spirit of the Army, and tampering with it would be disastrous; Templer, supported by others, including Stockwell, took this view. General Sir Charles Loewen was the Adjutant General, and the officer responsible, therefore, for determining which regiments would face extinction. As a gunner, he felt unqualified and unwilling to take such decisions. Templer therefore took personal charge. Rather than condemn some regiments to oblivion, Templer decided on a policy of amalgamation and a committee chaired by General Sir Lashmer Whistler was established to recommend the way forward. Whistler in due course recommended the disbandment of the third battalions of the Guards Brigade, and the amalgamation of thirty of the Regiments of the Line into fifteen new ones.

But the logic for regiments with more than one regular battalion, as had existed under Cardwell's scheme, still held good. To implement such a policy, however, would mean reducing still further the number of regiments. As a compromise, therefore, Templer decided to formalize and strengthen the existing brigade groups, which since 1949 had been responsible for co-ordinating matters such as manning and training between their regiments. Within each brigade, battalions would continue to preserve separate regimental identities, although they would wear a common cap badge. The Brigade Headquarters would henceforth handle many matters – mostly those affecting personnel – on a semi-regimental basis and indeed could if they so wished, evolve into Large Regiments. Some, like the Green Jackets and the East Anglians, did so almost at once. It was an ingenious compromise solution at the time, but in the long term, it produced muddle.

For Stockwell as Military Secretary and Colonel of the Royal Welch Fusiliers, all this had the potential for a conflict of interest. He was of course also Colonel of the Malay Regiment, which he held until 1959; in 1957 he was appointed Colonel Commandant of the Army Air Corps; and in 1959 he was appointed Colonel Commandant of the Royal Army Educational Corps. Given his long interest in, and encouragement for, helicopters, and his command of 6th Airborne Division, this last was an unsurprising appointment, and one which Stockwell treasured and worked at assiduously. He had to do so, for this was a time of great upheaval in army aviation. The Army Air Corps had been born during the Second World War, when it consisted of the Parachute Regiment and the Glider Pilot Regiment, but since then the Paras had been taken into the Infantry and although the Glider Pilot Regiment existed in name, the Army had given up gliders in favour of powered aircraft and helicopters.

The Glider Pilot Regiment was therefore disbanded and the Army Air Corps re-formed on 1 September 1957, with Brigadier Patrick Weston as the first Director of the AAC Centre, Middle Wallop. Stockwell was appointed as the first Colonel Commandant of the Corps. One of his first tasks was to take the Corps' light blue beret and its badge – based on that of the Glider Pilot Regiment – to Buckingham Palace for the Queen's approval. It is said that the Queen, who is noted for her dry sense of humour and quick wit, looked at the offerings and then said to Stockwell, 'Well General, I do think it might look better on *me* than on *you*.' The new corps assumed responsibility for the three Air OP squadrons and seven liaison flights,[1] to be equipped with the XP 820 De Havilland Beaver Mark I. Initially the RAF kept responsibility for first- and second-line maintenance, until the REME took this on in 1958. The corps was established at 1,500 all ranks, including non-technical staff supplied by the Royal Artillery, and attached specialists from the service corps. Officers and NCOs of all arms were eligible to apply for secondment or transfer to its permanent cadre of 200 pilots.

Despite the considerable time Stockwell spent on AAC matters, it was the Colonelcy of the Royal Welch Fusiliers that absorbed the greatest part of his energies. While the Suez operation was being planned he nominated a committee to state the Regiment's claim to various battle honours from the Second World War, and in the summer of 1957 the Regiment was granted twenty-seven honours. On a day-to-day basis, the two regular battalions, Regimental Depot at Wrexham, two TA battalions, companies of cadets across Mid and North Wales, and even, for a time, eight Home Guard units,[2] represented a considerable constituency for Stockwell as Colonel of the Regiment in addition to his job. However, the golden age of the Cardwell system was beginning to fade. When 2 RWF arrived home from Malaya by the last troopship around the Cape on 6 August 1957, it was earmarked for disbandment. The last acts came on 17 December 1957 when Stockwell led a representative party from 2 RWF to the Royal Hospital, Chelsea, to receive back a French Eagle captured by the Regiment at Martinique in 1809. The same group then went straight on to Buckingham Palace with the Eagle, where the Queen received them, making her own farewell to the 2nd Battalion as its Colonel-in-Chief. But as well as disbandments, there were resurrections. In July 1956, the two anti-aircraft artillery regiments which had been formed in the post-war years from the 6th and 7th Battalions of the Royal Welch Fusiliers (TA) were amalgamated, re-roled as infantry, and given back to the Regiment as its 6th/7th Battalion.

It should not be supposed, however, that in determining which Regiments would face amalgamation, royal connections – having, like the Royal Welch Fusiliers, the Queen as Colonel-in-Chief, for example – would save any one regiment's bacon in the forthcoming reductions in the infantry. In early 1957, the Queen's Private Secretary, Sir Michael Adeane, sent out a minute which said:

> The Queen is mindful of the effect which the declared defence policy of the Government may have on the size and shape of the Army. No doubt, cuts are inevitable . . . In the circumstances, she desires me to make it clear that she would not expect any special consideration to be given to those which, either through Colonelcies-in Chief or other ways, are connected with the Royal Family.

Templer retired in September 1958 and was succeeded as CIGS by another of Stockwell's former chiefs, Frankie Festing. To Festing would fall the task of implementing the cuts in the infantry and indeed it has been suggested that he had been appointed because he, better than anyone else, could sell the concept of brigades and Large Regiments to a sceptical Army. Festing brought a very different style to the War Office. He had a very low boredom threshold indeed: '90 per cent of the jobs in this world are boring, and boring people do them best,' he famously remarked. He was certainly a highly intuitive thinker, who arrived quickly at a decision and then preferred to leave the formal process of justification for a particular course of action to the staff. Among some, this caused him to be thought of as idle, or even slow in intellect. Lieutenant Colonel Cecil ('Monkey') Blacker, who was Festing's Military Assistant, wrote that:

> Festing had a natural quickness of mind, a breadth of knowledge and an intellectual depth, which certainly made him equal to, if not superior to his predecessor. This, added to a formidable down-to-earth common-sense enabled him to get to the root of any problem however complicated. The trouble was that he went out of his way to conceal these attributes.

Stockwell told a story that, when Festing first arrived in his new office it was bare of files, and Festing found himself with nothing to do. Hanging on the door, however, was a sheet of paper headed 'Fire Orders'. On reading these, he noted that in the event of fire, he should shout 'Fire'. So, going to the corridor, he did – twice. For a time nothing happened, but after an interval an orderly appeared with a shovel of hot cinders for his fire.

In Stockwell, Festing had a close associate and friend whom he knew and trusted, and who was very like him in approach and inclination – if not in looks. Stockwell was always dapper, while Festing went about looking, as someone remarked, like an unmade bed. The wartime link with

Mountbatten, who was now Chief of Defence Staff, a position much increased in power and influence under Sandys, was clearly useful during difficult times for the Army. What Festing succeeded in doing, and in which Stockwell certainly played a big part as Military Secretary, was to make service in an all-regular Army attractive as a career. 1958 and 1959 saw some of the best regular recruiting figures ever achieved – 35,000 and 28,000 respectively – which helped to make a successful case for raising the 165,000 manpower ceiling to 180,000.

In the midst of these deliberations, Stockwell completed his tenure as Military Secretary. There was, however, no escape from London – on 14 August 1959, he was appointed as Adjutant General to the Forces in succession to General Sir Charles Loewen, and promoted to the rank of General. He was also advanced in the Order of the Bath from KCB to GCB – Grand Commander – and made an Aide-de-Camp (General) to the Queen. The duties and responsibilities of the AG were in essence still those assigned to him in 1888 – discipline, interior economy, training, camps and schools. Under him came all the directorates of the War Office concerned with the employment, deployment, management, welfare, well-being and education of the Army. Finally Stockwell was also, as AG, a member of the Army Council.

Although Festing had been brought in with a view to pushing the infantry towards large regiments, he and the rest of the Army Board, while they encouraged brigades to migrate to a regimental structure, were unwilling to impose this. Festing's own Regiment had gone into the Green Jacket Brigade, and then the Royal Green Jackets, but even so, he preferred to leave it to individual regiments and brigades to determine their structure, while evolving a system which would allow the maximum flexibility for cross-posting of individuals and force generation of units and formations. Interestingly, Stockwell and his fellow Colonels of Regiments in Wales – Major General F.R.G. Matthews of the SWB (the Commandant whom Stockwell had succeeded at Sandhurst in 1948) and Lieutenant General Sir Charles Coleman of the Welch – considered going all the way. At meetings of the Council of Colonels of the Welsh Brigade on 16 December 1958 and 1 April 1959, the three decided that the correct course of action would be to merge the identities of their three regiments into a new single Regiment to be called 'The Royal Regiment of Wales', and this should be put into effect by 1 April 1960. The Adjutant General had been lukewarm when approached on the subject, feeling that it was too far, too fast. At the next Council meeting on 13 May 1959, Stockwell reported this to his fellow colonels, and added that there was no certainty that the new regiment would be a Royal regiment – only one of the three Welsh regiments had this distinction – nor that the Queen would consent to be Colonel-in-Chief. One possibility might be to form a regiment in which the three existing 1st Battalions would retain distinct identities as a prelude to full integration later, as the Green Jackets had done. Both Coleman and Matthews were in favour of pushing on, but Stockwell at this point put his foot down – the loss of the

Royal title and the Queen as Colonel-in-Chief were more than he and indeed the Royal Welch Fusiliers could swallow. Nevertheless he undertook to sound out the Director of Infantry, Major General Douglas Kendrew, on his views on the Regiment of Wales. Kendrew came out against the idea on the same grounds as Loewen: 'Many of the [other] Brigades are so involved in the first stage of their amalgamations that to amalgamate within the Brigade into one big regiment would give them the most terrible indigestion.'

It was August before the Colonels met again, having discussed the matter with their own regimental hierarchies. Coleman for the Welch would accept 1st, 2nd, and 3rd Battalions of the Regiment of Wales as a preliminary to full amalgamation, but not 1st, 2nd and 3rd Regiments of Wales. Matthews supported this. Stockwell was supportive, but cautious. The Royal Welch Fusiliers had clearly left him in no doubt that the Royal title and the Colonel-in-Chief were non-negotiable. However, he himself was still in favour of creating a new large regiment on the date at which the Prince of Wales was installed, and could therefore become Colonel-in-Chief. The other Colonels did not wish to wait that long – maybe ten years – and wanted to go public. Stockwell was again cautious and went on to say that:

> He did not advise this course as our intention must not be made public yet and in any event support in Wales could be assured. As there was a conflict of views in the War Office, he felt that the best plan was to obtain the advice of the Private Secretary to The Queen, Sir Michael Adeane, on the best form of approach.
>
> [he] said he was prepared to go ahead with representations to the War Office with the proviso which he had already stated, namely that there must be no question of jeopardising the Royal title of the Royal Welch Fusiliers or losing The Queen as Colonel-in-Chief.

A letter to the Under Secretary of State at the War Office was duly approved at the meeting of the Council in September.

As things turned out, the whole plan came to nothing. But the Royal Regiment of Wales did indeed later come into existence, as the result of the amalgamation of the SWB and the Welch in 1969, following a bitter but successful struggle by the Royal Welch Fusiliers, under the Colonelcy of Jack Willes, Stockwell's successor, to preserve its separate identity. Given the strength of support for Jack Willes's campaign within the Regiment, it seems inconceivable that even so popular a Colonel as Stockwell could have carried opinion within his Regiment. So why, one must ask, did he and the other Colonels try to go down this path? There are no documents to help and those involved are all dead, so we are forced to read between the lines of the minutes of the meetings of the Council of Colonels – which at the time were clearly highly sensitive, held as Confidential documents, and released only to the commanding officers of regular battalions and depots. The most likely explanation is that Stockwell, as a member of the Army Council, felt obliged to support the collective view of the Council, which was to encourage the formation of Large Regiments, and show a lead to others. He may also, genuinely, have felt that this was the way of the future. But there were limits to what he could give up, as the objections showed. And if a Large Regiment had been formed, it must be open to doubt as to whether Wales would now be represented in the Army by two regular battalions of the line. The fate of Large Regiments like the Green Jackets, the Royal Anglians, and in particular, The Queen's, has been one of steady reduction. Public opinion will take more easily the slicing of a battalion with an unfamiliar title, than it will the loss of an old and honoured name, in which generations of a community may have fought and died. Nor have the Large Regiments ever established in the hearts of the people the same place that the English county regiments, or the Scottish regiments, or distinctively national regiments like the Royal Welch Fusiliers, have held – or at least did hold until all were forced into a large regiment construct in 2006.

Army Air Corps matters were soon to claim Stockwell's attention once more. Shortly after its formation, moves began towards an integration scheme aimed at increasing the size of the Corps – and in particular its holdings of helicopters and pilots. Under this scheme, helicopters would be closely integrated into the establishments of combat and combat support units. The responsibility for providing pilots, ground crew and REME maintenance would fall on the holding unit, leaving the AAC to man squadrons and flights at army corps level and above. The first integrated flights were assigned to the Royal Armoured Corps, and in June 1960, 22 Recce Flight joined the order of battle of the Queen's Dragoon Guards. Others followed in BAOR, although the Home Commands remained lukewarm. In parallel with this, a general staff requirement for a unit light helicopter was generated, but it was not until April 1964 that the MoD ordered 156 Bell 47G-3BI Sioux helicopters from Augusta. The organization, which would have resulted from the long-term adoption of this scheme, would have been very broadly based, with a small cadre of AAC personnel. Indeed, Weston thought that the AAC as a corps would logically wither away. This idea so alarmed the General Staff Officer at the Directorate of Land-Air Warfare who was responsible for Army Aviation, Major Peter Mead, that he called an urgent meeting at Middle Wallop with Weston and Hughie Stockwell – who was by then Adjutant General and as such effectively had a veto on such matters. At this meeting, Mead outlined: 'in a few words my objections to the idea being circulated that the Army Air Corps was obsolescent. Without waiting for any further statement of my views, Hughie Stockwell came down emphatically and unequivocally . . . on the side of the Army Air Corps.'

Stockwell was not just being proprietorial here. He felt that allowing the AAC to wither away as a corps would risk losing aviation experience, and circumscribe the development of new ideas. Integration could produce some benefits, especially in attracting more pilots, but:

271

This should be done selectively, and be backed by various levels of flights and squadrons to provide for the many people requiring light aircraft from a pool . . . I did not know whether it was the answer for the long term but saw that it was probably the best way of coping with the difficulties just then.

The integration scheme lasted only until 1967, and Stockwell's insistence on maintaining the centrality of the AAC certainly gives him a place among the founders of Army aviation. But for him, it was arguable that the modern attack helicopter, had it entered service, would be operated by the RAF. Heavy transport helicopters have remained crewed by the RAF, however since 1999 a Joint Helicopter Command, part of the Army's Land Command, has exercised administrative control of all aviation across the three services.

There was certainly a possibility that having been Adjutant General, Stockwell might succeed to the post of CIGS, as professional head of the Army. He had the operational credibility, and after nearly four years in Whitehall, he knew the ways of the Ministry. However, in July 1960, he was nominated to succeed General Sir Richard Gale as Deputy Supreme Commander Europe (DSACEUR) – and thus the ultimate prize eluded him. Was this a surprise? Probably not. In his heart of hearts, Hughie Stockwell was, and knew himself to be, a field commander. The cut and thrust of the political interface was never really his style. Nor did he have the intellect or professional education required – Sir Richard Worsley remarked that when one compared Stockwell with Templer or Festing, there was no doubt who, intellectually, was the bigger man. And given the circumstances of defence at that time, he was certainly the wrong choice for the needs of the Army. Timing too was against him. Festing had succeeded Templer in September 1958 and would expect to serve for three years; Stockwell's appointment would end in the summer of 1960. All in all, Stockwell was probably relieved to leave London after four years and to have the chance for one last command appointment before he left the service.

Notes
1 651, 652 and 656 Squadrons, and 4 Independent AOP Flight.
2 These battalions were part of the resurrection of the Home Guard, on a cadre basis, between 1952 and 1957. See S.P. Mackenzie *The Home Guard – A Military and Political History* (OUP, 1996) and *Regimental Records,* Vol VI, pp. 281-9.

Chapter Twenty

Allied Command Europe, 1960–1963

When Hughie Stockwell moved to Supreme Headquarters Allied Powers Europe – SHAPE – in the Paris suburb of Rocquencourt near Versailles, he succeeded his old chief in BAOR, General Sir Richard 'Windy' Gale. Gale had been brought out of retirement to take over from Montgomery, and under him, the nature of the post of DSACEUR changed fundamentally. During the seven years that Montgomery had held the appointment, DSACEUR's office had concerned itself only with army business, mostly the annual SHAPEX, and had also been wholly British. It had thus been rather isolated from the rest of the SHAPE staff, which numbered about 400 personnel, of whom half were officers, from the then fourteen NATO countries. Stockwell's MA, Major (later Major General) Roy Redgrave, remembered that as a result of this isolation: 'much of the work in SHAPE by-passed DSACEUR's office. Nobody dared to show the Field Marshal any new plan or proposal because he could not resist fiddling with it and changing it.'

The relaxed, gregarious and Francophile Gale was a breath of fresh air, and the DSACEUR's staff was rapidly made multinational. Moreover, Gale and the SACEUR, US Air Force General Lauris (Larry) Norstad, as famous for his film star looks as he was for his undoubted political and military insight, hit it off straight away. Things had clearly changed and, reflecting this, Norstad directed that in future, DSACEUR would be a proper deputy, working in close co-operation with the two subordinate deputy commanders for Naval and Air matters, responsible for overseeing all land, sea and air commands declared to the Alliance. Even so, the job of DSACEUR was not then what it later became. In 1961 it was very much a diplomatic or representational post, almost ambassadorial. Most of the work of SHAPE was concerned with strategic plans to counter the threat from numerically superior forces of the Warsaw Pact, not only in the central region but also on the flanks. It was to the flanks that Gale had given most attention and Stockwell followed suit. Indeed, Stockwell loved the job and the lifestyle that came with it, and like Gale, he struck up an immediate rapport with Norstad, with whom he met daily. Captain (later Brigadier) Anthony Vivian, who was Stockwell's ADC in Paris and subsequently Colonel of the Royal Welch Fusiliers, recalled him thus:

> Hughie was just right as the Deputy SACEUR, for he had the air and looked like a model British General – a warrior, and a knight – and yet he retained the common touch, with no conceit or vanity. In a multinational, multi-cultural headquarters of thirteen different nations, and two at least not speaking to each other, Hughie was perfect for healing the wounds, or in the vernacular, just chatting up people, of whatever rank, and making them all feel better. He was liked by everybody and admired by most. He was himself a tremendously hard worker and while he knew how to treat officers and soldiers, he expected the same dedication from them: 'officers work twenty five hours a day,' he remarked, 'soldiers twenty-three.' Although he was never an intellectual, he had the ability to get to the root of a problem, and to see a way through.

Being, as ever, fond of female company, Stockwell decided that he must have some British Military Policewomen at SHAPE, for duty outside his part of the headquarters and in his car. Several extremely pretty girls duly appeared and it is said that the first time they drove down the Champs Elysées in an open-topped Austin Champ, wearing their red caps, they brought the traffic to a standstill. On one rather cold morning, Stockwell was greeted with a smart salute by one of the girls as he entered the SHAPE building. 'Well, Corporal,' he remarked conversationally, 'winter draws on.' She blushed as red as her cap and replied, 'Not today, sir.'

The Stockwells took up residence in the Villa de Marne in Marnes la Cocquette, a beautiful spacious nineteenth-century house across the Bois de Bologne in an area much favoured by millionaires. The house was enclosed by a secure compound, which it shared with Norstad's residence, that of the Chief of Staff, and a fourth owned by the actor Maurice Chevalier. This caused some interesting moments when some of Polly's more colourful artist friends arrived, looking like refugees from some distant disaster. The American guards at the security post refused admittance and Norstad himself directed that they should be taken to the back entrance – but Stockwell would have none of it. His daughter's friends were his guests and that was the end of it. Animals too were part of the establishment, and according to Anthony Vivian:

> Hughie adored his dogs . . . no longer able to ride, he switched his attention to dogs. In particular, the love of his life was his shorthaired brown Yorkshire terrier, Gertie. In the morning on his arrival at his office, he was preceded by Sergeant Hill the driver, carrying his large brief case, and followed by Gertie.

Official entertainment was the order of the day, with at least two dinners and lunches each week. Seating plans could have the potential to cause a diplomatic incident especially where Greeks and Turks were concerned. Among the guests at various times were the 'charming' President John F. Kennedy; and Verner von Braun, to whom Joan, not surprisingly, could hardly be persuaded to speak at all. Hughie's father, although getting on in years (he was eighty-four), was also a regular guest until his death in 1962. There were balls and dances too in plenty. Polly went with Stockwell to one ball at Versailles, at which the two – both superb dancers – took the floor to waltz solo, amid terrific cheers. Stockwell himself had limited interest in food: he was perfectly happy with nursery dishes, and taking him to a gourmet restaurant was a waste of time and money – although he was wont to remark, 'Never trust a man who has not had a good breakfast.'

Gale had spent little enough time in the headquarters; Stockwell spent even less. Roy Redgrave remembered that he had only to point to a map and say, 'I bet no general from SHAPE has ever been there.' Stockwell would invariably reply, 'If you can set it up, Roy, I will go.' One of his first visits was to Pothus in Norway where he had first seen action in 1940. He went on to visit Kirkenes in Finnmark, where Norway shared 196 miles of frontier with the Soviet Union, before returning to SHAPE by way of Denmark. On the Southern Flank, historical tensions remained high and there was marked reluctance by the Greeks and Turks to co-operate, even in the face of the unifying threat from the Warsaw Pact. In October 1961 he visited the headquarters of First Turkish Army on the Dardanelles, where he was proudly shown a huge railway-mounted artillery piece, which had been run out of its cave and stood overlooking the straits with its crew of sixteen gunners all straight as ramrods. Stockwell inspected the men and then had a look at the gun: 'Krupp 1903,' he snorted. 'Why, that is the same year I was born. We are both far too old for the next war. Push it into the sea.' Fortunately only the Turkish General heard and he agreed with a hearty laugh.

Visiting Greece, Stockwell was taken around the frontiers with Albania, Jugoslavia, Bulgaria and Turkey. The Bulgarians were clearly the most pressing danger, as they were strong enough either to drive through Greece to the Mediterranean, or to capture Turkish Thrace, so long as Greece and Turkey did not co-operate. Standing on the frontier by the bridge at Alexandroupolis, Roy Redgrave, described how Stockwell had the opportunity to bring his personal charm to bear on these ancient hatreds:

Sir Hugh asked the Greek general if he had ever spoken to his Turkish counterpart. He said he had not. Sir Hugh then asked a terrified Greek soldier to walk across the frontier bridge . . . with a field telephone cable and connect it to the Turkish military exchange. He then suggested that the Greek general should invite the Turkish general to a meeting in, say, a month's time. An initiative which succeeded.

Joan went on some of these official visits with Stockwell and there was also the opportunity to travel at leisure, as Anthony Vivian recalled:

> Both he and Joan had been passionate travellers all their lives. Now in Paris they had the springboard for journeys all over Europe, often driving themselves in his newly acquired sleeping home on wheels – 'the Jeep' – which had been built by Ford to his own specifications. I remember once when his former commander and friend, Field Marshal Festing, was staying in Villa de Marne, Hughie took great pride in showing off this new toy. Festing was not impressed: 'I spent the war being uncomfortable, and I do not intend to continue at this stage of life.'

A big issue was the continuing tension with the Soviets over Berlin – the so-called 'Berlin Crisis'. In November 1958 the Soviets had renewed their efforts to force the Allies out of Berlin by obstruction, intimidation and blockade. As is well known, US President John F. Kennedy refused to be bullied. The Soviet campaign was mounted not least to reduce the numbers of refugees leaving the German Democratic Republic – DDR – for West Germany and in particular, West Berlin. Between the end of the Blockade in 1949 and late June 1961, this figure reached 6.6 million people, of whom a high percentage were skilled workers or professional people that the DDR could not afford to lose. At 2.30 am on 13 April 1961, the border was closed and sealed. Roads were cratered or dug up with pneumatic drills and wire obstacles erected. Tear gas was used to disperse crowds, but even so, 1,500 people managed to escape into the West that day. By the following morning, the only way of crossing was through thirteen check points; this temporary barrier was, over the coming months, developed into the infamous Berlin Wall.

One important result of the Berlin crisis was the establishment by Norstad, initially wearing his hat as C-in-C US Forces Europe, of Live Oak, a tripartite staff established for planning and crisis management. For most of its existence, Live Oak was shrouded in secrecy and it was not until 1987 that the organization even put its name on a building. It was initially established inside US European Command at St Germain en Laye, but this forced the British and French contingents to collect their secure communications from SHAPE and the French Ministry of Defence respectively. Norstad and Stockwell quickly realized that communications needed to be improved, along with closer co-ordination between Live Oak and NATO, and the supervision of the Live Oak staff. Initially, the British government was reluctant to countenance any expansion of the organization on the ground that this 'would be taken as a sign of British agreement to Live Oak's plans [i.e. for military measures in and around Berlin]'. Stockwell, however, lobbied hard for greater involvement, proposing that a British two-star officer should be appointed as Chief of Staff Live Oak, working to its American commander, General Lyman L. Lemnitzer. This would, he said, allow the British government 'to know exactly what the US representatives in LIVE OAK were doing . . . and bring out any weaknesses in current LIVE OAK planning'. Stockwell's logic was solid and his argument carried the day. On 11 July 1961 the Chiefs of Staff not only supported Live Oak's expansion, but also agreed to the appointment of Major General (later Field Marshal Sir) Geoffrey Baker as its Chief of Staff. Baker was in post by the time of the construction of the Berlin Wall in August; the organization worked round the clock in order to keep up with the fast-moving situation.

The last showdown over Berlin was the autobahn crisis of 1963, during which the Soviets, paranoid over the perceived role of Allied convoys in dropping agents and picking up refugees, blocked Allied convoys to and from Berlin. The Soviets demanded advance notification of all convoys of more than three vehicles, the internal inspection of vehicles, and dismounting of personnel for headcounts. The Americans refused on all counts, the British on two. From 9 October, the Soviets began blocking Allied convoys, in some cases bringing up armoured vehicles. The Allies refused to co-operate and made very obvious military response preparations. This was probably the closest that Live Oak came to having to implement its contingency plans. On 6 November, the Soviets gave way, having had enough of confrontation.

Throughout the various Berlin crises, Norstad had taken a cautious, moderate approach, never raising the stakes but simply matching Soviet moves and wearing them down. This moderate approach went down well with the British and French, but found little support among US hawks, especially President Kennedy's Special Representative in Berlin, General Lucius D. Clay. Increasingly uncomfortable, Norstad discussed resignation with Kennedy as early as January 1962. In July, he was summoned to Washington. He was back in Berlin on the evening of the 17th and his resignation was announced the following day. He remained in Paris until the end of 1962, when Lemnitzer, who on 1 November had already taken over his responsibilities as C-in-C European Command, also assumed the post of SACEUR.

Lemnitzer was an experienced infantry officer with as much – or more – experience of field command as Stockwell. In contrast to the youthful Norstad, he was 71, down to earth and forever chewing a large cigar. The relationship between SACEUR and his deputy underwent a subtle, but immediate, change. Stockwell was no longer the older and more experienced of the two, and he treated Lemnitzer with the greatest personal respect and deference. But there was a great deal of common ground in the experiences of the two men and their relationship was if anything closer than that of Stockwell and Norstad. Lemnitzer for his part obviously thought of Stockwell as a very able field commander, continued to treat him as his deputy in all things and gave him his head.

Stockwell was of course still Colonel of the Royal Welch Fusiliers. He spent two days with the 1st Battalion in Tidworth over St David's Day 1960, and Granada Television filmed the proceedings. He made his last visit to the 1st Battalion as a serving officer on 13 November 1963. The battalion had only just moved to Iserlohn in Germany from Tidworth, and was now in the mechanized role, equipped with the new Saracen wheeled armoured personnel carrier. The whole battalion paraded for their Colonel with all its vehicles, and the impressive parade concluded with a drive-past. Pembroke Dock must have seemed a long time ago.

Stockwell's tenure as DSACEUR was due to end in December 1963, when he was to hand over to Air Chief Marshal Sir Thomas Pike. He was determined to mark his departure with a proper farewell dinner so as not to let down the British Army's image. There were to be fourteen guests – 'Anthony, tell me what you think.' Anthony Vivian had a moment of inspiration and suggested not only the British Ambassador, Lemnitzer and the obvious guests from the headquarters, but also the Duke and Duchess of Windsor. Stockwell was not at first in favour of the idea but obviously discussed it with Joan. The Duke was, as a Field Marshal, the senior British officer in Europe and the next day Vivian was again summoned: 'alright – you make the arrangements.' A date was fixed and a briefing on protocol arranged from the Ambassador, who also gave a few tips. The Duke had to be addressed as 'Your Royal Highness' and treated as royalty. The Duchess, however, should receive no such deference. If the Duke became bored, he would be sure to leave; and he ate quickly, so the food would have to be served rapidly. Moreover he drank only vodka and smoked Bronx cigarettes. The last two horrified Stockwell, who was very careful about expenditure.

On the night, all the other guests arrived in good time and were briefed by Vivian on the arrival procedure. However, no plan survives contact with the enemy and the Duke, having met Stockwell at the top of the stairs, sent Wallis ahead. The guests, expecting the Duke first and the Duchess afterwards, duly bowed forbidden bows to Wallis, while ignoring His Royal Highness. A waiter then approached and asked the Duke what he would like to drink, expecting the reply 'vodka'. Not so: 'A gin and tonic please,' was the answer. Sergeant Anderson then approached with a box of the famous Bronx cigarettes. 'I won't smoke, thank you.' Stockwell thought of the unnecessary expense and groaned inwardly.

Dinner was then announced. At the table, Joan sat on the Duke's right, with Mrs Lemnitzer on his left, and the Duchess opposite with Stockwell on her right. The Duke was of course served first and began to eat immediately. By the time service had reached Joan, the Duke had finished and the plates had to be cleared at once. Poor Joan had very little indeed to eat and no conversation either since the Duke addressed his remarks only to the gentlemen. After dinner, however, the Duchess made good the lack of conversation by talking at length to Joan, Polly and her husband about art. Next day, a special courier arrived from Hermes with a gold pen.

The day before he left the appointment, 19 December 1963, France honoured Stockwell with the award of the Grand Officer of the Legion of Honour. He was greatly pleased with this award, which not only recognized his achievements as Land Force Commander at Suez, and his role as DSACEUR, but also finally laid to rest any suspicion of lingering resentment over his part in the invasion of Madagascar. He received the decoration at a ceremony at the British Embassy in London, on the same day that Sir Richard Gale was similarly decorated; the occasion was made even more memorable by the Ambassador, who managed to stick the pin on the star of the order right through Stockwell's tunic and shirt, and into his flesh! On 20 December there was another ceremony at the SHAPE main building, decked out with Christmas decorations, where in front of a full multinational guard of honour, Lemnitzer bade farewell to his deputy. After the ceremony, Stockwell changed into plain clothes at Villa de Marne and he and Joan drove away. The Lemnitzer family was there to wave them off as Hughie Stockwell departed from SHAPE, from Paris, and after forty years' service, from the British Army.

Chapter Twenty-One

Canal Zone: Devizes, 1964–1974

The 87½ miles of the Kennet and Avon Canal link the navigable parts of the River Thames below Reading with the Avon at Bath, via the Kennet navigation. Commissioned by Act of Parliament on 17 April 1794, it was designed and built by the Scottish engineer John Rennie. It was completed on 28 December 1810, and includes among its 104 locks, one of the most famous flights of locks in the world, the twenty-nine locks of the Caen Hill flight at Devizes. But its heyday was brief, and by 1900, little traffic remained. What there was diminished further by the growth of road traffic after the First World War. One section was closed in May 1950 when the lock at Burghfield near Reading collapsed, and severe deterioration of other locks followed through disuse and neglect. By 1952, the Caen Hill flight was impassable. By 1956, while Hughie Stockwell was engaged with another canal far away, the Kennet and Avon was again threatened with extinction through legal closure.

But salvation was at hand through an idea for alternative use: recreation. The Inland Waterways Association (IWA) had been formed in 1946, and the Kennett & Avon was one of its first objects of interest. In 1948, the Kennet & Avon Canal Association was formed as a branch of the IWA, with the objects of working for the greater use, maintenance and development of the waterway, to promote greater knowledge and use of the canal, and to extend its amenities. One of the first to become involved was Captain Lionel Munk, who saw the potential of the canal for pleasure craft.

An important milestone was reached in 1958 when the Bowes Report was published. Although the report did not recommend the inclusion of the canal in the commercial navigation network, it did recognize the overwhelming interest in its redevelopment for recreation. The Association, welcoming the report, at once set about raising money. By 1962, the Kennet & Avon Association had become a Trust. In the following year, the newly formed British Waterways Board (BWB) took over responsibility for the canal, and the first restoration projects began, with limited public funds, and money raised privately by the Trust. In this it was helped by the Inland Waterways Redevelopment Advisory Committee, which the Bowes Report had recommended be set up.

Hughie Stockwell became engaged with the canal through the earlier purchase of Canal Cottage at Horton, near Devizes. The January 1962 K&A Trust Council meeting minutes noted that 'One other report, which was to be of tremendous importance to the future of the canal, was that General Sir Hugh Stockwell, Deputy Supreme Allied Commander Europe, had joined the association and offered any help in his power.' The story of the purchase of this cottage was typical of Hughie Stockwell's luck, for he was a lucky man. Having returned to his London house after Suez, he and Joan were besieged by the press. It was just after Christmas and he needed a break, so he decided to take Joan to a pub in Devizes that they knew from an earlier holiday, to get away from it all. The next day, they went for a walk down the canal and came across a former waterman's cottage, very run down. No one knew who owned it, but as usual Hughie knew how to get things done. He guessed that it belonged to the Waterways Board and wrote to his old friend Sir Brian Robertson, who was the chairman. Robertson replied that he did not previously know of this cottage, but since Hughie had found it, he could buy it at a very low price. This is just what Stockwell did, and Joan's creative talent rapidly turned it into a charming little house. Of course, he and Joan still had Erw Suran and the London house in Elgin Crescent, but Devizes became their main base. Polly tried hard to make Stockwell invest in more property in London, but he remained averse to the idea. Many people of that generation were of the same opinion, perhaps having grown up with the spectre of declining property values during the 1920s and early 1930s. But Stockwell would not even buy the land that gave access to the cottage, and so he and Joan had to get to it by rowing boat, after parking their car on the opposite bank of the canal.

Stockwell hated retirement, but he also refused to take on another high-pressure appointment in civilian life. Once he was retired, Joan proved adept at keeping him engaged in projects, travelling in the Jeep, canoeing on the canal and in visiting their other properties. He disliked London life, the only exception being the Army and Navy Club where he was sure to bump into old friends. He remained Colonel of the Royal Welch Fusiliers until 1965 when he handed over to Jack Willes, and thereafter he remained in touch and engaged with the Regiment and its institutions. He also remained involved with the Army Air Corps after giving up as Colonel Commandant in 1963. Stockwell Hall in the Museum of Army Flying at Middle Wallop was later named after him. In addition, he kept up his contacts with the Malay Regiment, the RWAFF Association and the Burma Star Association.

Stockwell was elected to the Kennet and Avon Trust Council in 1963. He was specifically appointed as chairman of the appeals committee, a vital task in view of the scale of the restoration project. This was meat and drink to Hughie Stockwell. A working party headed by Munk, who was by now Association Chairman, had surveyed the canal from Reading to Hungerford and, after consulting a contractor, came up with a figure of £100,000, of which £50,000 would come from the BWB. Although costs could be cut by using volunteer labour for unskilled jobs, this was a considerable sum at 1963 prices and required a national appeal. Fund-raising started, literally, by shaking tins in the street, but this was never going to produce the sort of amounts needed, and it quickly gave way to activities such as boat fairs at Newbury in 1965 and 1966. These fairs proved to be major money-spinners, raising around £1,200 each year. Stockwell himself seemed to be everywhere, always accompanied by his basset hound, Dudley, encouraging, motivating, shaking up the Council, talking to local authorities, using his extensive network of contacts to lobby politicians and the Waterways Board, raising money, and of course, rolling up his sleeves to work on restoration projects.

In March 1967, Lionel Munk, who was by now IWA Chairman, announced that pressure of work made it necessary for him to give up the chairmanship of the Trust. There was a clear favourite to succeed him and Hughie Stockwell agreed to do so as soon as he was asked. Less than a year later, the 1968 Transport Act set up the Inland Waterways Amenity Advisory Council. The Council superseded the old Advisory Committee and was a statutory body to advise the then Ministries of Transport, and of Agriculture, Fisheries and Food, and indeed the Waterways Board, on strategic policy for the use and development of the 2,000 miles of inland waterways managed by the Waterways Board. It included four BWB representatives. The Act also gave the BWB powers to enter into agreements with local authorities or other bodies, to help with improving and maintaining the canals. This was, for the K&A, a turning point that made the eventual complete restoration of the canal possible. All that was needed was determination and money – Hughie Stockwell had plenty of the first, and there was now no stopping him and his friends in getting the second. Moves began at once to enlist the support of local authorities and momentum picked up quickly. The funds raised saw a dramatic increase in the number of restoration projects on locks, bridges and the canal itself. By 1970, the Trust had spent £19,000 on restoration, with the same amount programmed for 1971 and £17,500 for 1972. In April 1969, Stockwell launched a publicity campaign to support all these moves by steering the paddle steamer *Charlotte Dundas*, recently acquired by the Trust, on her maiden voyage at Devizes. Stockwell's name alone was sufficient to produce coverage in most national newspapers.

In April 1971 Stockwell was appointed chairman of the IWAAC, with a seat on the British Waterways Board. John Morris,[1] a former Royal Welch Fusilier who was Joint Parliamentary Secretary at the Department of Transport from 1966 to 1968, and responsible for piloting through the House of Commons that part of the Transport Bill (later the Transport Act 1968) dealing with canals, recalled that: 'Canals were then very much a poor relation of the transport system, and it was exceedingly difficult to get political interest in the subject. In the absence of that, the only hope was to enlist and give a practical role to active enthusiasts.'

*   *   *

Stockwell's involvement with the wider waterways issue had begun two years earlier when, at a conference at New College Oxford on the future of the canals, he had met Illtyd Harrington. Harrington was at that time the Labour Leader of the Greater London Council. When he left the job in 1968, as the Transport Act was being passed, he was offered the chairmanship of the BWB by the then Minister of Transport, Barbara Castle. John Morris had played the leading role in securing his appointment:

> I first came across Harrington when I attended the Annual Dinner of the London Sector of the Waterways Association, held at Regent's Park Zoo. Despite Harrington's colourful political track record – and he and I were poles apart politically – I convinced myself and, more importantly, my Minister, Barbara Castle, that we should appoint him to the Waterways Board. It took some doing and I had to accompany Barbara for a late night brandy at No 10 with Harold Wilson. Despite Party opposition my presence, rather unusually, bolstered the approach of my boss. Wilson countermanded the Party advice.

Morris was also at the Oxford conference where he and Hughie were both speakers. Morris formed the view that Stockwell's zeal had to be harnessed and that he and Harrington would make an excellent partnership. He duly introduced them. 'I am rather proud,' he said later, 'to have played the part of Cupid.' Harrington, who had met Hughie Stockwell 'at Ismailia in the Canal Zone when he was GOC and I was a Leading Aircraftsman, on National Service, in an RAF guard of honour which marched past him,' subsequently received 'two pages of energetic handwriting asking what he could do to help'. The two agreed to meet for lunch in London to discuss matters:

> My entrance into the Army and Navy Club in St James's for lunch on a hot June day in 1968 was greeted coolly. The CND badge in my lapel possibly provoked an enraged major to snarl 'Who let that bloody communist in here?' A voice from behind, which had long commanded immediate authority snapped 'That bloody communist is my guest.' General Sir Hugh Stockwell . . . tolerated most things except intolerance. The major apologised and the general and I went in to eat our lunch: he to be greeted with a ripple of warmth and great respect, me to a long worrying gaze of curiosity. It was the beginning of a fast friendship.
>
> Stockwell looked like Douglas Fairbanks and had the humorous eyes of David Niven. He had invited me to talk about the future of Britain's inland waterways . . . at the end of the afternoon it was I who offered him the Queen's shilling. He readily agreed to help.

And so Hughie Stockwell became Vice-Chairman of the BWB. When Harrington met Gerald Templer for lunch not long afterwards, Templer gave Harrington a long, dark look and said, 'You and Hughie Stockwell are a

283

pair of bloody romantics. He'll persist – but will you?' When Harrington told Stockwell of this, he laughed, and replied, 'Next time you see him, remind him of the time he and I turned up to a party in Malaya dressed as French maids!' Together, Harrington and Stockwell – and of course, Dudley – travelled the length and breadth of Britain proclaiming the cause of the canals. They reopened the long, dark, slimy tunnel at, appropriately, Dudley: 'It took his nerve and my brandy bottle to get us through,' remembered Harrington. At one meeting in a smart marina near Chester, a tweedy lady asked Stockwell why he felt so strongly, especially about the Kennet & Avon. 'Madam,' the hero of Suez replied, 'I lost one canal, but I'll be buggered if I'll lose another.' Later they were at Bathampton on the K&A to reopen the lock there. The working party was commanded by a former Corporal in the Welsh Guards, who expected – and got – instant obedience from the two four-star officers under his command, Hughie Stockwell and Admiral Sir William (Bill) O'Brien. It was Harrington, too, who telephoned George Thomas, the then Secretary of State for Wales, when Stockwell and Joan were left off the guest list at the Investiture of the Prince of Wales in Caernarfon in 1969. Tickets appeared by return of post.

When Stockwell became Chairman in 1971 it was in succession to Harrington, who left the post for political reasons following the election of Edward Heath's Conservative government. Stockwell took to turning up to meetings with Dudley, and with Dudley's lunch in a bucket, giving him a good excuse to keep meetings short and to the point. The appointment was a tribute to Stockwell personally, and to the K&A, but it is possible that his appointment to the Board had been viewed by some as a sinecure – a famous name to add stature to the organization without any real contribution. If that was so, the reality was rather different. Hughie Stockwell was no businessman, but he had a shrewd suspicion that there were some on the Board who were using it as a means of property speculation, for as the canal network began to reopen, the property on it naturally became more attractive. Coached by de Cronin Hastings, Stockwell refused to keep his mouth shut, and there were some famous rows. Two years later he was also appointed to the Water Space Amenity Commission, which had been set up by the Water Act in 1973. This body was responsible for advising and co-ordinating with water boards on a range of issues, including water quality, wildlife, recreation, navigation, extraction, flood control and hydro-electric power. He took a stand at the Boat Show at Earl's Court, attracting much favourable attention, including that of Ted Heath. He did much to encourage the Devizes to London canoe race, which followed the length of the K&A. In 1981, Sir Ashley Brammall (brother of the Field Marshal) arranged for the Greater London Council, led by Ken Livingstone, to give a lunch to thank Stockwell, Harrington and O'Brien for their work. The chief guest was the Duke of Edinburgh, who was not amused when Livingstone rushed off early to learn the results of the Chancellor's budget speech.

Stockwell remained with the Waterways Board – and in his other related appointments – until 1974, by which time the Kennet and Avon project was well under way. He announced his decision to retire as Chairman of the K&A Trust at its AGM in April of that year and it was rightly remarked that:

> He had led the Trust through some of the darkest hours but his stead-fastness never wavered and his brilliant leadership gave courage to everyone with whom he made contact. The Kennet & Avon Canal restoration project owes its success to quite a small band of dedicated people and truly General Sir Hugh Stockwell was one of them.

Stockwell was immediately appointed President of the Trust in succession to Lord Methuen, who had died in January. He himself was succeeded by Bill O'Brien, whom Stockwell himself had persuaded to join. Soon after, dredging around Hungerford was completed which allowed the canal to be opened to navigation from Reading to beyond the newly restored Hungerford Lock.

Stockwell remained engaged with the Trust as its President until his death, and although he never saw the completion of his work, its success was never in doubt. His contribution was marked on the Trust's 21st birthday, and by coincidence, Stockwell's 80th birthday, in 1983, when Lock Number 44 at Devizes – one of the famous flight there – was named in his honour. The final completion of the restoration was achieved after thirty-four years of work – rather longer than the original construction. The Queen reopened the canal as a public amenity on 8 August 1990, at Devizes; final completion of restoration was achieved in 2003.

Notes

1 The Rt Hon John Morris, Lord Morris of Aberavon PC KG did his National Service in 1955–1957 and then served in 4 RWF (TA) in 1957–1959. He was Minister of Defence Equipment 1968, and later Attorney General 1997–1999. He became Lord Lieutenant of Dyfed in 2003. *Who's Who*, 2004.

Chapter Twenty-Two

Last Post, 1974–1986

At the age of seventy-one, real retirement loomed at last for Hughie Stockwell. He and Joan lived primarily at Devizes, but went regularly to Erw Suran, where he spent a good deal of time in a new hobby, painting. Neither went back to hunting. Elgin Crescent was sold to Anabel in 1975. They still travelled and he remained in close contact with the K&A, with the Snowdonia Society through Esme Kirby,[1] and with his various military associations. On 22 January 1978, for example, they were in Ghana for the 33rd Anniversary celebrations on Myohaung Day, in the El-Wak stadium in Accra. Stockwell Green was named after him when the old military quarters in Wrexham were redeveloped, along with other roads named in honour of the great Colonels of the Royal Welch Fusiliers.

He remained in close touch too with his family. Anabel and Harris were doing well at Blaise Farm; Polly and John Hope, however, parted company in 1974. She later married Theo Crosby, the hugely talented and distinguished designer, writer and architect, whom Hughie greatly liked.[2] Hughie's father had died in 1962, towards the end of his time as DSACEUR in Paris, but his sisters were all very much alive. Dorothy lived on until 1984 when the horrors of multiple sclerosis engulfed her, but Betty and Kitty were to outlive Hughie by six and eight years respectively. Then there were the grandchildren, in whom he took particular delight. Diccon Wright remembered that to the end of his life, his grandfather was 'fantastic . . . he was always interested, always wanted to talk and be kept in touch and up to date. He had such charm and charisma.' Then there were always dogs. When Dudley died, Hughie took on a Border terrier called Redford, who was soon his constant companion.

Despite occasional bouts of malaria, Stockwell's heath remained generally good. He had a bad attack of shingles soon after retirement, perhaps an allergic reaction to civilian life. He gradually slowed down and, once he was eighty, he began to shrink, almost to shrivel, as people who have been hale and hearty at seventy-five sometimes do. But in 1983 he was diagnosed with leukaemia. From then on he was on various courses of drugs and treatment at the military hospital at RAF Wroughton, where by coincidence the Queen had presented Colours to the Royal Welch Fusiliers in the great parade in 1954.

286

By 1986 he had become very weak, but in early November he insisted on attending the annual reunion of the Burma Star Association in Aberystwyth. Joan tried to dissuade him as she felt it might be too much, and she did not want him to appear undignified. However he insisted and in the end, Anabel took him. Joan was right, it *was* too much, and he came home worn out. He was well enough on Sunday, 23 November to see Gigi's new daughter – his great granddaughter. Nevertheless, it was approaching the 30th anniversary of the Suez operation, and he insisted on being interviewed on Tuesday 25 November. The strain of this, on top of the trip to Aberystwyth, brought on a collapse and he was rushed in to hospital. In the small hours of Thursday, 27 November, quite alone, Hugh Stockwell suffered a heart attack, and died. He could not be revived. Anabel arrived soon afterwards to take the death certificate and sign for his belongings. 'It was when I did that,' she said, 'that I knew it was final. His watch was still ticking though, and I kept it going. I still do.'

Obituaries appeared the following day in *The Times*, the *Daily Telegraph* and the *Independent*. His funeral, attended by the family and close friends only, took place at All Cannings Church, close to Horton. The church was filled with a thousand candles and Polly arranged the music, which was for violin and cello. His coffin, about which there had been furious disputes with the undertakers, was absolutely plain, and covered with a great Regimental flag. Six fusiliers from the Regiment carried it into the church. His dog Redford followed the coffin. Everyone wept.

The funeral service was followed by cremation at Chippenham, and Polly took the urn containing his ashes. His memorial service did not take place until Friday, 20 March 1987. There was some discussion over where this should be: the Royal Memorial Chapel at Sandhurst and the Royal Hospital, Chelsea, were possible; however as a Grand Commander of the Order of the Bath, he was entitled to have his memorial in Westminster Abbey. Moreover, it was obvious that a huge number of people would wish to attend the memorial to the most distinguished Royal Welchman of modern times, and one of the greatest field commanders of the century; only the Abbey would be big enough. Anthony Vivian, now Colonel of the Royal Welch Fusiliers, took the decision and with the help of the Regimental Secretary, Major Tim Herbert, made the arrangements, while Polly took on the music and aesthetic aspects. There were difficulties over introducing a photographer, but eventually it was agreed that one could be out of sight in the organ loft. Then there were objections from the recently appointed Dean, Michael Mayne, over the anthem. Polly wanted to commission a new piece, 'Death hath no Dominion', using words by Dylan Thomas and music by Malcolm Singer. The Dean did not like modern music and would not agree, but eventually the organist, Simon Paston, agreed that he and the choir could do it.

On the day, the Regimental flag flew high above the abbey which was, as expected, full to bursting. The Stockwell family were there in force. There were too, of course, many distinguished people. The Queen was represented, appropriately, by the Deputy Supreme Allied Commander Europe, General Sir Edward Burgess, and Prince Michael of Kent by Colonel Michael Farmer. Nicholas Edwards, Secretary of State for Wales, and a former Royal Welch Fusilier, was there. There were Lords Lieutenant, Colonels of Regiments, representatives of the many organizations and bodies of which Hughie Stockwell had been a member.[3] But there were, too, hundreds of ordinary men and women, to whom Hughie Stockwell had been quite simply a much-loved friend.

As the procession, led by the clergy, entered the abbey to begin the service, Hugh Stockwell's orders, decorations and medals were carried by his grandsons, Augustine Hope and Diccon Wright, and by Lieutenant James Dunn of the Royal Welch Fusiliers. The Dean conducted the service, assisted, among others, by Canon H.J. Lloyd, Honorary Territorial Army Chaplain to the Regiment. Brigadier Morgan Llewellyn read the lesson, Colonel Peter Reece, the only serving member of the Regiment to have won the DSO, read from John Bunyan's *Pilgrim's Progress*, and Illtyd Harrington read the poem *Rocky Acres*, by Robert Graves. The hymns were *Cwm Rhondda*, and *Onward Christian Soldiers*.

Anthony Vivian gave the address. It was, rightly, a long address and in it he spoke for all those present, and many others who could not be there in person but were certainly there in spirit.

> General Hughie. I wrote to him four days before he died, to ask for advice on a Regimental matter. I don't know whether he ever read the letter – but I hope he did – for he always said to me as Colonel of the Royal Welch Fusiliers: 'I don't mind what you do – provided you always tell me first.'
>
> I know that everyone here has his own personal memory of General Hughie, for everything about him was so striking and exciting. He was never dull or mundane – his strong and forceful manner; the twinkle in his eye and his impish sense of humour; his untiring energy . . . his impeccable standards; his kindness and his friendly manner which made people both respect and love him; his smart yet casual dress, whether on parade in Blues with sash, sword and medals, hat slightly at an angle, or more quietly at home, in an old pair of trousers and pullover. Whatever picture you have, not far behind would be his cars and his dogs.

In September 1987, a memorial to Hughie Stockwell was unveiled in the Royal Memorial Chapel at Sandhurst, which he had attended as a Gentleman Cadet and as Commandant. In 1989, the Burma Star Association dedicated a memorial containing a short book on his life in the church of St Padarn at Llanbadarn Fawr, near Aberystwyth. These, along with this book, constitute his physical memorials. He wanted no others.

But Polly still had the ashes, which he had asked in his Will should be scattered near Erw Suran – he had been on many walks to choose the right place.

After a year had passed, Polly knew that the time had come to complete the last act. But Hughie had already had a funeral and no clergyman could be found to conduct another. At last, the vicar of All Cannings agreed to conduct a service of blessing. On the appointed day, a small group gathered at Erw Suran: Joan, Polly, Anabel, Diccon and Augustine, Esme and Peter Kirby, Anthony Vivian, a subaltern from the territorial battalion of the Royal Welch Fusiliers, and a bugler. It was a beautiful day – bright, clear and windy – and the group scrambled up the rocky paths to the appointed place. The words were said, the Last Post echoed over the mountains, but then Polly could not get the lid off the urn. At last it came, and the wind took Hughie's ashes and scattered them far over the Welsh hills.

Those who walk there say that you can still hear him laugh.

Notes

1 Esme Kirby, née Cummins (1910–1999) married Tom Firbank in 1935, divorced and married Major E.L. (Peter) Kirby MC, curator of the RWF Museum, in 1945. She remained a passionate activist on behalf of rural affairs in North Wales to the end of her life. See her obituary in the *Daily Telegraph*, 25 November 1999.

2 Theo Crosby (1923–1994), born in South Africa, was a founder member of the Pentagram Design Group. He is best known as the designer of Shakespeare's Globe theatre in London.

3 For a full list of those attending see the account in *The Times*, Saturday, 21 March 1987.

Select Bibliography and Sources

Interviews

Major Nigel Anderson, 12 December 2004.
Lieutenant Colonel Neville Bosanquet, 19 July 2002.
Professor Nick Bosanquet, 5 June 2003.
Major General F.G. Caldwell, 16 March 2004.
Major General Peter Cavendish, 26 June 2003.
Captain W.P. Edwards, 30 March 2004.
Lieutenant Colonel L.J. Egan, 1 May 2002.
General Sir Anthony Farrar-Hockley, 16 May 2003; 12 February 2004.
Sir Philip Goodhart, 15 January 2004.
Major Barney Griffiths, 20 March 2003.
Rear Admiral E.F. Gueritz, 10 June 2002; 26 June 2002; 29 October 2002; 28 January 2004
Polly Hope, numerous occasions throughout 2002, 2003 and 2004.
Major H.J.E. Jones, 28 May 2002.
Mrs Susan Jonnak, 5 April 2002.
Major E.C. Lanning, 21 November 2002.
Mr Hugo Meynell, 15 April 2004.
Mr Ian Moody, 10 February 2003.
Lord Morris of Aberavon, 17 December 2004.
Lord Parry of Neyland, 12 November 2002.
Air Chief Marshal Sir Thomas Prickett, 19 July 2004.
Major B.G.B. Pugh, 3 September 2003.
Major General Sir Roy Redgrave, 14 June 2004.
Annette, Lady Reilly, 22 January 2002.
Major M.L.G. Robinson, 18 May 2003.
David Russell, 24 February 2004.
R.F.F. Simmonds, 21 February 2003.
Sir Anthony Tritton, 24 February 2004.
Brigadier Anthony Vivian, 19 November 2004.
Major General R.D. Wilson, 24 June 2003.
General Sir Richard Worsley, 6 February 2004.
Anabel Wright, 22 March 2004.
Diccon Wright, 22 March 2004.

National Archive (Public Record Office) Papers

EARLY SERVICE

CO 820/9/1, Nigeria; CO 820/9/9, Nigeria; CO 820/18/9, Nigeria; WO 166/1030, 158 (RW) Infantry Brigade War Diary, September 1939–April 1940.

NORWAY

DEFE 2/1 WO 106/1944, HQ North-West Expeditionary Force Instructions dated 2 May 1940; WO 166/1030, 158 (Royal Welch) Infantry Brigade War Diary, September 1939–
April 1941; WO 168/106 folio 84277, No. 2 Independent Company War Diary, May 1940.

MADAGASCAR

CAB 120/44.
CAFO 2491.
COS (41) 629.
DEFE 2/312; 2/314; 3/314.
WO 166/4625, 2 RWF War Diary, 1 July–31 December 1941; WO 166/8928, 174/36, 2 RWF War Diary, 1 January–31 August 1942.

INDIA AND BURMA

WO 230/53; WO 172/2078, 29 Independent Infantry Brigade War Diary, January–December 1943; WO 172/4404, 29 Brigade War Diary, January–December 1944; WO 172/9561, 82nd (WA) Division War Diary, January–June 1945; WO 172/9562, 82nd (WA) Division War Diary, 1 July–31 December 1945; WO 172/9563, 82nd (WA) Division War Diary AQ files, 1 July 1945–31 December 1946.

PALESTINE

WO 275/12, Moves of 6th Airborne Division HQ; WO 275/48. WO 275/90 Craforce Incident Reports 1948; WO 275/90 North Sector Incident Reports, April–May 1948; 6th Airborne Division Operations and Incidents, January–March 1948; 'History of the Transjordan Frontier Force' by Colonel G.W. Montgomery OBE, HQ 6 AB Div 401/16/G/SD dated 29 October 1947 in WO 275/112, Organisation and Employment of Transjordan Frontier Force; WO 275/113, Organisation and Administration of the Arab Legion.

MALAYA

WO 216/561; WO 216/630, 216/631; WO 216/874; PRO 1022/29, 'Resettlement of Squatters in Malaya'.

SUEZ

ADM 205/154, Psychological Warfare PSW (56).
CAB 134/1217 Terrapin EC(56) 47.
DEFE 13/47 'Limitations of Operation Musketeer'.
FO 371/118842/JE 1022/23; FO 371/118997, Minutes of the Egypt Committee.
WO 288/77, HQ II (British) Corps Report on Operation Musketeer.

Imperial War Museum

Inquiry on Whether the Japanese Ever Contemplated an Invasion of India in IWM Japanese Interrogation Reports, Box 8, AS 5002.

IWM 82/15/1, The Life and Times of Sir Philip Christison, Bart.

IWM 82/37/1, Captain D.M. Cookson, attached to the Gambia Regiment.

IWM 97/36/1, Lieutenant J.A.L. Hamilton, attached to 81st (WA) Division; Captain F.K. Theobald, attached to 82nd (WA) Division.

SOUND ARCHIVE

4383, HCS's interview on the 82nd (WA) Division.

20457, John Randle of the 7th/10th Baluch.

Liddell Hart Centre (King's College London) Papers

EARLY SERVICE

KCL/Stockwell/1/4; KCL/Clarke/1/9 and 2/5.

GENERAL

HCS's AB 439 in KCL/Stockwell/1/1.

NORWAY

KCL/Stockwell/2/1.

INDIA AND BURMA

KCL/Stockwell/3/1;   KCL/Stockwell/5/3;   KCL/Stockwell/5/7/5; KCL/Stockwell/5/8; KCL/Stockwell/10/12.

PALESTINE

KCL/Stockwell/6/1; KCL/Stockwell/6/2; KCL/Stockwell/6/3; KCL/Stockwell/6/5; KCL/Stockwell/6/7;   KCL/Stockwell/6/9;   KCL/Stockwell/6/12; KCL/Stockwell/6/14;   KCL/Stockwell/6/15;   KCL/Stockwell/6/24; KCL/Stockwell/6/26;   KCL/Stockwell/6/29;   KCL/Stockwell/6/30; KCL/Stockwell/6/33;   KCL/Stockwell/6/35;   KCL/Stockwell/6/39; KCL/Stockwell/25/1.

CANAL ZONE

KCL/Stockwell/10/13.

MALAYA

KCL/Stockwell/7/5; KCL/Stockwell/7/6; KCL/Stockwell/7/8; KCL/Stockwell/7/9.

SUEZ

KCL/Stockwell/8/1;   KCL/Stockwell/8/4;   KCL/Stockwell/8/6; KCL/Stockwell/8/6/12-13; KCL/Stockwell/8/6/14.

Churchill College Cambridge

RMSY 5/11 and 12, Imperial Defence College Exercise No. 5, 1933, para 242 in the Ramsay Papers.

St Anthony's College Oxford (Middle East Centre)

MEC GB 165-0128/1/1. Sir Henry Gurney, 'Palestine Postscript: a short record of the last days of the Mandate March–14th May 1948'.

MEC GB 165-0072/IV/5/34. General Sir Richard Cunningham's 'Appreciation of the Situation in Palestine' in his official papers and telegrams.

MEC GB 165-0282/I/19. Thames Television Collection, text of an interview with HCS covering the British withdrawal from Palestine.

MEC GB 165-0208/3/3, Letters of Miss S.P. Emery to her mother.

MEC GB 165-0208/1/3, excerpts from a general report (No. 8) to the Bishop in Jerusalem, 12 May 1948.

MEC GB 165-0208/1/3, Report on events in Haifa, April 20 to May 4 1948.

University of Southampton

'The First Sea Lord's Part in the Suez Canal Crisis up to 7 September 1956' in Mountbatten Papers.

Hagana Archive, Israel

Hushi Files, No. 4: HCS's Statement to the Haifa notables.

Israel State Archive

P/940/437, The Arab Committee's memo to HCS and the minutes of the Jewish delegation meeting with HCS; P/941/440/1, Testimony by Khousa and Sa'ad in David Ariel, 'The Arab States and the Refugee Problem: Documents and Testimonies on the Responsibility for Creating the Problem', 7 October 1951.

Israeli Defence Forces' Archive 128/51/70.

Supreme Headquarters Allied Powers Europe Archive

Gregory, W. Pedlow, 'Allied Crisis Management for Berlin: the Live Oak Organisation 1959–1963'.

——, 'Flexible Response before MC/14/3: General Lauris Norstad and the Second Berlin Crisis 1958–1962'.

Humphries, J.A.J., 'Memories of LIVE OAK 1959–1961' (unpublished MS 1986).

Royal Welch Fusiliers Archive (Caernarfon) Papers

EARLY LIFE

'A Welsh Fusilier: account by H.C. Stockwell of his early life and military service in Pembroke Dock, Germany and West Africa', 2RWF Digest of Service, 1923–6 and 1926–30.

NORWAY

5439, No. 2 Independent Company, Account by Captain B.G.B. Pugh dated 1 June 1940; 5168, No. 2 Independent Company 1940, account by Sgt W.A. Jones.

MADAGASCAR

L/2655/190 (A), Brian Cotton, 'A Short War History of 2 RWF'.

INDIA AND BURMA

Gordon Milne (late 236 Field Company RE, 29 Brigade), 'Reminiscences on General Sir Hugh Stockwell and Brigadier Ll Gwydyr-Jones'.

SUEZ

'Report on Operation Musketeer' by General Sir Hugh Stockwell.

Museum of Army Flying Archives

Chronology of Army Aviation.

Private Papers

NORWAY

Quintin Riley, Personal Diary, held by Mrs N.A.C. Owen (daughter).
Papers and Diaries of Brigadier T.B. Trappes-Lomax, held by Tessa Trappes-Lomax (daughter).

PALESTINE

Polly Hope, 'General Hughie Says "Tanks for the Memory", an Historical Opera' (1993).

SUEZ

An Account of the Events Leading up to and During the Suez Campaign 1956 – by Lieutenant General Sir John Cowley GC KBE CB (Cowley Papers).

Books

GENERAL

Blaxland, Gregory, *The Regiments Depart. A History of the British Army, 1945–1970* (London, 1971).

Chandler, David and Beckett, Ian (eds), *The Oxford History of the British Army* (OUP, 1996).

Farrar-Hockley, Anthony, *The Army in the Air: The History of the Army Air Corps* (London, 1994).

Godwin-Austen, Brevet Major A.R., *The Staff and the Staff College* (London, 1927).

Grenville, J.A.S. and Wasserstein, Bernard, *The Major International Treaties of the Twentieth Century* (London, 2001).

Mackenzie, S.P., *The Home Guard – A Military and Political History* (OUP, 1996).

McNish, Robin, *Iron Division: The History of the 3rd Division 1809–1989* (Revised Edition, HMSO, 1990).

Mead, Peter, *Soldiers in the Air: the Development of Army Flying* (London, 1967).

Messenger, Charles, *For Love of Regiment. A History of British Infantry,* Vol II, 1915–1994 (London, 1996).

Montgomery of Alamein, Field Marshal, *Memoirs* (London, 1958).

Parry, Clive and Hopkins, Charity, *Index to British Treaties,* Vol III (HMSO, 1970).

Pear's Cyclopaedia, 51st Edition.

Philip's *University Atlas* (London, 1975).

Riley, J.P., *Regimental Records of the Royal Welch Fusiliers,* Vol VI, 1945–1969 (Llandysul, 2001).

——, *Regimental Records of the Royal Welch Fusiliers,* Vol VII, 1970–2000 (Llandysul, 2001).

EARLY LIFE AND SERVICE

Bainbridge, W.S., 'A report on the present conditions in the Ruhr and the Rhineland' (New York, 1923).

Bamfield, Veronica, *On the Strength. The Story of the British Army Wife* (London, 1974).

Dennis, Peter, *The Territorial Army 1907–1940* (RHS, 1987).

Masters, John, *Bugles and a Tiger* (London, 1956).

Niven, David, *The Moon's a Balloon* (London, 1973).

NORWAY

The German Campaign in Norway. German Naval History Series BR 1840 (1) compiled by Tactical and Staff Duties Division of the Admiralty (27 November 1948).

Buckley, Christopher, *Norway, The Commandos, Dieppe* (HMSO, London, 1951).

Derry, T.K., *The Campaign in Norway. History of the Second World War, United Kingdom Military Series* (HMSO London, 1952).

Erskine, David, *The Scots Guards 1919–1955* (London, 1956).

Fell, W.R., *The Sea our Shield* (London, 1966).

Fitzgerald, Major D.J.L., MC, *History of the Irish Guards in the Second World War* (Aldershot, 1949).

Messenger, Charles, *The Commandos 1940–1946* (London, 1985).

Riley, J.P., *From Pole to Pole: The Life of Quintin Riley* (Cambridge, 1988 and 1999).

Verney, Peter, *The Micks* (London, 1970).

Wilkinson, Peter and Bright Astley, Joan, *Gubbins and SOE* (London, 1997).

MADAGASCAR

History of the Combined Operations Organisation 1940–1945 (Amphibious Warfare Headquarters, London, 1956).

Buckley, Christopher, *Five Ventures* (HMSO, 1977).

Churchill, Winston, *The Second World War*, Vol IV, The Hinge of Fate (London, 1951).

Glover, Michael, *That Astonishing Infantry. The History of The Royal Welch Fusiliers 1689–1989* (London, 1989).

Kemp, Lieutenant Commander P.K. and Graves, John, *The Red Dragon: The Story of the Royal Welch Fusiliers 1919–1945* (Aldershot, 1960).

Mocler, Anthony, *Our Enemies The French* (London, 1976).

Tute, Warren, *The Reluctant Enemies: The Story of the Last War between Britain and France 1940–1942* (London, 1990).

INDIA AND BURMA

Argyle, C.J., *Japan At War 1937–1945* (London, 1976).

Calvert, Mike, *Slim* (London, 1973).

Carver, Michael, *Out of Step* (London, 1989).

Cross, J.P., *Jungle Warfare: Experiences and Encounters* (London, 1989).

Foster, Geoffry, *36th Division, The Campaign in North Burma 1944–45* (Privately Printed, 1946), p. 51.

Hamilton, John A.L., *War Bush* (Norwich, 2001).

Kemp, J.C., *The Royal Scots Fusiliers 1919–1959* (Glasgow, 1963).

Liddell Hart, B.H., *History of the Second World War* (London, 1973).

Joslen, H.F., *Orders of Battle, Second World War,* Vol I (HMSO, 1960).

Macdonald Fraser, George, *Quartered Safe Out Here* (London, 1992).

Masters, John, *The Road Past Mandalay* (London, 1961).

Perrett, Bryan, *Tank Tracks to Rangoon* (London, 1978).

Skillen, Hugh, *Spies of the Airwaves* (Privately published, 1989).

Slim, Field Marshal Viscount, *Defeat into Victory* (London, 1999).

Stockwell, H.C., *Arakan Assignment: The Story of the 82nd West African Division* (Privately published).

Thompson, Julian, *War in Burma* (IWM, 2002).

Turnbull, Patrick, *The Battle of the Box* (London, 1979).

Woodburn Kirby, S., *The War Against Japan,* Vol III (Official History of the Second World War, HMSO, 1961).

——, *The War Against Japan,* Vol IV, The Reconquest of Burma (HMSO, London, 1965).

Ziegler, Philip (ed.), *The Personal Diary of Admiral the Lord Louis Mountbatten, Supreme Allied Commander South-East Asia 1943–1946* (London, 1988).

PALESTINE

Charteris, David A., *The British Army and Jewish Insurgency in Palestine 1945–1947* (London, 1959).

——, *The British Army and Jewish Insurgency in Palestine, 1945–1947* (Basingstoke, 1980).

Cohen, Michael J., *Palestine and the Great Powers*, Vol II, 1933–1951 (Princeton, 1982).

Gilbert, Martin, *A History of the Twentieth Century*, (London, 1998).

Gelber, Yoav, *The Emergence of a Jewish Army: The Veterans of the British Army in the Israeli Defence Forces* (Tel Aviv, 1986).

——, *Palestine 1948* (Sussex, 2001).

Harclerode, Peter, *"Go To It" – The History of the 6th Airborne Division* (London, 2000).

Hennesey, Peter, *Never Again. Britain 1945–1951* (London, 1993).

James, Lawrence, *The Rise and Fall of the British Empire* (London, 1994).

Kurzman, Dan, *Genesis 1948. The First Arab-Israeli War* (London, 1972).

Macmillan, Margaret, *Peacemakers. The Paris Conference of 1919 and its Attempt to End War* (London, 2001).

Mokaitis, Thomas, *British Counterinsurgency in the Post-Imperial Era*, Vol I (MUP, 1995).

Nowar, Maan Abu, *The Struggle for Independence 1939–1947: A History of the Hashemite Kingdom of Jordan* (Reading, 2001).

Royle, Trevor, *Glubb Pasha. The Life and Times of Sir John Bagot Glubb, Commander of the Arab Legion* (London, 1992).

Segev, Tom, *One Palestine, Complete* (London, 2000).

Shepherd, Naomi, *Ploughing Sand: British Rule in Palestine* (London, 1999).

Shlaim, Avi, *Collusion Across The Jordan. King Abdullah, the Zionist Movement, and the Partition of Palestine* (Oxford, 1988).

Wilson, Major R.D., MBE MC, *Cordon and Search. With the 6th Airborne Division in Palestine* (Aldershot, 1949).

MALAYA

Baynes, John, *Urquhart of Arnhem* (London, 1993).

Cloake, John, *Templer: Tiger of Malaya* (London, 1985).

Clutterbuck, Richard, *The Long War – the Emergency in Malaya 1945–1963* (London, 1970).

Mackay, Donald, *The Malayan Emergency 1948–1960* (London, 1997).

Niellands, Robin, *A Fighting Retreat: The British Empire 1947–1997* (London, 1996).

O'Balance, Edgar, *Malaya: The Communist Insurgent War 1948–1960* (Hamden USA, 1966).

Thompson, Sir Robert, *Defeating Communist Insurgency* (London, 1966).

SUEZ

Beaufre, André, *The Suez Expedition 1956* (translated by R.H. Barry) (London, 1969).

Eden, Sir Anthony, (Earl of Avon), *Full Circle: The Memoirs of Anthony Eden*, Vol III (Boston, 1960).

Ginat, Rami, *The Soviet Union and Egypt, 1945–1955* (London, 1993).

Horne, Alastair, *Harold Macmillan,* Vol I, 1894–1956 (London, 1988).

Jackson, Robert, *Suez, the Forgotten Invasion* (Shrewsbury, 1996).

Kyle, Keith, *Suez* (London, 1989).

Love, Kennett, *Suez – The Twice-Fought War* (London, 1970).

Lucas, W. Scott, *Divided We Stand: Britain, the US, and the Suez Crisis* (London, 1996).

Menzies, Sir Robert, *Afternoon Light* (London, 1967).

Nowar, Maan Abu, *The Struggle for Independence 1939–1947: A History of the Hashemite Kingdom of Jordan* (Reading, 2001).

Tal, David (ed.), *The 1956 War: Collusion and Rivalry in the Middle East* (London, 2001).

Thomas, Hugh, *The Suez Affair* (London, 1966).

Thorpe, D.R., *Eden: The Life and Times of Anthony Eden, First Earl of Avon 1897–1977* (London, 2003).

Newspapers and Periodicals

African Affairs: E.E. Sabben-Clarke, 'African Troops in Asia', Vol XLIV (1945).

Army Quarterly: Lieutenant Colonel J.R.L. Rumsey, 'Air Supply in Burma', Vol LV, October 1947–January 1948; Captain F.W.E. Fursdon, 'Draft Conductor to Togoland', Vol LVII, No. 1, October 1948.

British Army Review: Jim Stockman, 'Madagascar 1942. Part 1: Prelude to Assault', April 1986; Jim Stockman, 'Madagascar 1942. Part 2: The Battle', August 1986.

Caddick-Adams, Peter, *The Territorial Army before the Second World War*, No. 121.

Defence Studies (Joint Services Command and Staff College, 2003).

Dekho: E.C. Lanning, 'The 82nd (West African) Division, Royal West African Frontier Force', Winter 1995.

Essex County Telegraph, 10 March 1945.

Foreign Policy, Issue 137, July–August 2003.

Haaretz: Arazi Tovia, 'General Stockwell's Decision', 4 April 1972.

Independent, 28 November 1986.

Listener, 4 November 1976; 29 November 1979.

Palestine Post, 10 February 1948.

RUSI Journal: General Sir William Platt, 'The East African Forces in the war and their future', August 1948.

The RWAFF News – a home newspaper for West African troops serving abroad. 1 May 1946.

Sunday Graphic, 20 September 1942.

Sunday Telegraph, 30 October 1966; 6 November 1966; 13 November 1966.

The Times, 23 November 1944; 28 November 1986; 18 February 1993.

West African Review: December 1945, Captain J.A. Danford, 'The Empire's Largest Expeditionary Force'.

Y Ddraig Goch – The Journal of The Royal Welch Fusiliers, March 1987.

Military Publications, Studies and Pamphlets

Abraham, Kevin, Chapman, Chip and Plenty, Brian, HCSC, 'Campaign Case Study, Suez' (Joint Services Command and Staff College, 2003).

Field Service Regulations, December 1939, WO 26/GS Publications/176.

Higham, Major J.B. and Knighton, E.A., *The Second World War 1939–1945 Army Movements* (War Office Official Publication, 1955).

Infantry Training 1937 (WO26/1447).

Kennet A. and Clayton C.H.T., HCSC, 'Campaign Case Study, Madagascar' (Joint Services Command and Staff College, 2003).

Operations – Military Training Pamphlet 23 Part I. WO 26/GS Publications/602 (1942).

Periodical Notes on the Japanese Army, Nos 1 & 7. WO 26/GS Publications/1285.

Report to the Combined Chiefs of Staff by the Supreme Allied Commander South-East Asia 1943–1945 (HMSO, 1951).

RMA Sandhurst Study on Morale, Leadership and Discipline, 1950.

Serve To Lead (RMA Sandhurst).

The Royal Air Force: The Malayan Emergency 1948–1960. AP 3410 (MoD, 1970).

Other Official Publications

Memorandum of the Secretary of State for War relating to the Army Estimate for 1926 (Cmnd 2528), 1 March 1926.

Future Organisation of the Army (Cmnd 230), July 1957.

Defence: Outline of Future Policy (Cmnd 24), 1957.

Index

305

Index of Places

Index of Military Units and Formations

Naval Commands and Task Groups

HM Ships

311

Regiments and Corps

Index of General Subjects